THE INTERNET

NO EXPERIENCE REQUIRED™

SECOND EDITION

Christian Crumlish

SYBEX®

San Francisco • Paris • Düsseldorf • Soest

Associate Publisher: Amy Romanoff
Contracts and Licensing Manager: Kristine Plachy
Acquisitions & Developmental Editors: Sherry Bonelli, Richard Mills, Dan Brodnitz
Editor: Dann McDorman
Technical Editor: Tyler Regas
Book Designers: Patrick Dintino, Catalin Dulfu, Maureen Forys
Electronic Publishing Specialist: Nila Nichols
Production Coordinators: Blythe Woolston, Jeremy Crawford
Indexer: Lynnzee Elze
Cover Designer: Design Site
Cover Illustrator/Photographer: Jack D. Myers

Screen reproductions produced with Collage Complete.

Library of Congress Card Number: 98-88331
ISBN: 0-7821-2385-6

Manufactured in the United States of America

10 9 8 7 6 5 4 3 2

To Briggs, who's almost used to this routine

Acknowledgments

Of the numerous wizards I've met or asked advice of, through the Net or in the real world, I'd like to particularly thank Richard Frankel. I'd also like to thank Mitch Goldman for checking some e-mail program details for me and James "Kibo" Parry for allowing me to reproduce a Usenet article.

At Sybex, I'd like to thank the following people: Sherry Bonelli for envisioning a way to bring my Internet philosophy to a wider audience; Dan Brodnitz and Richard Mills for their timely and thorough attention to my project when Sherry was indisposed; Claudia Willen for her assistance in the revisions to the previous edition of this book; Dann McDorman for patiently shepherding the manuscript through the editorial and production processes and carefully editing the content; and Tyler Regas for checking the technical accuracy of the book. I'd also like to thank Blythe Woolston and Jeremy Crawford, production coordinators, and Nila Nichols, electronic publishing specialist, for their hard work putting this book onto the written page.

Contents at a Glance

Table of Contents

PART II • COMMUNICATING WITH E-MAIL 43

Introduction

Will the Internet hype never end? It seems like there's a newspaper article or magazine cover story every day. You probably saw hundreds of other Internet books on the shelf where you picked up this one. This book, however, is different from most of the other books out there. It's not a puff piece, full of generalities and futuristic hype. Instead, this book tells you the truth about the Internet and tells you exactly how to get things done on the Internet.

More and more people are connecting to the Net every day, and many businesses are beginning to rely on it for communication, for information, and even for the transportation of certain types of products, such as software or writing. Maybe you already have access to the Internet through your work or school, or maybe you're considering getting a modem and trying it out for yourself.

While you may be an Internet beginner, you will need some basic knowledge about computers and software to benefit most from this book. The step-by-step instructions in this book will walk you through many Internet software routines, but you should be familiar with personal computers, keyboard and mouse techniques, and basic file management processes (opening, editing, saving, and closing files, and finding files on your hard drive). If you've got that stuff down, get ready for your Internet odyssey!

How This Book Works

For most people, the basic appeal of the Internet is e-mail and the World Wide Web. I devote a lot of this book to those two topics because I realize that's all some people are going to want to know about. Eventually, though, you'll be tempted to look into some of the other resources available via the Net, and I cover some of the most interesting ones, such as newsgroups, conferencing, and FTP.

The Internet is a great resource, and you're bound to learn more about it once you're connected. For now, I'm just going to tell you enough to get you over the threshold. That's all you really need.

This book contains twenty-one skills, or chapters, and two appendices. Each skill is designed to be a lesson in some aspect of the Internet, the World Wide Web, or communicating online. The cover page for each skill summarizes what you will learn by reading that lesson. You will see numbered lists throughout the skills, as shown here. These lists give you the basic steps for performing functions such as searching the Internet, sending e-mail, or creating a home page for the Web.

1. The first step will be to start your program by clicking its desktop icon.
2. The next step may involve selecting a menu command, which is indicated like so—choose File ➢ Open. This means you should move your mouse pointer to the word File in the program's menu, click on it, and pull your mouse down through the drop-down menu until you reach the command after the arrow (➢) in the instructions. When this second command is highlighted, release the mouse button to activate the command.
3. Additional procedures may be listed in subsequent steps, depending on which task you are working on. You may also see keyboard shortcuts listed for either Windows or Macintosh computer users. These look like Ctrl+O for Windows, or Command+O for Macintosh. To use these shortcuts, hold down the Ctrl (or Command) key on your keyboard and type the letter in the shortcut. Ctrl+O (or Command+O) is the fast way to launch the File ➢ Open command.
4. The final step is usually to close the program or save the file you have created or downloaded.

You will also see useful notes scattered throughout the book in the steps and in the regular text. These brief notes are set off from the rest of the text because they convey related information about the material that you are reading. Here is an explanation of the three types of notes used in this book.

NOTE NOTE NOTE NOTE NOTE NOTE NOTE NOTE NOTE NOTE NOTE NOTE NOTE NOTE NOTE NOTE

Notes provide extra insights on the procedures or subjects being discussed. Notes may also suggest alternative approaches, different factors to consider when selecting dialog box options, or places you can go on the Internet to get more information.

TIP TIP TIP TIP TIP TIP TIP TIP TIP TIP TIP TIP TIP TIP TIP TIP TIP TIP TIP TIP TIP TIP TIP TIP TIP

Tips present a faster or better way to do something. Tips can also help you get around confusing interfaces or avoid convoluted procedures when a shortcut is possible.

WARNING WARNING WARNING WARNING WARNING WARNING WARNING WARNING

Warnings alert you to all kinds of problems before you undertake a potentially dangerous procedure. Warnings can assist you in saving your data, avoiding viruses, and ensuring your privacy on the Internet.

A Quick Tour of This Book

The next sections discuss what the lessons in this book cover.

Part I: Understanding Internet and World Wide Web Basics

Skill 1, *Understanding the Internet*, gives you a basic overview of the Internet, e-mail, and the World Wide Web. I introduce most of the basic terminology you'll need to start learning about these subjects.

Skill 2, *Getting on the Internet*, explains the different ways you might connect to the Internet and how the book will handle those alternatives.

Skill 3, *The Internet and Children*, discusses how you can incorporate Internet use into your family life without giving up control of the content or usage.

Part II: Communicating with E-mail

Skill 4, *E-mail Basics*, introduces the most basic e-mail concepts, essentially how to send, read, and respond to mail. If you've already used e-mail, you should be able to skim this chapter.

Skill 5, *Advanced E-mail Tricks*, explains some of the other useful and more elaborate uses of e-mail (such as attaching files).

Skill 6, *E-mail Programs*, explains how to use the most popular e-mail software.

Skill 7, *Signing Up for Mailing Lists*, shows you how to use your e-mail address and software to participate in online mailing list discussion groups. These lists can be your first taste of virtual communities of people united by common interests, no matter where they are geographically.

Part III: Browsing the World Wide Web

Skill 8, *Navigating the Web*, introduces you to the World Wide Web and how to get around it.

Skill 9, *Web Browsers*, explains the various programs that you might use to connect to the Web.

Skill 10, *Finding Stuff on the Web and the Net*, shows you how to search the Internet with your Web browser, so that you can find things on the Net without blindly hunting around. In this lesson, I also explain how to download files.

Skill 11, *Working with Multimedia*, explains how you can juice up your Web browser and connect to and play all kinds of multimedia content from the Internet.

Skill 12, *Push and the Desktop Web*, introduces the latest trends in Web browsing—*Webcasting* content *pushed* directly to your desktop—and covers the latest programs, such as Microsoft's Active Desktop in Internet Explorer.

Part IV: Conducting Group Discussions

Skill 13, *Joining Usenet Newsgroups*, explains the Usenet news network, a huge assortment of newsgroups devoted to interests and topics of every imaginable stripe, and outlines the practical details of running a newsreader program and reading and contributing to newsgroups yourself. No matter what newsreader you end up using—or even if you use your Web browser to read news—this lesson will have you covered.

Skill 14, *Chatting (and IRC)*, discusses live chatting using the IRC system.

Skill 15, *Conferencing and Collaborating*, discusses online conferencing and the new collaboration tools built into the major Web browsers, such as Netscape Communicator's Conference and Collabra applications and Microsoft Internet Explorer's NetMeeting.

Part V: Alternative Approaches to the Net

Skill 16, *Accessing the Internet with AOL*, covers much of the same material discussed elsewhere in the book, but with the instructions tailored for AOL users.

Skill 17, *Other Online Services, WebTV, and Free Web-Based E-mail*, discusses numerous other ways to obtain Internet access.

Skill 18, *Getting Around with FTP and Telnet*, explains how to use some of the older Internet protocols, such as FTP and Telnet, to find and connect to resources on the Net (because not everything on the Net is easily available via the World Wide Web).

Skill 19, *Making a Home Page or Web Site*, shows you how to easily create a simple home page and how to find a place to publish it on the Web.

Part VI: Troubleshooting

The final two lessons, Skill 20, *Problems with Connections, Providers, and Software*, and Skill 21, *Problems with Spam*, give you some advice to turn to when your Internet setup fails or when your e-mail Inbox is inundated with unwanted commercial solicitations.

Appendices

Appendix A, *Getting Started*, explains how to get an Internet connection (starting from scratch if necessary) and how to connect.

Appendix B, *Glossary of Internet Terms*, is an essential glossary of the Internet jargon you hear bandied about nowadays (and other things you'll hear on the Net and want explained).

Conventions I Use in This Book

When I want you to type something, I'll put it in **boldface**, and I'll use *italics* for new terms and jargon. When I want to give you useful Internet addresses or references, I'll put the information in `this font` or even

```
on a line by itself.
```

Sometimes, the specific text you need to type will vary from case to case. If so, I'll include some dummy text in *italics*. Don't type the italicized words! Instead, substitute the relevant filename, directory name, newsgroup name, etc. When the time comes, you'll know what to do. Usenet newsgroups also appear in `this font`. Program messages that appear on your screen are shown in quotation marks.

You'll notice (if you haven't already) that Web addresses (also called URLs) are often quite long, and it's important that you type them in exactly into your Web browser. Because many of them are too long to fit snugly on one line of this book, I've allowed URLs to break after any forward slash (/) or dot (`.`), without a hyphen ever being inserted. If you see a URL that breaks over a line and continues on the next line (such as `http://ezone.org/ez/e11/articles/conway/hoop.html`), just type it all on one line, without skipping a space for the line break!

Occasionally in this book I'll mention Unix programs. Because Unix is case-sensitive, the names of many of these programs are traditionally written all lowercase (such as pine, irc, gopher, tin, vi, and so on). I will refer to these programs by capitalizing their initial letter (Pine, Irc, Gopher, Tin, Vi) to make the sentences easier to read and understand, but remember that you have to type the program's name in all lowercase to run it.

Sorting Through the Many Programs

Because there are so many different ways to connect to the Net (at your office, through an online service, with an ISP) and so many different types of programs you can run to achieve many of the same goals, most of the lessons in this book are divided into two parts. In the first part, I usually explain the concepts you need to understand and, in generic terms, how to work the kind of program you'll need to send mail, browse the Web, post an article to a newsgroup, etc. In the second half, I'll cover the most popular and most common programs available for the feature in question and fill you in on the specific commands and idiosyncrasies of each.

You'll then have to read up on only one particular program (at least until you change to another one, at which time you can come back to the lesson and pick up the details for your new program).

Using *The Internet: No Experience Required* Web Page

Naturally, a book these days—especially, of all things, an Internet book—would have its own Web page, wouldn't it? Yes, of course, and there's an address on the Internet just for this book (at the site of our publisher, Sybex):

```
http://www.sybex.com/cgi-bin/rd_bookpg.pl?2385back.html
```

It's a very simple, straightforward Web page I like to call "The Internet: No Experience Required Update Web Site" to make it sound more grandiose. The site has just two sections, and one of them is empty (and I hope it stays that way). The sections are called *Web Resources Mentioned in This Book* and *Oops! Corrections and Updates.*

Web Resources Mentioned in This Book

The first section includes links to all the Web addresses and other Internet addresses I reference in the text. This means you can visit sites mentioned in the book without having to copy long tedious URLs from these pages. More importantly, it means I can furnish you with an up-to-date Web address if any of the URLs in the book change between the time we go to press and the time you read the book.

Oops! Corrections and Updates

This is that empty section I mentioned. Since, as far as I know at the moment, this entire book is perfect, it would give me great pleasure to predict that the second section of the book's Web page will remain pristine (or at least perfunctory). Chances are, though, that minute typographical errors might slip through our careful proofreading process. Furthermore, the Internet does change rapidly and resources or products covered in the book may change, disappear, or mutate. As needed, I will add updates to that page to correct mistaken or obsolete information in the book. I'll also include a link there to my address for this book in case you find something in need of correction or clarification and would like to bring it to my attention. If you discover an error, I'll fix whatever's wrong in the next edition of the book, and even thank you in the acknowledgments.

If you find anything incorrect or misleading, if you'd like to point me toward something you think I've overlooked, or if you'd just like to give me some feedback (or even flame me), please write me at the following address:

Christian Crumlish
c/o Sybex Inc.
1151 Marina Village Parkway
Alameda, CA 94501

Or send me e-mail at `InterNER@syx.com`.

PART I

Understanding Internet and World Wide Web Basics

I know, you're raring to go. You want to start sending and receiving e-mail, browsing the Web, and exploring the global library of fun stuff out on the Internet. Well, I don't want to hold you back. Feel free to skip to Part II, *Communicating with E-mail*, and start right in on e-mail (or even jump to Part III, *Browsing the World Wide Web*, to start messing around with the Web). However, if you're not clear on what the Internet actually is, how you get access to it, and what you can do once you're there, I'll try to answer those questions here in Part I.

SKILL 1

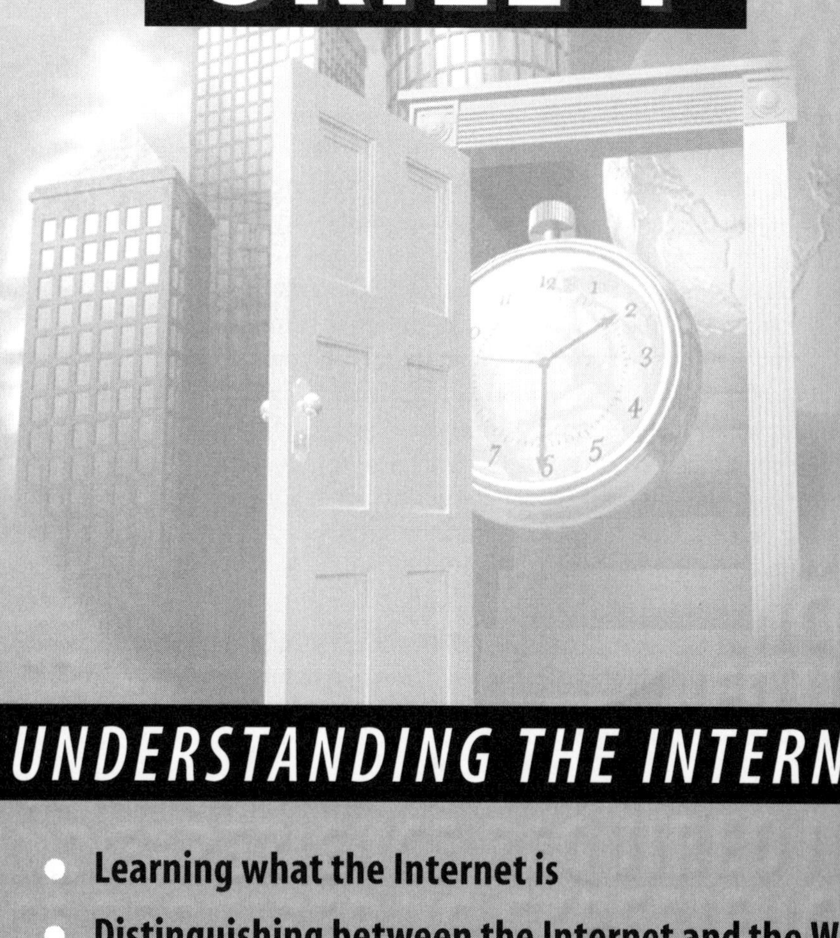

UNDERSTANDING THE INTERNET

- Learning what the Internet is
- Distinguishing between the Internet and the Web
- Discovering what you can do on the Internet and the Web
- Learning about the Internet's history and its future

In this book there are no dumb questions. Everybody talks about the Internet and the World Wide Web, but most people don't really know what the Internet is or what the differences between the Internet and the Web are. One reason for this is that the Internet looks different depending on how you come across it and what you do with it. Another reason is that everyone talks about it as if it's actually a network, like a local network in someone's office or even a large global network such as America Online. Fact is, it's something different. A beast unto itself. The Internet is really a way for computers to communicate.

Throughout this book I'll explain the jargon you hear when people start babbling about the Net, so you can figure out for yourself what you want to learn about and what you'd like to ignore. Notice that I just used the word *Net* and not *Internet*. For the most part, the words are synonymous, although some people will use the word Net to refer to just about any aspect of the global internetworking of computers. (Check out Appendix B—a glossary of Internet terms—to become more familiar with Internet jargon.)

NOTE NOTE NOTE NOTE NOTE NOTE NOTE NOTE NOTE NOTE NOTE NOTE NOTE NOTE NOTE

If you want a more thorough compendium of Internet jargon, terminology, and culture at your fingertips, look for one of my other books, *The Internet Dictionary*, also from Sybex.

As long as a computer or smaller network can "speak" the Internet lingo (or *protocols*, to be extra formal about it) to other machines, then it's "on the Internet." Of course, the computer also needs a modem or network connection and other hardware to make contact, too. But, regardless of the hardware needs, if the Internet were a language, it wouldn't be French or Farsi or Tagalog or even English. It would be Esperanto.

Having said that, I might backtrack and allow that there's nothing wrong with thinking of the Internet as if it were a single network. It certainly behaves like one in a lot of important ways. But this can be misleading. No one "owns" the Internet. No one even really runs it. And no one can turn it off.

Communicating through E-mail or Discussion Groups

In addition to being a network of interconnected computers, the Internet is also a collection of different tools and devices for communicating and storing information in a retrievable form.

Take e-mail, for example. If you work in an office with a local-area network, then chances are you have an e-mail account and can communicate with people in your office by sending them messages through the company's internal system. (See Skills 4, 5, and 6 in Part II, *Communicating with E-mail.*) However, office e-mail is not the Internet.

Similarly, if you have an account at America Online and you send a message to someone else at AOL, you're still not using the Internet. But, if your office network has a *gateway* to the Internet and you send e-mail to someone who does not work at your office, then you're sending mail over the Internet. Likewise, if you send a message from your AOL account to someone at CompuServe, or elsewhere, then again you are sending messages over the Internet (see Figure 1.1).

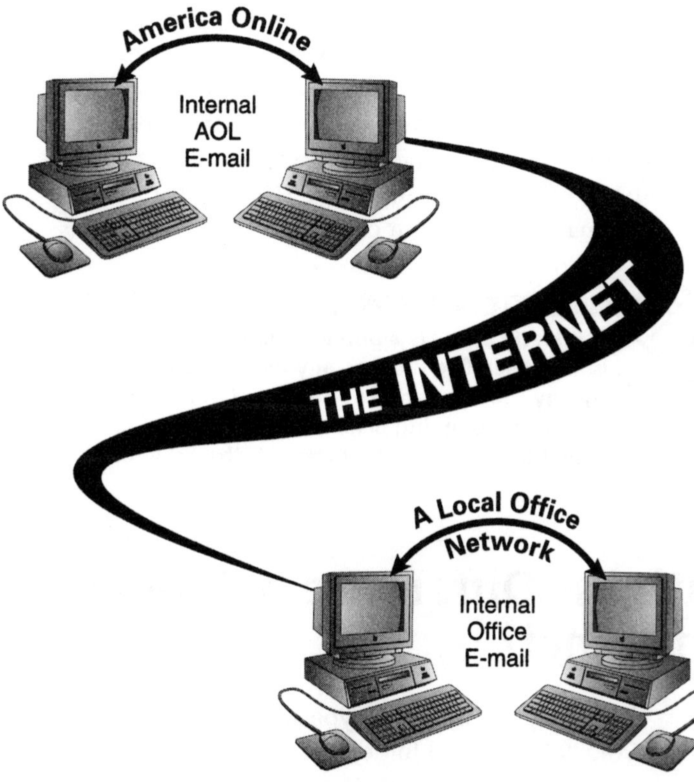

FIGURE 1.1: The Internet carries e-mail from one network to another.

NOTE NOTE NOTE NOTE NOTE NOTE NOTE NOTE NOTE NOTE NOTE NOTE NOTE NOTE NOTE

A *gateway* is a computer, or the program running on it, that transfers files (or e-mail messages, or commands) from one network to another.

But, from your point of view, the Internet is not just a collection of networks all talking to each other. A single computer can also participate in the Internet by connecting to a network or service provider that's connected to the Internet. And while the local office network I described and the big commercial online services are not themselves the Internet, they can and often do provide access through their gateways to the Internet. (I cover online services in Skill 2, in the section called "Cruising the Net at Home.")

All of this can be confusing to first-time Internet users (universally referred to as *newbies*). Say you have an AOL account and you join one of the *discussion groups* (bulletin boards) there. It may not be obvious to you right away whether you're talking in an internal venue—one only accessible to AOL members—or in a public Internet newsgroup. One of the benefits of an online service is the way various functions, including e-mail, Internet access, and online content, are brought together seamlessly so that they appear to be part of the same little program running on your computer.

NOTE NOTE NOTE NOTE NOTE NOTE NOTE NOTE NOTE NOTE NOTE NOTE NOTE NOTE NOTE

A *bulletin board* is a public discussion area where people can post messages—without sending them to anyone's individual e-mail address—that can be viewed by anyone who enters the area. Other people can then reply to posted messages, and ongoing discussions can ensue. On CompuServe, a bulletin board is called a *forum*. On the Internet, the equivalent areas are called *newsgroups*.

What's the Difference between the Web and the Internet?

Nowadays, most of the hype about the Internet is focused on the World Wide Web. It has existed for less than ten years, but it has been the fastest growing and most popular part of the Net for many of those years (except, perhaps, for the voluminous flow of e-mail around the globe). But what is the Web (also called *WWW* or *w3*) and is it the same thing as the Internet? Well, to answer the second question first: yes and no. Technically, the *Web* is just part of the Internet—or, more properly, a way of getting around part of the Internet. But it's a big part because a lot of the Internet that's not (strictly speaking) *part of* the Web can still be reached with a Web browser.

So the Web, on one level, is an *interface*. A window on the Net. A way of getting to where you're going. Its appeal derives from three different benefits:

- It disguises the gobbledygook that passes for Internet addresses and commands. (See Skill 2, *Getting on the Internet*.)
- It wraps up most of the different features of the Internet into a single interface used by Web applications.
- It allows you to see pictures, and even hear sounds or watch movies (if your computer can handle it), along with your helpings of text.

TIP

To play sounds or movies, your computer needs a sound card, speakers, and some kind of software (such as Microsoft Media Player for Windows or QuickTime 3.0 for Macintosh or Windows). For movies, you'll also want a lot of memory (or else the movies will play herky-jerky).

It helps to know a little bit about the history of the Net to understand why these three features of the Web have spurred the Internet boom. First of all, before the Web existed, doing anything beyond simple e-mailing (and even that could be difficult, depending on your type of access) required knowing weird Unix commands and understanding the Internet's system for numbering and naming all the computers connected to it. If you've ever wrestled with DOS and lost, then you can appreciate the effort required to surmount this type of barrier.

Imagine it's 1991 and you've gotten yourself an Internet account, solved the problems of logging in (with a communications program) to a Unix computer somewhere, and mastered the Unix programs needed to send and receive e-mail, read newsgroups, download files, and so on. You'd still be looking at lots of plain text, screens and screens of words. No pictures. Well, if you were dying for pictures you could download enormous text files that had begun their lives as pictures and then were encoded as plain text so they could be squeezed through the text-only pipelines that constituted the Net. Next you'd have to decode the files, download them onto your PC or Mac, and then run some special program to look at them. Not quite as easy as flipping through a magazine.

The Web uses a coding method called *hypertext* to disguise the actual commands and addresses you use to navigate the Net. Instead of these commands and addresses, what you see in your *Web browser* (the program you use to travel the Web) are plain English keywords highlighted in some way. Simply select or click on the keywords, and your browser program talks the Internet talk, negotiates the transaction with the computer at the other end, and brings the picture, text, program, or activity you desire onto your computer screen. This is how all computer functions should work (and probably how they *will* work one day).

NOTE NOTE NOTE NOTE NOTE NOTE NOTE NOTE NOTE NOTE NOTE NOTE NOTE NOTE NOTE

You may have already encountered a form of hypertext on your desktop computer. If you have a Macintosh, think of hypercard stacks—the cards in those stacks are hyperlinked to one another. If you have Windows running on a PC, think about the Windows Help system, where clicking on highlighted words connects you to definitions or tangentially related help topics.

Early Unix-based Web browsers, such as Www (developed at CERN, the European particle physics laboratory where the Web was invented) and Lynx (developed at the University of Kansas), were not especially attractive to look at, but they did offer the "one-step" technique for jumping to a specific location on the Net or for downloading a file or piece of software. Figure1.2 shows Lynx running on a Unix machine in a terminal window and connected to a PC by a modem.

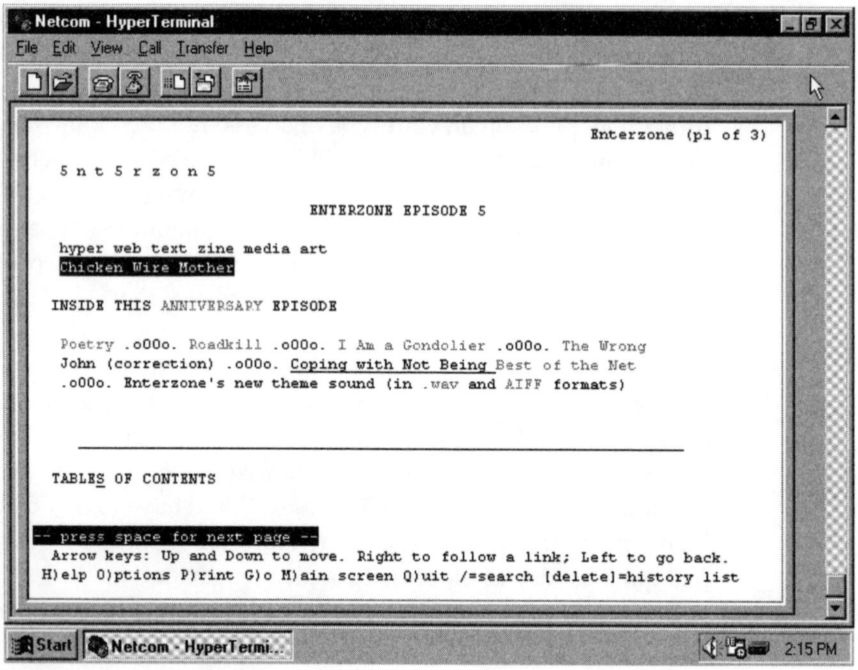

FIGURE 1.2: In Lynx, you can press Tab to get to and highlight a link, and then press Enter to execute the link and follow it to a file or another part of the Internet.

The next advance on the Web was the development of graphical Web browsers that could run on a desktop PC or Macintosh, permitting the user to employ the familiar point-and-click techniques of other software and incorporating text formatting and graphics into the browser screen. The first program of this type was NCSA Mosaic, which was developed at the National Center for Supercomputer Applications and distributed for free (see Figure 1.3).

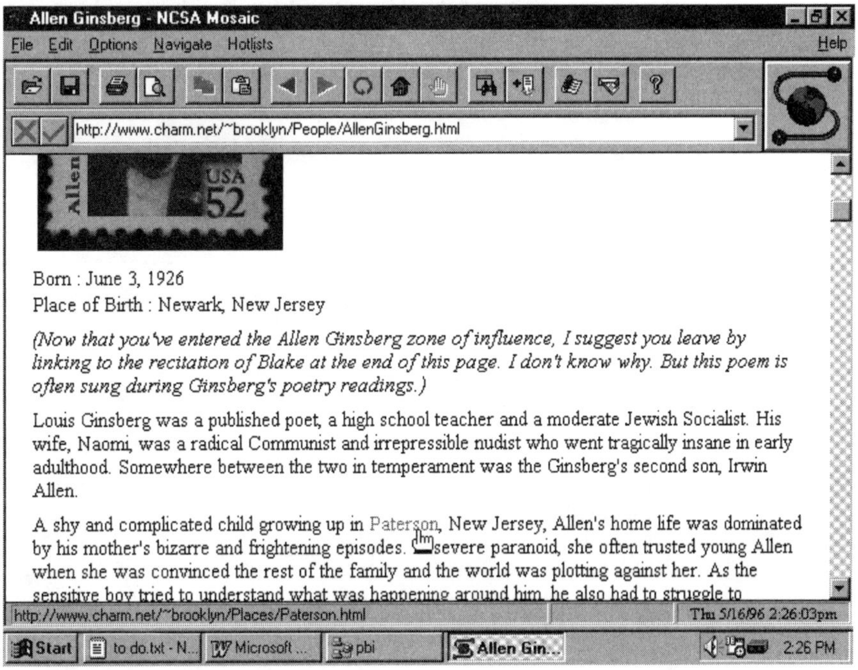

FIGURE 1.3: Mosaic made it possible to point to a link and click on it, making the Internet much more accessible to nontechnical users. It also pioneered the use of in-line graphics (meaning illustrations mixed in with text).

Furthermore, the various Web browsers can more or less substitute for a plethora of little specialty programs (such as Gopher clients, newsreaders, FTP programs, and so on) that you had to assemble and set up yourself "in the old days." The browsers all have their own little idiosyncrasies, but they're still remarkably uniform and consistent compared to the maze of different programs and rules you had to work your way through just a few years ago. These days, the most popular browser is Netscape Navigator (see Figure 1.4), although Microsoft's Internet Explorer is more popular on the Windows 95 and 98 systems.

NOTE NOTE NOTE NOTE NOTE NOTE NOTE NOTE NOTE NOTE NOTE NOTE NOTE NOTE NOTE

"Just a few years ago" is the old days on the Internet. Changes happen so rapidly in the online world that time on the Internet is like "dog years"—something like seven years go by for each one in the real world.

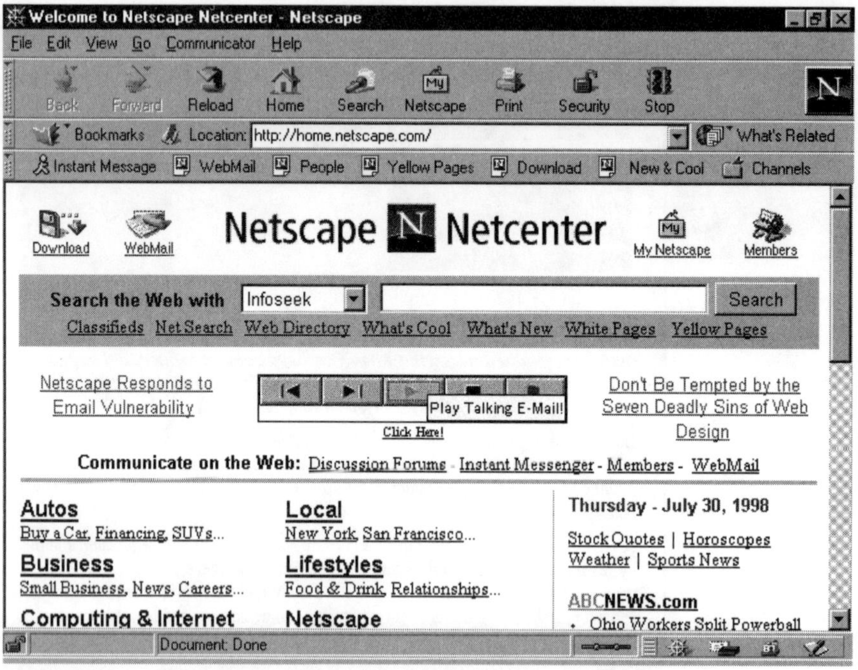

FIGURE 1.4: Netscape Navigator is the most popular World Wide Web browser program. It works very much the way Mosaic did, but with a number of additional features and improvements.

The Web has made it possible for browsers to display pictures right there in the midst of text, eliminating the need to decode files. A picture's worth a lot of words, and pictures look better in newspaper articles and on TV than scads of typewritten text. So this final ingredient made the Web seem both accessible and interesting to people who would never in a million years care to learn what a Unix "regular expression" is.

I have tried to answer the question that heads up this section: What's the difference between the Web and the Internet? Technically the Web and the Internet are not exactly the same, but for all intents and purposes they have a lot in common. Web browsers are the must-have programs that have made the Internet what it is today.

NOTE NOTE NOTE NOTE NOTE NOTE NOTE NOTE NOTE NOTE NOTE NOTE NOTE NOTE NOTE

You can use the Internet and the Web to find new friends and uncover fun facts and interesting Web sites. Individuals and groups all over the planet have gotten together on the Internet to explore mutual interests. Environmental and political causes, pets, sports, leisure activities, the arts, and the sciences are just some of the popular topics continually updated on the Internet.

Discovering What's New on the Net

These days, the latest Internet developments are mostly driven by the access tools. Browser makers Netscape and Microsoft are each trying to develop all-in-one solutions that make their own products the "platform" for everything you do on the Net. New companies are offering free Internet accounts with a Web-based e-mail interface. The catch? You have to keep the ad window open on the screen. There are even Internet solutions that don't require you to have a computer, such as WebTV (your TV plus a modem plus a keyboard plus a remote). Some solutions eliminate the need for a modem, such as DirectPC (your computer plus a special satellite hookup).

The Web on Your Desktop

From the user's point of view, the biggest change in day-to-day Internet and World Wide Web use is that Internet access is now built directly into computer operating-system desktops (as well as directly into many new applications). Both Netscape and Microsoft are trying to turn their browsers into substitute desktops, more or less merging your view of the Internet (out there) and your own computer (in here).

NOTE NOTE NOTE NOTE NOTE NOTE NOTE NOTE NOTE NOTE NOTE NOTE NOTE NOTE NOTE

The Internet has also become a great source of career information. Companies frequently list jobs and freelance opportunities online. You can research companies on the Internet and train yourself on a variety of topics that might come up in an interview. You can find business contacts and develop new ones through Internet e-mail, conferencing, and forums on particular subjects.

Webcasts Beamed onto Your Screen

The popularity of PointCast (see Figure 1.5), a program that displays news on your screen and automatically connects to the Internet for updates, has demonstrated a market for "Webcasting" software (programs that "broadcast" over the Internet directly to your computer screen). This use of the Internet is more passive, more like TV than the interactive, Web-browsing model, but it's possible to do both. Internet Explorer offers various Webcasting "channels" and Microsoft has cut a deal with PointCast to make their offerings one of those channels.

FIGURE 1.5: The PointCast Network (shown here in screen-saver mode) automatically downloads news from the Net and displays it on your computer screen.

NOTE

The type of news you can have Webcasted to your desktop ranges from sports to headline and financial news, as well as more specialized topics (science and technology, fashion, arts and entertainment) that you define and refine with your Webcasting software.

Applications with Internet Features

The growth of the Internet, coupled with the advent of smaller company or organization *intranets* running on Internet principles, has led users to expect their everyday business software to help them retrieve remote documents, collaborate with colleagues over network links, and save or publish documents to Web and intranet servers. To meet this demand, software publishers are adding Internet features to their programs left and right.

NOTE NOTE NOTE NOTE NOTE NOTE NOTE NOTE NOTE NOTE NOTE NOTE NOTE NOTE NOTE

***Intranets* are private networks running on Internet protocols so that, for example, an employee in one office may seek access to sensitive files stored at another office with the use of an ordinary Web browser.**

You can expect your next upgrade of various programs to include the ability to transfer files (open them from and save them to remote computers) and probably to create documents and reports in HTML (hypertext Web format) as well. See Skill 19, *Making a Home Page or Web Site*, for more on how to make Web documents.

NOTE NOTE NOTE NOTE NOTE NOTE NOTE NOTE NOTE NOTE NOTE NOTE NOTE NOTE NOTE

Knowing how to use Internet features in common business applications is a great job skill, even if you don't work in a high-technology field. All kinds of companies are depending more on the Internet and the World Wide Web to find information and promote their services and products. Companies and organizations are also developing in-house intranets to store policies, manuals, and other information. Having knowledge of the Internet is certainly a big plus in today's competitive job market.

What You Can Do on the Net

I've already touched on the most popular facilities on the Internet—e-mail and the World Wide Web—but now I'll run down some of the other useful features covered in this book. All of these things are interrelated, and you may notice me mentioning something before I cover it in detail. I don't want to leave you scratching your head when I'm forced to sputter terms of the trade, such as FTP, Telnet, and Gopher.

Once you start exploring the Web, you might get tired of its disorganization (imagine a library where every card-carrying member worked part-time as a librarian for one of the shelves, and each micro-librarian used their own system for organizing their section). Fortunately, there are a lot of useful *search engines* available on the Net, and I'll show you where to find them and how to use them.

NOTE NOTE NOTE NOTE NOTE NOTE NOTE NOTE NOTE NOTE NOTE NOTE NOTE NOTE NOTE

A *search engine* is a program or Web page that enables you to search an Internet site (or the entire Internet) for a specific keyword or words (see Skill 10, *Finding Stuff on the Web and the Net*).

The Web itself is becoming more of a whiz-bang medium with some of the bells and whistles we've come to expect in television advertisements and big budget movies. To take full advantage of some of the more dynamic Web offerings, though, you have to learn how to plug special tools into your browser. I'll show you where to find the tools and how to plug them in.

Those newsgroups I alluded to before, the Internet's public message boards, are organized (to use the term loosely) into a system called *Usenet*. I'll tell you how Usenet works, how to get and install a *newsreader*, and how to start participating in this public forum without getting called a jerk. If you plan to join the public discourse of the Net, you have to learn a thing or two about something called *netiquette*—the traditional rules of civilized behavior online. (Usenet and netiquette are explained in Skill 13, *Joining Usenet Newsgroups*.)

If you prefer the idea of communicating with people "live" rather than posting messages and waiting for people to reply later, then you'll want to know about the various chat facilities available on the Internet—particularly *IRC* (*Internet relay chat*). These are discussed in Skill 14, *Chatting (and IRC)*.

If you're willing to get your hands a little dirty and want to start tunneling your way around the Internet, connecting to computers all over the globe and moving files hither and yon, you might be able to do all that from your Web browser, or you may want to pick up the basics of *FTP* (*File Transfer Protocol*) and Telnet, systems that allow you to log in to remote computers over the Net. Read Skill 18, *Getting Around with FTP and Telnet*, to learn more about this technology.

Finally, if you want to join the ranks of people with their own home pages on the Web—to create a "presence" on the Net or publicize your favorite Internet sites—I'll show you how to do that as well in Skill 19, *Making a Home Page or Web Site*.

Downloading Files from the Internet

Another aspect of the Internet that you will especially enjoy is the ability to download files from a vast selection of sample applications, digital art and music, and many other offerings. Software companies promote their new products by maintaining sites where their customers can obtain samples, updates, and related information. Entertainment conglomerates supply sound and video files for movies, bands, and video games. Some organizations just collect information relevant to their interests, such as schedules of upcoming activities, databases of similar organizations, and the like.

WARNING WARNING WARNING WARNING WARNING WARNING WARNING WARNING

You can access files from the Internet, but before you attempt this, you should protect your computer (or your company's network) with anti-virus software. Computers downloading Internet files are the principal point of entry for computer viruses. We will learn more about viruses and how to defend against them in Skill 10, *Finding Stuff on the Web and the Net*.

The files obtained from the Internet can be quite large, so they often arrive compressed to a smaller size, and may also be coded for protection against unauthorized use or modifications. These files have to be decompressed and decoded before you can use them. Compression-decompression software and decoding applications are readily available, both as free Internet downloads (called freeware), and as commercial applications that you pay for. Again, Skill 10, *Finding Stuff on the Web and the Net*, contains more information about compression and encoding processes.

Many Internet users are concerned about their privacy while using the Net, especially if they are filling out forms or making purchases with credit cards over the World Wide Web. Programming geniuses have given us applications that try to protect our good credit and our privacy. Some of these efforts are even given away free on the Internet. Skill 10 will touch on some of the privacy precautions you can take on the Internet.

Using Web Sites to Gather Information About the Internet and the Web

You can visit the Internet itself to glean more details about its history, policies, and users. Use the Web sites listed below to get various interpretations of how to use the Internet, how it evolved, and how it should be regulated. These sites all contain links to even more sites that will take you surfing farther afield in your quest for knowledge about the Web. (See Part III, *Browsing the World Wide Web*, for more info on how to get around the Web.)

The Internet Society (`http://info.isoc.org/`) A simple site that includes Internet history and a timeline, as well as links to other technical organizations dealing with the Web and communication in general.

Netscape Home Page (`http://www.netscape.com/`) The Web site of an extremely popular Web browser company. Click the Assistance button in the button bar right below the Netscape banner at the top of the home page. This will take you to the Assistance and Customer Service page. Scroll way down through Netscape's product and technical support listings to the Learning About the Internet section, where you can select links of interest.

Electronic Frontier Foundation (`http://www.eff.org/`) A mainly civil-rights oriented site with many pages on free speech, privacy, and policy. Also home of the (Extended) Guide to the Internet, a lengthy document containing everything you might ever want to know about the origins of the Internet.

World Wide Web Consortium (`http://www.w3.org/`) A site hosted by MIT, the European Union, and DARPA (the defense agency that developed the Internet). This site has everything from very technical and lengthy documents to press releases and policy statements.

Are You Experienced?

Now you can...

- ☑ **explain what the Internet is and how it works**
- ☑ **understand how the Web and the Internet are related**
- ☑ **identify what applications you need to use the Internet**
- ☑ **anticipate how the Internet is changing to meet information demands**

SKILL 2

GETTING ON THE INTERNET

- **Accessing the Internet and the Web at work and at home**
- **Using Internet e-mail and addresses**
- **Understanding Internet addresses**
- **Connecting with different types of computers**

So what exactly does it mean to be "on the Internet"? Generally, if someone asks you, "Are you on the Net?" it means something like, "Do you have an Internet e-mail address?" That is, do you have e-mail and can your e-mail account be reached over the Internet? With the popularity of the Web being what it is, another common interpretation of what it means to be on the Net is, "Do you have the ability to browse the World Wide Web?" Often these two features—Internet e-mail and Web access—go hand in hand, but not always. In a short while, the concept of "being on the Internet" will likely include having your own home page, a "place" on the Web where information about you is stored and where you can be found. This is also sometimes known as having a "presence" online or on the Web.

Cruising the Net at Work

More and more companies these days (as well as schools and other organizations) are installing internal networks and relying on e-mail to share information. E-mail messages are starting to replace interoffice memos, at least for some types of announcements, questions, and scheduling purposes. The logical next step for most of these organizations is to connect their internal network to the Internet through a gateway. When this happens, you may suddenly be on the Net. This doesn't mean that anything will necessarily change on your desktop. You'll probably still use the same e-mail program and still send and receive mail within your office in the same way you always have.

WARNING WARNING WARNING WARNING WARNING WARNING WARNING WARNING

Some companies use Internet-usage monitoring programs that tell them how long employees have been using the Internet and what type of sites they are visiting. Use good judgment when you surf the Internet at work and try to explore only those sites that have potentially important work-related information.

What will change at this point is that you'll be able to send e-mail to people on the Internet outside of your office, as long as you type the right kind of Internet address. (Generally, this means adding @ and a series of words separated by periods to the username portion of an address, but I'll explain more about addresses at the end of this lesson.) Similarly, people out there in the great beyond will be able to send e-mail to you as well.

Depending on the type of Internet connection your company has, e-mail may be all you get. Then again, it might also be possible for you to run a Web browser on your computer and visit Internet sites while sitting at your desk. Of course, your company will only want you to do this if it's relevant to your job, but it works the same way whether you're researching a product your company uses or reading cartoons at the Dilbert site.

NOTE NOTE NOTE NOTE NOTE NOTE NOTE NOTE NOTE NOTE NOTE NOTE NOTE NOTE NOTE

Your ability to find information your company needs on the Internet will become a highly prized career asset, especially as more and more organizations contribute to the growth of the Internet.

Cruising the Net at Home

If you're interested in exploring the Internet as a form of entertainment or for personal communication, then a work account is not really the way to do it. (An account minimally consists of a username and an e-mail Inbox; it may also provide storage space on a computer or access to a Web server.) You'll need your own personal account to really explore the Internet on your own time, without looking over your shoulder to make sure nobody's watching.

TIP TIP TIP TIP TIP TIP TIP TIP TIP TIP TIP TIP TIP TIP TIP TIP TIP TIP TIP TIP TIP TIP TIP TIP TIP

If your office is sophisticated, you may actually be able to dial in to a company network from home via a modem to check your e-mail messages or even browse the Web; but again, unless it's work-related surfing or research, this might not be an appropriate use of your boss's resources.

Your best bet is to sign up for an account from a commercial online service or a direct-access Internet service provider. (Appendix A explains how to find and get your own Internet account.) What's the difference between those two choices? Well, an *online service* (such as CompuServe, America Online, Prodigy, Microsoft Network, and so on) is first and foremost a private, proprietary network offering its own content and access to other network members, generally combined with Internet access. An *Internet service provider* (also called an *ISP*) just offers access to the Internet and no proprietary content (or only limited local information and discussion groups). Figure 2.1 will help illustrate this distinction.

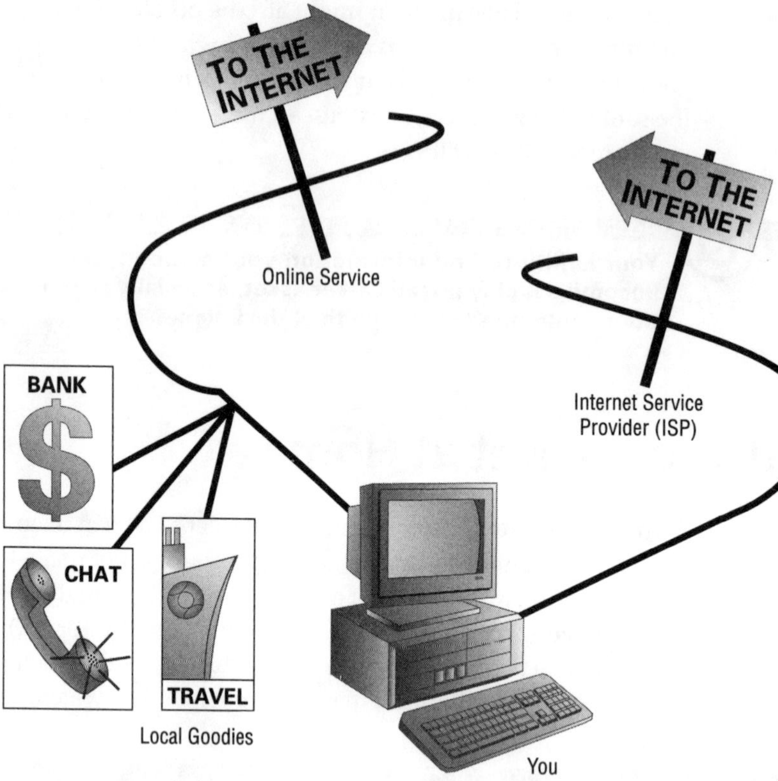

FIGURE 2.1: Online services connect you to the Internet but encourage you to explore their own offerings, whereas ISPs just connect you to the Internet and let you fend for yourself.

A few years ago, online services began to offer full Internet access as a normal part of the service. Because they are trying to do two things at once (sell you their own content *and* connect you to the Internet), they are generally more expensive than local ISPs. On the other hand, they tend to offer a single, simplified interface. I often recommend that people who just want to get their feet wet sign up for a free trial account at one of the online services. (See Skill 16 for detailed instructions for working with America Online.)

In the long run, you may decide you can save money by switching to a direct-access Internet service provider.

ISPs can be cheaper than online services, especially if you can find one that offers a flat rate—a monthly charge that doesn't vary no matter how much time you spend connected to the Net. They also don't try to compete with the Internet by offering their own content and sponsors. Instead, they function as a gateway, getting you onto the Internet and letting you go wherever you want.

What Kinds of ISP Accounts Are There?

An ISP account generally includes (along with the e-mail address) storage space on a computer somewhere on the Net. You will be billed monthly, and depending on the provider, there may be a surcharge based on the amount of time you spent connected that month or the amount of space you used on their hard drive (over a usually ample quota, often something like 5 megabytes of storage).

But how do you use an account? Well, you need a computer with a modem, and you need software that knows how to use that modem to call up (dial up) your provider and that allows you to log in to your account. Fortunately, most modems come with their own software. Appendix A has more on the nitty-gritty of connecting to an account.

TIP

You don't necessarily need a computer to connect to the Net. Another approach is to sign up for WebTV, a service that works with a television and a phone line, as discussed in Skill 17.

Your ISP will take care of all the technical details for you and will probably supply you with a setup disk and easy-to-use software for connecting to the Internet. Once you're set up, you won't have to think much about whether you have a PPP or SLIP account or any other kind of account, but I want to introduce the terminology now so you'll know what I'm talking about when I mention it again. If you want more than a connection to a Unix command-line and a plain-text account (and I suspect that you do), then you need something called a *PPP* or *SLIP account*. (The other kind is usually called a *shell account* or sometimes a *Unix shell account*.) Again, I'll explain more about these distinctions in Appendix A, if you're really interested.

A PPP (or SLIP) account lets your computer behave like it's connected directly to another computer on the Internet—when it's really connected over a phone line whenever you dial up—and it enables you to run software, such as a graphical

Web browser like Microsoft Internet Explorer or Netscape Navigator, that functions in your computer's native environment (for example, Windows or the Macintosh operating system) instead of forcing you to deal with plain-text programs like the text-only browsers Lynx and Unix (see Figure 2.2).

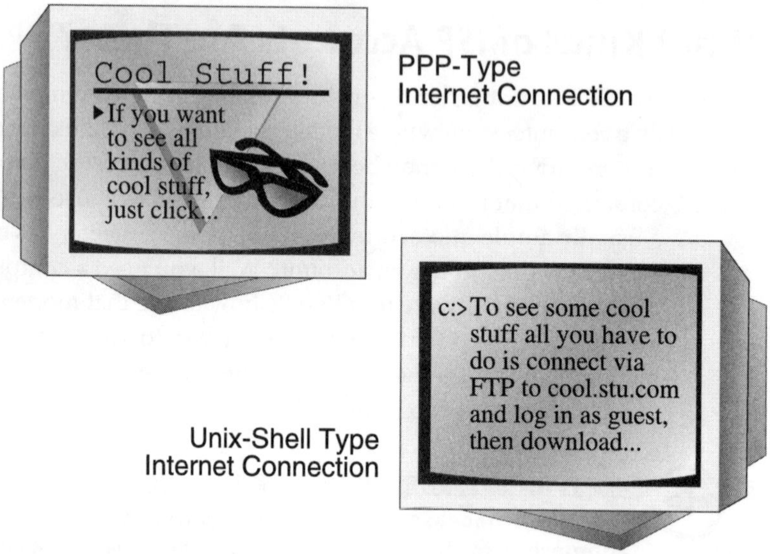

FIGURE 2.2: If you can get a PPP (or SLIP) account, then your connection to the Internet will be much more seamlessly integrated into your computer's normal environment (and much easier to use!).

WARNING WARNING WARNING WARNING WARNING WARNING WARNING WARNING

By the way, the speed of your modem—and that of the modem at the other end of the dial-up line (that is, your provider's modem)—determines the speed of your Internet connection, and even the fastest modems these days are still slower than a direct network connection to the Net, such as you might enjoy at your office.

The Anatomy of an Internet Address

One of the confusing things to Internet newbies is that the word "address" is used to mean at least three different things on the Internet. The most basic meaning—but the one used least often—is the name of a computer, also called a *host* or *site,* on the Internet in the form `something.something.something` (to really use the lingo properly you have to pronounce the periods as "dot"—you'll get used to it and it saves a lot of time over the long haul). For example, I publish a magazine (or 'zine) on the Internet called *Enterzone;* it's stored on a machine in San Francisco that is part of a collective. The address of that machine is

```
ezone.org
```

Reading from right to left, you first have the *domain,* `org`, which stands for (nonprofit) organization. Next you have a *subdomain,* `ezone`. Finally you sometimes have a *hostname* (often, but not always, `www`), which is the name (or *a* name) of the specific computer the magazine is stored on.

Another type of address is an e-mail address. An e-mail address consists of a *username* (also called a *login*, a *log-on name*, a *userID*, an *account name*, and so on), followed by an "at sign" (@) and then an Internet address of the type just described. So, for example, say you want to send e-mail to me in my capacity as editor of *Enterzone*. You could address that e-mail message to a special username created for that job (it will stay the same even if someone else takes over in the future):

```
editor@ezone.org
```

The third type of address is the kind you see everywhere these days, on billboards, on TV commercials, in the newspaper, and so on—a Web address, also called a *URL* (*Uniform Resource Locator*). I'll explain more about how to read (or ignore) URLs in Skill 8, *Navigating the Web*. For now, it's enough just to know what one looks like. The Web address of that magazine I told you about is

```
http://ezone.org/ez/
```

TIP

You can leave out the `http://` portion of the address when using certain Web browsers

Fortunately, you often can avoid typing in Web addresses yourself and can zip around the Web just by clicking pre-established *links*. Links are highlighted words or images that, when clicked or selected, take you directly to a new document, another part of the current document, or some other type of file entirely.

NOTE NOTE NOTE NOTE NOTE NOTE NOTE NOTE NOTE NOTE NOTE NOTE NOTE NOTE NOTE

The InterNIC committee attempting to govern the Internet has added some new domain name options. Now, in addition to `.org` for nonprofit organizations, `.com` for commercial users, `.net` for service providers, and `.edu` for educational concerns; you may see `.firm`, `.store`, `.web`, `.info`, `.rec`, `.arts`, and `.nom`. The `.mil` designation is reserved for the military and `.gov` for government agencies.

Getting on the Net with Mac, Windows, or Unix

One of the nice things about the Internet is that it makes some of the seemingly important distinctions between types of computers a lot less important. Sure, if you use a Macintosh, you have to run Macintosh software, and if you use Windows 95, you have to run Windows software, but the information out on the Internet, the public discussion areas, and the World Wide Web look and act more or less the same, no matter what kind of computer you use.

In fact, the Web is quickly becoming a sort of universal computer platform now that certain types of programs and services are being designed to run on the Web, rather than to run on one specific type of computer. In this book, most of the screen shots (such as in Figure 1.2) show Windows 95 screens because that's the kind of computer I do most of my work on, but many of the programs featured also exist for the Macintosh, and when they do I'll be sure to fill you in on the Macintosh versions and where to find them. Figure 2.3 shows a Netscape Navigator window on a Macintosh. Notice how similar it looks to the Windows 95 version shown in Figure 1.4.

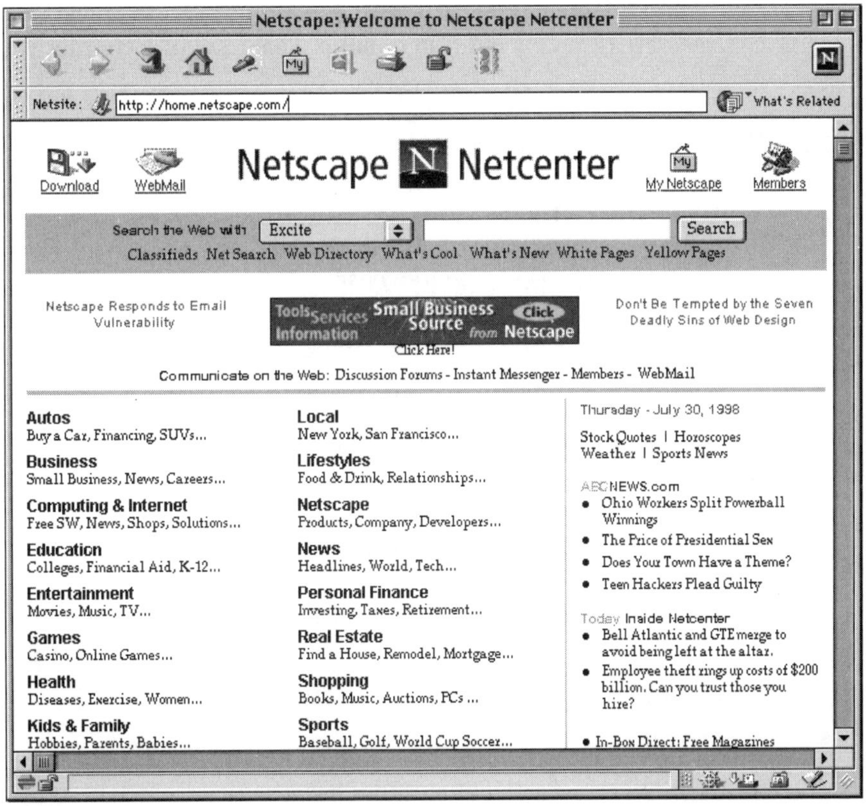

FIGURE 2.3: Netscape Navigator for the Mac works almost exactly the same way as the PC (and, for that matter, the Unix) version of the program, except for the normal Macintosh user-interface features, such as the menu bar being at the top of the screen instead of below the title bar.

Part of the elegance of the Internet is that much of the heavy-duty processing power and storage of large programs and dense information takes place "out there," and not on your computer. Your computer—whether it's a PC, a Mac, or a Unix workstation—becomes just a convenient beanstalk to climb up to the land of the Internet giants. You'll sometimes refer to this common structure of Internet facilities as *client-server* (sorry for the jargon). In this scenario, you are the client (or your computer or the program running on it is) and the information source, World Wide Web site, or e-mail-handling program is the server. Servers are centralized repositories of information or specialized handlers of certain kinds of traffic. All you (as a client) have to do is connect to the right server and a wealth of goodies are within your reach—without overloading your machine. This is a major reason why it doesn't matter what kind of computer you prefer.

Are You Experienced?

Now you can...

- ☑ get on the Internet at work
- ☑ get on the Internet at home
- ☑ understand Internet addresses
- ☑ connect with any type of computer

SKILL 3

THE INTERNET AND CHILDREN

- Internet stuff for kids
- Education and entertainment
- Supervising your children online
- Blocking out salacious material
- Protecting the privacy of your family

Naturally, you want what's best for your children. This has always included literacy, some understanding of numbers, and an appreciation for the finer things in life. Now, in our highly technological age, this also includes some facility with computers and the Internet. If you want your child to excel, both in school and in the job market of the future, you've got to encourage her to explore the Internet. But the Net is a public place, and young children should not be permitted to wander around in public unattended. You need to educate yourself about the Internet first, and take some precautions, so that your child is not exposed to the raw and seamy side of the Net without any guidance. (Even if you don't have children of your own, you may still want to familiarize yourself with the special concerns parents have about the Internet.)

In this lesson, first you'll discover what benefits and features are available for child and family participation on the Net (and particularly on the Web). Next, I'll explain some of the methods you can use to block undesirable Web content. Finally, I'll show you how to look into the privacy policies of various Web sites to make sure you are not exposing your child to unwanted commercial solicitation.

TIP

If you are an AOL user, you can learn about the Parental Controls available to you in Skill 16, *Accessing the Internet with AOL*.

Good Stuff for Kids

You'll learn a lot more about the Web and how to use it in Part III, *Browsing the World Wide Web,* but for now I want to give you an idea of what's available for kids on the Web. (So don't worry if you don't understand how to use a Web browser yet.) The best stuff for kids falls into one of two categories: education and entertainment. They each have their place in your child's online experience.

Education Resources

Sure, the Internet can be a huge waste of time, but don't forget that it originally started as a way for scientists, academics, and other researchers to share their work and collaborate on projects. Universities and schools were some of the first stable institutions on the Net and there's still a wealth of useful educational resources online if you just know where (or how) to look.

TIP TIP TIP TIP TIP TIP TIP TIP TIP TIP TIP TIP TIP TIP TIP TIP TIP TIP TIP TIP TIP TIP TIP TIP TIP

To learn more about how to find online resources on your own, see Skill 10, *Finding Stuff on the Web and the Net,* where you can learn how to search the Web and the rest of the Net.

School Stuff

Colleges and universities haven't been the only educational institutions online. The Net has always had resources created by and for kindergarten through 12th grade schools, teachers, and students. I ran a quick search using the keyword "k12" in the Netscape Web browser and came up with a few good starting places, lickety-split (see Figure 3.1).

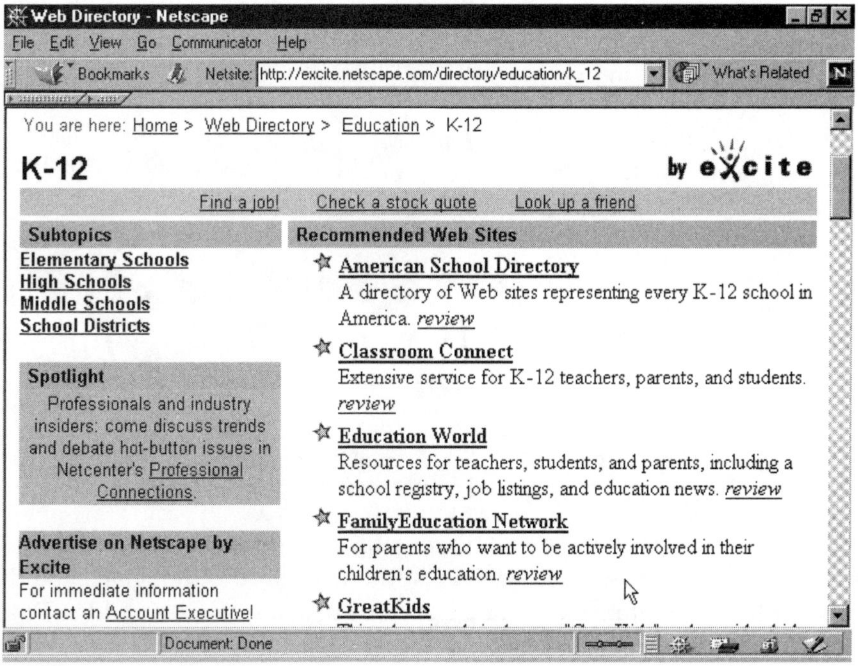

FIGURE 3.1: K–12 Web sites suggested by Netscape

Wicked Cool Web Pages

You and your child can also use the Net to research topics of interest directly. If you get tired of watching a grown-up in a purple dinosaur suit talking baby talk, perhaps you can entice your child into reading about (or looking at pictures of) "real" dinosaurs on the Web (see Figure 3.2).

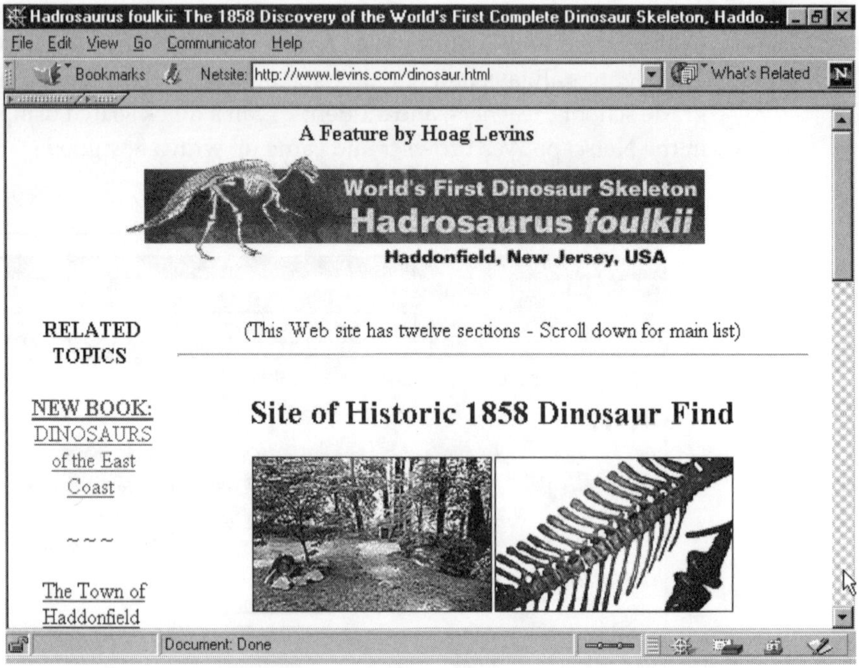

FIGURE 3.2: As you might imagine, there are dinosaur sites galore on the Web.

The Web can also represent an inexpensive supplement to conventional information sources like books and magazines (although it shouldn't be construed as a substitute for reading any more than television should be). Millions of people viewed images of the comet Shoemaker-Levy as it crashed into Jupiter in 1994, posted at a NASA site more or less as the event happened (for many people, this was the first time they realized that the Internet could be used to disseminate information). Figure 3.3 shows the site that still remains to document that astronomical event.

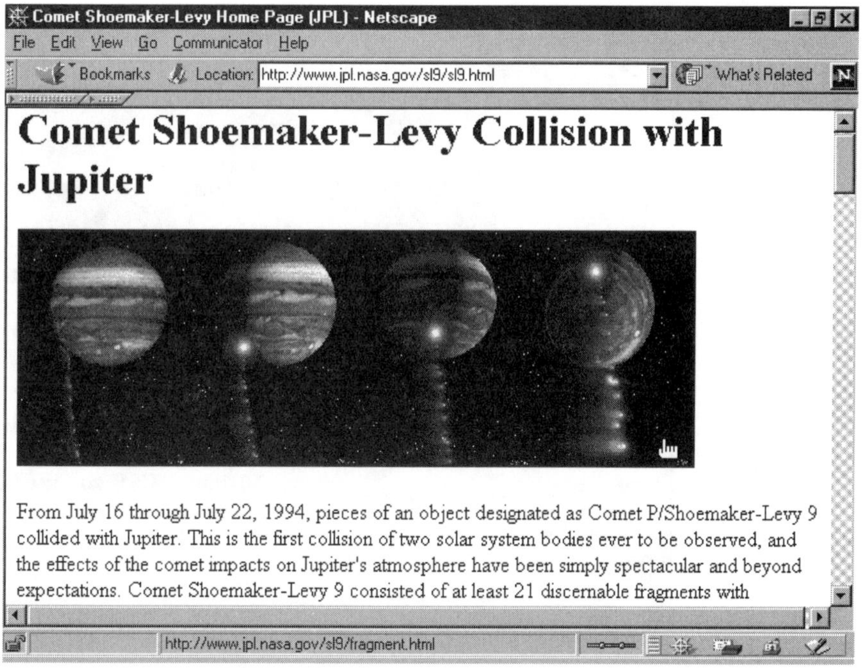

FIGURE 3.3: Even if you can't afford that telescope yet, you can still whet your tyke's appetite for science with the Web.

Help with College Admissions

Just recently, a number of graduate schools agreed to share a common online interface for applications. For the time being, most prospective college students will still submit their applications on paper, but that doesn't mean you can't do a little research about potential college choices on the Web. Some schools, such as the University of California at Santa Barbara, offer special Web resources tailored to the needs of prospective students (see Figure 3.4).

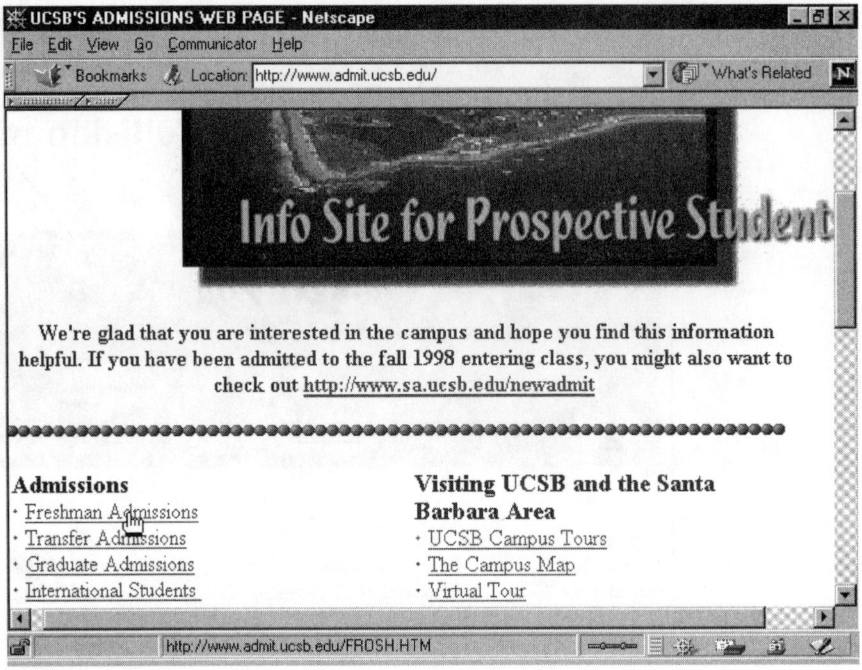

FIGURE 3.4: If you're thinking of attending UC Santa Barbara, here's a good place to start.

Entertainment Resources

There are all kinds of entertaining Web sites for children. Some are dedicated to specific topics and others function as "portals" or jumping-off points to interesting destinations of all kinds. Yahoo! (a popular Web directory site) has an excellent Web site made especially for children, called Yahooligans! (see Figure 3.5).

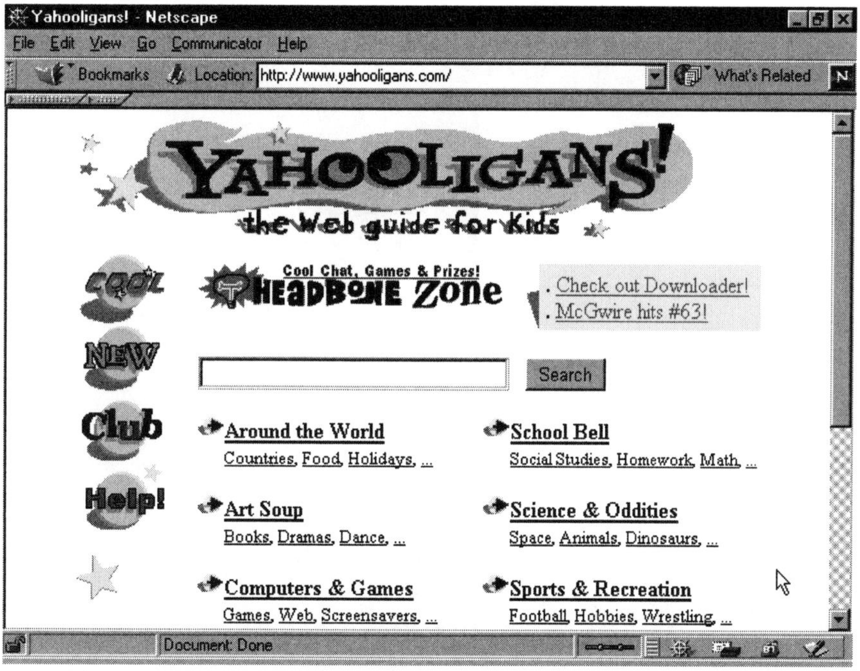

FIGURE 3.5: Yahooligans! is a Web site designed especially for children.

It's easy to find Web sites dedicated to children (you can start by searching for the word *kid* or *child*, using the browsing skills explained in Skill 10), but you will have to do some work weeding out the worthy sites from those that lack appropriate content or offer thinly disguised commercial come-ons. One way to judge a site is to look at who put it together or who has endorsed it. Two sites that look credible and on the up-and-up to me are Kids Domain (see Figure 3.6) and Great Sites (see Figure 3.7).

Kids Domain was created by parents (you can read about them on the Who We Are page at `http://www.kidsdomain.com/who/`). Great Sites is a guide to numerous Web sites especially selected by the ALA (American Library Association) for use by children.

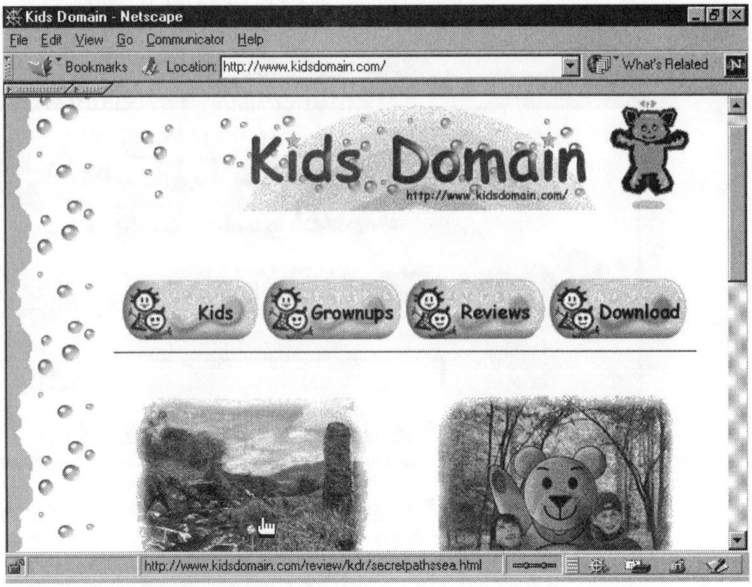

FIGURE 3.6: Kids Domain looks like a safe and wholesome place for a child to spend some time.

FIGURE 3.7: The American Library Association has culled over 700 "Great Sites" for kids.

There's No Substitute for Supervision

As with any other part of the outside world, the best guidance you can provide for your child is on-the-spot supervision. Especially when you are first exposing him to computers or the Internet, try to be there the whole time, even if there's not much for you to do. Your presence will provide support, and if your child finds anything confusing or questionable you'll be right there to help solve the problem or give the needed advice. Of course, in the long run, you can't always be there while your child is on the Web or reading e-mail, but the time you spend at the beginning will pay off in the long run, after you've had a chance to impart "the rules of the road" in a hands-on context.

No matter how much you try to limit your children's exposure to these new technologies, you can't evade the responsibility of preparing them for it in the long run. Even if you keep no TV in the house, your son or daughter will see the *Simpsons* or *Ren & Stimpy* at a friend's house. Likewise, even if you try to keep the flow of the Internet out of your home (which is your prerogative, of course), your child will encounter unsupervised access eventually, either in a public library (if only!) or, again, at a friend's house. Make sure you prepare your family members for what to expect on the Net, so they'll know how to behave when presented with opportunities and temptations.

NOTE NOTE NOTE NOTE NOTE NOTE NOTE NOTE NOTE NOTE NOTE NOTE NOTE NOTE NOTE

Be sure to tell your children that the information available on the Internet should not be considered reliable unless it can be confirmed elsewhere, and warn them about the temptations of plagiarism when the time comes for them to research their first term papers on the Net.

Blocking What You Don't Want

One way to extend your ability to supervise beyond the time you can be physically present is to install software that limits or blocks what material your child (or anyone without the password) can see on the Net. These methods are not foolproof, as pornographers and commercial vendors change their verbiage and strategies all the time, but it's one way to exercise control over the flood of information without clamping down on free expression. To get more information about blocking undesirable material online—and other strategies for guarding your child's exposure to the Net—check out the Net Parents Web site (see Figure 3.8).

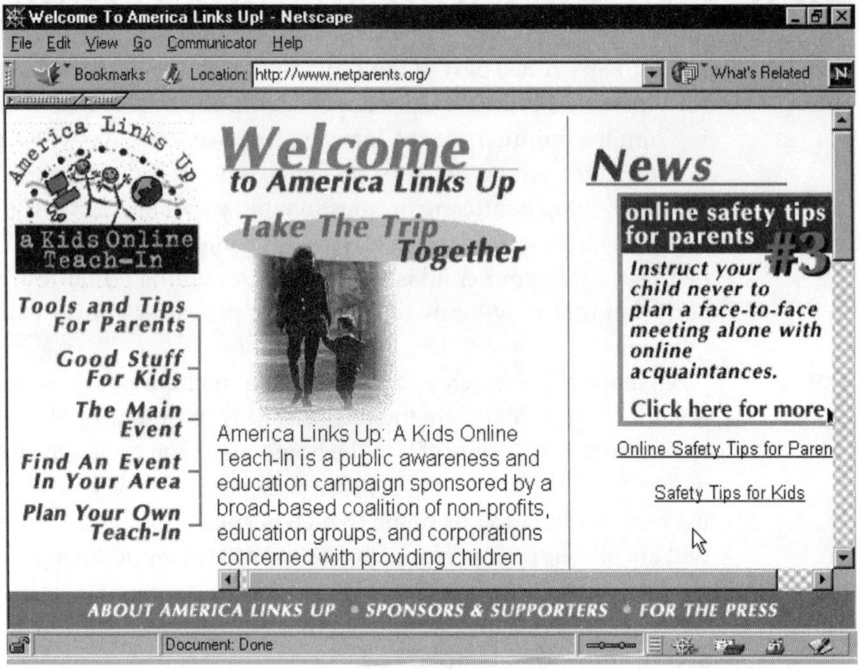

FIGURE 3.8: The Net Parents site at `http://www.netparents.org/` gives a helpful overview of the issues confronting parents whose children use the Internet.

Rating Content

The emerging standard for rating and filtering out content on the Net is *PICS*, which stands for Platform for Internet Content Selection.

In the PICS system, sites either rate themselves or are rated by third parties. This permits a fine level of control over a wide range of questionable content. The details of the PICS standard can be read at the Web Consortium's site (see Figure 3.9).

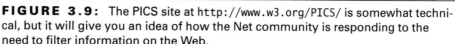

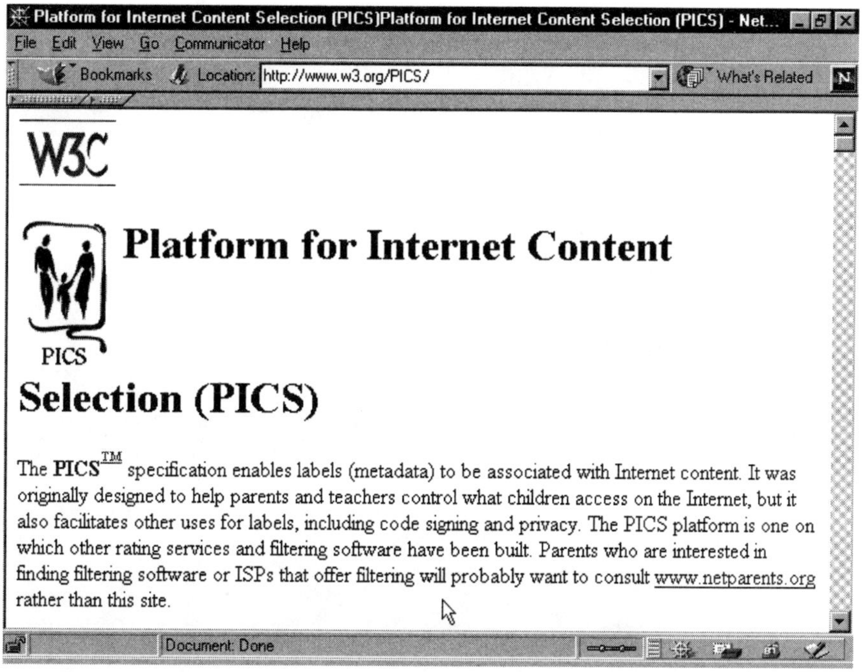

FIGURE 3.9: The PICS site at `http://www.w3.org/PICS/` is somewhat technical, but it will give you an idea of how the Net community is responding to the need to filter information on the Web.

Microsoft's Web browser, Internet Explorer, fully implements the PICS system. Figure 3.10 shows the Content Advisor dialog box with which you can establish thresholds of acceptable content in four problematic areas: language, nudity, sex, and violence.

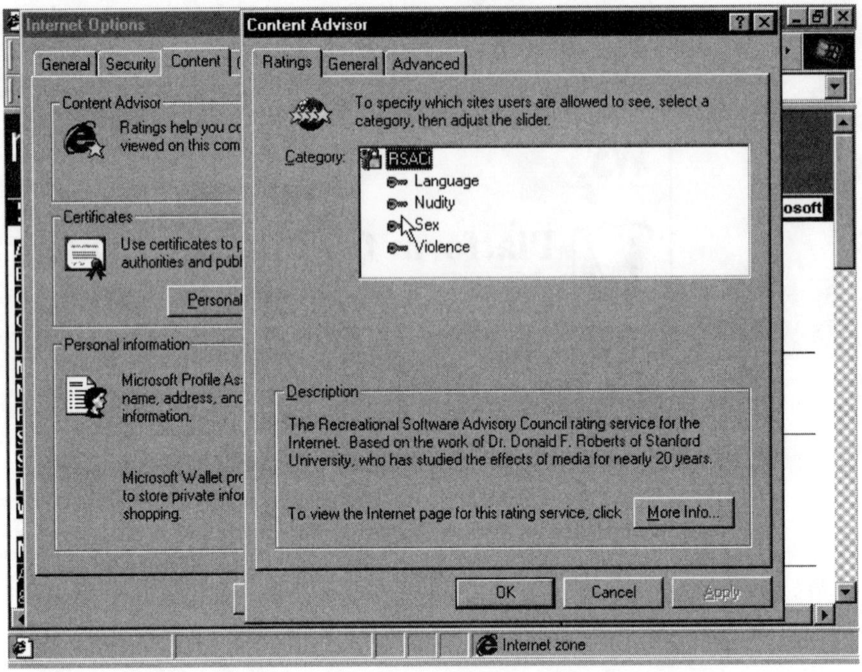

FIGURE 3.10: Microsoft Internet Explorer incorporates controls that permit you to set acceptable levels of several types of problematic content.

Software Filters

There are also a number of stand-alone programs that can be used alongside your Internet connection to weed out the unsavory material. For example, to download trial software from Cyberpatrol, just visit the `http://www.cyberpatrol.com/` Web site and click the Download button (see Figure 3.11).

Other popular software filter programs include Netnanny (`http://www.netnanny.com/`) and Surfwatch (`http://www.surfwatch.com/`).

However, if you're the type of parent who has to ask your children to program your VCR for you, beware of any system that relies on you outsmarting them! Filtering material is all well and good (in fact, it's part of exercising your supervisory responsibility with your children), but it's no substitute for establishing what's right and wrong in advance.

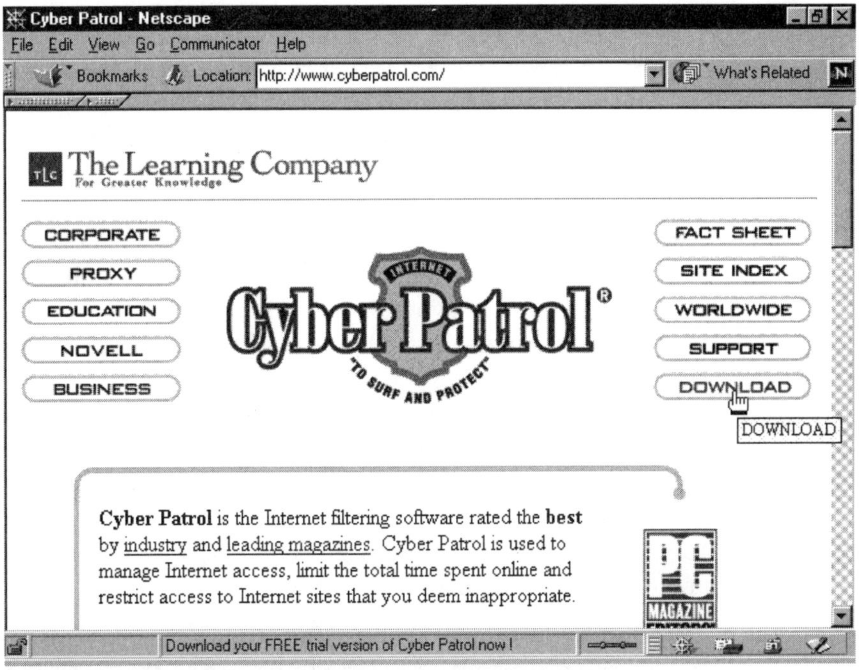

FIGURE 3.11: CyberPatrol offers its software for a trial download.

Protecting Your Child's Privacy

Your child's exposure to unfriendly strangers or inappropriate content should be your primary concern, but you must also recognize that the Internet is a heavily commercialized public space (something like television in this respect), and that your child will be vulnerable to commercial solicitation while online. You wouldn't permit a traveling salesperson to make a pitch to your child at your front door, so you should take steps to limit your child's exposure to sales pitches online as well. (See Skill 21 for some tips on how to minimize unwanted commercial e-mail, called *spam*.)

TIP

AOL users, see Skill 16 for instructions on how to exert Parental Controls over what your children see via America Online.

Any Web site that requires users to sign in has the capacity to retain their personal information and target them for advertisements (or even to sell the information to mass marketers). Therefore, it's important that a Web site disclose precisely what it intends to do with any information it requests. Before you fill out forms at any Web sites (and especially before you fill anything out on behalf of your child or permit your child to fill in her own information), consult the Web site's statement of its privacy policy, which is required by law, at least in the United States.

If a Web site says nothing about privacy or about how it uses the information it collects, steer clear of it. Any scrupulous site, particularly if it caters to children, will have its policy posted in an easy-to-find place.

Figure 3.12 shows the Web page that contains the privacy policy of the Yahooligans! Web site. There's a link to this page at the bottom of the site's home page (its main page, that is).

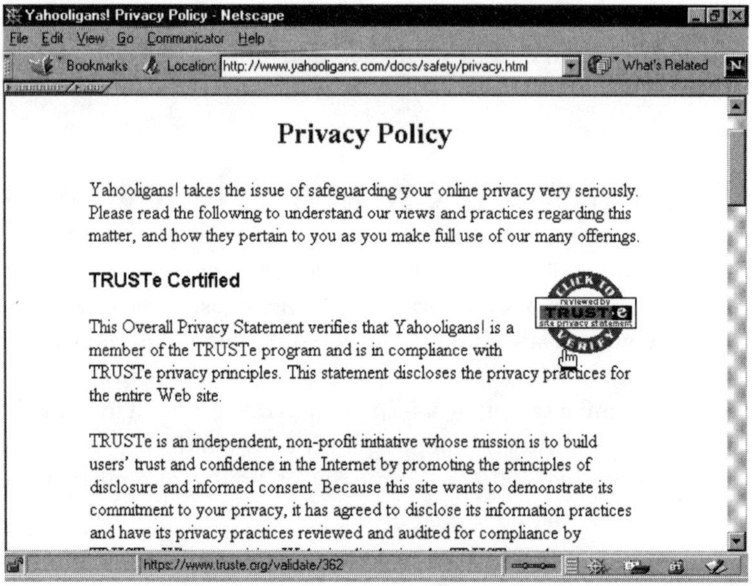

FIGURE 3.12: Yahoo! takes pains to reassure you that its Yahooligans! site for children will not misuse any of the information it accrues.

Are You Experienced?

Now you can…

- ☑ explore the Internet together with your children
- ☑ help your children find educational resources online
- ☑ discover entertainment sites on the Web
- ☑ block content you don't want your children exposed to
- ☑ safeguard the privacy of your family

PART II

Communicating with E-mail

This is the real stuff. The reason why you're on the Net. E-mail! Instant (more or less) communication with people all over the globe. Sure, we'll get to the World Wide Web soon (see Part III, *Browsing the World Wide Web*), but first things first. Once you can send and receive e-mail, you're wired. Whether you have a Mac, PC, or more exotic type of computer, whether you connect by modem or from a network, and no matter what e-mail program you have, you can still send and receive e-mail over the Internet.

SKILL 4

E-MAIL BASICS

- **Sending e-mail**
- **Reading e-mail**
- **Replying to e-mail**
- **Deleting e-mail**

This lesson will cover the most basic e-mail concepts—mainly, how to send and receive e-mail. If you have an internal network at your office and you're already familiar with how to send and receive mail, you can probably skip this lesson (though you might want to read the parts about how to write an Internet e-mail address to send mail beyond your network). If you don't yet have an e-mail account or Internet access, look in Appendix A for how to get connected to the Internet and how to get started once you are connected.

NOTE

When you get used to sending e-mail, you'll find that it's as useful a form of communication as the telephone, and it doesn't require the other person to drop whatever they're doing to answer your call. You can include a huge amount of specific information, and the person you sent mail to can reply in full in their own good time. And unlike the telephone, with e-mail you can write your message and edit it first before you send it.

Working with E-mail

These are the things that you will do most often with e-mail:

- Run the mail program
- Send mail
- Read incoming mail
- Reply to mail
- Delete mail
- Exit the mail program

In Skill 5, *Advanced E-mail Tricks*, I'll show you some additional e-mail techniques you might find useful, such as how to forward mail and create an electronic address book.

Running an E-mail Program

You start most e-mail programs the way you do any program, usually by double-clicking an icon or by choosing a program name from a menu (the Start menu in Windows 95/98, the Apple menu or Launcher on a Mac). If your Internet connection is not already up and running, your e-mail program may be able to start that process for you. (If not, see Appendix A for how to connect to the Net.)

TIP TIP TIP TIP TIP TIP TIP TIP TIP TIP TIP TIP TIP TIP TIP TIP TIP TIP TIP TIP TIP TIP TIP TIP TIP

If you have to log in to a Unix shell, then you'll start your mail program (probably Pine) by typing its name at the Unix prompt and pressing Enter.

Your e-mail program will start and either show you the contents of your Inbox (the mailbox where your new messages arrive) or show you a list of all your mailboxes (in which case you'll want to open the Inbox).

NOTE NOTE NOTE NOTE NOTE NOTE NOTE NOTE NOTE NOTE NOTE NOTE NOTE NOTE NOTE

There are some free Internet accounts (such as HotMail and Juno.com), that offer Web-based e-mail access. The accounts are paid for by advertising that you have to keep on your screen while you're connected. To find out more about them, see Skill 17, *Other Online Services, WebTV, and Free Web-Based E-mail* after reading Part III, *Browsing the World Wide Web*.

In addition to an Inbox where new messages appear, you'll also have an Outbox in which copies of your outgoing messages can be saved (some programs will do this automatically), and usually a deleted-messages or Trash mailbox where discarded messages are held until they are completely purged. Figure 4.1 shows a Microsoft Outlook Inbox and an Inbox for Microsoft Outlook Express, which is part of Microsoft Internet Explorer.

Mailboxes generally list the sender's name and the subject line of the message (and often its date as well). When you double-click a message in any of your mailboxes, the message will open up in a window of its own.

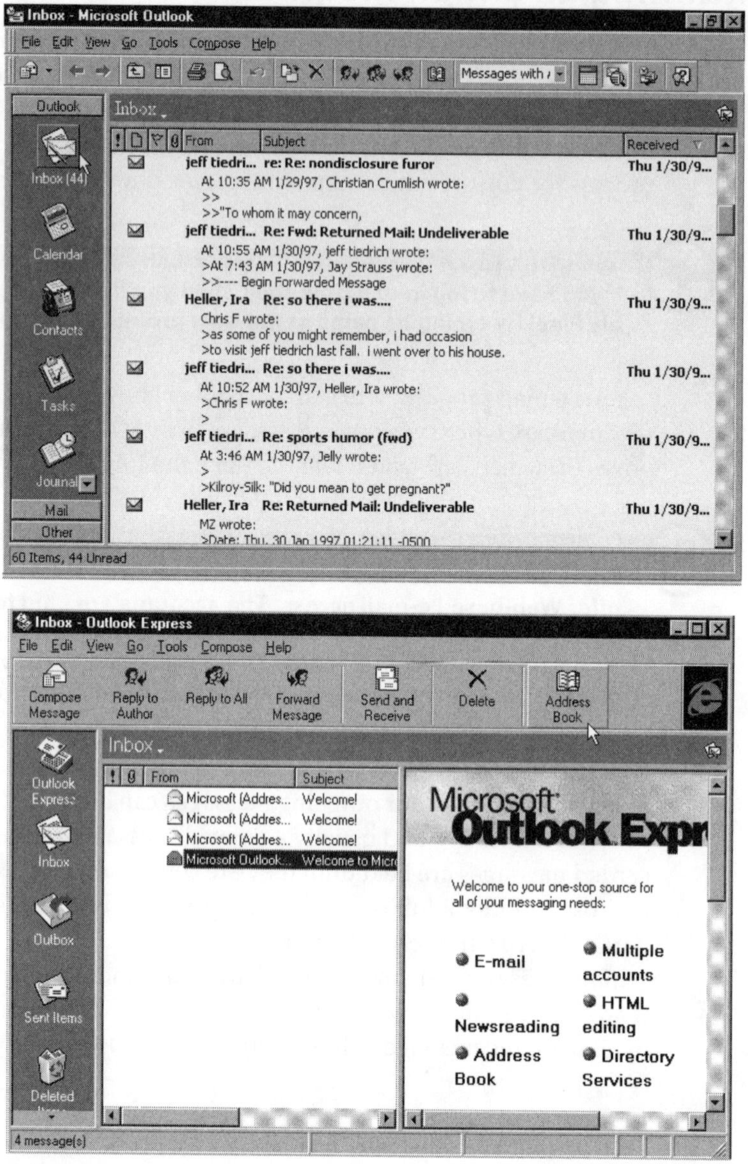

FIGURE 4.1: The first screen shows my Microsoft Outlook 97 Inbox with messages listed in the order they were sent, from the most recent to the oldest. Compare that Inbox to the one shown next for Microsoft Outlook Express, which comes with Microsoft Internet Explorer 4.

Sending Mail

All mail programs have a New Message or Compose E-mail command, often located on a message menu, and they usually have a keyboard shortcut for the command as well, such as Ctrl+N for New Message. When you start a new message, your program will open a new window. Figure 4.2 shows a new message window in Eudora, a popular e-mail program.

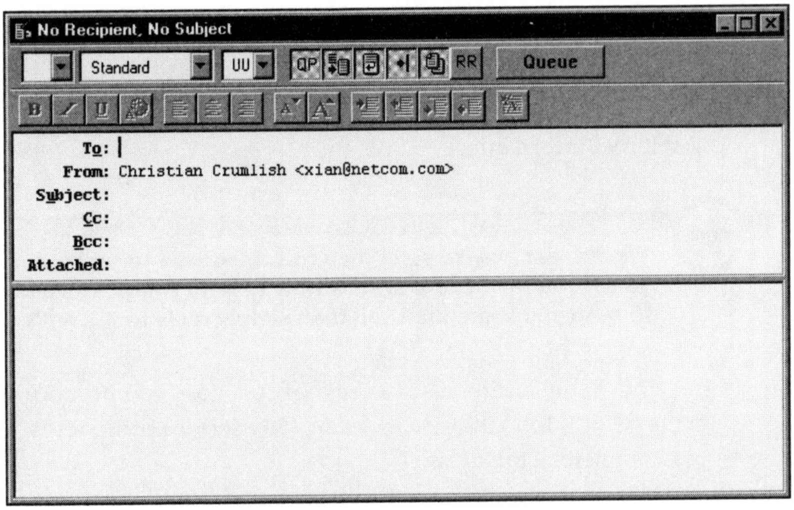

FIGURE 4.2: A blank new message window

TIP

Most e-mail programs enable you to save addresses and then select them from an address book or list of names rather than type them in directly. See Skill 5, *Advanced E-mail Tricks*, for more on this.

Type the address of the person to whom you wish to send the mail. The person's address must be of the form `username@address.domain`, where *username* is the person's identifier (the name they log in with); *address* is the identifier of the person's network or machine on the network (the address might consist of several words—the host and subdomain—separated by dots); and *domain* is the short code at the end indicating whether the address is a business (`.com`), a non-profit organization (`.org`), a university (`.edu`), a branch of the government (`.gov`), a part of the military (.mil), and so on. (Some e-mail programs require special text before or after the Internet e-mail address.)

NOTE NOTE NOTE NOTE NOTE NOTE NOTE NOTE NOTE NOTE NOTE NOTE NOTE NOTE NOTE

Would you rather write up your message ahead of time and then just paste it in when it comes time to send it? See Skill 5, *Advanced E-mail Tricks,* for how to include a text file you've already prepared.

By the way, all the rules mentioned in the previous category apply only to sending mail over the Internet. Generally, if you're sending mail to someone on your own network (or another member of your online service or a subscriber of your service provider), you only have to specify the username, not any of the Internet information.

TIP TIP TIP TIP TIP TIP TIP TIP TIP TIP TIP TIP TIP TIP TIP TIP TIP TIP TIP TIP TIP TIP TIP TIP TIP

The easiest way to send mail to someone is to reply to mail that they've sent you. If you're not sure exactly how to form someone's e-mail address, ask them to send you some mail and then simply reply to it. That's what I always do.

One of my addresses is xian@netcom.com (you pronounce the "@" as "at" and the "." as "dot"). I log in as "xian," my service provider is Netcom, and Netcom is a commercial business.

Sending Mail to People on Other Networks

Many people have Internet addresses even though they are not, strictly speaking, on the Internet. Most other networks have gateways that send mail to and from the Internet. If you want to send mail to someone on another network, you'll need to know their identifier on that network and how their network address appears in Internet form. Here are examples of the most common Internet addresses:

Network	Username	Internet Address
America Online	Beebles	Beebles@aol.com
AT&T Mail	Beebles	beebles@attmail.com
AT&T WorldNet	Beebles	beebles@worldnet.att.net
CompuServe	75555,5555	75555.5555@compuserve.com
Fidonet BBS	1:2/3	f3.n2.z1@fidonet.org
MCI Mail	555-7777	555-7777@mcimail.com

Network	Username	Internet Address
Microsoft Network	Beebles	`beebles@msn.com`
Prodigy	Beebles	`beebles@prodigy.com`

As you can see, the only tricky ones are CompuServe, for which you have to change the comma in the CompuServe address to a dot in the Internet address; and Fidonet, for which you have to reverse the order of the three numbers and then put them after `f`, `n`, and `z`, respectively. (If you are only given two numbers, in the form `a/b`, then assume that they are the `n` and `f` numbers and that the `z` number is 1 (one).)

Creating an E-mail Message

Here's how to create an e-mail message:

1. After entering the recipient's address in the Address box, press Tab and then type a subject in the Subject box (keep it short). This will be the first thing the recipient of your mail sees.

TIP TIP TIP TIP TIP TIP TIP TIP TIP TIP TIP TIP TIP TIP TIP TIP TIP TIP TIP TIP TIP TIP TIP TIP TIP

The subject you type in the subject line should be fairly short, but should be a good description of the contents of your message. Good subject lines can help recipients categorize their mail and respond more quickly to your messages. If they are using Inbox filters, described in Skill 5, *Advanced E-mail Tricks,* they may be presorting their e-mail according to the contents of the subject line, making the subject even more important for getting your mail noticed.

2. If you want to send a copy of the e-mail message to more than one recipient, you can either:
   - Type additional addresses on the Cc line.
   - Add addresses to the To line (usually separated by commas, although some programs, such as Outlook, use semicolons instead).

TIP TIP TIP TIP TIP TIP TIP TIP TIP TIP TIP TIP TIP TIP TIP TIP TIP TIP TIP TIP TIP TIP TIP TIP TIP

In almost all e-mail programs, you can press Tab to jump from box to box or from area to area when filling in an address and subject. You can also just click directly in the area you want to jump to in most programs.

3. Press Tab until the insertion point jumps into the blank message area, and type your message.

4. When you are done, send the message or add it to a *queue*, a list of outgoing messages to be sent all at once. (A queue is useful if you have a lot of mail to write and send and you don't want to wait for each message to go out before drafting the next one.) Press the Send button, or select File ➢ Send.

TIP

Most e-mail programs can word-wrap your message, so you only have to press Enter when you want to start a new paragraph. I recommend leaving a blank line between paragraphs, to make them easier to read. Figure 4.3 shows a short e-mail message.

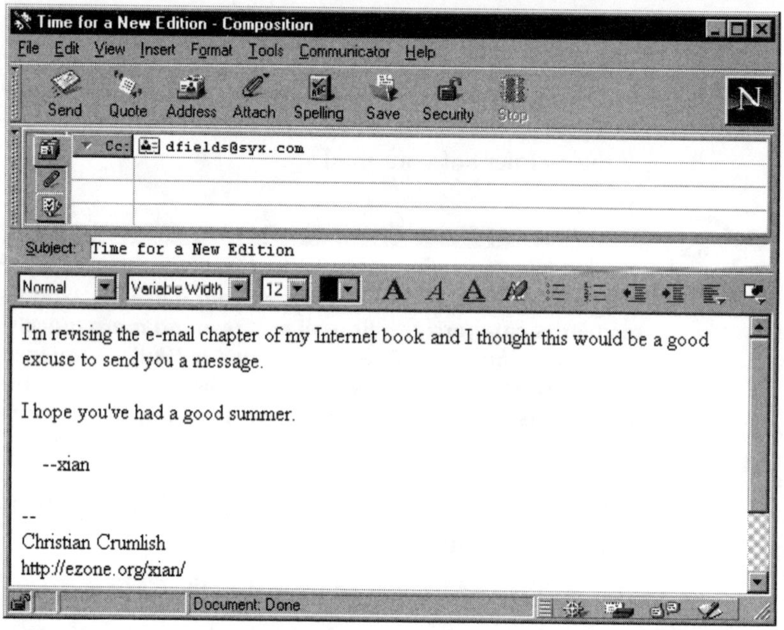

FIGURE 4.3: A short e-mail message to a friend

Some e-mail programs allow you to filter messages, meaning you sort them according to some criteria as they come into your Inbox. The post office sorts regular mail according to zip code; similarly, you can use your e-mail program to automatically sort messages according to who sent them, the subject, the date they were sent or received, or any other category that is useful to you from an organizational standpoint. See Skill 5, *Advanced E-mail Tricks*, for more on message filters.

TIP TIP TIP TIP TIP TIP TIP TIP TIP TIP TIP TIP TIP TIP TIP TIP TIP TIP TIP TIP TIP TIP TIP TIP TIP

You can sort your messages in many e-mail applications, according to categories and other criteria. Certain e-mail programs also allow you to flag messages according to the urgency of the response needed or other priorities. Check in your application's Help menu or under the File or Edit menus (in Windows programs) for commands such as Sort or Categorize. These options provide you with powerful organizational tools and transform your messages into valuable records that can be filed and retrieved for later reference. See Skill 5, *Advanced E-mail Tricks*, for more about sorting.

Reading Mail

Whenever I connect to the Net, the first thing I do is check my e-mail. It's like checking your mailbox when you get home, except the contents are generally more interesting—and usually don't contain bills! Some mail programs combine the process of sending queued messages with checking for new mail. Most also check for new mail when you first start them.

Unread (usually new) mail typically appears with some indicator that it's new: the Subject line may appear in bold, or a bullet or checkmark may appear next to the new messages. This is supposed to help you pick out the messages you haven't read yet, so you don't miss any.

Here are the steps for reading an e-mail message:

1. Open your e-mail program by double-clicking its shortcut icon or selecting it from the Start menu. Some programs begin by displaying your Inbox contents, but with others you will need to click a Get New Mail button, or select File ➢ Get Mail or Get New Mail. Others have a special Mail menu selection, where you choose Mail ➢ Get New Mail or Mail ➢ Read Incoming Mail. Display your Inbox with the command appropriate for your program.
2. To view the contents of a mail message, highlight it in the Inbox window and press Enter (or double-click it). The message will appear in its own window, much like an outgoing message. Figure 4.4 shows an example of an incoming message.
3. If the message continues beyond the bottom of the window, use the scroll bar to see the next screenful.
4. After reading the message, you can close or reply to the message.

TIP TIP TIP TIP TIP TIP TIP TIP TIP TIP TIP TIP TIP TIP TIP TIP TIP TIP TIP TIP TIP TIP TIP TIP TIP

I keep my mail around until I've replied to it. I could save it to a mailbox (as I'll explain in Skill 5, *Advanced E-mail Tricks,* soon) but then I might forget about it. When my Inbox gets too cluttered, I bite the bullet, reply to mail I've been putting off, and then delete most of it.

Replying to Mail

Somewhere near the New Message command (probably on the same menu or button bar), you'll find the Reply command. When you reply to an e-mail message, your new message is automatically addressed back to the sender, and depending on your e-mail program, you may be able to easily quote the message you received.

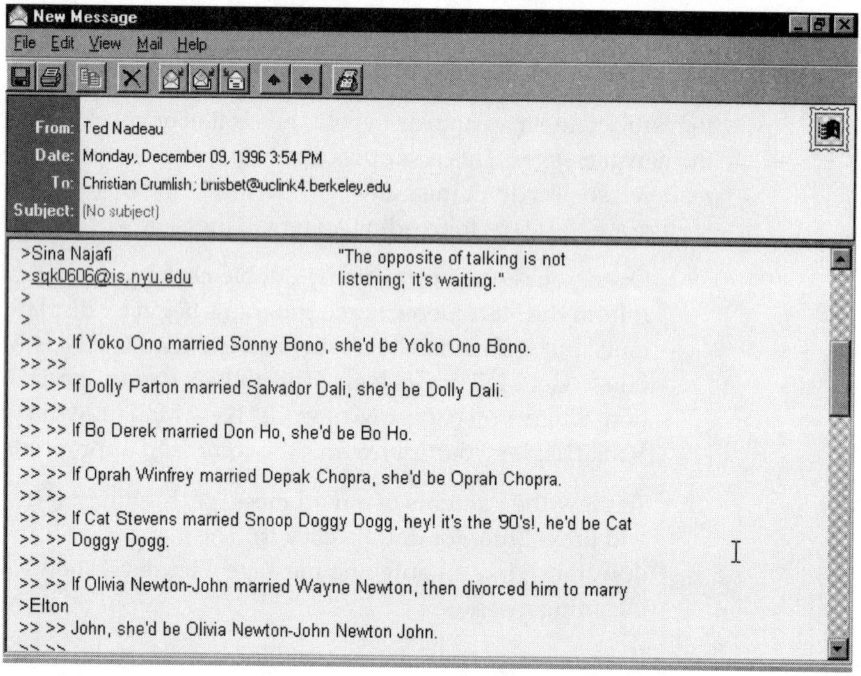

FIGURE 4.4: Here's an e-mail message I received.

TIP TIP TIP TIP TIP TIP TIP TIP TIP TIP TIP TIP TIP TIP TIP TIP TIP TIP TIP TIP TIP TIP TIP TIP TIP

If you start to reply by mistake, just close the message window and don't save the reply if prompted.

To reply to an e-mail message, follow these steps:

1. Highlight the received message in the Inbox or open the message, and then select the Reply command.
2. Your program will create a new message automatically addressed to the sender of the message you're replying to. Some mail programs will also automatically include the contents of the original message (or will give you the choice of including the contents or not). Often, especially with e-mail programs that were designed primarily for use on the Internet, the included message will appear with a ">" character at the beginning of each line to indicate that it is quoted text, although different mail programs have different ways of showing quoted messages. Some, for example, just indent the quoted material (see Figure 4.5).

TIP TIP TIP TIP TIP TIP TIP TIP TIP TIP TIP TIP TIP TIP TIP TIP TIP TIP TIP TIP TIP TIP TIP TIP TIP

Any Web addresses mentioned in e-mail messages can function as clickable links in many of the newer programs, such as Netscape Messenger, Microsoft Outlook and Outlook Express, and Eudora Light and Pro. To use these links, click the highlighted address, which will probably be underlined or depicted in a different color, such as blue. You will be transported to the Web site using that address. Microsoft Outlook and Outlook Express users can also add Web shortcuts as file attachments. Just click the Web icon to head for that site. For more information on the Web, see Part III, *Browsing the World Wide Web.*

3. Sometimes, you'll want to reply to everyone who was sent a copy of the original message. Most e-mail programs offer a variation on the normal Reply command that includes all original recipients in your reply. Select Reply to All or a similar command to send your reply to everyone.
4. Tab to the subject line and type a new subject if the old one isn't very meaningful anymore. (People often fail to change the subject line of messages, even when the conversation has evolved its way onto a new topic.)
5. Add other recipients if necessary, tab your way into the message area to type your reply, and then choose the Send (or Queue) command when you are done.

TIP TIP TIP TIP TIP TIP TIP TIP TIP TIP TIP TIP TIP TIP TIP TIP TIP TIP TIP TIP TIP TIP TIP TIP TIP TIP

E-mail tends to take on a life of its own, with people forwarding you messages from other people asking for help, information, you name it. Sometimes people send you long chains of related messages, often called *threads*. To avoid confusion when replying to a message forwarded to you, or when replying to many recipients, direct the mail program to "retain the original text," or however the command is worded, so that people reading the message will know what you are talking about and will know the history of the issue. However, if the thread starts getting too long, try to abbreviate it as described later in the "Using Proper E-mail Netiquette" section of this lesson.

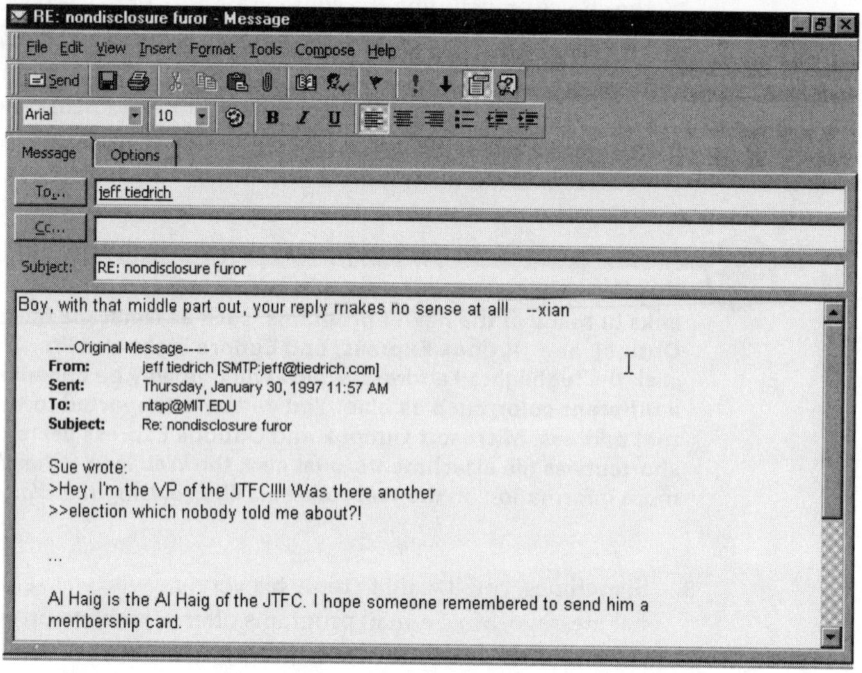

FIGURE 4.5: A reply with the original message included

Deleting Mail

If you have read a piece of mail and you're positive that you have no need to save it, you should delete it so it doesn't clutter up your Inbox (and waste precious hard-disk storage space). To delete a message, you typically highlight it and press the Delete key on the keyboard (or click the Delete or Trash button, if there is one). In most programs, this moves the message to the Deleted Mail or Trash mailbox until you empty the trash (or quit the program).

WARNING WARNING WARNING WARNING WARNING WARNING WARNING WARNING

In some programs, you don't get a chance to undelete a message, so be sure you know how your program works before deleting messages willy-nilly.

If you change your mind, try opening the Trash mailbox (or Deleted Mail mailbox) and then looking for a command that allows you to transfer mail from one mailbox to another. It may even be called Transfer (as it is in Eudora). When you find it, transfer the mail back to your Inbox.

I cover ways to save messages in Skill 5, *Advanced E-mail Tricks*. The next section of e-mail etiquette, or *netiquette*, is an important aspect of communicating on the Internet.

Using Proper E-mail Netiquette

Like any social system, the Internet has evolved to the point where its users observe a variety of informal rules for interacting politely. Collectively, these rules are known as *netiquette*, and most of them can be inferred through the application of some common sense to various social situations.

For example, it's generally not considered good manners to misquote what someone said when talking to someone else, to take their words out of context, or to repeat something that was told to you in confidence (though the media and gossips often commit such acts!). Think of e-mail as a kind of online conversation. If people send you messages containing sensitive material, don't forward them to others without the author's permission.

If you retain only part of the original text of messages in your replies (to keep the replies from becoming too long), be sure it is not misleadingly taken out of its full context (and likely to be misinterpreted). And please do not intersperse your own comments with the retained pieces of other people's messages so that it's not clear to the recipients who wrote what.

Keep Your Messages Brief and Tactful

When you write messages to business associates and colleagues, stick to the point and be informative. Break up large blocks of text into smaller paragraphs. Reread your messages and run a spellcheck before sending them—this will give you a chance to minimize mistakes, fix poorly organized sentences, and reconsider bad word choices.

If you are writing to friends (or potential friends in usegroups or chat rooms), you can relax a little more, but still hold back on anything that could be considered offensive, even if you think it's funny and you are sure that your friends will, too. Seemingly innocuous statements said in spoken conversation can take on a whole new meaning when written down. Figures of speech, jokes, and your own private way of referring to situations or people seem a lot more serious when viewed in writing.

Save Connect-Time Charges by Going Offline

If the message is going to be a long one, it might be better to write it up in your word processing application and take advantage of all the formatting features (bulleted lists, columns, tables, etc.) that are not usually available in e-mail programs. Save the long message (as a text file if you are sending it to someone who does not have a word processing program compatible with yours) and send it as an attachment to a brief message that simply states, "attached you will find my comments on …" Not only will the message look better, but you will save lots of connect-time charges because you are writing it offline, while not connected to your service provider's network. The recipient will also save connect-time charges by quickly downloading the long message and reading it offline too.

If your e-mail application, online service, or Internet access provider has an offline reader or an option for working offline, you can use that feature to save connect-time charges while reading or composing mail. For example, Microsoft Internet Explorer has a File ➢ Work Offline command, and Microsoft Outlook Express's Tools ➢ Send and Receive function asks you if you want to hang up when finished collecting and transmitting your mail.

WARNING WARNING WARNING WARNING WARNING WARNING WARNING WARNING

The old adage about never saying or putting anything in writing that you would not want to see in a headline the next day also applies to e-mail and the Internet. Now you also have to worry about your words appearing on someone's Web page or showing up when someone searches the Web, a chat service, or a newsgroup. Journalists search the Web for juicy opinions every day. There's no law preventing potential employers from checking you out on the Web and uncovering some embarrassing thing you wrote or posted years ago.

When replying to messages, try to minimize the amount of quoted text that you keep in your return message. Leave enough so it's clear what you're replying to (people don't always remember exactly what they wrote to you). However, as mentioned at the beginning of this section, don't send abbreviated message bits attributed to other people that could be taken out of context. Just use your good common sense!

Don't Fly off the Handle

In this book I'm trying not to give you too much advice about how to behave on the Net, for a couple of reasons. First, I assume you are an adult and can decide for yourself how to behave. Secondly, the Net has a strongly interactive culture, and you will receive plenty of advice and cues from others if you overstep the bounds of good behavior.

NOTE NOTE NOTE NOTE NOTE NOTE NOTE NOTE NOTE NOTE NOTE NOTE NOTE NOTE NOTE

Issues of netiquette arise even more frequently when you are communicating with large numbers of people on mailing lists or Usenet. See Skill 7, *Signing Up for Mailing Lists*, and Skill 13, *Joining Usenet Newsgroups*, for more details.

Nevertheless, I will point out that e-mail is a notoriously volatile medium. Because it is so easy to write out a reply and send it in the heat of the moment, and because text lacks many of the nuances of face-to-face communication—the expression and body cues that add emphasis, the tones of voice that indicate joking instead of insult, and so on—it has become a matter of course for many people to dash off ill-considered replies to perceived insults and therefore to fan the flames of invective.

This Internet habit, called *flaming*, is widespread and you will no doubt encounter it on one end or the other. All I can suggest is that you try to restrain yourself when you feel the urge to fly off the handle. (And I have discovered that apologies work wonders when people have misunderstood a friendly gibe or have mistaken sarcasm for idiocy.)

TIP

If you are the sort to flare up in an angry response, or if you find yourself getting emotional or agitated while composing a response to a message that upsets you, save your message as a draft rather than sending it right away. Most e-mail programs provide the option to save a draft message. You can review the draft message later when you have calmed down and decide then whether you want to send it, or you can send the draft to a disinterested third party and ask them if it is too harsh before you send it out.

Exiting an E-mail Program

When you are finished sending, reading, and replying to mail, you can quit your program or leave it running to check your mail at regular intervals. You can quit most mail programs by selecting File ➢ Exit or File ➢ Quit.

Are You Experienced?

Now you can...

- ☑ check for new e-mail messages
- ☑ open your messages and read them
- ☑ reply to messages
- ☑ send messages to people via the Internet
- ☑ delete old messages to keep your Inbox uncluttered
- ☑ write tactful messages and observe Internet etiquette

SKILL 5

ADVANCED E-MAIL TRICKS

- **Forwarding e-mail and sending it to multiple recipients**
- **Composing e-mail messages in your word processing program**
- **Sending attachments with your messages**
- **Saving e-mail messages and addresses**
- **Spell-checking an e-mail message**
- **Attaching signatures to e-mail messages**
- **Finding Internet e-mail addresses**

Once you've mastered the basics of e-mail—sending, reading, and replying to messages—there are just a few more e-mail functions you'll want to know about. Some of them are basic and available in just about every e-mail program, such as forwarding a message to a new recipient, sending mail to more than one person at a time, and saving old messages somewhere besides in your Inbox. Other, more advanced features vary from program to program.

What's New with E-mail?

The competition among software companies to provide the best, or most popular, e-mail tool is fierce, so most programs are revised at least yearly, and any useful new feature that appears in one program is sure to crop up in the competition the next time around. Some e-mail capabilities that are becoming standard include message filtering (automated sorting of mail as it comes in), receiving mail from multiple e-mail accounts, managing address books, and adding HTML (hypertext codes and links) and other types of formatting to messages.

In upcoming releases of mail programs, look for special routines to help you filter out or respond to spam (junk e-mail).

First, let's start with some straightforward tricks.

Sending Mail to More Than One Person

Sometimes you'll want to send a message to more than one recipient. You can usually do this in one of several ways. E-mail message are always preceded by a number of "headers"—lines of information telling who the message is from, who it has been sent to, and what the subject of the message is. Most programs allow you to list multiple recipients in the To line, usually separated by commas (some programs require that you use a different character, such as a semicolon, to separate addresses). Most also have a Cc line. As with traditional paper office memos, the Cc line in an e-mail message is for people who should receive a copy of the message, but who are not the primary recipient.

NOTE NOTE NOTE NOTE NOTE NOTE NOTE NOTE NOTE NOTE NOTE NOTE NOTE NOTE NOTE

When you reply to a message, if you select the Reply To Sender option, your reply will be sent only to the person in the To line. If you select Reply To All, your reply will be sent to everyone in the Cc list as well.

Some programs also offer a Bcc line, which lets you list one or more people to receive blind copies of that message. This means that the primary (and Cc) recipients will not see the names of people receiving blind copies.

WARNING WARNING WARNING WARNING WARNING WARNING WARNING WARNING

You can typically include as many names on the address lines as you want, but some mail servers will choke on a message if its headers are too long.

Sending Files via E-mail

It sounds too good to be true. Just "attach" a file to an e-mail message and it zips across the globe to your recipient, without having to be put on a disk and sent by mail or courier. Naturally, it's not that simple. Some files are just too big to send this way (anything close to a megabyte is probably too big). But even with files of a more appropriate size, you may encounter hitches. Most of the problem is in coordinating between computer types, file types, compression formats, and encoding formats. Getting all the elements to work out can be a little like trying a combination lock. But I'm getting ahead of myself. Let's start with what an attachment really is.

NOTE NOTE NOTE NOTE NOTE NOTE NOTE NOTE NOTE NOTE NOTE NOTE NOTE

Each online service or Internet service provider is a little different, so you can experiment with the size of files you can send. Some services limit the size of files you may attach to messages, while others will take anything, but the transmission may become extremely slow. You can compress files to make them smaller and you can send a group of files by attaching each one to a separate message to keep the sizes low. (For more on compressing files, see the section called "Compression Programs" in Skill 10, *Finding Stuff on the Web and the Net*.)

How Attachments Are Created

One of the most important functions of e-mail is its ability to let you send files called *attachments* along with your messages. An attachment is a data file, in any form, that your program will send along with your e-mail message—it could be a word processor file, a picture, a spreadsheet, or any other kind of file. Each e-mail program is different in the way it handles file attachments. Also, because different programs have different ways of *encoding* attached files (translating the files into a form that can be shipped over the Internet), you may have to compare details with your sender or recipient to make sure that both of your programs can "speak" the same code. For example, a big part of writing this book involved transferring files between a Macintosh, running one version of Eudora, and my PC, which was running another version. It took several file transfers before things worked seamlessly.

Internet mail generally consists of only plain text files, although there are some protocols for sending other forms of information. For example, some mail programs use *MIME* (*Multipurpose Internet Mail Extensions*) to send other kinds of data, including color pictures, sound files, and video clips. If you are sent e-mail with a MIME attachment, you may not be able to see the pictures, hear the music, or view the movies, but the text in the attachment should come through just fine. You'll be asked if you want to view the file or save it.

Working with Different File Formats

Quite aside from e-mail issues, you might be trying to send a file that your recipient doesn't have the right application for reading, so that's another thing you may have to work out in advance. For example, if you use Word for the Macintosh and your recipient uses WordPerfect for DOS, then you may have to save your file in a format that your recipient's program can understand (or a common format that many programs can understand, such as RTF, which stands for Rich Text Format); this may involve both of you poking around your programs' Open and Save As commands to see what options are available.

When you receive a file attachment, your e-mail program will usually decode it and tell you where it's been placed (unless it doesn't recognize the coding format, in which case you'll get a bunch of garbage at the end of the message and no file attachment—if this happens, you'll need to negotiate with the sender as I just discussed). We will look at techniques for sending and attaching files in Skill 6, *E-mail Programs*.

TIP

See Skill 18, *Getting Around with FTP and Telnet*, to learn about some of the other ways to send and receive files.

Forwarding Mail to Someone Else

If someone sends you an e-mail message and you'd like to send a copy of it to someone else, most mail programs let you select a Forward command.

WARNING WARNING WARNING WARNING WARNING WARNING WARNING WARNING

Never send received mail to a third party without the express permission of the original sender. Also, be sure to use a *reply separator*, such as a solid horizontal line, between all of the forwarded e-mail messages, to delineate where one person's response ends and another begins (most e-mail programs add reply separators automatically). This will avoid confusion about who wrote what and will avoid uncomfortable situations for both you and those who send you e-mail.

The Forward command is often on the same menu or toolbar as the Reply command, and it works in almost the same way. The difference is that your mail program won't insert the original sender's e-mail address into the To line. Instead, the To line will be blank so you can fill in the address of the person you are forwarding the message to. The original message will automatically be included in the new message, often with some characters (like the standard ">" Internet e-mail quoting character) or other formatting to distinguish it from what you yourself write.

Here's how to forward e-mail messages:

1. Open your e-mail program and either highlight or open the message you want to forward.
2. Click the Forward command in the toolbar of your e-mail program, or use a command such as Message ➢ Forward or Mail ➢ Forward. A new message window will appear with the forwarded message included in the text area.
3. Type the recipient's e-mail address in the To line and then Tab your way down to the message area.
4. Edit the message if you want, or add your own note to the beginning, perhaps explaining why you are forwarding the message.
5. Then send the message as usual.

Enhancing Your E-mail with HTML Formatting

For a long time, network e-mail programs have permitted the addition of formatting enhancements to e-mail messages for the benefit of recipients on the same network (who, presumably using the same program, could see the formatting as it was intended). Internet mail has long been an "unformatted" medium, with only a guarantee that basic text would be transmitted from site to site. Formatted messages typically lose their formatting as soon as they pass through an e-mail gateway.

Some mail programs can understand or create formatting that conforms to the Internet's MIME standard, but again, not all programs recognize MIME, so the point of the formatting may be lost.

More recently, mail programs have appeared that are more closely integrated with Web browsers, such as Netscape Messenger, part of the same Netscape Communicator suite that contains Netscape Navigator 4. Microsoft Internet Mail, which is designed to look like and work smoothly with Microsoft Internet Explorer 3 and earlier, and Microsoft Outlook Express, which comes with Microsoft Internet Explorer 4, are also tightly meshed with their browsers. Overall, e-mail programs (such as the popular Eudora Pro and Eudora Light) have become more "Web-savvy": able to recognize Web addresses (URLs), hyperlinks, and now most HTML formatting.

WARNING WARNING WARNING WARNING WARNING WARNING WARNING WARNING

Don't rely too heavily on any "brand" of formatting to make your point, because you can't be sure your audience will see the pulsing, blinking green text or other effects you may add. Your careful selection of just the right font may also backfire when the message arrives, because some programs substitute basic fonts for less common fonts, resulting in poorly aligned text at the message's destination.

As HTML, the coding language used to create Web documents, becomes a sort of universal Internet standard, you'll be able to compose mail messages much the same way you can Web pages, inserting images and links to pages on the Web or other Internet resources. In most programs, you won't need to "know the code" either, because the software will make it as easy to add HTML formatting as it now is to change font styles with your word processor. Similarly, e-mail can link directly to an intranet site on your local network.

See Skill 19, *Making a Home Page or Web Site*, for more on HTML and Web-style formatting.

Writing E-mail with Your Word Processor

If you're more comfortable writing in a word processing program than you are writing in your e-mail program, you can write your message there, copy it using the Copy command, and then switch to your e-mail program and paste it into a new message window.

One problem with putting word-processed text into e-mail messages is that some e-mail programs substitute special characters for apostrophes and quotation marks. If they are not correctly interpreted by the receiving program, these special characters come out as garbage characters that make your mail harder to read. (Eudora used to do this but in a recent version "learned" how to change those characters back into acceptable typewriter-style characters automatically.) Also, there are sometimes problems with line breaks, either with lines being too long or with extraneous characters (weird stuff, such as ^M or =20) appearing at the end of each line.

Here's how to copy a message from your word processor to your e-mail:

1. In your word processor, create your message. When you are done, save it as a text file. (Figure 5.1 shows a text file I created in Word 97 for Windows.)
2. Close the file and open it again to ensure that none of the special (non-text) characters are still in the file. Look for odd characters that you would not see on a standard keyboard and delete them.
3. Select the entire document and copy it (usually you press Ctrl+C in Windows programs, or Command+C on a Macintosh, to do this).
4. Then switch to your e-mail program.
5. Create a new message as usual, go to the message area, and paste the text you copied (usually you press Ctrl+V or Command+V).
6. The text will appear in the e-mail program as if you had typed it there.

TIP TIP TIP TIP TIP TIP TIP TIP TIP TIP TIP TIP TIP TIP TIP TIP TIP TIP TIP TIP TIP TIP TIP TIP TIP

If you are a dedicated Word for Windows user and you have Microsoft Outlook 97 or Exchange installed, then you can install WordMail (you have to re-run the Office setup program) to use Word as your e-mail program. Look up WordMail in Outlook's online help or in the Office Assistant to find out how to do so.

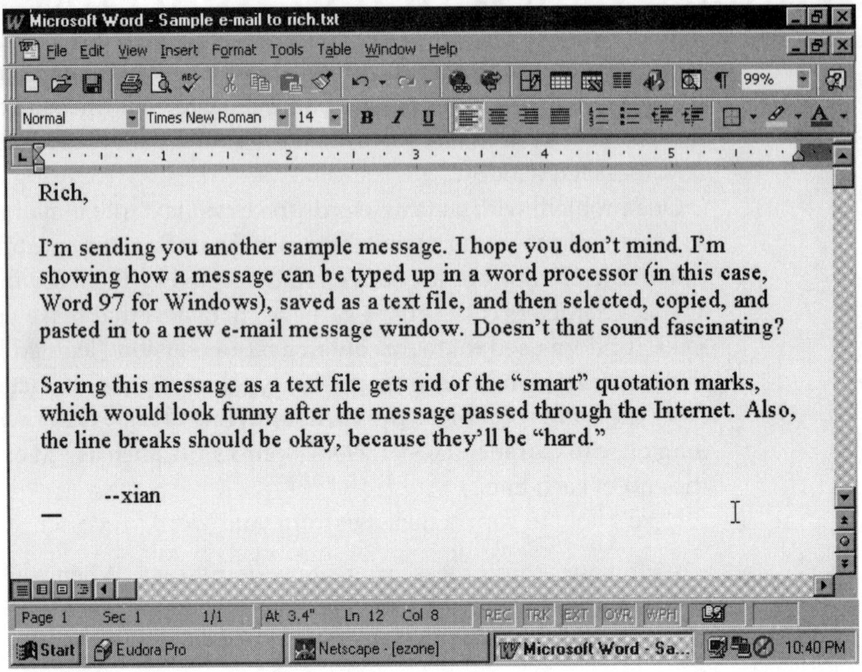

FIGURE 5.1: I created this file in Word 97 for Windows. Now I'm going to save it as a text file.

Checking Your Spelling

Most e-mail programs now offer spell-checking (so the traditional excuses for sloppily edited e-mail messages are vanishing fast!), but the specific techniques vary from program to program (as you might expect). It's a good idea to check the spelling in a message before sending it, especially if the message is long, formal, or for some business purpose.

NOTE NOTE NOTE NOTE NOTE NOTE NOTE NOTE NOTE NOTE NOTE NOTE NOTE NOTE NOTE

For more on using specific e-mail programs, see Skill 6, *E-mail Programs*.

If you write your messages ahead of time using a word processing program, then you can use your word processor's spell checker to check the message. You may find this easier than working with two different spell checkers.

Attaching a Signature

On the Internet, it's traditional to include a short *signature* at the end of each message. An e-mail signature is a few lines of text, usually including your name, sometimes your postal (*snail mail*) address, and perhaps your e-mail address. If you are including a signature in a business message, you might wish to include phone and fax numbers, and maybe the company Web page address. Many people also include quotations, jokes, gags, and so on. Signatures (also called *sig blocks*, *signature files*, *.signatures*, or *.sigs*) are a little like bumper stickers in this respect.

TIP

You can never be too careful when using company online resources, so consider adding a disclaimer to your signature block if you post to Usenet groups or mailing lists from a corporate e-mail address. The disclaimer can identify your views as solely your own and not those of the company.

Some e-mail programs do not support signature files, particularly those designed for local networks and those of some online services where signatures are less common, but many do and more are adding the feature all the time. Here's my current signature (I change it from time to time):

```
Christian Crumlish                  http://www.pobox.com/~xian
Internet Systems Experts (SYX)      http://www.syx.com
Enterzone                           http://ezone.org/ez
```

It includes my name, the address of my home page on the Web, the name of my company and its home page address, and the name of my online magazine with its address.

WARNING

Test your signature block with various e-mail systems to see if it still looks good at the receiving end, especially if it uses unusual fonts, has a logo or other graphic, uses tabs, or is formatted in columns. Some of these features do not translate well to other programs, where monospaced fonts may be substituted for fancier proportional fonts.

I'll show you how to create your own signature when I discuss the specific programs that support them.

NOTE NOTE NOTE NOTE NOTE NOTE NOTE NOTE NOTE NOTE NOTE NOTE NOTE NOTE NOTE

Some e-mail programs let you include a graphic, such as a company logo, in your signature. For example, Microsoft Word, Outlook 97, and Outlook Express all have commands you can use to import graphics files into your signature file. Just be sure to format the signature in such a way that it looks good even for those who do not have graphics support in their e-mail setup, so that the absence of the logo or graphic will not detract from the appearance of your message. This is an easy way to cultivate a professional presence on the Internet.

Filing Your Messages

Even after you have deleted all the messages you've replied to or that you no longer need to leave lying around in your Inbox, your undeleted messages can start to pile up. When your Inbox gets too full, it's time to create new mailboxes to store those other messages.

NOTE NOTE NOTE NOTE NOTE NOTE NOTE NOTE NOTE NOTE NOTE NOTE NOTE NOTE NOTE

Your e-mail storage should conform to your general scheme of organization. I arrange mine alphabetically, chronologically, and/or by project, depending on the person involved. Think about the best system for yourself before you find your Inbox filled with 200 messages to sort. If your e-mail program allows you to save the messages that you have sent to other people, you will also need to organize them before they accumulate and become unmanageable.

Different programs offer different commands for creating mailboxes and transferring messages into them, but the principles are more or less the same as those used for real-life filing. Don't create a new mailbox when an existing mailbox will suffice, but do file away as many messages as you can (even if you have to create a new mailbox to do so) to keep the number of messages in your Inbox manageable. When you find yourself scrolling up and down through screenfuls of message lists trying to find a particular message, you know that your Inbox has officially become disorganized.

TIP TIP TIP TIP TIP TIP TIP TIP TIP TIP TIP TIP TIP TIP TIP TIP TIP TIP TIP TIP TIP TIP TIP TIP TIP

You can also save your messages as text files or word processing files to move them outside of the e-mail program. This way you can store them with other files related to the same topic. Select File ➢ Save As in your message window and select a text file type. Or select the message contents, press Ctrl+C (or Command+C) to copy it to the Clipboard, open your word processor and paste the message into a document with Ctrl+V (or Command+V), then save the new file.

Filtering Messages as They Come In

When you start developing carpal-tunnel syndrome from "hand-filing" all your mail as it comes into your Inbox, it's time to start looking for an e-mail program with filters. The most basic use of a filter is to recognize a type of mail, usually by one of its headers (such as who it's from, who or what mailing list it was sent to, or what it's about), and to automatically transfer it out of your Inbox and into the appropriate folder (or mailbox, depending on what your program calls it). More sophisticated filters can send automatic replies, forward mail to other recipients, perform multiple actions (such as both replying to a message and saving the message in a specific folder), and so on.

NOTE NOTE NOTE NOTE NOTE NOTE NOTE NOTE NOTE NOTE NOTE NOTE NOTE

Your e-mail filters can also be used to automatically clear the old messages out of your Inbox. Depending on what type of functionality is built into your program, you can tell the filters to delete all of the messages older than a certain date. Even better, some programs, such as Microsoft Outlook 97 and Outlook Express, allow you to automatically archive old messages in a special file that you can move to a different directory or to storage media (tape cartridges, floppies, and so on).

Setting up a filter to work usually takes just a small investment of time compared to the donkey work you save yourself from doing in the long run. Once you start relying on filters to keep your mail manageable, you'll wonder how you ever got on without them (or you'll just up and subscribe to twelve more mailing lists!).

Dealing with E-mail from Several Accounts

You may find yourself with more than one e-mail account. It can happen more easily than you might think. All you need is to get a personal e-mail account and then get Internet access at work (or vice versa), and voilà!, you've got multiple accounts to manage. How do you keep things straight?

There are several approaches. One is to try to keep any e-mail accounts you may have totally separate. This approach is ideal for keeping work and personal life separate or for keeping a public address and a private backchannel for friends and emergencies.

On the other hand, some people get a personal account just to get access to an existing work account, in which case there's no reason to store the mail in separate places. Then the problem becomes how to consolidate all your mail and make sure you're not missing any of it. (A related problem is how to look at your mail when at home without deleting it from your main workspace.)

There are two ways to consolidate mail from multiple accounts, both of which will make sure you get all your e-mail. One is to set the secondary account (or all the accounts but one) to automatically forward mail to your primary address. However, this is not always possible. Even if it is, the methods vary from system to system, and you should check with your system administrator and ask about "automatic forwarding of e-mail."

Even easier, some mail programs can be set up to check multiple addresses (or check some automatically and others only when you manually request it). If you have to deal with multiple accounts, and you prefer to commingle all your mail, I'd suggest getting your hands on a mail program (such as Eudora or any of the Microsoft brood) with this capability.

When you want to check your work mail from your home computer, you need an e-mail application that supports remote mail connections. Microsoft Outlook 97 has this capability (but only if your company is using Microsoft Exchange Server), and it even allows you to quickly download just the message headers from your work account. Then you can select the specific messages you want to download, minimizing connection time.

Managing an Address Book

Once you start using e-mail regularly, you will probably find yourself writing to a few people over and over, fumbling to remember some long and confusing addresses. Fortunately, most e-mail programs enable you to create *aliases* (sometimes called *nicknames*) for these people. Aliases are shorter words that you type instead of the actual address. These lists of addresses and aliases are usually grouped together in something called an *address book*. Modeled on real-world address books, these windows or modules often have room for other vital information (such as street addresses and phone and fax numbers).

Some e-mail and groupware programs share a single address box with other applications on your computer, so your contact information is available to various programs.

When you type an alias or choose a name from an address book, your e-mail program inserts the correct address into the To line of your message (some programs can also insert an address into the Cc line).

You can also set up an alias for a list of addresses, so you can send mail to a group of people all at once. I've got an alias for a group of people to whom I send silly stuff I find on the Net (no one's complained yet) and another one for contributors to my online magazine.

TIP TIP TIP TIP TIP TIP TIP TIP TIP TIP TIP TIP TIP TIP TIP TIP TIP TIP TIP TIP TIP TIP TIP TIP TIP

When you make up an address book entry or alias for an e-mail address, keep it short—the whole point is to save yourself some typing—and try to make it memorable (although you can always look it up if you forget).

Finding Internet E-mail Addresses

Because the Internet is such a large, nebulous entity, there's no single guaranteed way to find someone's e-mail address, even if you're fairly sure they have one. Still, if you're looking for an address, here are a few things you can try.

TIP TIP TIP TIP TIP TIP TIP TIP TIP TIP TIP TIP TIP TIP TIP TIP TIP TIP TIP TIP TIP TIP TIP TIP TIP

See Skill 10, *Finding Stuff on the Web and the Net*, for more tips on searching for people and their e-mail addresses, especially via the Web. Or just jump right in and try `http://www.whowhere.com`.

Say "Send Me E-mail"

If you're not sure how to send mail to someone but you know they're on the Net, give them a call and ask them to send you some mail. Once their mail comes through okay, you should have a working return address. Copy it and save it somewhere, or make an alias for it, or just keep their mail around and reply to it when you want to send them mail (try to remember to change the subject line if appropriate, not that I ever do).

TIP TIP TIP TIP TIP TIP TIP TIP TIP TIP TIP TIP TIP TIP TIP TIP TIP TIP TIP TIP TIP TIP TIP TIP TIP

Really, the best way to collect e-mail addresses is from people directly. Many people now have their e-mail addresses on their business cards, so you can get people's addresses this way too.

Send Mail to Postmaster@

If you know someone's domain, such as the company where they work, or you know they're on one of the online services, you can try sending mail to `postmaster@`*`address`* and asking politely for the e-mail address. Internet standards require that every network assign a real person to `postmaster@address`, someone who can handle questions and complaints. So, for example, to find someone at Pipeline, you could send mail to `postmaster@pipeline.com` and ask for the person by name.

Are You Experienced?

Now you can...

- ☑ **send your messages to more than one person**
- ☑ **forward mail to others and create a chain of replies**
- ☑ **attach files, graphics, signatures, or Web links to your messages**
- ☑ **create an address book and update it with new people**
- ☑ **use the address book to instantly add names and addresses to your messages**
- ☑ **file your messages where you will be able to find them when you need them**
- ☑ **automatically sort your messages by subject or other factors**
- ☑ **polish your messages with spell-checking and special formatting**

SKILL 6

E-MAIL PROGRAMS

- **Eudora**
- **Microsoft Outlook and Outlook Express**
- **NETCOMplete**
- **Netscape Messenger**
- **Pegasus Mail**
- **Pine**

There are so many different e-mail programs available that I can't hope to cover each one in detail, which is why I discussed e-mail in generic terms in the last two lessons. Nevertheless, it's quite likely that you'll end up using one of a handful of popular e-mail programs at one time or another, and I'll discuss the most common ones here, so that you can learn some specific skills as well.

In the unlikely circumstance that you have none of the specific programs that I cover, the previous two lessons will still give you a sense of what features to look for in the Help portion of your e-mail program or to discuss with your system (or network) administrator.

If you get your mail via America Online, skip to the AOL lesson, Skill 16. (Skills 17 and 18 discuss other alternative ways of getting and sending e-mail.) Remember, you may still jump to Skill 8, *Navigating the Web*, if you're impatient to get onto the World Wide Web.

Eudora

Eudora is one of the most popular and dependable Internet e-mail programs available. It can work on a network connection, with a PPP or SLIP dial-up account, or as an offline mail reader with a Unix shell account.

TIP TIP TIP TIP TIP TIP TIP TIP TIP TIP TIP TIP TIP TIP TIP TIP TIP TIP TIP TIP TIP TIP TIP TIP TIP

A free copy of Eudora (called Eudora Light) can be downloaded from `http://www.eudora.com/`**. See Skill 10, *Finding Stuff on the Web and the Net*, for instructions on how to download files from the Net. Qualcomm, the company that now owns Eudora, makes improvements to the program all the time, to Windows and Mac versions in both the Professional and the free Light editions. Therefore, if you've been using Eudora for a while, you may have a slightly out-of-date copy of the program, and some of your specific commands or menu names may differ from my instructions. Either upgrade to the latest version of Eudora or poke around the menus for similar commands.**

The professional edition of Eudora, Eudora Pro, has just about every state-of-the-art Internet e-mail feature you could wish for (in both the Windows and Macintosh versions). The freeware Light version continues to develop gradually as well and is a bargain at the price.

Before trying out the features below, be sure to start the Eudora program by double-clicking on its desktop icon.

Most of the useful Eudora commands are available on the Message menu (shown here).

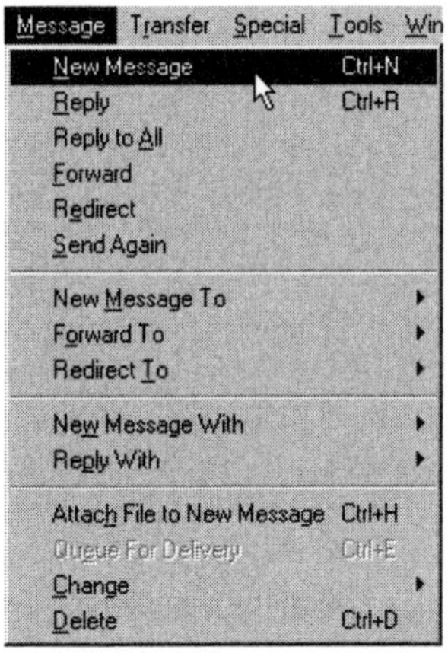

Creating Eudora Messages and Checking E-mail

Here's how to create and send e-mail using Eudora:

1. Select Message ➢ New Message (or press Ctrl+N in Windows, Command+N on the Mac).
2. Type the address of the person to whom you wish to send the mail and press Tab a few times until the insertion point jumps to the area below the gray line. Figure 6.1 shows a short e-mail message.
3. When you are done, click the Send button in the upper-right corner of the message window. The button might read Queue instead of Send. This means that the message will be added to a list (a queue) of messages to be sent all at once when the program checks for new mail.

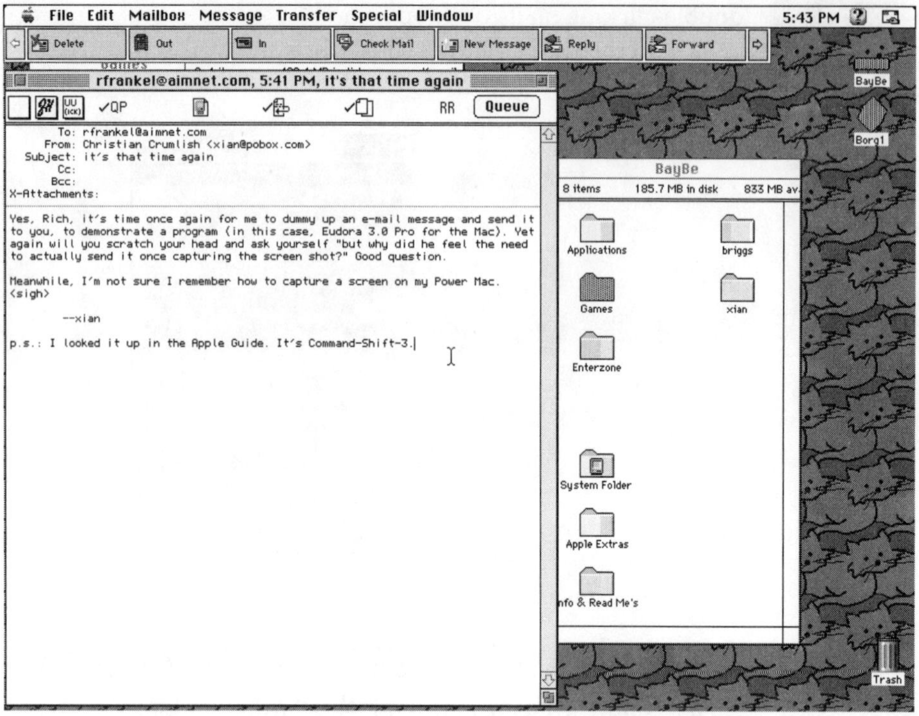

FIGURE 6.1: A new message window in Eudora for the Macintosh

Eudora makes it easy to check your Inbox for new mail, too:

1. Select File ➢ Check Mail or press Ctrl+M (or Command+M on a Mac). Eudora will connect to something called a *POP server* (POP stands for *Post Office Protocol*, but you can forget that) to pick up all your mail.
2. Unread mail will appear with a large dot (or bullet) in the left column of the Inbox (see Figure 6.2). To view the contents of a mail message, highlight it in the window and press Enter (or double-click on it).
3. After reading the message, you can close its window or select Message ➢ Reply (or Ctrl+R) to reply to the message. If you start a reply by mistake, just close the message window and don't save it when prompted.

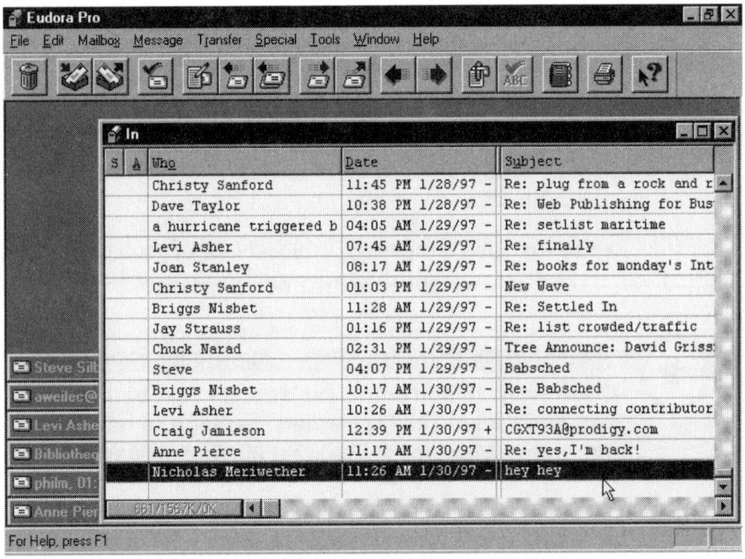

FIGURE 6.2: The Inbox of the Windows version of Eudora

TIP TIP TIP TIP TIP TIP TIP TIP TIP TIP TIP TIP TIP TIP TIP TIP TIP TIP TIP TIP TIP TIP TIP TIP TIP

If you want to reply to everyone who was also sent a copy of the message, press Ctrl+Shift+R instead of Ctrl+R (or select Message ➢ Reply to All).

Deleting Eudora Messages

After you have sent and received a number of messages, you may need to clean up your Eudora Inbox by deleting old messages. Use the following options to delete messages and undelete (restore) messages that you deleted by mistake.

- To delete a message, place the highlight on it and click Delete (or click the Trash icon at the top of the mailbox window). This moves the message to the Trash mailbox. It won't actually be deleted until you empty the trash (Special ➢ Trash).
- If you change your mind, select Mailbox ➢ Trash to open the Trash or mailbox and look at the list of deleted messages. Highlight the message you want to rescue, and then select Transfer ➢ In to move the message back into the Inbox.

Sending, Forwarding, and Formatting Eudora Messages

Eudora's messaging features provide all of the basic e-mail functions, along with some extras that you may find useful. Here are some of the Eudora options:

- To send a message to additional recipients, type their e-mail addresses on the Cc or Bcc lines, separated by commas if there are more than one on any single line.
- To forward a message you have open, select Message ➢ Forward. Then proceed as you would with a new message.

TIP

If you want to add some explanatory text before the forwarded message, but you don't want the forwarded message to have the ">" symbol before each line, select Message ➢ Redirect instead of Message ➢ Forward.

- If you wish to format your message, you can add MIME-encoded formatting with the Pro version of Eudora. Use the formatting button just above the To line in the message window or select the formatting options from the Edit ➢ Text submenu.

NOTE

Eudora does not create HTML formatting, but it does treat any URL (Web address, as explained in Skill 8, *Navigating the Web*) as a live hyperlink.

Transferring a Eudora Message to a New Mailbox

You can transfer messages to a different mailbox, such as the one on your notebook or home computer. Transferring works much like sending or forwarding a message, except that the message itself is moved to the new mailbox, not a copy of the message. You will need the e-mail address of the mailbox on the computer you are transferring the file to.

Follow these steps to transfer a message to a new mailbox in Eudora:

1. Select the message and pull down the Transfer menu.
2. Either choose an existing mailbox from the menu or select New.
3. In the New Mailbox dialog box that appears, type a name for the mailbox and then click OK.

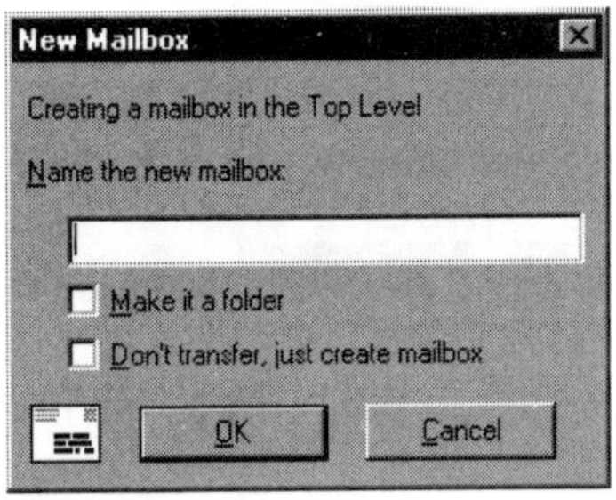

Filtering Incoming E-mail in Eudora

To set up a simple filter for keeping your messages neatly filed, follow these steps:

1. Select Tools ➢ Filters to open the Filters dialog box.
2. Click the New button.
3. Checkmark the Incoming and Manual checkboxes by clicking them. Checkmark the Outgoing checkbox as well, if you plan to sort your own outgoing mail with this same filter.
4. Click the Header drop-down list box and choose the header by which these e-mail messages can be recognized. Select Any Header for the broadest possible net. Headers can be any name in the To line, any name in the From line, or any topic in the Subject line.
5. Choose a criterion in the next drop-down list (usually Contains will work well, but there are many interesting choices), and then type the text to be found (or avoided or compared with) in the box to the right.
6. To further qualify the filter, add a second criterion by clicking the drop-down list box that currently reads Ignore and change it to And, Or, or Unless.
7. Select an action in the first Action drop-down list box (you will probably want Transfer To, but again, there are many interesting options).
8. If you choose Transfer To, click the button to the right and select a folder into which the filtered mail should be transferred automatically (see Figure 6.3).
9. Add up to four additional actions, if you are ruthless enough.
10. Close the window and save the changes when prompted.

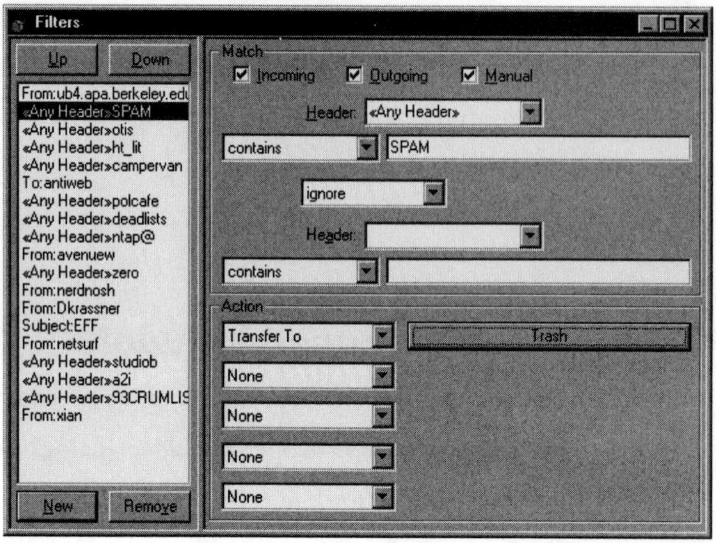

FIGURE 6.3: The simplest filter you can make with Eudora—straight to the circular file.

Checking Multiple E-mail Accounts with Eudora Personalities

You can set up Eudora (at least in the Pro version) to check multiple accounts with the Personalities feature.

1. To set up a new "personality," first find and select the Options or Settings command. (Its exact location on the menu differs in the various versions of the program, but it's over on the right somewhere!)
2. Choose the Personalities category in the dialog box. Now you can add additional addresses to your original, or "dominant," personality.
3. Click the New button to create a new personality. Enter the basic e-mail server and address information required for any account.
   - Click Check Mail if you want Eudora to look for mail on this account any time you tell it to check for mail.
   - Click Leave Mail on Server if the mail will have to be accessible to some other e-mail program as well—one at home or work, perhaps.

Attaching Files to Eudora Messages

Eudora messages can also have files attached to them. Eudora's design lets you work intuitively with the drag-and-drop method, or you can use the keyboard or menu commands to add attachments, as explained here:

1. When you want to attach a file, first start a new message.
2. Then use one of these actions to attach the file:
    - Drag the file from a folder window into the Eudora message window
    - Select Message ➢ Attach File
    - Press Ctrl+H or Command+H
3. Choose a file from the Attach File dialog box (it's just like a normal Open dialog box).
4. Click OK to attach the file.

Depending on your version of Eudora, you might have the choice of several different formats for attached files, including MIME, *UUencode*, and *BinHex*—all different ways of translating files into a format that lets them travel across the Internet. Discuss the options with your intended recipient to find a format in common. The person you send the coded file to will need a program that decodes the file into a format usable in standard programs. See Skill 10, *Finding Stuff on the Web and the Net*, for more on decoding and decompressing files.

Adding a Name to Your Eudora Address Book

Eudora's address book feature is great for saving the e-mail addresses of people you correspond with frequently. It is not easy to remember e-mail addresses, so remember to enter the address in your address book as soon as you get a message from someone new. Here are the steps for adding addresses in Eudora:

1. Highlight a message from the person whose e-mail address you want to save and then select Special ➢ Make Address Book Entry (or press Ctrl+K).
2. Type a short, memorable name in the Make Address Book Entry dialog box that appears.
3. Click the Put It on the Recipient List checkbox if you want to be able to select the address book entry from a pop-up menu (this is useful if you expect to send mail to this address regularly).

4. Click OK to add the new name to your address book.

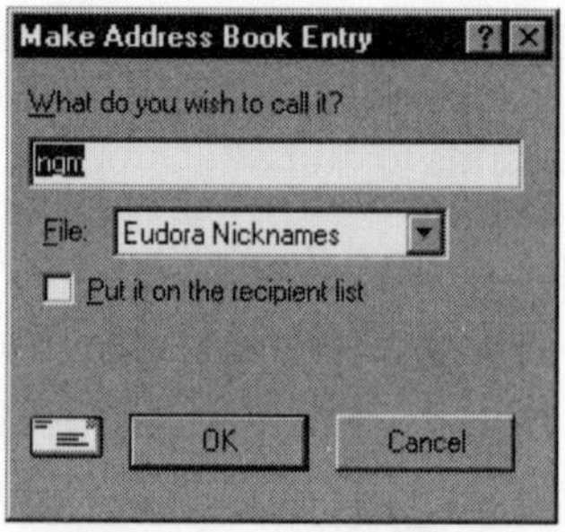

Now, whenever you want to use the address book entry, just type the short name instead of the full Internet address. You can also use address book entries in a couple of other ways, as outlined here:

- If you added the address book entry to the recipient list, then you can send or forward mail to the address by selecting Message ➢ New Message To ➢ *Short-Name* or Message ➢ Forward To ➢ *Short-Name*, where *Short-Name* is the name of the address you want. Eudora will do the rest.
- If you forget an address book entry, select Tools ➢ Address Book (in earlier versions of Eudora, it was Window ➢ Nicknames—so poke around a little if you can't find the command), select the address book entry you want, and click the To button. Eudora will copy that address into a new message window.

NOTE NOTE NOTE NOTE NOTE NOTE NOTE NOTE NOTE NOTE NOTE NOTE NOTE NOTE NOTE

Until the most recent versions of Eudora, saved addresses were called "nicknames." Now, more in line with other e-mail programs, Eudora calls them "address book entries." (They really work the same as before, if you're used to the older versions of the program.)

Using Eudora's Spell Checker

To check the spelling in a message, select Edit ➢ Check Spelling. Eudora will scan the message for words it doesn't recognize. If you've ever used the spell checker in any standard word processor, then you should be familiar with this drill:

- To skip a suspected word, click Ignore.
- To accept a suggested correction, click Change.

- To make your own correction, type it in the Change To box and then click Change.
- To add the word in question to the spell checker's dictionary, click Add.

Creating an E-mail Signature with Eudora

Eudora also has a signature feature, which I introduced in general terms in the previous lesson (see the "Attaching a Signature" section of Skill 5). Here's how to use it:

1. Select Tools ➢ Signatures ➢ New (the free version of Eudora only permits one signature).
2. Type your signature and then close the window and agree to save it when prompted. If you create multiple signatures in Eudora Pro, you can set which one you want as the default in the Signatures category of the Options dialog box (the Settings dialog box on a Macintosh).

Eudora will automatically append this signature to all your outgoing mail unless you choose None in the Signature drop-down list box at the top of the new message window.

Quitting Eudora

When you are finished sending, reading, and replying to mail, you can quit Eudora or leave it running so you can quickly go back and check your mail. To quit Eudora, select File ➢ Exit (or File ➢ Quit in the Macintosh version of Eudora), or select Ctrl+Q (Command+Q for the Mac).

Microsoft Outlook

When Windows 95 came out, Microsoft Mail was superseded by the Microsoft Exchange program distributed with the new operating system. (They were similar, but Exchange had more Internet capabilities, among other improvements.) With the release of Office 97, Microsoft has once again distributed a renamed and upgraded e-mail program, Outlook 97. But Outlook is more than an e-mail reader. It's also a groupware program, suitable for collaboration, discussions, scheduling, and so on.

Internet Mail (often distributed along with its sister program Microsoft Internet News, or in a jumbo package with Internet Explorer 3 as well) was Microsoft's first true Internet-oriented mail program, but since Internet Explorer 4, it's been replaced with Microsoft Outlook Express, a custom version of the Outlook groupware program that comes with Office 97. You can download Microsoft's latest e-mail software from the Microsoft Internet Explorer Web site (`http://www.microsoft.com/ie`), shown in Figure 6.4. See Skill 10, *Finding Stuff on the Web and the Net*, for an explanation of how to download files.

FIGURE 6.4: Microsoft's Internet Explorer Web site is the source of free trial versions of new Internet software, but it can take a while to download the software, and you have to answer a bunch of questions for the marketing department.

Fortunately, the e-mail features of Outlook 97 and Express are similar to those of Exchange and Internet Mail (with, again, a few improvements here and there). I'll use Outlook 97 and Outlook Express for my examples here, but you can follow along even if you use Exchange (or, for that matter, Microsoft Mail).

Outlook can handle Internet mail, network mail, and mail from MSN (the Microsoft Network online service). You can start Outlook 97 by double-clicking the Outlook 97 icon on your desktop or by selecting Start ➢ Programs ➢ Microsoft Outlook. You can open Outlook Express by selecting Start ➢ Programs ➢ Internet Explorer ➢ Outlook Express, or by clicking on the miniature Launch Outlook Express icon in the taskbar tray near the Start button.

Both versions of Outlook start you off in a window showing two panes. The pane on the left shows the various features of the program that are available, with your Inbox first and foremost (see Figure 6.5). The pane on the right shows you the contents of your Inbox (but you can click the large Inbox button at the top of the list of messages to choose another mailbox and Outlook will show its contents below).

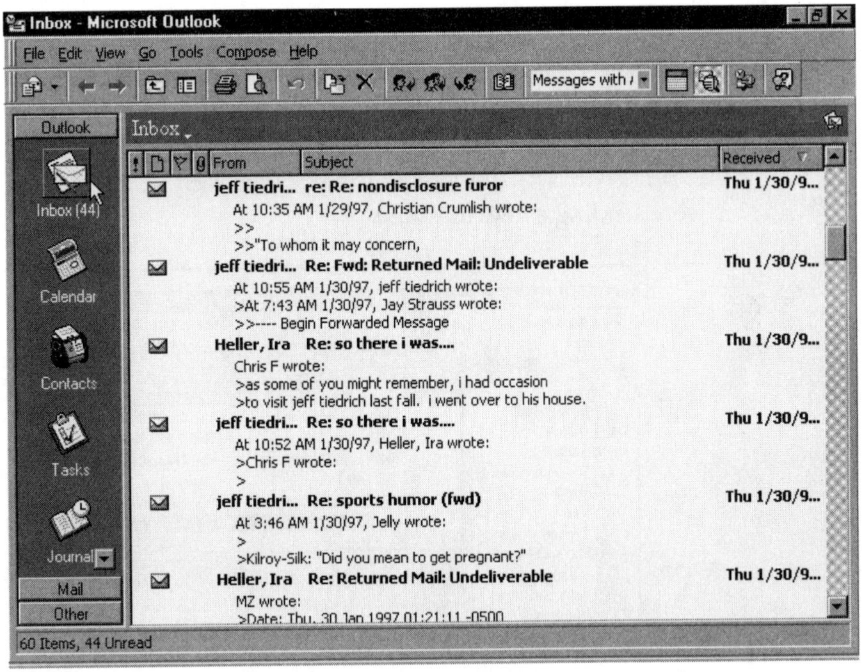

FIGURE 6.5: The opening window of Outlook Express

NOTE NOTE NOTE NOTE NOTE NOTE NOTE NOTE NOTE NOTE NOTE NOTE NOTE NOTE NOTE

Outlook Express has a big Preview pane that shows you the contents of the highlighted message. You can turn this Preview on or off, and change its appearance and location with the View ➢ Layout menu selection.

Creating Outlook Messages and Checking E-mail

Here's how to create a new Outlook e-mail message:

1. Select Compose ➢ New Mail Message (Ctrl+N). This will open up a new message window.

2. Type an address and press Tab to get down to the Subject box where you can type a subject.

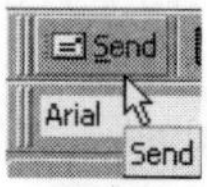

3. Tab down to the message area and type your message. Click the Send button in either Outlook 97 or Express. If you are accumulating messages to send in bulk with Outlook Express, select File ➢ Send Later, then click the Send and Receive button in the main Outlook Express window when you are ready to send them all.

To read a message in your Inbox (see Figure 6.6), just double-click its subject line. The message will appear in its own window. To reply to the message, select Compose ➢ Reply in Outlook 97 or Reply to Author or Reply to All in Outlook Express (Ctrl+R). Outlook will supply the recipient's address. Proceed as if you were sending a new message.

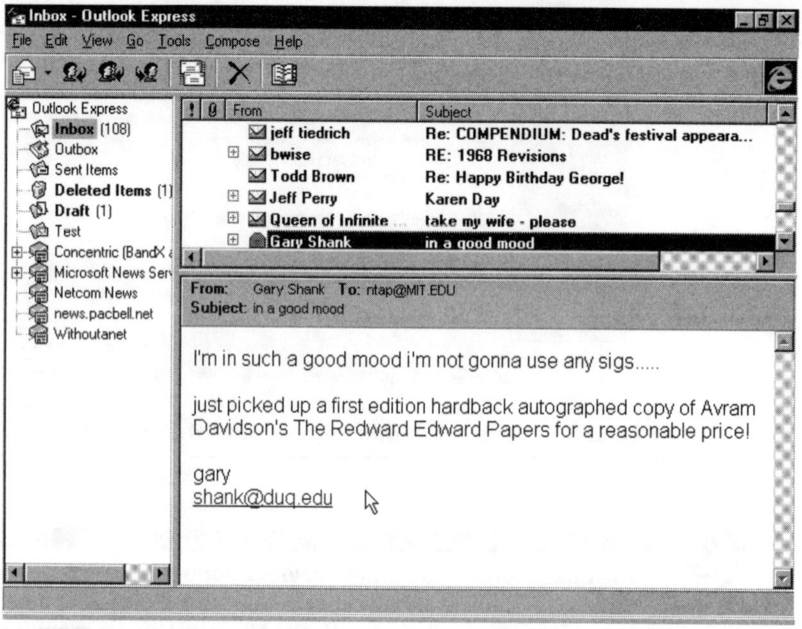

FIGURE 6.6: My Inbox as shown by Microsoft Outlook Express

TIP

If you want to reply to everyone who was also sent a copy of the message, press Ctrl+Shift+R instead of Ctrl+R (or select Compose ➢ Reply to All).

Deleting Outlook Messages

To delete a message, just highlight it and click the Delete button or press the Delete key on your keyboard. It will be moved to the Deleted Items folder until you specifically open that folder and delete its contents (even then Outlook will warn you that you are permanently deleting the message).

TIP TIP TIP TIP TIP TIP TIP TIP TIP TIP TIP TIP TIP TIP TIP TIP TIP TIP TIP TIP TIP TIP TIP TIP TIP

To undelete a message, open the Deleted Items folder and select the message you want to restore. Then select File ➢ Move, choose the Inbox folder from the dialog box that appears, and click OK.

Sending and Forwarding Outlook Messages

Here are some commands you will probably use a lot:

- To forward a message in Microsoft Outlook 97 or Express, click Forward Message (in Outlook Express) or Forward (in Outlook 97). You can also choose Compose ➢ Forward or press Ctrl+F in any of these programs and then proceed as you would with a new message
- To send mail to multiple recipients, type their addresses in the To box—separated by semicolons, not commas—or type additional addresses in the Cc box.

Using Microsoft Word in Outlook

Outlook 97 and Express can take advantage of all of Microsoft Word's formatting power for creating sophisticated messages with fonts, graphics, and many other features. However, the person receiving the message needs Outlook 97, Outlook Express, or Microsoft Word to view the enhanced formats.

If you have Microsoft Word and would like to use it for composing and formatting Outlook 97 or Express mail, follow these procedures:

1. Select Tools ➢ Options and select the E-mail tab.
2. Click Use Microsoft Word as E-mail Editor.
3. Click OK.

Creating More Message Folders

As you begin to accumulate messages, replies, and copies of original messages you sent to others, you will need additional folders to store them in for easy retrieval.

In Outlook 97 or Express, it's quite easy to add new message folders to your set of personal folders:

1. Select File ➢ New Folder (or press Ctrl+Shift+E) in Outlook 97. In Outlook Express, choose File ➢ Folder ➢ New Folder.
2. In the New Folder dialog box that appears, type a name for the folder and click OK.

Once a folder is created in Outlook, moving a message into the folder is even easier. In both Outlook 97 and Outlook Express, simply click on the message and drag it to the folder (in the left pane).

Sorting Outlook Express Messages with Filters

Microsoft Outlook Express has the simplest type of filtering possible: Mail with specified text in one or more of four headers can be automatically filed in a specified folder.

NOTE

Outlook 97 has no filtering, but you can download the Inbox Rules Assistant from Microsoft's Outlook Web page to give it filtering capabilities "after the fact." Select Help ➢ Microsoft on the Web ➢ Free Stuff in Outlook 97 to get there, or go to `http://www.microsoft.com/OfficeFreeStuff/Outlook`.

These steps will get you started with the setup of an e-mail message filter in Outlook Express.

1. Select Mail ➢ Inbox Assistant, then click Add.
2. In the Properties dialog box that appears, type text in one (or more) of the top four boxes to single out the messages you want to filter. Any message that has the text you typed in its corresponding header field(s) will be moved where you specify.
3. Select the folder you want the e-mail transferred to in the Move To drop-down list (see Figure 6.7).
4. Click OK to save the filter and then add more filters if you wish. Outlook Express lists your filters in the Inbox Assistant dialog box (in plain English, such as "Move to 'Likely Spam' if Subject contains 'Money'").

You can also set up Outlook 97 to check mail from multiple online services (select Tools ➢ Services to see the options), but you can't set it up to check for mail on, say, two different Internet e-mail accounts.

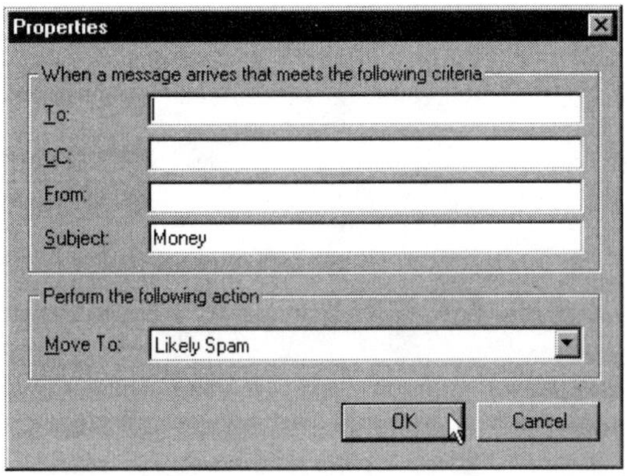

FIGURE 6.7: With Outlook Express you can sort your messages as they arrive.

Attaching Files to E-mail Messages in Outlook

In Outlook 97 and Outlook Express, use one of these options to attach files to your messages:

- Use Explorer, My Computer, or File Manager to open the window the file is in, click on the file, and drag it into the new message window.
- Select Insert ➢ File and choose the file you want from the Insert File dialog box that appears and then click OK. Figure 6.8 shows an attached file in an Outlook message.

Using the Outlook Address Book

Outlook's address book is useful for keeping track of all the e-mail addresses associated with your friends and business associates. Here's how to update the address book with new names:

1. To add a name to your address book, select Tools ➢ Address Book (or press Ctrl+Shift+B) and then select File ➢ New Entry (or press Ctrl+N).
2. In the New Entry dialog box that appears, choose Internet Mail Address and click OK.
3. Type a name for the address, press Tab, and type the e-mail address.
4. When you're done, click OK.

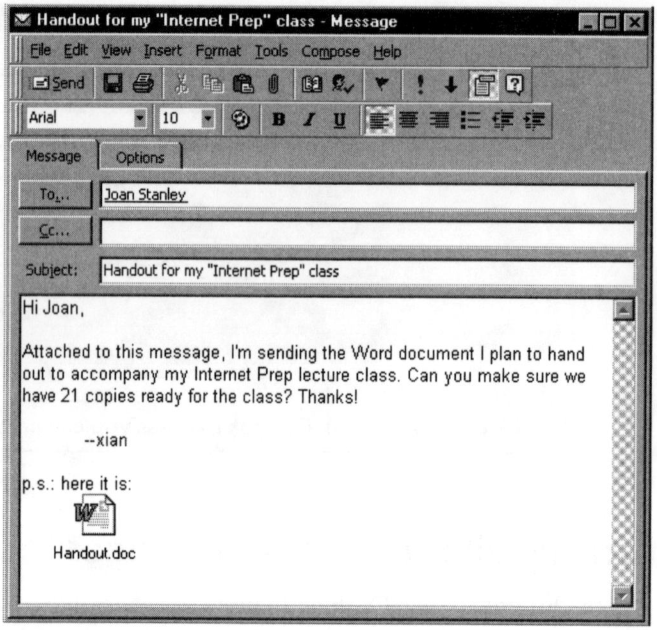

FIGURE 6.8: Outlook inserts an icon representing the attachment into your message at the insertion point. Your recipient double-clicks the icon to open the attached file.

Using address book names in Outlook messages is even easier than adding them, as you can see from these steps:

1. To send a message to someone in your address book, create a new message as usual, but instead of typing a recipient's address, click the To button to the left of the To box.
2. Select a name from the address book list and click the To button.
3. Then click OK to copy the address to the e-mail message.

Correcting Spelling Errors in Outlook

All of the Microsoft e-mail products have spell checkers. In the Outlook 97 or Express message window, select Tools ➢ Spelling (or press F7) to check the spelling of a message.

Outlook will start scanning the message for words it doesn't recognize. If you've ever used the spell checker in Word or any other standard word processor, then you should be familiar with this drill:

- To skip the word in question, click Ignore.
- To accept a suggested correction, click Change.
- To make your own correction, type the correct word in the Change To box and click Change.
- To add the word in question to the spell checker's dictionary, click Add.

Formatting an E-mail Message with HTML in Outlook Express

Outlook Express is set up by default to permit HTML formatting in your messages. If you don't see the HTML formatting toolbar, you can add it by selecting Format ➢ HTML.

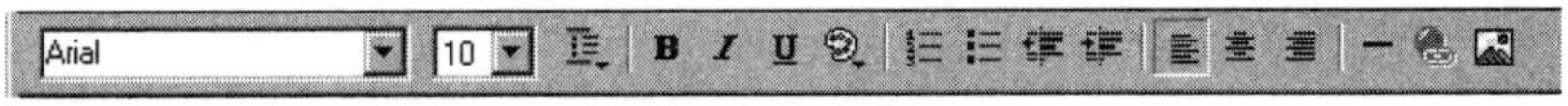

Then just select text to be formatted and use the buttons on the toolbar to apply HTML formatting, such as bold and italic, bulleted lists, alignment (center, flush left, or flush right), and text color.

WARNING WARNING WARNING WARNING WARNING WARNING WARNING WARNING

Bear in mind, though, that not everyone will be able to see the formatting you apply, and some mail programs may even mangle your message trying to represent the formatting. The message may even get displayed twice, once in plain text and once with HTML tags.

Outlook 97 does not provide HTML formatting, but it does feature extensive non-HTML formatting. There are even templates (try Compose ➢ Choose Template to see some examples) with preset formatting.

Using E-mail Signatures in Outlook

Microsoft Outlook Express and Outlook 97 all support signature files. These files retain your personal or professional information and add it to your messages according to your instructions.

Here are the steps for creating a standard e-mail signature in Outlook:

1. Select Tools ➢ AutoSignature. This brings up the AutoSignature dialog box.
2. Type your signature and click Add to put this signature at the end of new messages. (You can also prevent the signature from being added to messages you reply to or forward.)
3. Then click OK.

Quitting Outlook

To exit Outlook 97 or Express, select File ➢ Exit.

NETCOMplete

NETCOMplete (formerly NetCruiser) is an all-in-one Internet program from Netcom for both Windows and Macintosh. NETCOMplete has its own e-mail program, but it also allows you to run third-party programs, such as Eudora, Pegasus, or Outlook.

Basic NETCOMplete Functions

Here's how to activate the NETCOMplete mail module:

1. Click the E-mail button (or select Internet ➢ E-mail).
2. To send mail, click the Compose button (or select E-mail ➢ Compose). This brings up a Compose window.
3. Type the recipient's address and press Tab twice. Type a subject and press Tab twice again.

4. Type your message and click the Send button when you are done (see Figure 6.9).

The E-mail window has three panes. The top two show the list of folders (with your Inbox selected) and the subjects of messages in the current folder. The bottom pane shows the contents of the currently selected message.

When you want to reply to messages, delete messages, or exit from NETCOMplete itself or just from the mail module, use these commands:

- To reply to a message, click the Reply button.
- To delete a message, click the Delete button (the Trashcan icon).
- To exit the mail module of NETCOMplete, just close the window.
- To exit NETCOMplete, select File ➢ Exit.

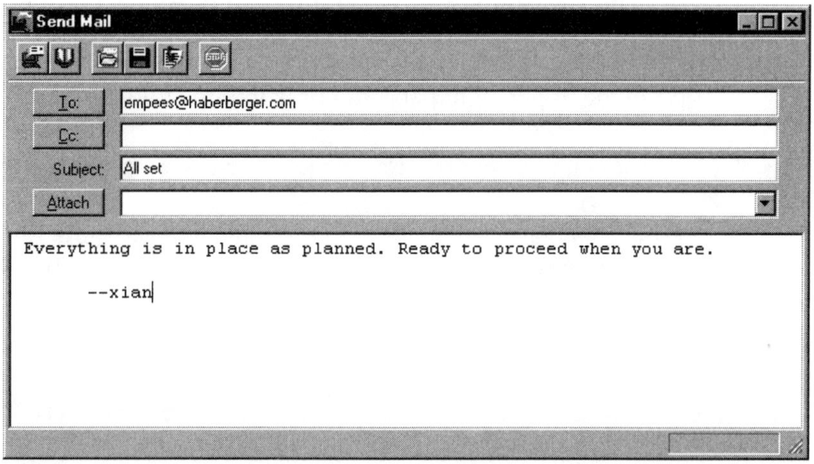

FIGURE 6.9: NETCOMplete's Compose window has all the standard e-mail trimmings.

Forwarding Mail or Sending Mail to More Than One Person with NETCOMplete

You can easily forward mail with NETCOMplete or send mail to more than one person with these commands:

- To forward mail in NETCOMplete, click the Forward button or select Message ➢ Forward. Then proceed as you would for a new message.
- To send mail to multiple recipients, just type additional e-mail addresses on the To line, separated by commas, or press Tab and add the additional addresses to the Cc line.

Creating a New NETCOMplete Mailbox Folder and Moving Messages to It

Keep your NETCOMplete Inbox organized by moving messages into specific folders. These folders can be named according to message subjects, work projects, message senders, message recipients, or dates.

1. Select Mailbox ➢ Folder Setup and then click the Add button on the Folder Setup dialog box that appears.
2. Type a name for the new folder and then click OK twice.

To transfer a message to this new folder or a different folder just click on its subject in the upper-right pane and drag it to the folder icon in the left pane.

> NOTE
>
> **NETCOMplete does not offer filters for sorting your incoming mail, nor does it have any facility for checking multiple mail accounts (though you can use a program such as Eudora for this purpose instead of NETCOMplete's built-in mail module).**

Attaching a File to a NETCOMplete E-mail Message

NETCOMplete's Send Mail window features a toolbar with an Attachment button used expressly for attaching files to your messages, as described here:

1. When you want to send an attached file with an e-mail message, click the Attachment button in the Send Mail window.
2. Select a file in the Open dialog box that appears and then click OK.

Adding Names to the NETCOMplete Address Book and Using Them in Messages

When you receive e-mail from someone new and you want to keep the address available, NETCOMplete provides a quick way to get it into the address book. Use these steps to add addresses:

1. To add an address to your address book you must first have a mail window open, and then select Settings ➢ Address Book.
2. Click the Add button.

3. Type a name for the address, press Tab, and type the e-mail address.
4. Click OK twice.

Using the address book when sending new messages is also easy:

1. Select E-mail ➢ Compose.
2. Click the To button in the compose window.
3. Select the name you want, click To, and then click OK.

NOTE NOTE NOTE NOTE NOTE NOTE NOTE NOTE NOTE NOTE NOTE NOTE NOTE NOTE NOTE

NETCOMplete currently does not have a built-in spell checker, it doesn't permit formatting of e-mail messages (HTML or otherwise), and it does not allow you to attach signature blocks to messages.

Netscape Messenger

Netscape Communicator 4 sports a full-featured mail program called Netscape Messenger.

NOTE NOTE NOTE NOTE NOTE NOTE NOTE NOTE NOTE NOTE NOTE NOTE NOTE NOTE NOTE

You'll learn more about Netscape's Web capabilities in Skill 8, *Navigating the Web*.

Basic Messenger Functions

Using Netscape Messenger for e-mail is a lot like using many of the other programs I've mentioned. Here's how to create and send an e-mail message:

1. Select File ➢ New ➢ Message (or press Ctrl+M or click the New Message button).
2. Type an address in the To box. Press Tab and type a subject.
3. Press Tab again to enter the message area and type your message.
4. When you're done, click the Send button.

If you receive mail while working in Netscape (the little envelope in the lower-right corner of the Netscape window will alert you), select Communicator ➢ Messenger. (The first time you do this, Netscape may require you to enter your password.) Just highlight a message in the upper-right pane to see its contents in the lower-right pane (see Figure 6.10).

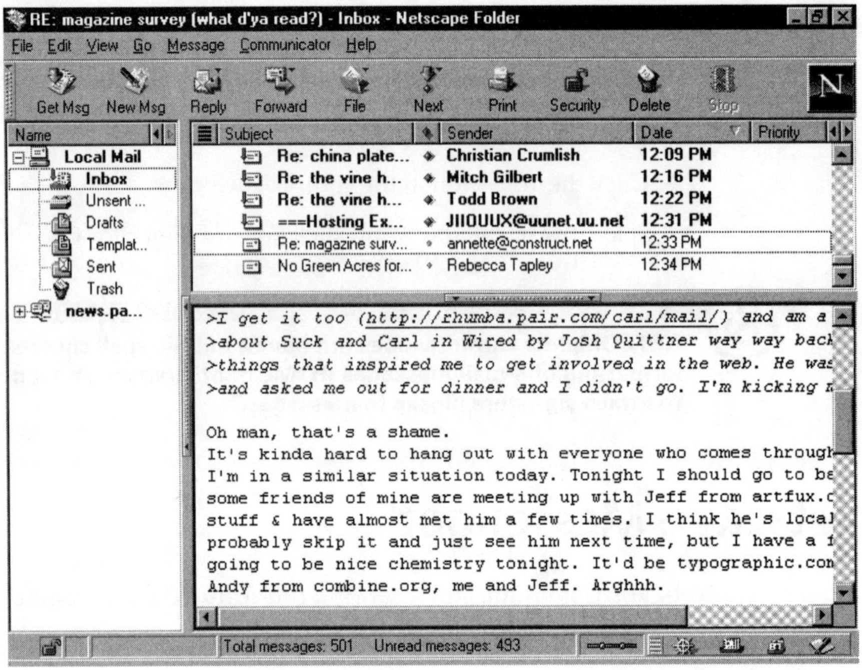

FIGURE 6.10: The Netscape Messenger window lists messages in the upper-right pane and shows the contents of the current message in the hideable lower-right pane.

TIP

Remember that any Web addresses mentioned in Netscape Messenger e-mail messages you receive will function as clickable links. That means when you finish reading, all you have to do is click on a highlighted word to go to that Web page and start surfing. For more information on the Web, see Skill 8, *Navigating the Web*.

Here are some other Netscape Messenger commands you will find useful:

- To reply to a message, click the Reply button, press Ctrl+R (Command+R on the Mac), or select Message ➢ Reply ➢ To Sender Only.

- To delete a message, just highlight it and click the Delete button. Netscape will move the message to a Trash folder.
- To undelete a message, select the Trash folder in the drop-down folder list just above the top pane, select the message, and then choose Message ➢ Move Message ➢ Inbox.

You can close the mail window and keep Netscape running if you want—in Windows 95, click the close button in the upper-right corner; on the Mac, click the close button in the upper-left corner—or you can quit Netscape entirely by selecting File ➢ Exit (or, on the Mac, File ➢ Quit).

Forwarding and Sending Mail to More Than One Person with Netscape Messenger

Netscape Messenger has a full complement of messaging features, including mail forwarding and the means to send mail to more than one person at a time. Here are the basic forwarding and sending options:

- When you want to forward a message, click the Forward button (or select Message ➢ Forward Quoted or press Ctrl+Shift+L or Command+Shift+L). Then proceed as you would with a new message.
- To send mail to multiple recipients, type the addresses in the Mail To box, separated by commas, or enter additional addresses in the Cc box.

Creating New Folders for Filing Messenger E-mail

Messenger also allows you to create new folders for filing messages. Here's how you do it:

1. Select the folder in the left pane in which you want the new folder to appear (or select Local Mail to create an upper-level folder).
2. Then select File ➢ New ➢ Folder.
3. Type a name for the new folder in the dialog box that appears and then click OK.

Filing Netscape Messenger Messages in Folders

Netscape Messenger (and the rest of the Communicator suite) has a revamped menu structure that gives toolbar buttons mini-menus of their own. This means that it is even easier and faster to file messages in Messenger than it is in other e-mail programs, because you do not have to open a folder window or use a dialog box to find the folder where you want to put the message.

1. Highlight the message to be moved.
2. Click the File button (or select Message ➢ Move Message).
3. Choose the destination folder from the menu that pops up (subfolders appear on submenus).

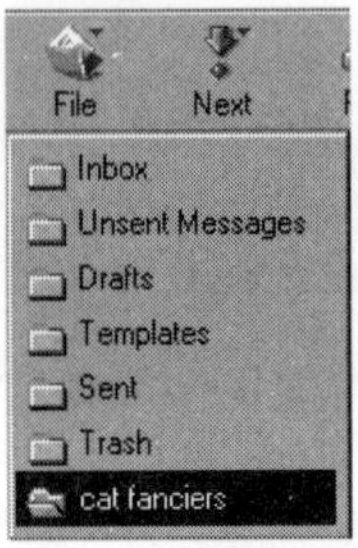

Filtering Netscape Messenger E-mail

Netscape Messenger's rules for filtering e-mail are quite specific and give you more flexibility in organizing your mailbox than other mail filters. Most of the time you can use the existing rules provided by Netscape. If none of these rules are customized enough for you, you can construct unique rules for your own mail management needs.

Here's how you create a new filter for incoming messages:

1. Select Edit ➢ Message Filters.
2. Click the New button on the Message Filters dialog box.
3. In the top half of the Filter Rules dialog box that appears, enter a name for your filter (see Figure 6.11).
4. Choose one of the nine different aspects of the message to base your filter on (such as the subject, the priority, or who's on the Cc list).
5. Choose one of the six different comparison criteria (Contains, Doesn't Contain, Is, Isn't, Begins With, and Ends With) and then enter the text to look for or avoid in the third box.
6. Click the More button if you want to add additional criteria.

7. Below the More button, choose from six actions (usually you'll want Move to Folder—some of the instructions are more suited for discussion groups than for private e-mail), and then choose a folder (if applicable).
8. Finally, enter a description (if you wish), and click OK.

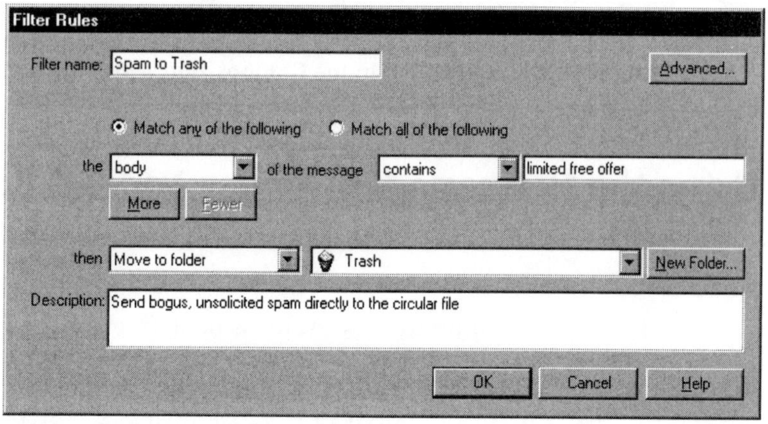

FIGURE 6.11: You can put together sophisticated filters easily with Netscape Messenger.

NOTE

Netscape Messenger has no provision, as of yet, for checking mail from multiple accounts.

Attaching Files to Messenger E-mail

Netscape Messenger's provisions for attaching files to e-mail are quite simple. You can also attach Web page links to your messages with these commands:

1. Select Message ➢ New Message to open the Composition window. Or you can click the New Message button in the Messenger toolbar or press Ctrl+M.
2. Address your e-mail and type your message in the message body. To attach a file to the message, click the Attach button.
3. Choose File (as you can see, you can also attach Web pages, among other things).

4. In the dialog box that appears, choose the file you want to send, and then click Open.
5. Click the Save or the Send button to save a draft or to send your message on its way.

TIP TIP TIP TIP TIP TIP TIP TIP TIP TIP TIP TIP TIP TIP TIP TIP TIP TIP TIP TIP TIP TIP TIP TIP TIP TIP

To check the spelling of your e-mail message in Netscape Messenger, choose Tools ➢ Check Spelling in the Composition window.

Using the Netscape Messenger Address Book

You can add names to Netscape Messenger's address book by following these steps:

1. Select Communicator ➢ Address Book from any of the Messenger windows.
2. In the Address Book window that appears, click the New Card button.
3. Enter the name, e-mail address, and nickname, and then click OK.
4. Select File ➢ Close to close the Address Book window.

To use the addresses in your new messages, do one of the following, depending on how good your memory is:

- In the Composition window, type the nickname on the To line.
- If you don't remember the nickname you made up, click the Address button, select the name, click To, and then click OK.

NOTE NOTE NOTE NOTE NOTE NOTE NOTE NOTE NOTE NOTE NOTE NOTE NOTE NOTE NOTE

You can add HTML formatting (or insert hyperlinks or even graphic images) to your message using the convenient toolbar in the Composition window. (Insert links and images with the Insert Object button furthest to the right.) See Skill 19, *Making a Home Page or Web Site*, for more on HTML formatting.

Adding a Signature File to Messenger E-mail

Messenger's signature file feature does not include much formatting support, but you can create basic signature files and add them to your messages with a minimum amount of fuss.

Here are the steps for creating and adding a signature file:

1. First, use a text editor or word processor to create and save a text file containing the signature you want to have at the end of your e-mail messages.
2. Then, in Netscape Messenger, select Edit ➢ Preferences. Double-click the Mail & Groups item in the Category list of the Preferences dialog box.
3. Click Identity in the Mail & Groups list item and type the full path and filename of your signature file in the Signature File box (or click the Browse button to find and select the file, and then click OK).
4. When you're done, click OK.

TIP TIP TIP TIP TIP TIP TIP TIP TIP TIP TIP TIP TIP TIP TIP TIP TIP TIP TIP TIP TIP TIP TIP TIP

If your signature exceeds the recommended four lines (this rubric is a widely accepted netiquette standard, though many people violate it), Netscape will warn you, but all you have to do is click OK again to accept it.

Pegasus Mail

Pegasus is a popular, free e-mail program that can run on networks and over dial-up Internet connections. Pegasus employs all of the usual e-mail commands and features. Use the Pegasus buttons and menus as described in the following steps to do everything from forwarding mail to using your address book.

TIP TIP TIP TIP TIP TIP TIP TIP TIP TIP TIP TIP TIP TIP TIP TIP TIP TIP TIP TIP TIP TIP TIP TIP

You can download Pegasus from its Web site at `http://www.pegasus.usa.com/`**. See Skill 10, *Finding Stuff on the Web and the Net,* for tips on downloading files from the Net.**

Basic Pegasus Functions

When you are ready to send Pegasus messages, here's how to compose and send them:

1. Select File ➢ New Message (or press Ctrl+N).
2. Type the recipient's name, press Tab, and type a subject. Then press Tab two more times to get down to the message area and type your message.

3. When you're done, click the Send button to either send your message immediately or put it in a queue, depending on how your version of Pegasus is set up.
4. To send all queued messages, select File ➢ Send All Queued Mail.

To read new mail, select File ➢ Read New Mail (or press Ctrl+W). This opens the New Mail folder. (Once you've read a message, it will automatically be moved to the Main mail folder after you close the New Mail folder or exit Pegasus.)

The following commands will help you check for new Pegasus messages, read, reply, or delete messages you've received, and finally exit Pegasus:

- To check for new messages, select File ➢ Check Host for New Mail.
- To read a message, double-click on it.
- To reply to an open message, click the Reply button.
- To delete a message, click the Delete button.
- To exit Pegasus, select File ➢ Exit.

Forwarding Pegasus Mail or Sending Messages to More Than One Person

Your Pegasus Mail messages can be forwarded to other people and you can send forwarded messages or other types of messages to more than one person with the following options:

- To forward a message, just click the Forward button at the top of the message window. Then proceed as you would with any new message.
- To send an e-mail to multiple recipients, type the addresses in the To box, separated by commas, or enter additional addresses in the Cc box.

Managing Pegasus Mail with Folders

Like most of the other mail programs profiled in this lesson, Pegasus Mail has a folder feature for storing messages so that you can find them later when you want to refer back to them.

Here's how to create a new folder:

1. Select File ➢ Mail Folders to open the Folders dialog box.
2. Click the New button, type a name for the new folder, and click OK.

To move a message from one folder to another, double-click the folder currently containing the message, highlight the message you want to move, and drag it to the new folder.

Attaching Files to Pegasus Messages

File attachments are an important part of Pegasus Mail messages because the program supports many different Internet file types. When you start sending messages with attachments to many different people on many different systems, you might have to experiment with these file formats to see which one works best and gets the information to your recipients in a usable format. These steps will get you started:

1. Click the Attach button on the left side of the message window.
2. Select a file in the bottom part of the window that appears, and then click the Add button (top right).
3. Choose one of the wide variety of file-encoding formats from the Encoding drop-down list, or allow the mailer to choose one for you.
4. Then click the Editor button (on the left side of the window) when you're ready to return to typing your message.
5. When you're done typing the message, you can just click Send.

TIP

If you use a PC—especially on a local-area network—and you sometimes have trouble accessing the path the folder is in, you may have to move the file around with Windows Explorer.

Creating and Using a Pegasus Address Book

The address book feature in Pegasus Mail is a little different than other e-mail address books because you have to create the address book before you can add names to it. The advantage to this setup is that you can have more than one address book. For example, you could have Business and Personal address books to store the names and addresses of business associates and friends separately. Some people might get listed in both books, however, if you are fortunate enough to have friends at work!

1. To create an address book, select Addresses ➢ Address Books, and then click New in the Select an Address Book dialog box that appears.
2. Type a name for the address book and then click OK.
3. To open an address book, select Addresses ➢ Address Books and double-click on the name of the address book you want to open.
4. To add a name to the address book, click the Add button. Pegasus suggests the name and e-mail address from the currently selected message, but you can type in any name.
5. Press Tab seven times to get to the E-mail Address box and type a different e-mail address, if you like. Then click OK.

When you want to send e-mail to someone in one of your address books, you have two choices:

- Type their name in the To box.
- Open the address book (as just described), scroll down to select the person you want, and click the Paste button. Then click Close.

Correcting Misspelled Words in Pegasus Messages

You can access the spell-checking feature by selecting Edit ➢ Check Spelling. Pegasus will start scanning the message for words it doesn't recognize. If you've ever used the spell checker in any standard word processing program, then you should be familiar with how it works:

- To skip the word in question, click Skip.
- To accept a suggested correction, click Change.
- To make your own correction, type the correct word over the suggestion and click Change.
- To add the word in question to the spell checker's dictionary, click Add.

Pegasus will tell you when you've reached the end of the message and ask if you want to start over from the top. Click No (unless you want to). Then click Close.

Creating and Adding Signatures to Pegasus Mail

Use the Pegasus Mail Signature feature to create signature blocks that you can use repeatedly in different messages. This is especially useful for business messages, because it saves you the time of retyping your name, title, company name, address, phone and fax numbers, e-mail address, and all the other contact information usually included on a business card. Just type it once and save it in a signature file, then reuse this file in all your messages.

Follow these steps to make your signature file:

1. Select File ➢ Preferences ➢ Signatures ➢ For Internet Messages.
2. Type your signature in the dialog box that appears and click the Save button.

Pine

If you're determined to get your hands dirty and log in directly to a Unix account to read mail with a Unix mail reader, then here's a quick rundown of the most useful commands in everybody's favorite Unix mail program, Pine. (Pine uses simple letter commands rather than menus and buttons to implement e-mail features, but the end results are the same as for the programs that run under Windows and the Mac OS, described earlier in this lesson.)

TIP

Another popular Unix e-mail program is Elm. For information about Elm, send mail to `mail-server@cs.ruu.nl` **with no subject and type the two lines** send NEWS.ANSWERS/elm/FAQ **and** end **on separate lines as your message.**

Basic Pine Functions

Here's how you create and send e-mail using Pine in the Unix environment:

1. Start Pine by typing **pine** (yes, all lowercase—it matters) at the Unix command prompt and press Enter.
2. Pine starts you off at a main menu. To enter your Inbox, type **i**.
3. To send mail, type **c**—and don't press Enter. Pine will start a new message (see Figure 6.12).
4. Type the recipient's address, press Tab, and type a subject. Press Tab again until you're in the message area. Then type your message. Pine will handle word-wrapping, so you only have to press Enter when you're starting a new paragraph.
5. When you're done, press Ctrl+X to send the message.

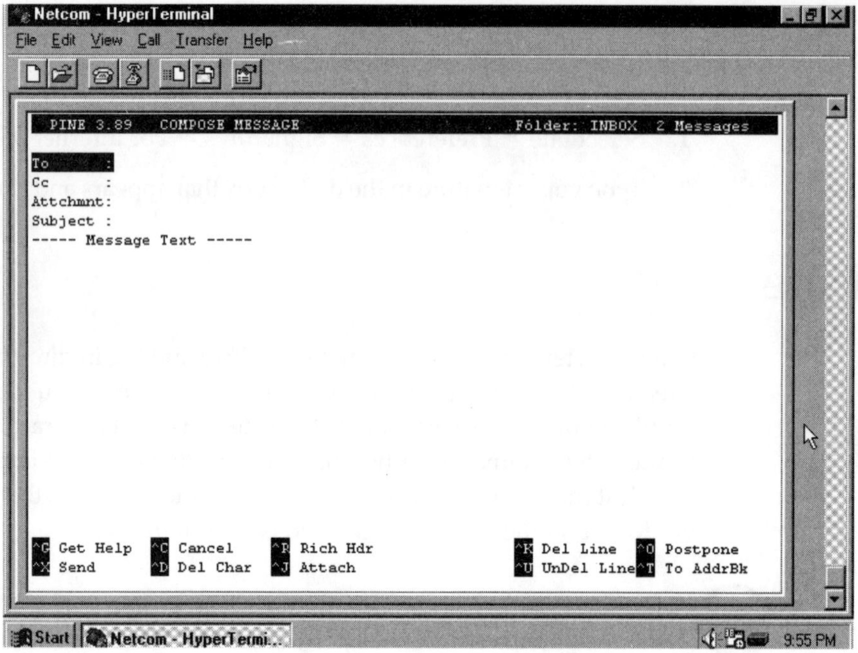

FIGURE 6.12: Pine is a full-screen editor, so it works something like a normal Windows or Mac program, even though it's text-only and runs in Unix

The following list summarizes the commands for some specific Pine functions:

Function	Type
To run Pine	Type **pine** and press Enter
To move between listed messages	Press the up and down arrow keys
To read a message	Highlight it in your Inbox and press Enter
To send mail	Type **c**
To return to your message list	Type **i**
To reply to a message	Type **r**
To delete a message	Type **d**
To undelete a message	Type **u**
To quit Pine	Type **q**

Forwarding a Message in Pine

Pine may be a simple mail program, but you can still forward messages, and Pine even adds a reply separator between the message you type and the message you are forwarding. Use these steps to forward Pine messages to other Pine users:

1. When you receive a message you want to forward to another person, type **f**.
2. Pine will put you in the Forward Message screen, which is exactly the same as the Compose Message screen except that the message area will include the original message, preceded by

   ```
   -----Forwarded Message-----
   ```

3. Proceed as you would with a normal message.

Sending Pine Messages to More Than One Person

Pine also supports sending mail to many people at one time. You can add more than one address to either the To line or the Cc line in the Pine message using one of these options:

- Type each e-mail address on the To line, separated by commas.
- Type additional e-mail addresses on the Cc line, separated by commas.

TIP

You can always go back to your Inbox folder by typing g **(for Go to) and then Enter to accept the default.**

If you want to save a piece of mail for future reference, press **s** either in the index or while reading the mail. Pine will suggest Saved-Messages as a folder name, but you can replace it with anything you like.

Looking at Message Folders with Pine

Pine provides message folders for storing messages in an orderly manner. You can file messages in folders that reflect the message subject, sender, or other topics and revisit them later with these procedures:

1. To look at the contents of a folder, type **l** to see a folder list.
2. Press the Tab key to get to the folder list you want to see, and then press Enter.
3. When you are done and want to go back, type **l** to get back to the folder list and choose the Inbox folder.

Attaching Files to Pine Messages

You can also send a file with Pine. Here are the steps for adding file attachments to Pine messages:

1. In the Compose Mail screen, press Tab twice to get to the Attachment line.
2. Then press Ctrl+T. This will bring up a list of the files in your Unix directory.
3. Using the arrow keys, select a file and press Enter. Pine will send the file as a MIME attachment.

TIP TIP TIP TIP TIP TIP TIP TIP TIP TIP TIP TIP TIP TIP TIP TIP TIP TIP TIP TIP TIP TIP TIP TIP TIP

Okay, but how do I get the file to my Unix directory? You can use an FTP program, as explained in Skill 18, *Getting Around with FTP and Telnet*. Or check with your Unix system administrator to find out which modem protocol and commands to use on your system.

Creating and Using a Pine Address Book

To create an address book—a list of e-mail addresses you regularly send mail to—type **a** (from the Main Menu screen). This brings up the Address Book screen.

To add a new address to the Pine address book:

1. Type **a**. Pine will prompt you with

   ```
   New full name (last, first):
   ```

2. Type the last name, a comma, and then the first name of the person whose Internet address you want to add to your address book. Then press Enter and Pine will prompt you with

   ```
   Enter new nickname (one word and easy to remember):
   ```

3. Type a short nickname and press Enter. Then Pine will prompt you to

   ```
   Enter new e-mail address:
   ```

4. Type the person's address and press Enter. The new address will be added to the address book.
5. Type **i** to return to the Inbox folder index, or type **m** to return to the Main Menu.

Now, whenever you want to use the nickname in the address book, just type it instead of the full Internet address. Pine will do the rest.

Adding Addresses to the Pine Address Book

Pine's address book supplies all of the usual address book functions and even has a nickname feature for storing address book entries. All you have to remember is the nickname and Pine will retrieve the person's e-mail address.

You can also take an e-mail address off a recent message and send it to the Pine address book with these steps:

1. To automatically add the sender of the current message to your address book from the Folder Index screen, type **t**.
2. Type an address book entry for the sender and press Enter.
3. Press Enter twice to accept the full name and address of the sender.

NOTE NOTE NOTE NOTE NOTE NOTE NOTE NOTE NOTE NOTE NOTE NOTE NOTE NOTE NOTE

Pine does not permit you to add formatting to message text (HTML or otherwise). Pine has no message filtering capabilities, either.

Checking Message Spelling with Pine

Even though Pine may not have all the bells and whistles of its non-Unix counterparts, it does provide the essential spell-check feature for proofing your messages before they "go public." Here are the steps involved:

1. To check the spelling of a message, press Ctrl+T (while in the message area itself).
2. Pine will highlight any suspicious word and prompt you to correct it and press Enter—but Pine won't suggest any possible spellings. Press Enter to make the correction.

Adding Signature Files to Pine Messages

Pine's signature file function operates much like that of other e-mail programs. You can add all of your professional information to the signature file and it will be added at the end of all your Pine messages. The only disadvantage to the signature file is that it will appear on all your messages, not just the ones you select to have signatures.

1. Create a text file named `.signature`. To do so, type **pico.signature** at the Unix prompt and press Enter.
2. Type whatever you want for your signature (but keep it under four lines as traditional netiquette dictates).
3. Then press Ctrl+X, type **y**, and press Enter.

TIP TIP TIP TIP TIP TIP TIP TIP TIP TIP TIP TIP TIP TIP TIP TIP TIP TIP TIP TIP TIP TIP TIP TIP TIP

The required location of the signature file might vary from one system to the next, so if your signature file does not appear at the end of your messages, ask your system administrator where it should be stored.

Your signature will appear at the end of your e-mail messages. When you reply to a message and quote the text in your reply, Pine will put your signature at the beginning of your new message, before the quoted text. The idea is for you to write your message before the signature and then delete as much of the quoted text as possible (while still letting it make sense).

Whew! You have just completed a very thorough examination of the e-mail capabilities of some of our most celebrated Internet programs. Now that you are an e-mail "expert," you're ready to learn about mailing lists, where you can correspond with large numbers of like-minded people at once.

Are You Experienced?

Now you can...

- ☑ **handle mail with Eudora**
- ☑ **handle mail with MS Outlook and Outlook Express**
- ☑ **handle mail with NETCOMplete**
- ☑ **handle mail with Netscape Messenger**
- ☑ **handle mail with Pegasus Mail**
- ☑ **handle mail with Pine**

SKILL 7

SIGNING UP FOR MAILING LISTS

- Finding interesting mailing lists
- Subscribing to mailing lists
- Getting off mailing lists
- Putting in your two cents worth

Apart from using e-mail to keep in touch with friends, another benefit of e-mail is that it gives you the opportunity to participate in mailing lists. I'm not talking about what you might usually think of as a mailing list—the kind you're put on after buying once from a department store and that results in two hundred catalogs sent to you the next year. No, subscribing to an electronic mailing list is voluntary, and the communication is interactive (unless you want to stay silent). Each list has its own particular topic, so you can sign up for several if you have a variety of interests.

Electronic mailing lists enable people to send e-mail to a list of e-mail addresses ("broadcasting the e-mail," it's sometimes called), and these mailing lists usually function as discussion forums for people who are interested in the same topics. The simplest kind of mailing list is an alias (or address book entry) that corresponds to a list of several e-mail addresses (see "Managing an Address Book" in Skill 5, *Advanced E-mail Tricks*, for a more in-depth explanation of aliases and address books), but the more interesting kind of mailing list (or *list* for short) allows anyone to send mail to a central list address and have it forwarded to everyone else on the list. These lists function as discussion groups on any subject you can imagine, with subscribers all over the globe.

Anyone with an Internet mailing address can participate in lists of this sort. And every subscriber can be a contributor as well. Sending a message to a mailing list is called *posting*.

Once you've posted your message, one of two things will happen to it. If the list is unmoderated, your message will be immediately re-sent to everyone on the list; if it is a moderated list, your message will go to the moderator (a volunteer) who determines if it's *on-topic* (directly related to the subject of the list), and then either sends it along to the entire list if it is or sends it back to you if it isn't. Most lists are unmoderated, however, and rely on peer pressure to keep posts in line.

NOTE NOTE NOTE NOTE NOTE NOTE NOTE NOTE NOTE NOTE NOTE NOTE NOTE NOTE NOTE

Mailing lists are free and are great sources of opinion and information. There are mailing lists on all sorts of topics. Keeping current with a mailing list related to your work is a good way to meet colleagues, pick up tips on work-related topics, and learn about the latest developments and debates in your professional field.

If you subscribe to a busy list or to several lists and then don't read and clear out your mailbox for a while, it can fill up and even exceed your system's limitations. This could result in some mail being lost, and some messages being returned as undeliverable. Many mailing lists will also automatically unsubscribe you when that happens. So if you *do* subscribe to some lists, be sure to check your mail regularly.

Mailing Lists versus Usenet Newsgroups

Another way for people to share common interests over the Internet is by participating in Usenet newsgroups.

Mailing lists have been around longer than Usenet and are more universal, as anyone with Internet access—even without Usenet—can participate in mailing lists. Lists generally have less traffic (fewer posts) than newsgroups, but there are some very large, very busy lists and some pretty dead newsgroups. Busy lists fill up your mailbox, whereas newsgroup posts are not sent to you directly. In Skill 13, *Joining Usenet Newsgroups*, I explain how to "read" Usenet.

Sometimes mailing lists become newsgroups. Usually this means that there is a gateway between a list and a corresponding newsgroup, and all posts are shared between them. Most of these decisions are made by polling the readership. Some people feel that lists are more private, even when they are open to anyone, because they are harder to find—if you don't know where to look.

TIP TIP TIP TIP TIP TIP TIP TIP TIP TIP TIP TIP TIP TIP TIP TIP TIP TIP TIP TIP TIP TIP TIP TIP TIP

Some lists are available as digests. This means that posts are grouped together and sent out less often. You might receive ten or twenty posts in a single mailing rather than ten or twenty individual messages. If you subscribe to a list and then find that the traffic is too much for you to handle, look into whether it is also available in a *digest* form. If your e-mail has filtering and sorting capabilities, you can also manage posts and messages with these tools.

Exploring Lists of General Interest

So how do you find the lists you'd be interested in? There's no single way. To some extent, all information on the Net flows by word of mouth (or by e-mail, more likely). People will tell you about mailing lists. I've heard about some of the lists I subscribe to in Usenet newsgroups. There are also some large "lists of lists" out there that you can consult and peruse. Some Web sites have links to mailing lists or newsgroups on subjects related to the topic of the site. Professional organizations and clubs also maintain lists and newsgroups.

TIP TIP TIP TIP TIP TIP TIP TIP TIP TIP TIP TIP TIP TIP TIP TIP TIP TIP TIP TIP TIP TIP TIP TIP TIP

These lists are long and will take up a lot of disk space. If you find what you're looking for, delete the files. You can always get the updated versions in the future using the same method described here.

A General List of Lists

I know of two e-mail addresses you can send to and have lists of lists mailed back to you. The first one is so large that it is broken into twenty-seven parts. (The second address is mentioned in the next section, "More Specific Lists of Lists.") Send mail to `mail-server@rtfm.mit.edu`. The Subject line can be anything—blank is fine. For the message, type just this line:

send usenet-by-group/news.answers/mail/mailing-lists/part01

You will receive part01 as e-mail.

Then send the same message, but substitute **part02**, **part03**, and so on, all the way up to **part 27**, to obtain the entire list.

NOTE NOTE NOTE NOTE NOTE NOTE NOTE NOTE NOTE NOTE NOTE NOTE NOTE NOTE NOTE

This list is always growing, so there may be more than 27 parts to this list of lists by the time you get around to sending for it.

If you'd rather peruse this same listing of mailing lists on the Web, point your browser at `http://www.neosoft.com/internet/paml` (that's the letter "l" at the end, not the numeral one). This site is shown in Figure 7.1. These lists are also posted regularly to the `news.announce.newusers` newsgroup. (See Skill 13, *Joining Usenet Newsgroups*, for more on Usenet newsgroups.)

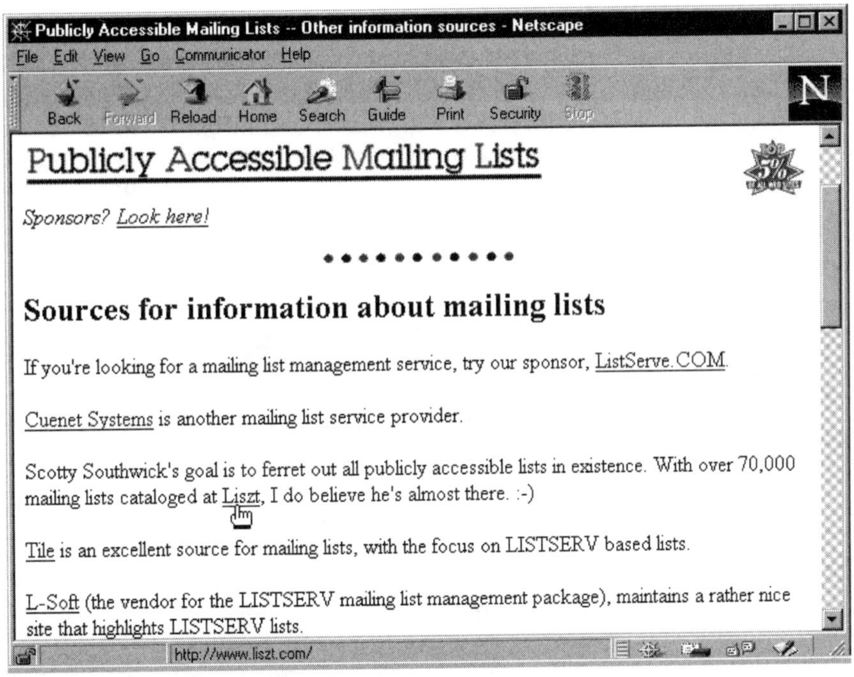

FIGURE 7.1: Even pioneering Internet mailing lists are now available on the Web at sites such as the Publicly Accessible Mailing Lists site shown here.

More Specific Lists of Lists

You can seek out lists that relate to a specific topic by sending mail to `listserv@listserv.net`. Leave the subject blank. Type the line **list global/*topic*** in your message and substitute whatever topic word you want for *topic*. (Also, don't include your signature if you've got one. The Listserv program will try to interpret it as a command.)

NOTE

You can send mail to this address and just include the line `list global` without specifying a topic, but then the message sent back to you will be incredibly long. You're much better off limiting the responses in some way.

Figure 7.2 shows the mail I got in response when I sent the message **list global/auto** to the Bitnic Listserv.

TIP

If you are interested in music, you might want to see the List of Musical Mailing Lists, which is updated regularly. Send mail to `lomml@arastar.com` **and the current list will be sent to you, or look for it on the Web at** `http://server.berkeley.edu/~ayukawa/lomml.html`.

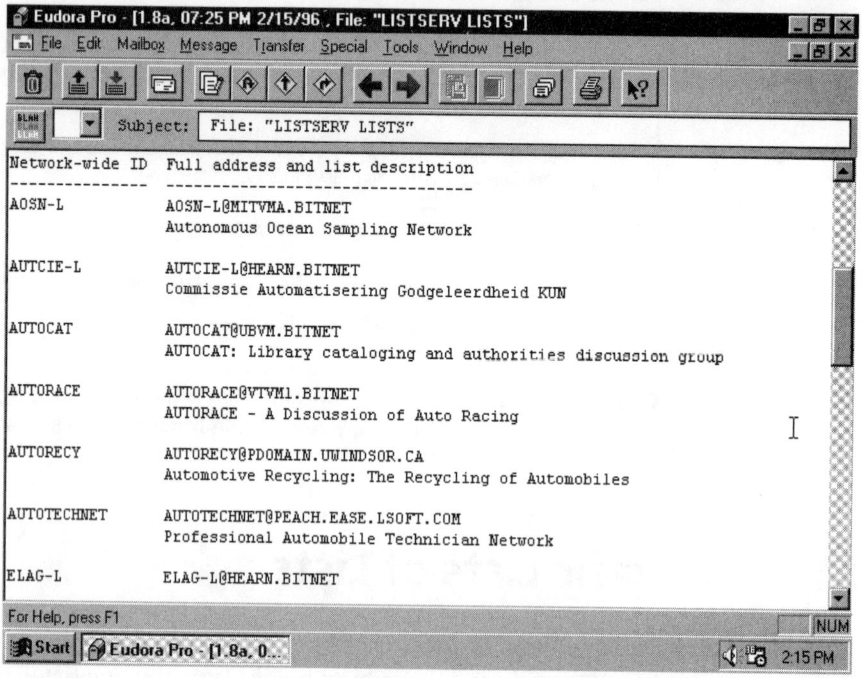

FIGURE 7.2: By using the topic word *auto* I got information about automobile mailing lists along with other lists related to words that start with *auto* (such as automatic).

Table 7.1 is a quick reference guide for getting general and specific lists of lists.

TABLE 7.1: Reference guide for mailing lists

To Get Lists of Lists	Address	Message
General list of lists	`mail-server@rtfm.mit.edu`	**send usenet-by-group/news. answers/mail/mailing-lists/part01** (then substitute **part02**, **part03**, and so on, all the way up to **part27** for future messages)
	`http://www.neosoft.com /internet/paml`	no message
	`news.announce.newusers` (a Usenet newsgroup)	no message
Specific lists of lists	`listserv@listserv.net`	**`list global/`*`topic`*** (substitute whatever word you want for topic)

Subscribing to Lists

The first and most important thing I can tell you is that to subscribe to a mailing list, you send a message to an address *different* from the mailing list address. People constantly make the mistake of sending their subscription requests directly to the lists in question. This forces everyone on the list to read your mistaken post.

SKILL 7

WARNING WARNING WARNING WARNING WARNING WARNING WARNING WARNING

It's embarrassing to you and annoying to everyone else on a mailing list when you send your requests to the list itself instead of to the administrative address. Be careful.

The next thing you need to know is that there are two different kinds of lists. Once you're on the list, it won't make any difference to you. There are lists administered by real live people and there are automated lists. Lists that are run by programs are called *listservs* (or, by their full name, *list servers*).

If possible, try to determine what sort of list you're subscribing to ahead of time. There are two types:

- If the address you've found for subscribing to a list is of the form `list-request@`*`address`* (with *list* representing the name of the mailing list), then the list is handled by a person.

- If the address starts with `listserv@` or `majordomo@`, then the list is handled by a program (or robot—'bot for short).

People-Administered Lists

To subscribe to a people-administered list, send e-mail to the request address for the list. This address should be of the form `list-request@address`.

Since this message will be read by a human being, you can write a normal sentence to the effect that you'd like to subscribe to the list. Include your e-mail address, just to be sure it comes through okay. The administrator will acknowledge your mail and send you the actual address of the list (for posting). He might also send you some additional information, such as where to find the list's FAQ or archive of posts.

So, for example, to join the "they-might-be" list to discuss the rock band They Might Be Giants, I sent a message to the address `they-might-be-request@super.org` that said something like

> **Hi, I'd like to subscribe to the they-might-be list. My e-mail address is xian@netcom.com. Thanks!**

When you subscribe to a list, you'll receive a message about list commands, how to unsubscribe, and guidance on what is and is not acceptable for posting to that list. Save these messages in a clearly labeled folder or file so that you can refer to them later.

Robot-Administered Lists

Subscribing to robot-administered lists is a little more involved, unless you subscribe by clicking a link in a Web page. To subscribe to a robot-administered list:

1. Send mail to the contact address of the list, which should be of the form `listserv@address` (or `majordomo@address`).
2. Leave the subject line blank.
3. Include in your message only the following line:
   subscribe *listname Your Name*
   Use the name of the list for listname. Then include your real first and last name, not your e-mail address. You will receive a confirmation and a welcome message in response.

NOTE NOTE NOTE NOTE NOTE NOTE NOTE NOTE NOTE NOTE NOTE NOTE NOTE NOTE NOTE

Only a computer program will read your message, not a human being, so don't gussy up the language to make it sound natural. Include only the keywords listed here. To get help, send a message to the same address with just the word *help* in it.

So, for example, to join the Screen Writing Discussion List Top-Ten list, I sent a one-line message to the address `listserv@tamvm1.tamu.edu` that said, **subscribe SCRNWRIT Christian Crumlish**.

Canceling Your Subscription

If you tire of a list, you can simply cancel your subscription to it. Again, it's different for people and robots.

People-Administered Lists

Send an e-mail to the original list-request address, asking "Please unsubscribe me" or something to that effect.

Robot-Administered Lists

Send an e-mail to the original `listserv@`*`address`*, with no subject and only the line **signoff *list***, substituting the name of the list for *list*, of course.

SKILL 7

Temporarily Unsubscribing

If you're going on vacation, you can temporarily cancel your subscription by sending to the `listserv@`*`address`* the message **set *list* nomail**. When you return, send the message **set *list* mail** to start up your subscription again.

NOTE NOTE NOTE NOTE NOTE NOTE NOTE NOTE NOTE NOTE NOTE NOTE NOTE NOTE NOTE

Certain lists may have slightly different commands for temporarily unsubscribing, such as `mail postpone`.

Posting to Lists

There are two ways to post to mailing lists. The first is to send mail to the list address. The other way is to reply to a message from the list, when the return address is set to the list itself. How the return address is assigned varies from list to list, so watch out you don't do this by mistake when you mean to reply to someone directly.

TIP TIP TIP TIP TIP TIP TIP TIP TIP TIP TIP TIP TIP TIP TIP TIP TIP TIP TIP TIP TIP TIP TIP TIP TIP

Always look at the header of a message before replying to it. Normally, your reply will go to the return address, but sometimes there's a Reply To line, and then your reply will go to that address. Check the address in your reply, too, if you are not sure where it is going.

Remember that you always have the option of sending mail just to the person who wrote the post you are replying to, though you may have to copy that person's address into the To box yourself.

WARNING WARNING WARNING WARNING WARNING WARNING WARNING WARNING

In general, remember that many people will read your post. If you post, it is like speaking in public. You never know who is listening or who is saving what you've written. Try to ensure that your posts are on-topic and that you won't regret sending them afterwards.

Participating in a List

Everybody was a newbie once, and while there's no such thing as a dumb question, there are such things as frequently asked questions. Most lists eventually get around to compiling a *FAQ*, a document of answers to frequently asked questions. Look for or ask for the FAQ for your list and read it before posting the first questions that come to mind. FAQs are usually fun and interesting to read—they are some of the best resources on the Net.

WARNING WARNING WARNING WARNING WARNING WARNING WARNING WARNING

Some people just like to make trouble and post messages designed to arouse indignation, resentment, or anger. After a while, it's easy to tell when someone has posted *flame bait*, and you learn to just ignore it until it goes away. Unfortunately, there are always too many people too ready to jump in and debate even the most obviously insulting posts. Oh well. Fortunately, this seems to happen on mailing lists less often than it does on Usenet.

I highly recommend *lurking*—reading the list without posting to it for a while—to get caught up on the various threads of conversations that are going on. Once you've made a reasonable effort to get up to speed, plunge right in and start gabbing. Many people lurk most or all of the time. It's easy to forget how many people are out there when only a small number of them post regularly.

Lists are like communities and often have their pet peeves, their unassailable truths, their opposing parties, and so on. You might experience some campaigning if someone is taking a poll or a vote. Rules of e-mail netiquette become especially important in a one-to-many forum such as a mailing list (look back at "Using Proper E-mail Netiquette" in Skill 4, *E-mail Basics*). Bear in mind that sarcasm and other subtleties that are easy to communicate when face-to-face do not translate well in cold, hard text. Try to say exactly what you mean and read things over before posting them. Ask yourself if what you've written might be misinterpreted. And if the subject is heated or emotional, then remember that you don't have to send it immediately (that's one advantage of e-mail). Write your post and put it aside for a while, then read it over again before you send it.

Are You Experienced?

Now you can...

- ☑ **find interesting mailing lists through Web sites, newsgroups, or other lists**
- ☑ **lurk on a list to learn more about it and its participants**
- ☑ **review a list's FAQ for additional enlightenment**
- ☑ **post replies to lists using the correct protocol**
- ☑ **subscribe to lists and temporarily or permanently cancel subscriptions**
- ☑ **avoid mailing list disputes by ignoring flame bait**

PART III

Browsing the World Wide Web

When most people speak of the Internet, they are thinking of the World Wide Web (or just Web for short). The program used to get around the Web, a Web browser, is the closest thing we have at the moment to a universal Internet interface, so once you've learned to operate one, you instantly have direct access to tons of information and resources online.

The lessons in Part III explain how to get around the Web, how to operate the most popular Web browsers, how to find things on the Net (and what the difference is between the Net and the Web), how to work with multimedia formats, and how to have Web content "beamed" directly to your desktop.

SKILL 8

NAVIGATING THE WEB

- **Understanding the World Wide Web**
- **Deciphering Web addresses**
- **Distinguishing between various types of Web browsers**
- **Using Web browsers**

The most famous part of the Internet is the World Wide Web. The Web (or sometimes WWW, w3, or W3) is a huge collection of interconnected hypertext documents. (See the sidebar, "What Is Hypertext?" to learn more about hypertext.) Hypertext documents can contain links to other documents, to completely different kinds of files, and to other sites on the Internet. With a Web browser, you can jump from one link to the next, following the trail of links in any direction that interests you. Not everything on the Internet is available via the Web, but more and more of it is being linked together.

The beauty of the Web is that the browser programs with which you "read" the Web are incredibly easy to use. This gives you access to all kinds of data, programs, news, pictures, and so on, without having to master the syntax of difficult protocols and arcane Unix commands.

Throughout the rest of this book, there will be references to the Web. It has become such a ubiquitous *front end* (way to connect) to the Net that much of your interaction with the Net will take place through a Web browser.

WHAT IS HYPERTEXT?

On the Web, hypertext is simply text with *links*. Links are elements of the hypertext documents that you can select—often presented as underlined words or icons. Click on a link and you'll be transported to the document it's linked to (or to a different part of the displayed document). As I mentioned in Skill 1, *Understanding the Internet*, if you use Windows, then you've got hypertext right in front of you, in the form of Windows help files. Whenever you select options from the Help menu of a Windows program, you are shown a hypertext help document with definitions and links available at the click of a mouse.

In addition to taking you to other documents, links can take you to Gopher servers, FTP sites, Telnet sites, Usenet newsgroups, and other Internet facilities. Links can also take you to other programs and connect you to pictures, sounds, movies, and other binary files.

Once we start considering other media besides text, the term hypertext is replaced by the word *hypermedia*. But the basic idea is the same: links. An advantage of hypertext (or hypermedia) over traditional media is that it allows you to navigate through all kinds of related documents (and other kinds of files), using one simple procedure—clicking on a link.

continued

One limitation of hypermedia is that, for now, you generally must follow links that other people have created, so the medium is not yet fully interactive. Of course, you can always make your own Web page—see Skill 19, *Making a Home Page or Web Site*. Also, there's a lot more text out there than hypertext. A Web browser can lead you to a plain text document as easily as to a hypertext document. You won't be able to jump anywhere else from a plain text document, so it's a sort of cul-de-sac, but you can always turn around.

How Is the Web Being Used?

More and more day-to-day applications are gaining the capability to browse the Web and display documents in Web format (HTML). The competition among Web browsers is fierce, with Netscape and Microsoft duking it out for the dominant share of the market. Every sought-after browser includes e-mail and news modules as well, with Web (HTML) editors being another common feature. Upcoming releases of popular browsers will blend together your desktop view of your own computer with the Web interface. (More on that in Skill 12.) Meanwhile, in-house "intranets" incorporate most of the features of Web sites while local, small-scale networks operate much like the Internet.

Those are the changes taking place in the world of tools. On the Web itself, commercial sites keep sprouting up like mushrooms, although there is no proven business model yet for making money on the Web.

Cramming the Web with Content

Companies have rushed to post their own Web sites, where they provide everything from customer service to upcoming product information and online ordering capabilities (if you can get through). Any information or material added to a Web site, even fiction and graphics, is referred to as *content*. The Web has more content than a single university or library because the Web is a collection of data from many different universities, libraries, businesses, and individuals.

All kinds of companies have set up shop on the Web—not just megacorporations like Coca Cola and IBM. Any organization that can afford space on a Web server can display its wares (or its philosophy, or both) online. This gives Web users access to many new products, services, and business ideas that would have been difficult to find before Internet use became so widespread.

If you are in the market for energy-saving compact-fluorescent lighting or solar panels for your home, for example, check out the Real Goods Solar Living site at `http://www.realgoods.com/` (see Figure 8.1). This site has its own set of specialized Web links that will lead you to sites sponsored by the U.S. Environmental Protection Agency, including Solstice: Internet Information Service of the Center for Renewable Energy and Sustainable Technology (CREST) at `http://www.solstice.crest.org/`. Explore Solstice for a little bit and you can reach the CREST Global Energy Marketplace (GEM) at `http://gem.crest.org/`, where you can click on a link to your state to find local energy information. Chances are, if you have a special interest or purchase to make, there is a site out there that you can use, with links to other related sites that might help you out, too.

FIGURE 8.1: Find everything from compact-fluorescent lighting to worm composters at the Real Goods Solar Living site at `http://www.realgoods.com/`.

Business needs aside, the Web's greatest strength may be its capacity for entertainment. You can find everything from literary 'zines to science fiction film guides. Sports enthusiasts, of course, have many Web sites to choose from, including sites supporting the growing field of fantasy franchises, where players have their own fantasy teams and create rosters from real players. You can find out about the local activities of your favorite organization by following links from the organization's parent Web site, such as the Habitat for Humanity site shown in Figure 8.2.

This overabundance of Web content brings problems, too, such as slower browsing speeds and information overload. Run a search for the term "computer" on the Web and you could wind up far too many *hits*. Each hit is an individual site that matches your search term and, in this case, has something to do with computers. Fortunately, you can refine your searches, as you will learn in Skill 10, *Finding Stuff on the Web and the Net*.

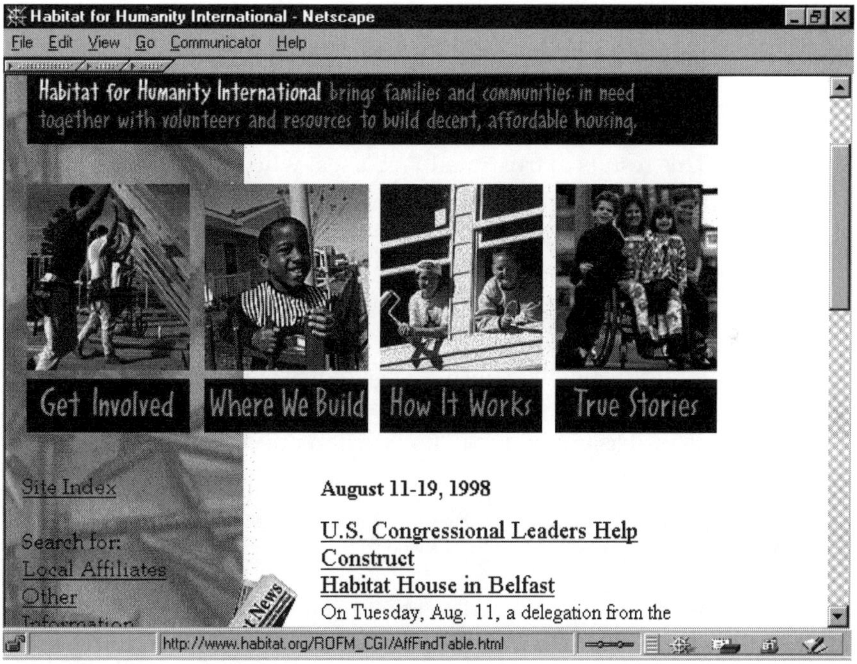

FIGURE 8.2: Find out about local branches or organizations from the Web page of their headquarters. Habitat for Humanity's Web site at `http://www.habitat.org/` has many links to pages about its work.

You don't always have to go out and look for things on the Web, though. Now there is also *push* technology (also called Webcasting), which allows you to direct your browser to find and obtain information from specific sites for you while you are off doing something else. This innovation is available in Microsoft Internet Explorer versions 4 and after, and is discussed briefly in the next section and in more detail in Skill 12, *Push and the Desktop Web*.

Saving Time with Webcasting

A brave new method for delivering content to your screen via the Web, called *Webcasting*, allows your browser to surf the Web for you. You can set up your Webcasting software, such as Internet Explorer's Active Channels, to deliver any kind of information you like to your desktop, including stock market reports, up-to-the-minute sports results, and even weather reports. This new "push" technology promises to give Web users finer control over their Web surfing activities and improve the quality of the information pulled in.

As Web content expands and draws in more Web users, the amount of time spent waiting to get through to sites and waiting for Web pages to load has increased. This results in frustrated Web users who are sick of waiting around on the Web to see new sites or popular pages. Webcasting is one possible solution to this problem, and is covered in Skill 12, *Push and the Desktop Web*.

Next week, something new will appear on the Web's horizon because the Web is in a constant state of change. When you learn how to browse the Web, you will have a valuable skill that will enable you to stay informed about new developments in all kinds of subjects, not just computers. Your ability to browse the Web and develop effective search strategies for finding things could lead to personal, as well as professional, growth and opportunities.

Web Addresses (URLs)

If you've ever noticed an advertisement that says "check out our Web site," you've seen the arcane way they describe how to find it, giving you the address, or *URL*, which almost always begins with the characters `http:`. (*URL* stands for *Uniform Resource Locator*.) A Web address starts with the name of a protocol, which lets the computer know how to communicate with the computer at the other end—on the Web it is usually `http`. *http* stands for *Hypertext Transfer Protocol* and means that the resource at that address will be found on a Web server. This protocol is followed by `://` (the oft-heard "colon slash slash," or even more cumbersome, "colon forward-slash forward-slash"), and then by an Internet address of the form `site.subdomain.domain`, as explained in "The Anatomy of an Internet Address" in Skill 2. After that, you might find a colon and a port number (this is fairly rare), or a path comprised of a list of folders or directory names leading to the resource in question, separated by more forward slashes. After the path, you might find a file name, which often ends with the extension `.html`. An *HTML* file (or *Hypertext Markup Language* file) is the primary type of document on the Web.

Fortunately, most of the time you won't have to type in Web addresses yourself (after the first one) because you'll be following links that have the URL encoded into them. You can also copy Web addresses from e-mail and other sources and paste them into your browser. Another beautiful feature of most Web browsers is URL-saving bookmarks, which we will cover later in this lesson.

Enterprising search engine companies have also given us Web sites designed around their search software, such as Yahoo!, Excite, AltaVista, and Infoseek. You can go to these sites, use the interactive search form to find a list of Web addresses relating to your search criteria, and click on the links in the search list to go to the sites. You still have to type in some of the search terms, however.

NOTE NOTE NOTE NOTE NOTE NOTE NOTE NOTE NOTE NOTE NOTE NOTE NOTE NOTE NOTE

While graphical browsers such as Netscape Navigator are certainly a pleasure to use and a great way to surf the Net, reading the Web with Lynx or Www can be just as fascinating—after all, it's the information itself that is most interesting on the Net.

Web Browser Basics

Generally, when you start a browser, you begin at a home page, a starting place you designate (or your browser designates) for your Web-crawling sessions. This will either be the default home page for your browser or a custom home page that you have specified. Some e-mail programs, such as Eudora, now allow you to double-click a URL in an e-mail message to automatically start up your most recently installed browser and bring up the selected Web page.

HTTP, HTML, AND URLs

Don't get thrown by the alphabet soup of acronyms you're confronted with when you start looking into the Web. URL, as I mentioned before, stands for Uniform Resource Locator and is simply a form of address that all Web browsers can understand. URLs always take this form: `protocol://host:port/dir/filename`.

The www you see in Web addresses is part of the host name and refers to the World Wide Web portion of the Internet.

So, the URL `gopher://gopher.spinaltap.micro.umn.edu:70/00/fun/Recipes/Balls/tofu-balls` tells a browser to "use the gopher protocol to connect to the host machine called `gopher.spinaltap.micro.umn.edu` (somewhere at the birthplace of Gopher in the University of Minnesota), connect to port 70 there, look in folder `00/fun/Recipes/Balls`, and get the file containing the tofu-balls recipe."

The protocol generally used to connect to hypertext documents is called HTTP. HTTP stands for Hypertext Transfer Protocol, so called because browsers use it to transfer you to hypertext documents. If this protocol is called for, the URL will begin with `http:` (other protocols are `ftp:`, `telnet:`, and so on—there's also a protocol called `file:`, which is equivalent to `ftp:`).

The other confusing acronym you might come across is HTML. HTML stands for Hypertext Markup Language, and it is the code used to mark up text documents to turn them into hypertext documents. Hypertext documents from the Web generally end in the extension `.html` and contain funny-looking text tags, like this: <TITLE>.

NOTE

Hypertext documents on the Web are commonly referred to as *pages*. All of the Web pages linked together and maintained in the same file on a server (network computer) comprise a Web site. Companies, organizations, and individuals maintain Web sites, either on their own servers or on a server maintained by an online service or access provider.

Most online services offer access to the Web in two ways: with a built-in, licensed browser (usually Microsoft Internet Explorer), or with an external browser program that you can launch alongside the main access program. Direct-access ISPs also permit you to run whichever Web browser you like over the dial-up connection (and most people opt for Netscape Navigator).

NOTE NOTE NOTE NOTE NOTE NOTE NOTE NOTE NOTE NOTE NOTE NOTE NOTE NOTE NOTE

The Web is growing more popular all the time, and you may experience delays connecting to busy addresses. Attempts to follow links may even result in *timing-out*, meaning that some computer along the line gives up and you get an error message. If this happens, just try again—first right away and then, if necessary, during off-hours (late at night or on the weekend).

Figure 8.3 shows the Netscape home page that comes up automatically when you start Netscape Navigator (unless you change it to start at a different page).

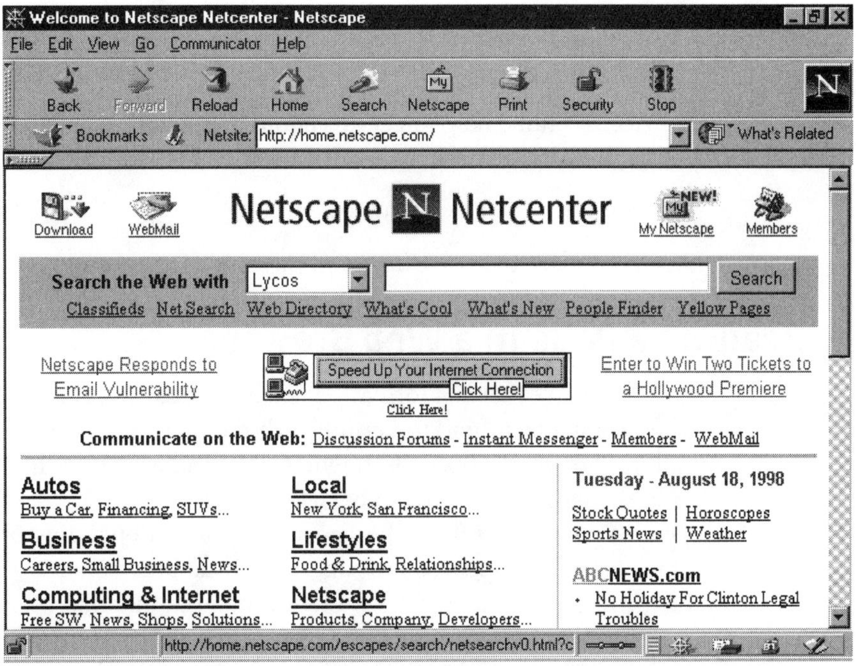

FIGURE 8.3: Unless customized, Netscape Navigator starts you off at the Netscape home page.

Now that you're connected, you can:

- Follow the links that interest you. At any point, you can retrace your steps or bring up a complete history of where you've been this session and then jump immediately back to one of those pages. However, if you back up to any main page of links during the session and branch off on another series of links, that new sequence of links will replace the previously visited sequence in your history list.
- Go to a specific Web address (URL) when you start your browser. Generally, to stop it from loading the default home page, you click the Stop button and enter an address directly.
- Insert bookmarks that enable you to jump back to an interesting page without having to retrace your steps or bring up a history of where you've been.
- Save (download) or e-mail interesting documents and files.
- View the hidden URL (Web address) that a link points to.
- Customize your program's home page so that you always start at a page with links that interest you, rather than at a generic home page.
- Access online help to get tips about using the program and information about the Web itself.
- Find out what's new on the Net.

Read on to discover how to do all these things…and more.

Reading a Page in a Web Browser

Web pages can consist of formatted text and headings, illustrations, background art and color effects, and hyperlinks, which can be highlighted text or art. In most graphical browsers, links are shown in blue and are underlined (unless the creator of the page has decided otherwise).

Often a page won't fit on the screen all at once, depending on the design used by the person who created the page. Graphical browsers use scroll bars, just as other programs do, to enable you to see material that doesn't fit on the screen. If you're hunting for a specific piece of information on a long document page, try searching for keywords, which can usually be done with a menu command.

TIP TIP TIP TIP TIP TIP TIP TIP TIP TIP TIP TIP TIP TIP TIP TIP TIP TIP TIP TIP TIP TIP TIP TIP TIP

If you find browsing too slow, if pictures take too long to load, or if your browser has trouble displaying some of the art on some of the Web pages, consider turning off automatic picture loading. Most browsers have an option on one of their menus for doing so. You'll still be able to load any specific pictures you want to see, or even see all the art on a page at once, but it will make your browsing go much more quickly and smoothly.

Following a Link

In graphical browsers, following a link is as simple as positioning the mouse pointer over the link and clicking once. You will know the pointer is over an active link, because it will change shape—in Netscape Navigator it changes to a little hand. Keep in mind that you only need to click once on Web links—we are all so used to double-clicking that at first it may be difficult to get out of the habit.

All browsers have a Back command, often a shortcut button, for retracing your steps back to the previous page. Once you've gone back, you can also go forward, using the Forward command, to return along your original path to the furthest point you had gotten to. Also, you can usually bring up a *history list* (on a menu in a graphical browser; on a separate page in a text-only browser) of all the pages you've been to since you started the most recent series of links.

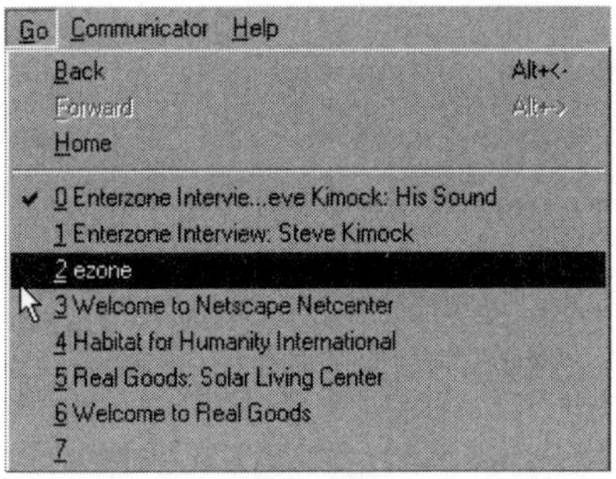

WARNING WARNING WARNING WARNING WARNING WARNING WARNING WARNING

The history list will actually show you only the pages you've visited sequentially from your starting point. Any time you back up and then follow a different link, you will lose the history path beyond the point you backed up to. For example, if I go to sites A, B, C, and D, then back up to B and then go to E, my history path will read A, B, E.

Knowing Where to Go

It's hard to get oriented in the Web because there's no real starting point. Your default home page should provide some pretty useful places to start. I recommend surfing around for a while to see where these points lead.

NOTE NOTE NOTE NOTE NOTE NOTE NOTE NOTE NOTE NOTE NOTE NOTE NOTE NOTE NOTE

For pointers toward directories and methods of searching the Web, see Skill 10, *Finding Stuff on the Web and the Net.*

In most browsers, if you have a specific Web address in mind (perhaps one you saw in an advertisement or one that was e-mailed to you), you can type in the URL and visit the Web page directly, without having to follow a trail of links to get there.

Also, at any time, you can return to your default home page. Graphical browsers have a Home button, often decorated with an icon representing a house, for this purpose.

Saving or Mailing a Document

If a Web page contains information that you want to send to someone or that you want to save on your own computer, you can either use your browser's mail command to send the document to yourself or to someone else, or you can use the save command (File ➢ Save As in graphical browsers) to save a copy of the document on your hard disk, much the same way you'd save a file in a word processor.

NOTE NOTE NOTE NOTE NOTE NOTE NOTE NOTE NOTE NOTE NOTE NOTE NOTE NOTE NOTE

For more on downloading documents, see Skill 10, *Finding Stuff on the Web and the Net.*

Clicking Image Maps

One of the most common navigation devices at Web sites is the image map. An image map is a clickable image with different regions, each of which sends the browser to a different destination. At well-designed Web sites there are often two main image maps: a clickable banner at the top of the site's home page, and a smaller navigation menu at the bottom of every other page. Some image maps are actually maps, such as those found at Web sites that function as city or regional guides.

Dealing with Frames

More and more of the Web pages you'll see are divided up into frames—sections of the screen with separate content devoted to different purposes. These frames actually partition the Web page into multiple windows, some of which may have their own sets of scroll bars. All of these windows can be a problem if you do not have a huge monitor, because you can only see a small portion of the contents of each frame without extensive scrolling through the frame. Even worse, you cannot drag the frames around or resize them like you can drag and resize windows in your desktop applications. Sometimes you have to use one frame's set of scroll bars to scroll around enough in that frame to access the scroll bars of another frame, the one with the content you actually wanted to see.

Most sites have kept at least their home pages frame-free, so as not to alienate the people whose browsers don't "do" frames, not to mention those who find them cumbersome or distracting. Hopefully frame technology will become more advanced so that you can move the frames or close the ones you do not want to look at, but for now, they can be challenging.

NOTE NOTE NOTE NOTE NOTE NOTE NOTE NOTE NOTE NOTE NOTE NOTE NOTE NOTE NOTE

Some sites use frames to keep you oriented to their site regardless of where you link to. The frame from the original site stays on the screen even when you are looking at content from another site reached by following a link from the first site.

Basic frame types include a narrow navigation frame and a full content frame. Sometimes frames are also used to keep an advertisement on the screen as you scroll through the content of a site.

Keeping Track of Floating Windows

Another recent Web-interface development is the use of additional floating windows. While many browsers allow you to right-click (or, on the Mac, click and hold) a link to pop up a list of options, and then choose to open the linked page in a new window, Web developers are now also creating links that automatically open a new window for you. Some sites also pop up a small window without a menu that you can use as a control panel. It can get confusing if you're surfing the Web for a while and end up with multiple windows open on your screen.

Remember to close secondary windows when you're done with them, to minimize the confusion of having multiple windows open. As you practice browsing the Web, you will figure out which method for switching among windows works best for you. Three ways of window switching that do work well are clicking on another window, using Alt+Tab in Windows, or selecting a window from a menu. Remember to use your Back button anytime you've ended up somewhere you didn't mean to go.

NOTE NOTE NOTE NOTE NOTE NOTE NOTE NOTE NOTE NOTE NOTE NOTE NOTE NOTE NOTE

Site maps are becoming more common for complex commercial Web sites with many subordinate pages. These maps are generally reached via an icon in the frame or on the home page. The maps can be graphical depictions of a site or a simple outline of the site showing the way subpages branch off from main pages. The maps usually have live links, so that you can click on any location in the map and go immediately to that page. See Figure 8.4 for an example of a site map.

Browsing an Intranet

Organizations, companies, and other groups that share space and networked computers are creating smaller versions of the Internet in the form of internal *intranets*. These intranets contain documents formatted with HTML, like those you find on the Web, and are a good place to store policies, manuals, databases, and every other type of record that used to be on a piece of paper in a filing cabinet.

The whole point of an intranet is that once it's set up, you can browse it (or transfer files, or send mail, or print on shared printers, and so on) just as you would over the "real" Internet. This means you can use the same software, the same type of browser. The content and uses of an intranet naturally differ widely from the content and uses of public Web sites. However, if your intranet is set up well, you won't ever notice where you're connecting to. You'll just grab the files you want, send your messages, set up meetings, and join discussions without pausing to think about whether you're doing so on your local intranet or on the Internet "out there."

WARNING WARNING WARNING WARNING WARNING WARNING WARNING WARNING

Then again, you *should* pause to think about whether you're about to communicate with a private group, such as your colleagues or supervisors, or with a public group on the Net, no matter how familiar the software tools feel.

See Skill 15, *Conferencing and Collaborating*, for more on the collaborative potential of intranets and the Internet.

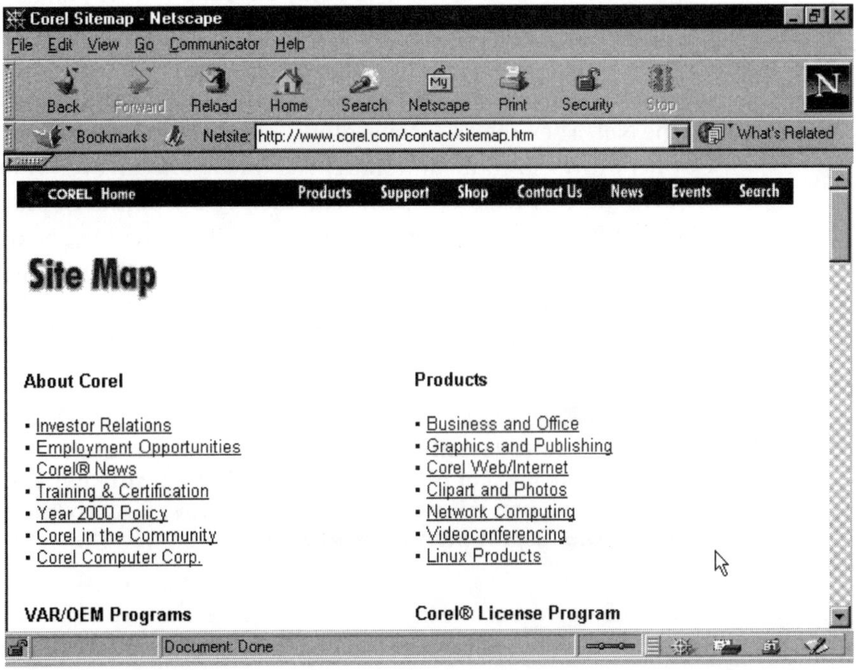

FIGURE 8.4: Corel, a Canadian software publishing firm, has a detailed site map with links to all of its Web pages. Corel's site is at `http://www.corel.com/`.

Wandering in Gopherspace

Gopher is a sophisticated Internet system that lets you look at data and files from different computers and networks without regard to the type of computer the client (you, more or less) is running on. If you run Gopher from a character-based Unix account, you see things as lists consisting of text entries. If you run a Gopher client on another platform, the menus and items will look appropriate to that type of computer. (For example, a Macintosh Gopher program will show the menus as folders that open up into windows.)

NOTE NOTE NOTE NOTE NOTE NOTE NOTE NOTE NOTE NOTE NOTE NOTE NOTE NOTE NOTE

Skill 10, *Finding Stuff on the Web and the Net*, explains how to search for items that are locked in Gopherspace using the Veronica and Jughead search programs. Many Gopher items can only be found this way and are invisible to conventional Web browsers.

At one time, the Internet Gopher was one of the most useful and seamless tools on the Net. Then the Web came along and Web browsers could do everything Gopher browsers could and more. Web browsers can even connect to Gopher sites, so there's precious little reason to have a separate Gopher program now. Many dedicated Gopher programs come with extensive bookmarks that make it easier to find specific information in Gopherspace, though, so you may want your own Gopher program. Even if you plan to use your Web browser when entering Gopherspace, you'll still want to read up on Gopher at this point.

NOTE NOTE NOTE NOTE NOTE NOTE NOTE NOTE NOTE NOTE NOTE NOTE NOTE NOTE NOTE

Gopher is so-called either because it can "go fer" stuff and bring it to you or because the mascot of the University of Minnesota (where Gopher was created) is a gopher; it is not named after the Love Boat character played by (now former U.S. Representative) Fred Grandy.

All Web browsers make perfectly adequate Gopher clients as well. One way to end up in Gopherspace from the Web is to click on a link that (whether you realize it or not) is linked to a Gopher address. This process is a little like tumbling down a rabbit hole. You'll leave the graphics and formatting of the Web behind and enter a limited (but still hyperlinked) world of folders and documents.

The other way to start browsing Gopherspace with a Web browser is to type a Gopher address into the address box, for example,

```
gopher://gopher.netcom.com/
```

Documents are shown with a document icon. Menus are shown with a folder icon.

Getting around the Gopher Menus

Browsing Gopherspace is simply a matter of pointing and clicking on links, just like anywhere else you visit using a Web browser. Clicking any icon or link takes you to a subdirectory or opens a document. If you wish to leave a subdirectory or document and go back to the main menu, just click the Back button, as you would on the Web.

Reading Gopher Documents

Eventually, your selections will lead you to a document, which will appear unformatted and in a typewriter-like typeface. Read the document as you would any Web page, scrolling down if necessary.

Bookmarks in Gopherspace

If you find your way to or stumble upon an interesting Gopher site, you can make a bookmark to it as you would for any Web page or other resource in your browser. (More about bookmarks a little later on in this lesson.)

NOTE NOTE NOTE NOTE NOTE NOTE NOTE NOTE NOTE NOTE NOTE NOTE NOTE NOTE NOTE

Gopher has been around almost as long as the Internet. Many universities, government agencies, and organizations have a long-established Gopher "presence." That's why Gopherspace is a fascinating archive of information, some of which is not available on the Web. However, Gopher sites may not be updated as often as you would like, so the information culled from this resource may not be completely current. However, some Web sites contain incorrect out-of-date information, too.

Peeking behind the Scenes

If you need to see the URL associated with a specific link, you can do so. For instance, in most browsers, when you place the pointer over a link, the associated URL appears in the status bar at the bottom of the program. Some browsers enable you to copy a URL by right-clicking or clicking-and-holding the link. You can then paste it into another document for future reference or paste it into an e-mail message to tell someone else how to get to the page in question.

If you want to see how a Web page was constructed, you can generally view the source file underlying a page. In graphical browsers, you do this by selecting View ➢ Page Source (or something similar). Figure 8.5 shows the source underlying the Netscape home page.

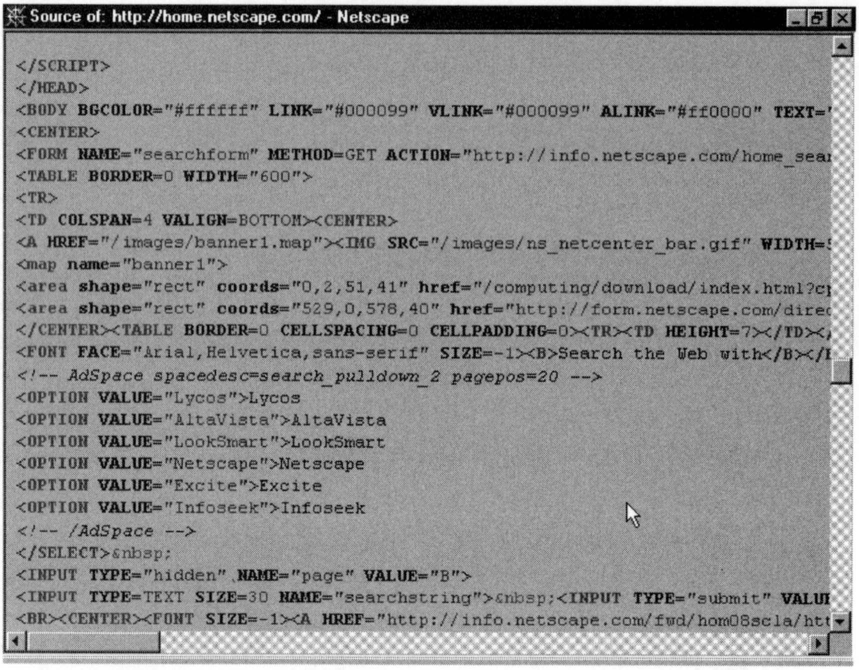
Source of: http://home.netscape.com/ - Netscape

```
</SCRIPT>
</HEAD>
<BODY BGCOLOR="#ffffff" LINK="#000099" VLINK="#000099" ALINK="#ff0000" TEXT='
<CENTER>
<FORM NAME="searchform" METHOD=GET ACTION="http://info.netscape.com/home_sea
<TABLE BORDER=0 WIDTH="600">
<TR>
<TD COLSPAN=4 VALIGN=BOTTOM><CENTER>
<A HREF="/images/banner1.map"><IMG SRC="/images/ns_netcenter_bar.gif" WIDTH=
<map name="banner1">
<area shape="rect" coords="0,2,51,41" href="/computing/download/index.html?c
<area shape="rect" coords="529,0,578,40" href="http://form.netscape.com/dire
</CENTER><TABLE BORDER=0 CELLSPACING=0 CELLPADDING=0><TR><TD HEIGHT=7></TD><
<FONT FACE="Arial,Helvetica,sans-serif" SIZE=-1><B>Search the Web with</B></
<!-- AdSpace spacedesc=search_pulldown_2 pagepos=20 -->
<OPTION VALUE="Lycos">Lycos
<OPTION VALUE="AltaVista">AltaVista
<OPTION VALUE="LookSmart">LookSmart
<OPTION VALUE="Netscape">Netscape
<OPTION VALUE="Excite">Excite
<OPTION VALUE="Infoseek">Infoseek
<!-- /AdSpace -->
</SELECT> 
<INPUT TYPE="hidden" NAME="page" VALUE="B">
<INPUT TYPE=TEXT SIZE=30 NAME="searchstring"> <INPUT TYPE="submit" VALU
<BR><CENTER><FONT SIZE=-1><A HREF="http://info.netscape.com/fwd/hom08scla/ht
```

FIGURE 8.5: The HTML document that makes the Netscape home page look the way it does. (Don't let it spook you!)

Storing and Managing Your Favorite Web Sites as Bookmarks

As you travel around the Web, you can record interesting destinations by making bookmarks (also called Favorites or Favorite Places in some browsers, and Items in a Notebook or Hotlist in others). Once you've made a bookmark, you've created your own personal shortcut to a favorite destination. You won't have to find your way back to the page in question next time you want to go there.

Make bookmarks as often as you want. You can always weed out your bookmark list later, but it's very difficult to find a page you stumbled across by trying to retrace your steps later.

Organizing Bookmarks

At first, all your bookmarks will fit on a menu, but eventually you'll have too many to fit and you'll have to open a window to see them all (each browser has its own version of these features). Once the bookmark window is open, you can usually cull the list by clicking on and deleting (or dragging to the trash) any out-of-date, duplicate, or no-longer-interesting bookmarks.

As your bookmark pile grows, it becomes something like an address book—another thing to manage! The easiest way to deal with bookmark overflow is to create folders (they usually appear as submenus on the bookmark menu) for different categories your bookmarks fall into, and then occasionally sort them out.

Changing Your Start Page

The commands differ from browser to browser, but most Web browsers allow you to change your start page (the first page that comes up when you start the program) to a different page (or even to a list of your bookmarks) so you can start exploring the Web from any vantage point.

Generally, the way you change your home page is to go into the Options or Preferences area of your browser and either specify an exact URL or tell the browser to use the current page as the new home page. Why would you change your page? Well, you might find a useful page out there on the Net that connects to most of your favorite sites. Or you might want to use one of the directory or search pages (as discussed in Skill 10, *Finding Stuff on the Web and the Net*) as your new starting page.

Get EFF's Internet Guide as Hypertext on the Web

The Electronic Frontier Foundation has published a hypertext version of its Internet Guide on the World Wide Web. You could hunt around for it by looking in one of the many indexes or other jumping-off pages on the Web, but why don't I just give you the URL? Point your browser at `http://www.eff.org/papers/eegtti/eegttitop.html` to go to the main page for the Guide.

Web Help and Info

There are a number of helpful resources for the Web, both hypertext and plain text documents. Try the WWW FAQ, an excellent document. Its URL is `http://www.boutell.com/faq/`. The W3 Consortium is the official source of information about the Web, and you can connect to their home page at `http://www.w3.org/`. (But be forewarned, much of their information is highly technical!) Many individual browsers also offer dedicated help files, accessible through a menu command.

Are You Experienced?

Now you can...

- ☑ understand the difference between URL, HTTP, and HTML
- ☑ follow Web links to little-known Internet byways and return to your starting point
- ☑ use Web addresses through links, cut-and-paste, history lists, and shortcuts
- ☑ head for Gopherspace to find fascinating documents and data
- ☑ click on image maps, site maps, or document frames for intuitive Web page browsing
- ☑ find cool Web sites and Web-based help when you need it
- ☑ create and use bookmarks to keep track of your favorite Web sites

SKILL 9

WEB BROWSERS

- Browsing the Web with Lynx
- Browsing the Web with Microsoft Internet Explorer
- Browsing the Web with Netscape Navigator

The program you choose to travel the Web with is largely a matter of taste, need, and budget. In fact, you may eventually end up with more than one browser on your hard drive. I'll discuss a few of the more common browsers now and tell you how to surf with each.

Lynx

If your connection to the Internet is through a character-based Unix account, then the best Web browser for you is Lynx. Lynx is a full-screen program that is very easy to use. Ask the system administrator if Lynx is available.

You run Lynx by typing **lynx** at the Unix prompt and pressing Enter. This will start you off at Lynx's default home page for your system. At one of my providers (Netcom's shell service), Lynx starts off at the University of Kansas home page. At another (a2i), Lynx starts off at a page called Basic Web Links for Lynx Users, shown in Figure 9.1 (`http://www.rahul.net/startup/lynx.html`).

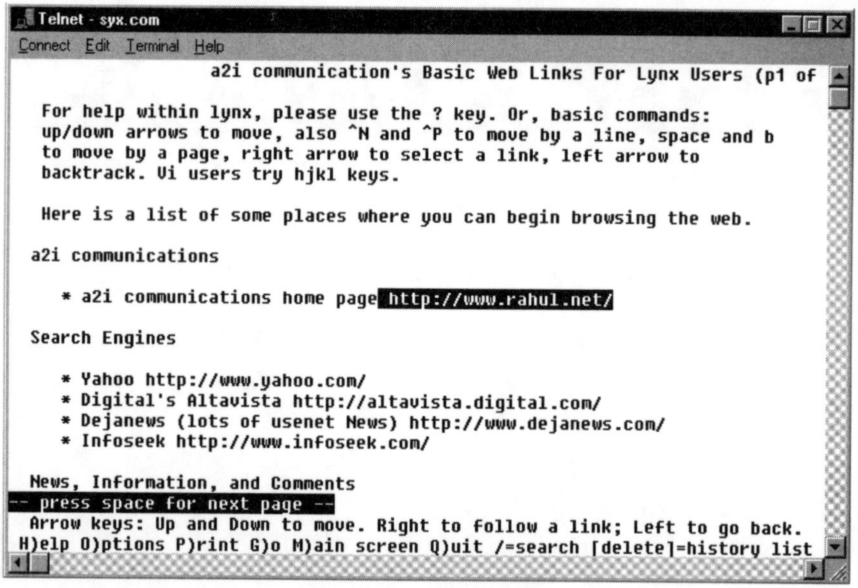

FIGURE 9.1: Basic Web Links for Lynx Users, a start page set up by one of my Internet service providers, a2i (Rahul.net)

As you work with Lynx, keep these important commands in mind:

- To get Lynx help at any time, type **?**.
- To quit Lynx at any time, type **q**, and press Enter.
- To quit without being prompted, type **Q**.

Running Lynx via Telnet and a Public Access Browser

If you don't have Lynx installed on your system, Unix will tell you "lynx: Command not found." You can still run Lynx by "Telnetting" to a public-access browser. Here's how to do it:

1. At the Unix prompt, type **telnet ukanaix.cc.ukans.edu** and press Enter.
2. At the `Enter user name:` prompt, log in as **www** (no password required).

For more on Telnet, see Skill 18, *Getting Around with FTP and Telnet*.

Pointing Lynx Directly to a Web Address

If you have a specific Web address (URL) in mind, you can also start Lynx by pointing it at that URL:

1. Type **lynx *url***, substituting the actual URL for *url*, of course.
2. Press Enter to open the page at that URL.

TIP TIP TIP TIP TIP TIP TIP TIP TIP TIP TIP TIP TIP TIP TIP TIP TIP TIP TIP TIP TIP TIP TIP TIP TIP

Different installations of Lynx may function differently. Lynx is sometimes set up to prevent users from entering URLs directly. If you run into problems trying to follow these instructions, ask your system administrator for help.

Most of a Web page will be displayed as regular text and headings. In Lynx, hypertext links are shown in boldface, and the current link is shown in reverse video (white text on black, instead of vice versa). The first link on the page is the current link when you arrive at a page.

Often a Web page won't fit on the screen all at once. The commands necessary to move around a Web page in Lynx are detailed in the following table.

TABLE 9.1: Lynx Commands for Web Page Navigation

Action	Commands
To move one screen down a page	Press the spacebar or type **+** (or press PageDown or 3 on your numeric keypad with NumLock on)
To move one screen up a page	Type **b** or – (or press PageUp or 9 on the numeric keypad with NumLock on)
To move down to the next link	Press Tab + ↓ (or press 2 on the numeric keypad with NumLock on)
To move up to the previous link	Press ↑(or press 8 on the numeric keypad with NumLock on)
To fix a messed-up screen (for example, if reverse video is left all over the screen)	Press Ctrl+W to redraw the screen
To search for specific text	Type **s** or **/**. Then type the text you want to search for and press Enter
To repeat a search	Type **n**
To select the current link (and jump to the address it refers to)	Press Enter (or press → or 6 on the numeric keypad with NumLock on)
To return to the previous link	Press ← (or 4 on the numeric keypad with NumLock on)

TIP TIP TIP TIP TIP TIP TIP TIP TIP TIP TIP TIP TIP TIP TIP TIP TIP TIP TIP TIP TIP TIP TIP TIP TIP TIP

If the arrow keys don't work and you have a numeric keypad, try turning NumLock on and then using the number keys on the numeric keypad. Your communications program might be reserving the arrow keys (along with some Control keys and scrolling commands) for their standard uses in your operating environment. Check the terminal-emulation settings to see if you can change this (these settings are found in the HyperTerminal applet in Windows reached via Start ➢ Programs ➢ Accessories ➢ HyperTerminal).

Returning to Previous Jump Points in Lynx

Though you can always retrace your steps in Lynx by pressing 4 (with NumLock on) repeatedly, you can also jump back to any previous point in just three steps:

1. Press Delete to see your history page, a list of all the links you've followed in this session (try Backspace if Delete doesn't work).

2. Select the page you want to return to by using the arrow keys to reach it.
3. Press Enter to move to that page.

Moving to Different URLs in Lynx without Backtracking

Lynx has other commands for moving through the Internet, all of which are activated by typing a single letter. Here are the options:

- At any point, you can type **i** to go to the Internet Resources Meta-Index, which includes many more starting points for you to try.
- At any point, you can also type **g** to enter a URL directly by using these steps:
    1. Lynx will prompt you with `URL to open:`. Type (or paste in) the URL and press Enter.
    2. If you've done this once already, the previous URL will already be there. Delete it by pressing Ctrl+U before typing in the new one.
- Also, at any time, you can return to the default home page by typing **m**.

Creating and Viewing Lynx Bookmarks

You can save interesting Web destinations by adding bookmarks to your bookmark page. (Lynx will create one for you if you don't have one.) Here are the instructions for using Lynx bookmarks:

- To add a bookmark for the current page, type **a**.
- View your collection of bookmarks at any time by typing **v**.
- Use the arrow keys to highlight a bookmark, then press Enter to go there.

Printing and Saving a Document with Lynx

If you want to save a copy of a document you're reading on the Web, you can print it and save it in Lynx by following these pointers:

1. Type **p** to bring up the Printing Options page.
2. Press Enter to save the document to a file. Lynx will prompt you to `Please enter a file name:` and will suggest one.
3. Press Enter, or type in a different name for the file and press Enter.

NOTE NOTE NOTE NOTE NOTE NOTE NOTE NOTE NOTE NOTE NOTE NOTE NOTE NOTE NOTE

To send mail to the owner of the page you're on, type c. (The *owner* just means the person who created and maintains the page.)

Mailing a Lynx Document to Yourself for Safekeeping

At some point you may want to mail a Web document to yourself (sometimes that's the easiest way to store a copy of a document). Here's how to send a copy of the document to your mailbox.

1. Press Tab to go to the next link (Mail the File to Yourself) and then press Enter. Lynx will prompt you with `Please enter a valid Internet mail address:`
2. If you've told Lynx your address, it will appear on the line as a default. If not, type your address.
3. Press Enter to send the document to yourself.

Viewing Document URLs or HTML Formatting in Lynx

You will frequently want to view at least the URL of the document you are looking at. Sometimes you may also want to see the HTML code used to create the document (also known as the document source). These actions can be easily accomplished in Lynx.

- To see the URL associated with the current link, type =. Type = again to go back to the normal view.
- To see the actual HTML text of the current page, type \. Type \ again to go back to the normal view.

Additional Important Lynx Commands

Follow these steps to change some of the Lynx settings:

1. Type **o**. This brings up the Options Menu.
    - Type **e** to change the default editor for sending e-mail to mail to URLs.
    - Type **b** to change your bookmark file.
    - Type **p** to enter or change your e-mail address.
2. When you are done, type > to save your changes. Or, to return to where you left off without saving the changes, type **r**.

To select a different default home page, first open your startup file (usually called `.login`, `.profile`, or `.cshrc`). Then, type the line **setenv WWW_HOME *url*** (replacing *url* with the correct URL for the page you want) in your startup file.

Microsoft Internet Explorer

Internet Explorer works seamlessly with Windows 95 and Windows 98, but it also stands alone as a Web browser that can work with any Internet connection. It's available for both Windows and Macintosh, though it's much more popular on the Windows side.

TIP TIP TIP TIP TIP TIP TIP TIP TIP TIP TIP TIP TIP TIP TIP TIP TIP TIP TIP TIP TIP TIP TIP TIP TIP

You can download a trial version of Microsoft Internet Explorer for free from `http://www.microsoft.com/ie/`. However, be prepared to answer some questions about yourself to satisfy the Microsoft marketing department before you get the freebie! Be prepared for some lengthy download times, too.

Figure 9.2 shows the page that comes up automatically when you use Internet Explorer to connect to the Web without specifying a particular site.

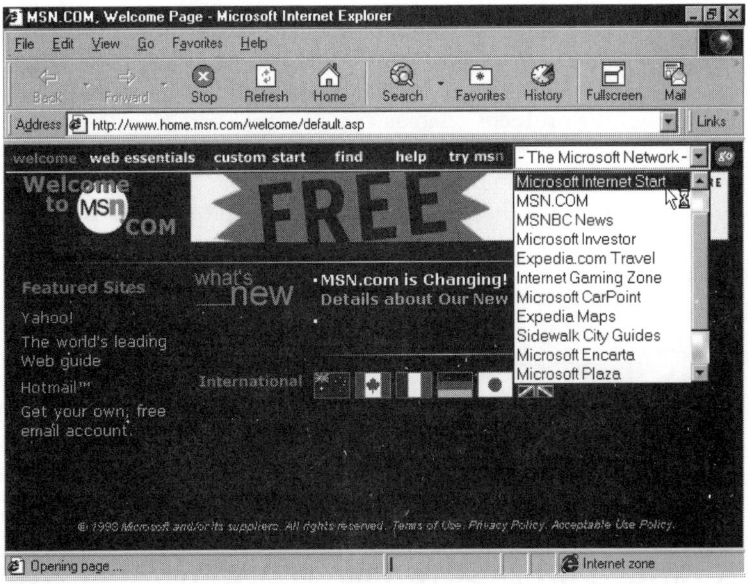

FIGURE 9.2: Internet Explorer currently starts you off at the MSN.COM Welcome page or a page called Internet Start, depending on when you got your copy of the program and how it was initially set up. As you can see from the MSN welcome page, the site is in transition even as I'm snapping this screenshot for you.

SKILL 9

Easy Ways to Get Around with Internet Explorer

Internet Explorer has some clearly marked buttons and commands for browsing the Web, so you are never far from finding your way back to your home page. Here are some of the easily accessed functions:

- To search a long Web page, select Edit ➢ Find (On This Page…), type the text you're looking for, and press Enter.
- Use the Back and Forward buttons to return to pages you've visited this session.
- Return to any of the recent sites you've visited by pulling down the File menu and selecting the page name from the list near the bottom of the menu (just above the Exit or Quit command).
- Click the arrows (triangles) next to the Back and Forward buttons to select a page from the list of pages you have visited during the current Internet Explorer session.
- To go somewhere directly, type the URL into the Address box (it will change to an Open box when you click in it).

NOTE NOTE NOTE NOTE NOTE NOTE NOTE NOTE NOTE NOTE NOTE NOTE NOTE NOTE NOTE

You can leave off the `http://` part of any Web URL when typing it into the Address box, but if it is not a Web (`http://`) address, you will have to type in the protocol, such as `ftp://`, `gopher://`, and so on.

- Click the button at the right end of the Address box to drop down a list of all the addresses you've entered recently.
- Click the Home button to return to your starting page.

TIP TIP TIP TIP TIP TIP TIP TIP TIP TIP TIP TIP TIP TIP TIP TIP TIP TIP TIP TIP TIP TIP TIP TIP TIP

You can save interesting Web destinations by selecting Favorites ➢ Add to Favorites. The page you add will instantly become a menu item on the Favorites menu. To go to a Favorite, just select it from that menu.

Saving and Mailing Web Documents and Shortcuts in Internet Explorer

Internet Explorer makes good use of Windows *shortcuts*, small icons depicting a particular type of file or program. Clicking a shortcut will send you directly to that file or load the program. You can accumulate many Web site shortcuts in Internet Explorer and distribute them as desired to help yourself and your friends get around the Web.

- To save a Web document with Internet Explorer, select File ➢ Save As.
- You can also save a shortcut to a file—a tiny file containing the Web address—by selecting File ➢ Send ➢ Shortcut to Desktop.
- To mail a shortcut to someone, select File ➢ Send ➢ Link By Email. Internet Explorer will open a Microsoft Outlook Express new message window with the shortcut already attached.
- To view the HTML source of a Web document, select View ➢ Source.

Working with Internet Explorer Favorites (Bookmarks)

Internet Explorer refers to bookmarked Web sites as Favorites, but the idea is the same as making bookmarks in other programs. New favorites appear at the bottom of the Favorites menu, and can also be placed in folders with the Organize Favorites option.

Adding a Web page you are viewing to your list of Favorites is easy. Just select Favorites ➢ Add to Favorites. The page will be listed at the bottom of your Favorites list in the Favorites menu.

Organizing your Favorites is also easy:

- To move a Favorite into a Favorites folder, select Favorites ➢ Organize Favorites so you can see the Organize Favorites dialog box, shown here. Click the icons of loose pages and drag them into existing folders.

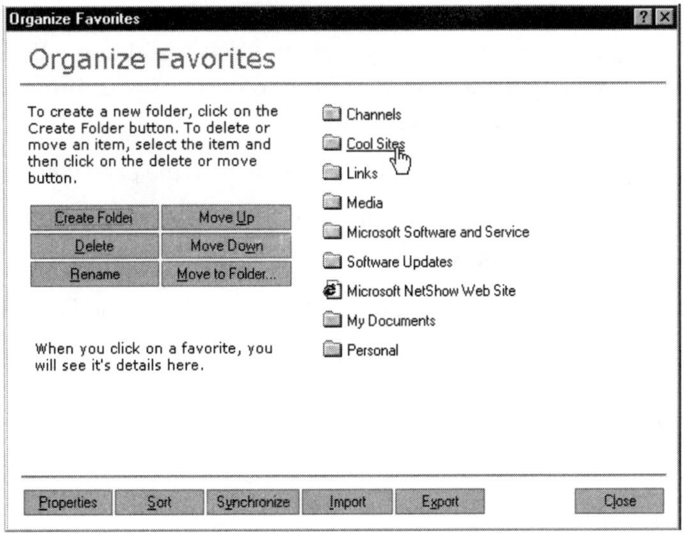

- If you want to create a new folder, click the Create Folder button. A new folder with a label containing the name "New Folder" will appear, with the text already selected. Type a more descriptive name.
- Click Close when you are finished organizing.

Changing Your Start Page

Every six months or so a new business model gains ascendancy on the Web, most of which are closely tied to notions of traditional advertising. Web sites that deliver "eyeballs" (yours) to commercial messages will be compensated, based on the "impression" or the "click-through rate." Lately, everyone seems to have noticed that certain Web pages see astronomical traffic, head and shoulders beyond even the most popular entertainment sites. These are now referred to as "portal sites," partly because they frequently serve as helpful starting points for directed use of the Web, either in total or in some specific area of niche popularity.

A few portal Web sites receive their traffic as the default starting page for popular Web browsers. The rest have to earn their eyeballs by reputation (Yahoo! and a few other search and directory sites, as discussed in Skill 10) or through strategic alliances with other popular sites. The two top Web-browser companies, Microsoft and Netscape, have begun to regard the start pages wired-in to their browsers as perhaps the most valuable intellectual property (at least in the Web sense) under their brand.

Microsoft, however, cannot force you to start at their preferred page. (They don't need to, really, since very few people ever tinker with the settings in *any* of their software.) If you like starting off at their current "portal" concept, then there's nothing to worry about. But if you eventually find another site that you're always returning to, perhaps visiting frequently for updates or to get news in an area of particular interest to you, then you should know that you can change Internet Explorer's start page and take control of your browsing experience. Changing your start page is simple:

1. First use Internet Explorer to go to the page you want to use as your start page.
2. Select View ➢ Internet Options and click the General tab in the dialog box that appears.
3. Click the Use Current button in the Home Page area of the General tab.
4. When you're done, click OK.

TIP

To get help with Internet Explorer, select Help ➢ Content and Index. To keep up with what's new, click on the What's New MSN.Com active area on the Microsoft Network welcome page. You can also click the Today's Links button in the Internet Explorer Links toolbar, which features a "pick of the day" and other useful links. The Links toolbar slides over the Address Bar from the right side, or you can drag it down below the Address Bar to display it as an additional bar.

Netscape Navigator

The latest version of Netscape Navigator is 4.5, but don't let that half-step in the numbering system fool you. Netscape has added some significant new features to this release, the most notable of which is an array of tools that together they call Smart Browsing. These capabilities range from smarter URL-guessing when you simply type key words into the address box to a "What's Related" button that lists similar Web sites culled from a constantly evolving database. These features constitute the latest salvo in a features war still underway between Netscape and Internet Explorer. (The What's Related database is adapted from a browser add-in made by a company called Alexa.) Microsoft may have to find an analogous or better service to offer if Smart Browsing proves useful for people trying to navigate the thickets of the Web.

You can start Netscape by double-clicking any of the Netscape desktop shortcuts, or by selecting Start ➢ Programs ➢ Netscape Communicator ➢ Netscape Navigator (or by choosing Netscape Navigator from your Apple menu). By default, it will take you to the Netscape home page.

Roaming the Web with Netscape

Navigator's buttons and menus make Internet and Web travel fairly painless. In the following points, you will recognize many commands similar to those described for other applications.

- Click the Back and Forward buttons to move between pages you've already visited in the current session.
- Click the Go menu to view a list of all the pages you've visited in the current session—your history list. Select a page to return to it.
- To go to a specific Web page, type its address in the Location box. You can pull down a list from that box to see every page you've ever typed in directly.

Adding Netscape Bookmarks

Here are the ways you can add bookmarks with Netscape:

- Click the Bookmarks button below the toolbar, and select Add Bookmark from the menu.
- Right-click (or, on a Mac, click-and-hold) in the main window and choose Add Bookmark from the shortcut menu.
- Click and drag the Page button on the status bar (the bar at the bottom of the screen) over to the Bookmarks button.
- Press Ctrl+D (or Command+D on the Mac).

TIP TIP TIP TIP TIP TIP TIP TIP TIP TIP TIP TIP TIP TIP TIP TIP TIP TIP TIP TIP TIP TIP TIP TIP TIP

Remember, you must open Netscape Navigator first, log on to the Internet with your service provider, and open up the Web site or page you want to add as a bookmark before you can use the bookmark features.

To go to a bookmarked site, click the Bookmarks button and choose the item from the drop-down list, or select Edit Bookmarks to see your entire bookmark collection. In this Bookmark window you can drag bookmarks from one folder to another, delete old ones, and create folders for storing bookmarks.

To reorganize your bookmarks, click the Bookmarks button and select Edit Bookmarks. In the Bookmarks window that appears (see Figure 9.3), you can drag bookmarks into folders, delete folders you don't use (just select them and press Delete, Ctrl+D, or Command+D), or create new folders by selecting File ➢ New Folders, typing a name, and clicking OK.

Saving and Mailing Netscape Navigator Web Documents

When you find a Web document of interest, you can send it to other people or save it for later review. The document will be saved as a text file with accompanying graphics files.

- In order to save a Web document with Netscape, select File ➢ Save As.
- To mail a document to someone, attach it to a message and click Send in the Composition window, or select File ➢ Send Now.
- Click the Attachment button in the message window to control how the document is sent—as an HTML source file (the default) or as plain text.

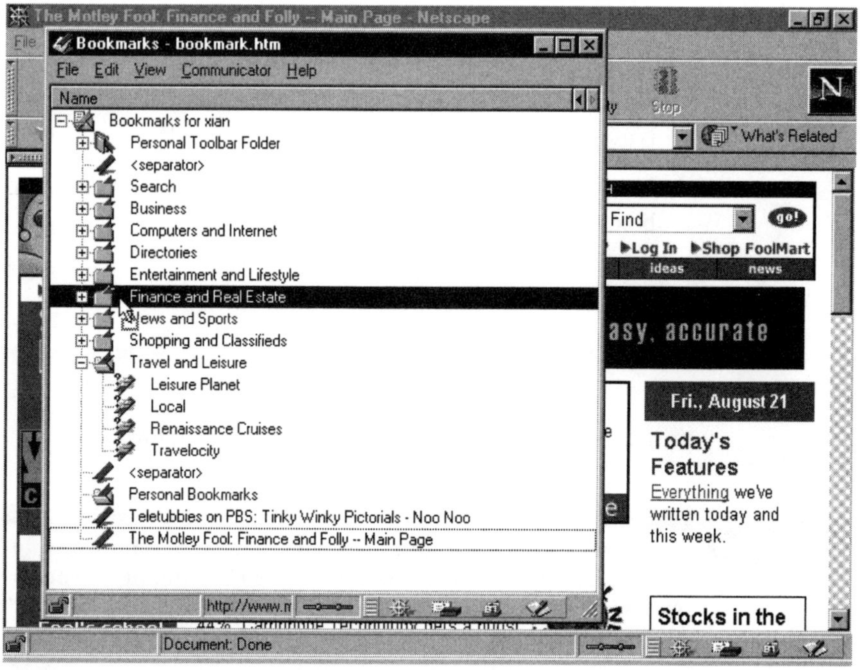

FIGURE 9.3: Netscape starts you off with a lot of folders and a number of suggested bookmarks that you may or may not find useful. Feel free to delete anything that's just taking up space.

TIP

When you want to view the underlying HTML source of a Web page displayed in Netscape, select View > Source.

Switching Start Pages in Netscape

Netscape has recently reconstituted its browser's default start page as a "portal site" designed to earn advertising dollars in exchange for making itself useful for you as a jumping-off point. (See the Internet Explorer section of this lesson for more on this latest development in the world of the Web.) If the Netscape page works for you, that's great. If you prefer a different start page to the one supplied by Netscape, you can change your page with these procedures. The new start page will also become your home page and will be the page where you are deposited if you click the Home button in Navigator's toolbar.

Here's how to change your starting page in Navigator:

1. Select Edit ➢ Preferences and the Preferences dialog box will appear. Select Navigator in the list on the left side of the Preferences dialog box.
2. In the Home Page section, type the new URL (Web address) in the location box, or use one of these options:
   - Click the Use Current Page button to change the start page to the page currently displayed in your browser.
   - Click the Browse button to search for other pages on the Web or on your network or hard drive.
3. Click OK to confirm the changes you've made.

TIP TIP TIP TIP TIP TIP TIP TIP TIP TIP TIP TIP TIP TIP TIP TIP TIP TIP TIP TIP TIP TIP TIP TIP TIP

Any time you want to get help with Navigator, choose Help ➢ Help Contents (or any of the other commands on the Help menu). To see what's new on the Net, click the Places button and choose What's New?, What's Cool?, or any of the other choices.

"Smart Browsing" with Netscape

Smart Browsing provides two new features in Netscape Navigator that help you find your way around the Web or find your way to sites even when you don't know their exact addresses. First of all, the address box now does double-duty as a keyword lookup textbox. This means that you can type any number of words (separated by spaces) into the address box, press Enter, and Netscape will analyze your request as a search. You will either be sent to the site most likely to accord with your wishes or offered a results page with possible sites (much like those returned by Yahoo! and other directory and search sites discussed in the next lesson).

For example, you could type the words **apple pie recipe** into Netscape's address box and Netscape will produce a page of links to sites that have such recipes.

More importantly, Netscape has teamed up with the folks at `http://www.alexa.com/` to offer a value-added service suggesting additional similar sites in the form of a menu that pops up when you press the What's Related button at the right side of the address box.

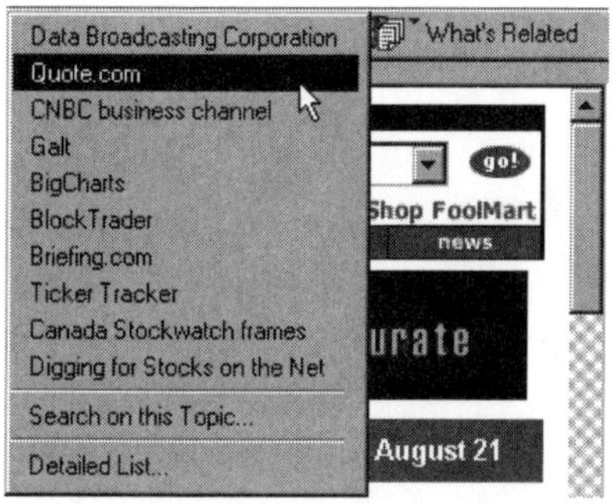

The database that serves up the similar pages is being updated all the time, based on how people actually use the Web, so the suggestions should get more sophisticated as the system comes into more widespread use.

Now that you have completed this lesson, you know all about Internet and Web browser basics, but that's only the beginning. The next lesson will introduce you to powerful search strategies for ferreting out all kinds of information on the Internet.

Are You Experienced?

Now you can...

- ☑ **travel the Web with Lynx**
- ☑ **travel the Web with Microsoft Internet Explorer**
- ☑ **travel the Web with Netscape Navigator**

SKILL 10

FINDING STUFF ON THE WEB AND THE NET

- Looking in Web directories such as Yahoo!
- Searching the Web from pages such as Lycos
- Visiting the Netscape directory pages
- Adding virus protection to your computer
- Downloading files and updating your software
- Looking for e-mail addresses
- Searching Usenet and the rest of the Internet
- Buying things online
- Using security features

Once you've had the chance to explore the Web a bit, you may start wondering how you're ever going to find anything there. As easy as it is to follow tangents and get lost wandering from interesting site to interesting site, there's no clear path through the Web and no obvious way to find a destination if you don't know its address.

Fortunately, various clever individuals and companies have set up sites to help you find information on the Web. While there's no single, definitive location for searching, there are, in fact, quite a few ways to search the Web (and more coming online all the time), and the Net is changing so rapidly that any central listing of sites is bound to be out of date in some ways. Still, the process of "mapping the Net" is ongoing, and the work in progress is usually useful enough to help you find what you're looking for.

Because there's no single, definitive way to search the Web, it's sometimes best to try several different approaches. In this lesson, we will look at different ways to search (by subject, keyword, date, or language) and different search engines that each have their own search strategy, such as AltaVista and Yahoo!

Also in this lesson, I'll show you how to download (save) files from the Web to your own computer, how to hunt for information on the Net that might not be directly on the Web, and how to buy stuff online.

What's New with Searching?

In Skill 9 I told you a little about the current "big idea" on the Web, the *portal* Web site. A portal is a site that many people visit to begin their browsing. Netscape realized they were sitting on a portal site at `http://home.netscape.com/`, where Netscape Web browsers are set to start by default. Microsoft keeps squirming around, it seems, with each new release of Internet Explorer, but they're starting to put all their eggs in a basket called "Microsoft Internet Start," currently at `http://home.microsoft.com/`. Both of these sites are now jacks-of-all-trades, offering search services leveraged from other sites.

Meanwhile, popular search and directory sites (we'll get into that distinction in a moment) such as Yahoo! are now trying to capitalize on their de facto portal status, with more aggressive use of advertising, news wires, travel services, and other features designed to get folks to show up at their sites *and stay*. Fortunately, it's still up to you when to stay and when to go, and if you haven't learned to ignore advertising by now, the Internet is not your biggest problem.

As mentioned in Skill 9, Netscape Navigator 4.5 includes a small set of new features lumped together under the rubric "Smart Browsing," the most visible manifestation of which is a button labeled "What's Related," located to the right of the address box. Click it to download a short menu of related sites or to search for related sites (by selecting the Search on This Topic item).

Netscape has also tweaked the functionality of the address box itself (the one that says Go To). Instead of simply adding `http://www.` and `.com/` to plain-English words, Netscape now treats the words as search terms and applies a little good old-fashioned artificial intelligence to the case, to avoid—for example—delivering the porno site at `http://www.whitehouse.com/` to folks looking for the President's house at `http://www.whitehouse.gov/`. Ordinarily, you have to visit a search or directory Web page (or, for that matter, a portal site) for search-type services. But these are now built directly into the Netscape browser.

Searching the Web

There are a number of pages on the Web that offer one of two models for finding specific information. One model is that of a directory, where Web sites are organized by topic and subtopic, something like a yellow pages phonebook. The other model is that of a searchable index, where you enter a keyword to search for, and the search page gives you a list of suggested sites that seem to match what you're searching for. I'll show you an example of each approach.

Searching through a Directory

One of the best directories on the Web is the Yahoo! site. To see it for yourself, type `www.yahoo.com` into the address box at the top of your Web browser. Figure 10.1 shows how Yahoo! looks as I'm writing this. Remember, most Web sites update their design and layout from time to time, so the site may look slightly different to you today.

TIP TIP TIP TIP TIP TIP TIP TIP TIP TIP TIP TIP TIP TIP TIP TIP TIP TIP TIP TIP TIP TIP TIP TIP TIP

Make a bookmark (or Favorites listing) for Yahoo!, as discussed in Skill 8, *Navigating the Web*, so you can come back here easily any time you want to start looking around.

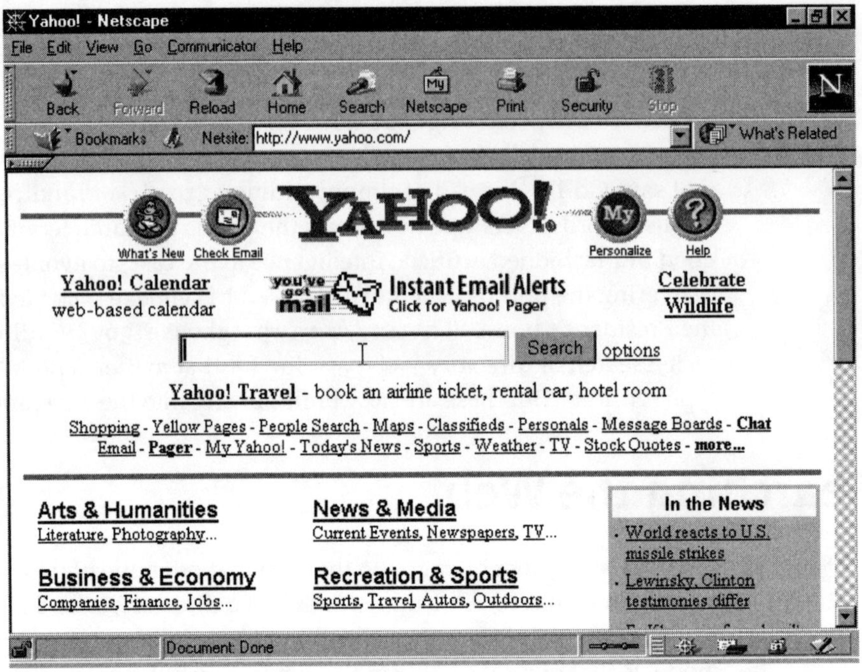

FIGURE 10.1: The popular Yahoo! directory site

Searching by Topic

Yahoo! is organized hierarchically, which means that you can start with a general topic area and then narrow it down to more specific topics as you go. Some of the major subtopics are listed under each topic as well, so you can skip one step, if you like.

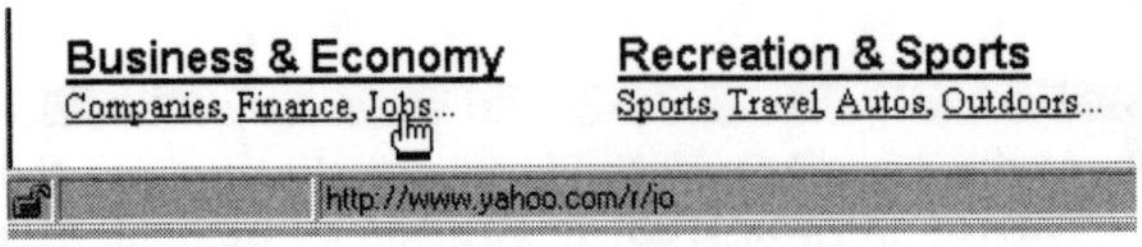

NOTE

At Yahoo!, category listings are in bold type, whereas *endpoint* listings (that don't lead to further subcategories) are in plain type.

Let's say you're interested in the subject of media ethics, specifically the topic of how fair and accurate journalists should be when reporting controversial events or when probing into the private lives of citizens. You could start by choosing the News & Media link on Yahoo!'s main search page. This will take you to Yahoo!'s News and Media page (see Figure 10.2).

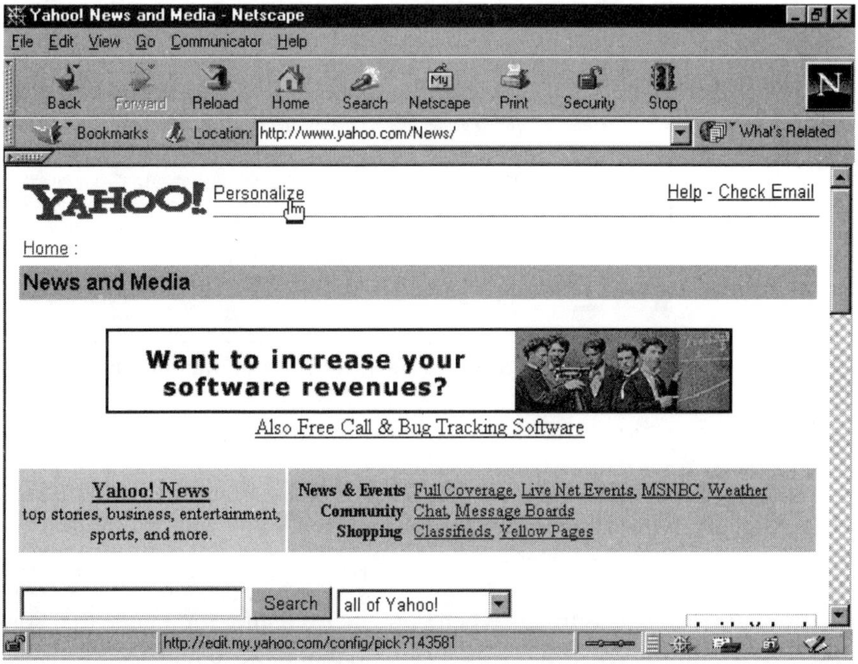

FIGURE 10.2: The Yahoo! News and Media page.

One of the sub-subtopics of News and Media is Media Ethics. (The @ sign after the listing means that topic appears in several different places in Yahoo!'s listings, allowing you to reach topics of interest by more than one route, without having to read the minds of the people who set up the site.) Click on Media Ethics to go to the list of pages on that subject (see Figure 10.3).

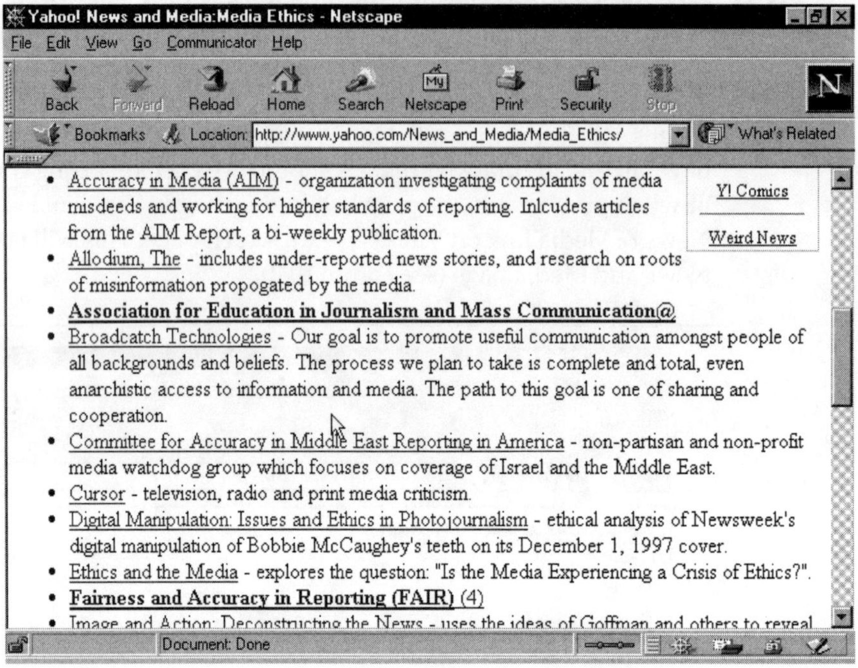

FIGURE 10.3: The News and Media: Media Ethics page at Yahoo!

TIP TIP TIP TIP TIP TIP TIP TIP TIP TIP TIP TIP TIP TIP TIP TIP TIP TIP TIP TIP TIP TIP TIP TIP TIP

Remember to use the Back button if you want to return to a previous topic in Yahoo!'s hierarchies.

Needless to say, when you reach a listing for a page that sounds interesting, simply click on the hyperlink to that page to jump to it.

Searching by Keyword

Of course, it's not always easy to guess where a page or topic might be listed in an organized structure such as Yahoo!'s. Fortunately, the site also includes a search feature at the top of each page.

To perform a search, type a word (or a few words, to make the search more specific) in the box near the top of the page and then click the Search button.

TIP TIP TIP TIP TIP TIP TIP TIP TIP TIP TIP TIP TIP TIP TIP TIP TIP TIP TIP TIP TIP TIP TIP TIP TIP TIP TIP TIP TIP

If you perform your search from any of the pages besides the home page, you have the choice of searching the entire Yahoo! directory (Search All of Yahoo!) or just the items in the current category (Search Only in *Topic*).

So, let's say you're interested in campaign finance reform and want to see if there are any good resources for political reformers on the Net. Type the words **campaign finance** into the search box and click the Search button. Yahoo! quickly returns a list of categories relating in some way or another to your keyword (in fact, the word will appear in bold type in a blurb for each category), as shown in Figure 10.4.

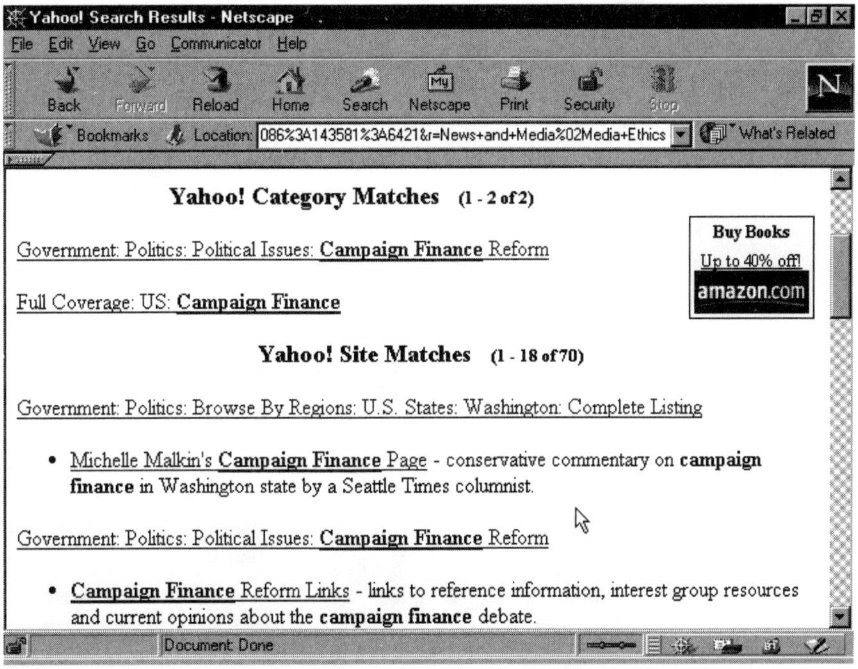

FIGURE 10.4: Some of the campaign finance related pages listed as the result of a Yahoo! search.

From there, all you have to do is start clicking on the interesting-looking sites you want to visit.

Searching with a Search Engine

Now that you know how to search the contents of a directory site, it's easy to perform a search of the entire Net from a search site. A search engine is just a Web site designed to perform searches of the Net. Conceptually, the only difference is that a site like Yahoo! is organized into hierarchies that have been edited, meaning that only "worthy" sites are listed. Most of the search engines attempt, instead, to reference every single page on the Web—although that's obviously impossible. Either way, of course, you're searching someone's list of sites, but the search engines generally return results from a broader pool.

Most search engines allow you to enter very specific, even complicated, search queries, much like ones you would submit to a database program. Fortunately, for your everyday searches you shouldn't need those advanced features. Instead, a single keyword—or a couple, for a narrower search (such as *medical ethics*)—will usually do the job.

One of the more popular search engines is Lycos. Everyone has their favorites, but Lycos, which has been around for a while, seems to crop up most often when I ask around. (Another popular one is AltaVista at `http://altavista.digital.com/`. See the sidebar "Zeigen Speaks" to read the opinion of an Internet expert on these two search engines.) Lycos is at (where else?) `http://www.lycos.com/` (see Figure 10.5).

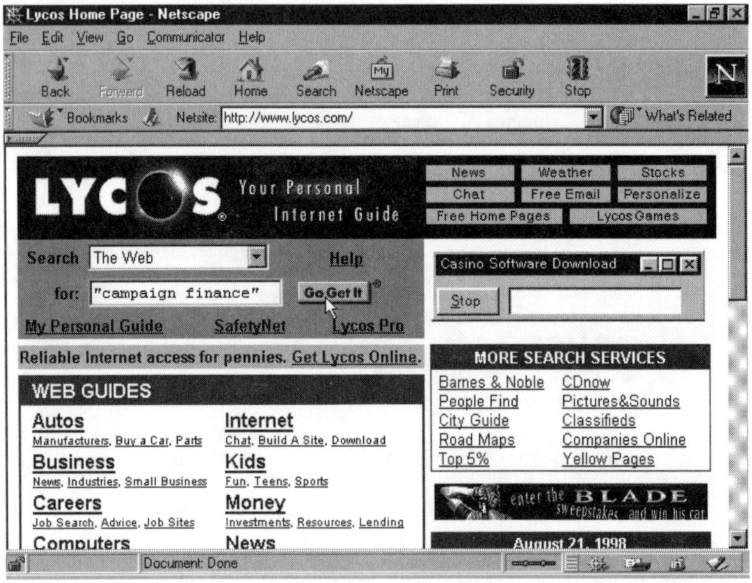

FIGURE 10.5: The Lycos search engine is powerful and easy to use.

TIP TIP TIP TIP TIP TIP TIP TIP TIP TIP TIP TIP TIP TIP TIP TIP TIP TIP TIP TIP TIP TIP TIP TIP TIP TIP TIP TIP

Make a bookmark (or Favorites listing) for the Lycos site as well.

As with the search feature in Yahoo!, just type a keyword (or several words) into the box and click the Go Get It button. Lycos will return a list of sites, ranked in order of their likeliness to match your keywords (this is especially useful when you've entered more than one word). Figure 10.6 shows the results of a Lycos search on the words *campaign finance*.

Zeigen Speaks

From: Zeigen <estephen@emf.net>

Subject: Re: best search engine(s) for beginners?

X-URL: `http://www.emf.net/~estephen`

Let me put in one final plug for AltaVista over Lycos:

Lycos is *seriously* out of date in many places. Their backlog of new indexing to be done is way greater than their robot machine's capacity to index. The frequency of their garbage collection (that is, removing the old/removed/moved pages from the index) is far less than AltaVista's. I don't mean to decry someone else's desert-island favorite-searcher, but I think objectively AltaVista has a larger and more updated catalog. Plus there's that Usenet searching side. It's funny to watch the frequency of the indexers as they come by my place. Scooter (from Digital, for AltaVista) comes by every month if not more often, and grabs EVERYTHING. The Lycos robot hasn't come by in several months, and when it does, it only gets a small fraction of the four megabytes that constitute chez Zeigen.

It's not like I own stock in Digital or anything. If they started charging to access AltaVista I would start insulting them like crazy. Like for limiting basic searches to 200 hits.

—Zeigen

P.S. Heck—why not put them both up?

Click on any of the hyperlinked listings to visit the listed site. (Lycos boldfaces the keyword in the page abstracts only to show you where your search words turned up.)

Refining Your Search

Sometimes your first attempt to search for a topic will fail. You won't find what you're looking for or you'll get so many results that you won't have time to review them all (like the search in Figure 10.6 that found thousands of sites). When this happens, you need to refine your search. If you're getting no results or too few, you'll have to come up with an alternative search term that's more general than whatever you tried at first. (Check the spelling first, though—you may have mistyped!)

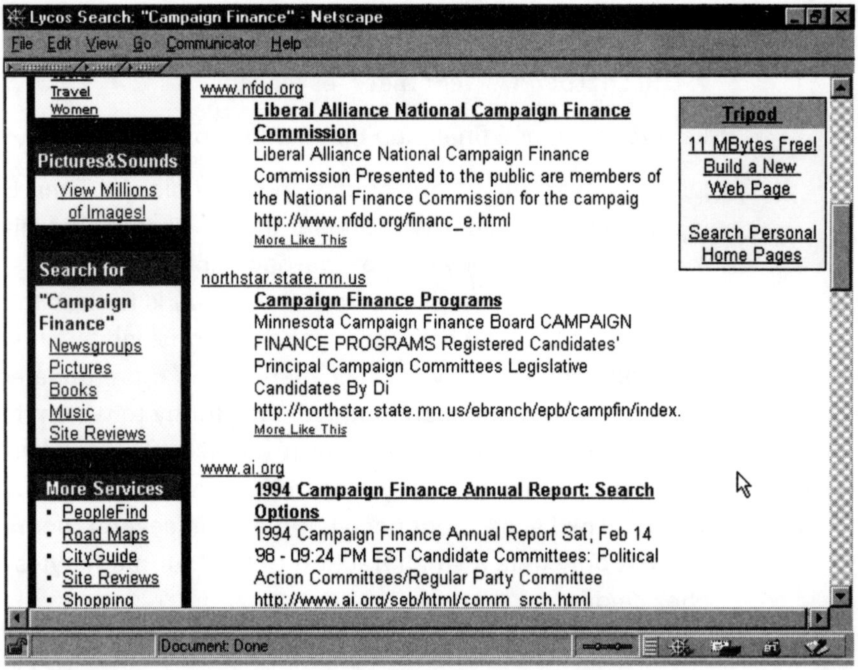

FIGURE 10.6: Web sites turned up by Lycos in a search using the words *campaign finance*

If you're getting too many results, you can try to narrow your search. At any search site (or directory), you can enter more than one keyword to get results containing any one of the words you enter. This broadens the search, though, instead of narrowing it. To limit the pages you find to those that match more than one word, you need to require that *each* word match, not just *any*. At most search pages, you do this by preceding each required keyword with a plus sign, but check the help or hints section of the search engine you prefer to see what options are available to you there.

NOTE NOTE NOTE NOTE NOTE NOTE NOTE NOTE NOTE NOTE NOTE NOTE NOTE NOTE NOTE

At some search sites, you can also narrow your search by date (type in a very recent range to get only the sites that were updated a short time ago), by language (English is a good place to start), or by stringing together search words with the *logical operator* "AND" (*kayak AND Pacific Northwest*, for example, will only give you sites that have both of these terms). AltaVista's Advanced Search feature at `http://altavista.digital.com/` can narrow searches with these methods.

Visiting a Central Search Page

Most of the popular Web browsers have a shortcut to one or more directories or search pages built into the program.

TIP TIP TIP TIP TIP TIP TIP TIP TIP TIP TIP TIP TIP TIP TIP TIP TIP TIP TIP TIP TIP TIP TIP TIP TIP

Even Lynx, the character-based Unix browser, has a searching shortcut. Type `i` to go to a directory site.

With Netscape Navigator, you can click the Search button to jump straight to Netscape's own central search page, which has links to the sites already mentioned in this lesson along with many others. Figure 10.7 shows Netscape's Net Search page.

As in the previous examples, enter a keyword in the Infoseek Guide textbox and click the Seek button, or choose a category and start browsing.

Lower down on the page, there's a list of other good search sites and directories. There's no need to bookmark this page if you use Netscape Navigator since you have a built-in shortcut. If you're using another browser, go to `http://home.netscape.com/home/internet-search.html` and create a bookmark so it will be easy to return any time you want.

NOTE NOTE NOTE NOTE NOTE NOTE NOTE NOTE NOTE NOTE NOTE NOTE NOTE NOTE NOTE

Microsoft Internet Explorer has a built-in search page, called Find It Fast. You can also change your preferences to specify a different default search page, if you have a favorite.

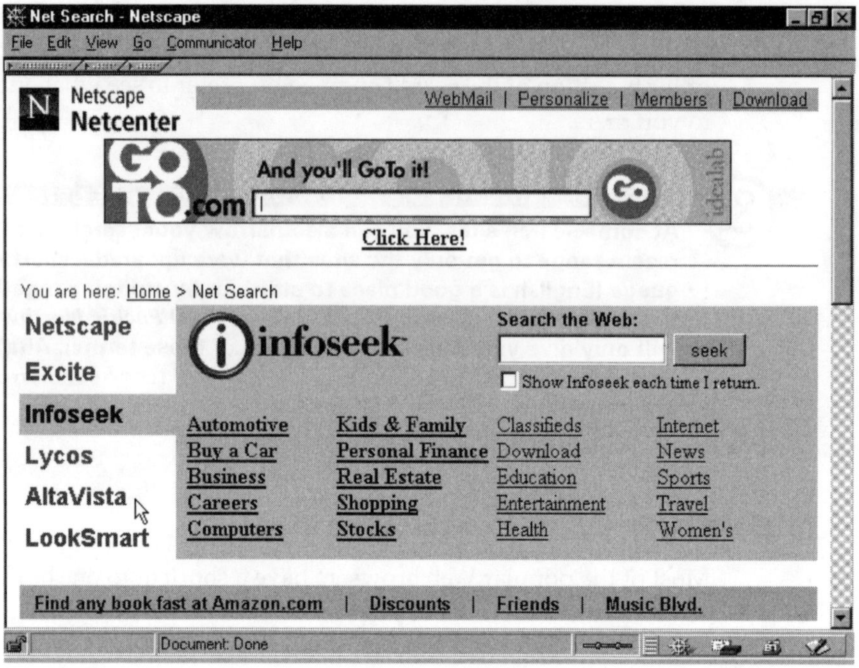

FIGURE 10.7: Netscape's Net Search page shows a direct search box for one of five sites (currently Infoseek) and then links to other good sites below.

Some Search Addresses

Here are the Web addresses of a bunch of other good directories and search pages:

Resource	Web Address
AltaVista	`http://altavista.digital.com/`
Amazing Environmental Organization WebDirectory!	`http://www.webdirectory.com/`
Berkeley Public Library's Index to the Internet	`http://www.sunsite.berkeley.edu/InternetIndex/`
Electric Library	`http://www.elibrary.com/id/2525/`
Excite	`http://www.excite.com/`

Resource	Web Address
HotBot	http://www.hotbot.com/
Infoseek	http://www.infoseek.com/
Lycos	http://www.lycos.com/
Magellan	http://www.mckinley.com/
Open Text	http://index.opentext.net/
Point	http://www.pointcom.com/
World Wide Arts Resources	http://www.wwar.com/
Web Crawler	http://www.webcrawler.com/
Yahoo!	http://www.yahoo.com/

Downloading Files and Keeping Your Software Up-to-Date

Sometimes when you search the Net you're looking for information, but other times you're looking for files to download from the Internet to your computer. For example, there's a lot of software out there available either for free or as *shareware* (meaning you're expected to pay for it after evaluating it, if you decide to keep using it). Also, a lot of programs, especially Internet-related software programs, are updated from time to time, with newer versions made available for downloading from the Net.

NOTE NOTE NOTE NOTE NOTE NOTE NOTE NOTE NOTE NOTE NOTE NOTE NOTE NOTE NOTE

Coming soon are programs that can update themselves whenever the developer adds a new feature. This may lead to more programs sold on a subscription basis instead of as a one-time license. There are already programs, such as online service interfaces, that you can upgrade by choosing commands within the program itself.

Once you start using Internet software (such as Web browsers, newsreaders, mail programs, and so on), you have to get used to the idea that if you want to have the latest version of the program, you occasionally have to check the software manufacturer's Web site to download the newest update.

No matter what your reason for downloading a file, the procedure with most Web browsers is pretty much the same. It generally involves finding your way to the appropriate site, working your way through a few links, and ultimately clicking on a link that connects directly to the file in question. When you do this, your browser will realize that you've requested something that can't be displayed in a browser window, and it will offer to download or even try to run the file for you.

TIP TIP TIP TIP TIP TIP TIP TIP TIP TIP TIP TIP TIP TIP TIP TIP TIP TIP TIP TIP TIP TIP TIP TIP TIP

The file you're downloading may be a compressed file. See "Compression Programs," later in this section, for tips on how to unsquish files.

Netscape Navigator will display a dialog box that when you click on a link to download a file.

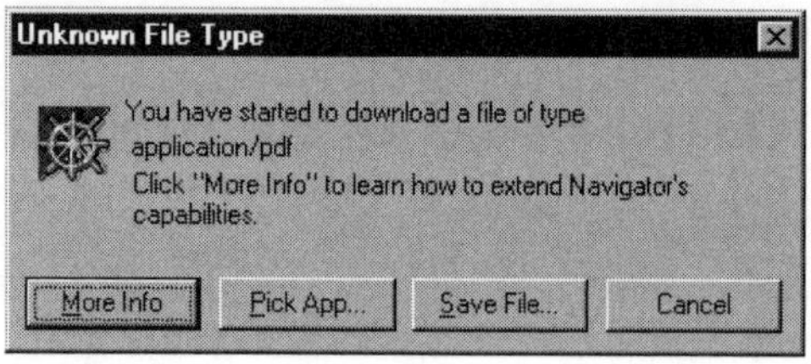

Click the Save File button and then select a folder to save the file to in the Save As dialog box that appears. Usually a Temp folder is best, since most of the time you'll be unpacking a compressed file or running an installation program to actually set up the software you're downloading.

Your browser will then download the file, showing you its progress either in a special dialog box or in the bottom-right corner of the browser window.

WARNING WARNING WARNING WARNING WARNING WARNING WARNING WARNING

Be careful when downloading files from the Internet. Only take files from reputable sources. If you download a file from some unofficial archive, it could easily contain a virus or other software designed to damage your computer. If you're downloading from a well-established company site, though, you usually have nothing to worry about.

For more on transferring files, see Skill 18, *Getting Around with FTP and Telnet*. For more on "teaching" your browser how to use an external application to open a file (like Navigator's Pick App option shown in the graphic above), see the full discussion in Skill 11, *Working with Multimedia*.

Protecting Your Files with Anti-Virus Programs

Viruses are prankish computer programs written by renegade programmers to play tricks on your files and your system. Most viruses enter your system from files downloaded from the Internet, although some viruses can be picked up from contaminated files sent to you via e-mail or on a floppy disk or other storage media.

An entire software industry has sprung up to deliver products to protect computers, programs, and company networks from viruses. These programs can scan files for viruses, remove the viruses, and notify you if you are about to download a file containing a virus. You can buy these programs, but one prominent anti-virus manufacturer, McAfee and Associates, allows you to download an evaluation copy of its software from its Web site. You can try it out for 30 days before deciding whether you want to buy it.

Downloading a Sample Anti-Virus Program

McAfee is not the only place where you can get free anti-virus programs, but it is fairly reputable and, if you like the program after trying it out, you can buy it to get more features, online help, and regular updates. If you want to visit other anti-virus sites to find out what they have to offer, search for *antivirus software* with your favorite search engine and you will turn up plenty of sites.

If you want to check out McAfee's VirusScan (available for most computers), just follow these steps:

1. Open your browser and log on to your Internet service. In the browser Address window, type **`www.macafee.com/`**. McAfee's home page is shown in Figure 10.8.
2. Click the Download button in the right-hand corner of McAfee's page to begin the download process. First you will have to fill out some information about yourself for McAfee's marketing department (that's how you pay for your "free" download).
3. Continue clicking on the download pages until you reach the page where you can specify what program you want and what operating system you have. VirusScan is a good one to try, and McAfee also has a WebScan program for detecting Internet viruses as you download.
4. Tell your browser where to download the file when the download dialog box appears. Wait about 12 minutes (with a 56.6 Kilobits per second, or 56,600 bits per second, modem) and you will have the zipped-up software file.
5. Log off of the Internet and exit your Web browser.

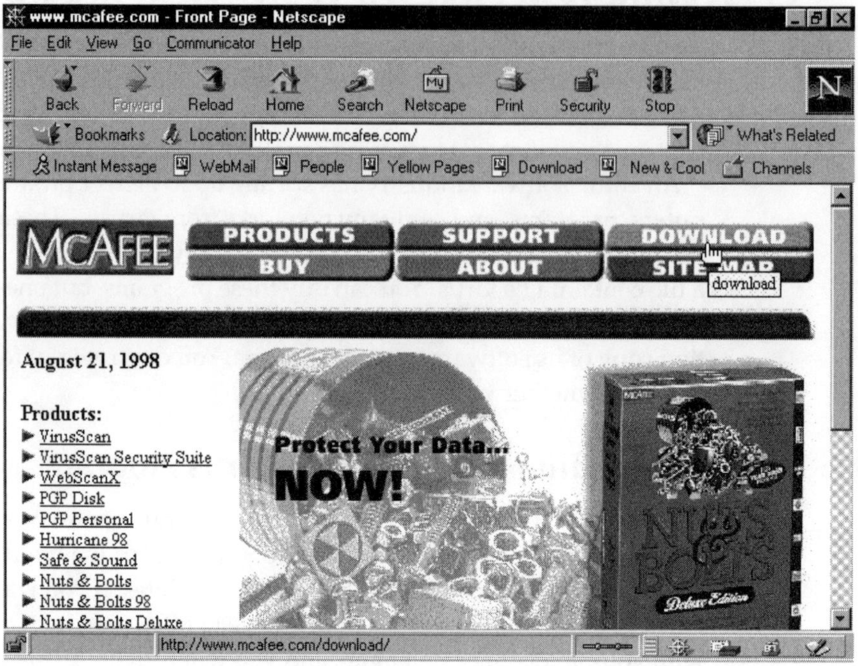

FIGURE 10.8: Click the Download button on McAfee and Associates' home page to begin downloading an evaluation copy of VirusScan.

Now that you have the McAfee file (called something like `v35i310e.zip`), you will need to unzip, or decompress it, to get to the setup file and install the program. Please see the section entitled "Compression Programs" to download a copy of WinZip (if you do not already have one) and install it, then return here to use VirusScan.

Using the Sample Anti-Virus Program

First, you need to unzip your McAfee archive as discussed in the "Using the WinZip Program" section further along in this lesson. After you unzip your archive, use these steps to install VirusScan:

1. Close all of your Windows programs.
2. Double-click the `setup.exe` file extracted from the zip archive. This will activate the Setup Wizard, which first displays the license agreement. Read the agreement, then click I Agree if you wish to accept its terms and proceed with the setup.

3. Click Next in the Welcome to Setup window. In the Setup Type screen, select either the Typical, Compact, or Custom setup, although Typical, which is preselected for you, is generally fine.
4. Click Next in the Confirm Install Settings screen after you review which VirusScan components will be added to your hard disk.
5. While McAfee is installing, it scans the system area of your hard disk and notifies you of the results. Hopefully you will receive the "No viruses were found" message and you will click OK to continue. If VirusScan finds viruses, follow the instructions to clean them.
6. If you would like to create an emergency start disk, which will give you the ability to restart and repair your computer if a virus crashes it, insert a floppy disk and click OK. If not, click Cancel and Finish to complete the installation.

McAfee VirusScan's installation will not be complete until you restart your computer, which you can do immediately, or at a later time by selecting the appropriate option in the last setup screen.

After you have installed McAfee, you can scan your entire hard drive or selected files by operating VirusScan with these procedures:

1. Start VirusScan by selecting Start ➢ Programs ➢ McAfee VirusScan ➢ VirusScan. You will see the VirusScan window shown here.

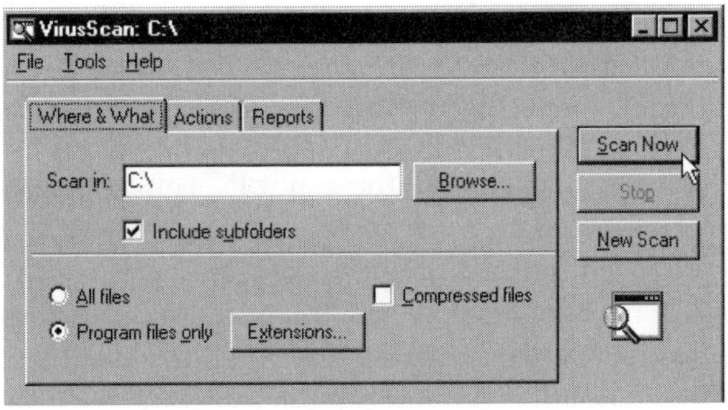

2. Specify the folders to be scanned in the Scan In textbox on the Where & What tab. If you want to scan the entire hard drive, leave the `C:\` in the Scan In textbox, otherwise use the Browse button to find the folders to scan.

TIP

You can download files from the Internet to a particular folder and then have McAfee VirusScan or another anti-virus program scan the files in that folder before using or installing them. This will help prevent the introduction of Internet viruses.

3. Click the Scan Now button to begin the scan. After the scan is complete, VirusScan will give you a report on what it found. If VirusScan finds any viruses, the program will ask you what actions you want to take, and will clean the viruses during the scan if you select that option.

To set options for VirusScan's behavior when it detects viruses, use the Actions tab. Select the Reports tab to modify what information will be included in the VirusScan report. You can also select Tools ➢ Advanced to display additional tabs containing options for how VirusScan alerts you to the presence of a virus and how VirusScan makes exceptions while conducting its scans. Select Help ➢ Help Topics to find more information on all of VirusScan's features.

Compression Programs

Files archived for downloading are usually stored in a compressed format. Each of the major platforms (Windows, Macintosh, and Unix) have their own compression standards. Fortunately, files intended for a specific platform are invariably compressed in a format favored on that platform.

Compressed Windows (or DOS) files usually end in `.zip`, `.arc`, or `.lhz`, with `.zip` being by far the most common. If you're a Windows user, get yourself an up-to-date copy of WinZip (and pay for it—it's shareware and a bargain at the price). It "speaks" all the major PC compression formats and is easy to use. Compressed files that end in `.exe` are self-extracting. Just double-click the icon when it's finished downloading.

In the Macintosh world, the primary compression program is StuffIt, from Aladdin Systems. Aladdin lets you download their software to evaluate it, and they provide a decompression tool, StuffIt Expander, for Windows users. Expander opens up Macintosh StuffIt files on Windows computers, but it can only decompress files, it cannot compress them.

Downloading WinZip

If you do happen to download a file ending in `.zip` instead of `.exe`, you have obtained a zip *archive*, or a file that contains many other files in compressed format. You need to unzip this archive with the WinZip program (or another unzipping program) before you can use the files inside it. The following steps will take you through the process of downloading WinZip:

1. Open your browser and log on to your Internet service. In the browser Address window, type **www.winzip.com/**.
2. Select the version of WinZip you want, such as version 6.3 for Windows 95. Instruct your browser where on your hard drive you want the file downloaded.
3. When the file is finished downloading you will have WinZip in an `.exe` (self-extracting) archive called `winzip95.exe` or something similar, depending on which version you downloaded.
4. Exit your Web browser and disconnect from the Internet.

NOTE NOTE NOTE NOTE NOTE NOTE NOTE NOTE NOTE NOTE NOTE NOTE NOTE NOTE NOTE

WinZip is a shareware program. It's OK to evaluate it for 30 days, but after that, you should pay Niko Mak Computing for an official copy. The WinZip Web site has information on online ordering of an official copy at `http://www.winzip.com/`.

Using the WinZip Program

After you download WinZip and exit your browser, use My Computer or Explorer to open the folder you downloaded WinZip into. When you find the `.exe` file, such as `winzip95.exe`, follow these directions:

1. Double-click `winzip95.exe` to begin installing WinZip. Then click the Setup button in the WinZip 6.3 Setup dialog box. (The name of the dialog box will be different if you downloaded a different version.) In the second WinZip Setup box, type in a different directory name in the Install To textbox if you prefer something other than `C:\WinZip`, then click OK.
2. You will see the first WinZip Wizard screen, extolling the virtues of WinZip. Click Next when you are finished reading.
3. Select View License Agreement in the License Agreement and Warranty Disclaimer dialog box. You can print out the agreement or just read it on the screen. Click Close when you are finished and click Yes if you agree to the agreement's terms.
4. In the second WinZip Wizard screen, you have two choices:
    - Select the Start with the WinZip Wizard option if you are new to this program and would like to be guided through its basic features.

- Select the Start with WinZip Classic to use all of WinZip's features with less wizard help.

5. In the next screen, select either of these search options:
   - Choose Search Entire Hard Disk (Recommended) to find all of the zip folders for your Favorites list. WinZip will add all of these folders to the Favorites menu item so that you can open them by pointing to Favorites, highlighting the zip archive and clicking it.
   - Choose Quick Search (Faster) if you are pressed for time.
6. After WinZip searches for zip files to put in favorites, the setup is complete and you can click Next to start the program or Close to exit from Setup.

It's easy to switch back and forth between the WinZip Wizard, which guides you through the entire zipping process, and WinZip Classic, which just brings up the standard program. If you selected Start with the WinZip Wizard during the installation, you will be greeted by the Wizard screen each time you start the program.

Click the Options button to specify how your zip folders will be handled, or select Next to proceed with the Wizard, which will assist you in unzipping archives and installing programs from zipped archives, such as the McAfee program downloaded earlier. You can also click the WinZip Classic button in the WinZip Wizard to close the Wizard and proceed with the basic program, shown next.

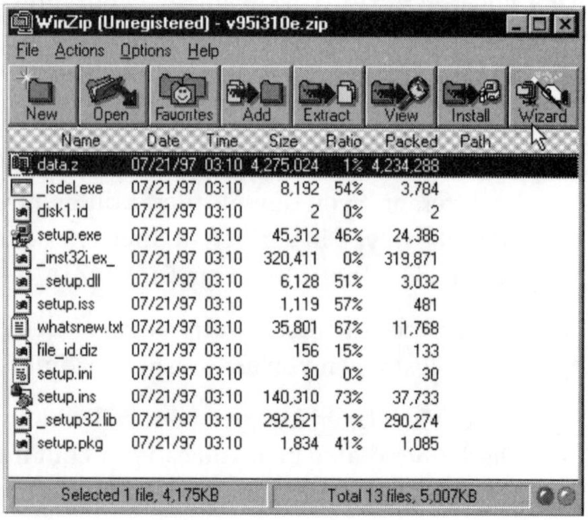

WinZip's interface is very simple and you can learn more about it by using the WinZip Wizard or by selecting Help ➢ Brief Tutorial, or Help ➢ Hints and Tips. You can activate the WinZip Wizard at any time by clicking the Wizard button at the far right end of the WinZip toolbar.

TIP TIP TIP TIP TIP TIP TIP TIP TIP TIP TIP TIP TIP TIP TIP TIP TIP TIP TIP TIP TIP TIP TIP TIP TIP

If you use the WinZip Wizard to open your archive and extract files, it will also activate the Setup program (if there happens to be one in the zip archive you obtained or downloaded).

To open a zip archive and unzip, or *extract*, the files inside of it, use these steps in WinZip Classic:

1. Double-click the WinZip desktop shortcut, or select Start ➢ Programs ➢ WinZip ➢ WinZip 6.3 32-bit (or whichever version you have).
2. Click the Open button in the WinZip Classic toolbar, or select File ➢ Open Archive.
3. Browse through your hard drive in the Open Archive dialog box until you find the zip archive, then highlight it and click the Open button.
4. Click the Extract button or select Actions ➢ Extract.
5. Browse through your folders in the Extract dialog box to specify where the unzipped files should be placed, then click Extract.
6. Select File ➢ Close Archive, and then File ➢ Exit to leave WinZip.

Downloading StuffIt Expander

If you use a Macintosh, or swap files between Windows and Macintosh computers, you will probably encounter some StuffIt files sooner or later. StuffIt is a popular Macintosh compression program. Compressed Mac files usually end in `.hqx`, `.bin`, `.sit`, or `.sea`. If your Mac is a fairly recent model, it will probably have the right decompression tools installed, and downloaded files will seem to extract themselves. If this doesn't happen, download an up-to-date version of StuffIt Expander from the Internet and install it.

StuffIt Expander's manufacturer, Aladdin Systems, also offers a Windows version of StuffIt Expander that can be used to decompress StuffIt files created on Macs. Here's how to download it:

1. Open your browser and log on to the Internet. In the Web address box, type **`http://www.aladdinsys.com/`** and press Enter.
2. You will see the home page for Aladdin Systems. Click the Get StuffIt Expander button to go to the page for downloading this program.
3. Scroll down on the StuffIt Expander page until you reach the download table. Click any of the cells in the table to try and download the program.

Sometimes one or more of these sites are busy, so keep clicking until you find one that's available.

4. In a matter of moments (if it's a good day on the Internet), the program will be in your download directory in a file named `sitex.exe`. Close your browser program and disconnect from the Internet.

Working With StuffIt Expander

After you have downloaded Aladdin Systems' free program, you can install it and get ready to unstuff some files. Here are the steps for installing the program:

1. Use Explorer or My Computer to find the `sitex.exe` file you downloaded. Double-click on this file.
2. You will see the multipurpose StuffIt Expander Setup window, shown next, which contains options you can change, such as the Program Group and the location where StuffIt Expander will be installed. Click Install when you are satisfied with the settings.

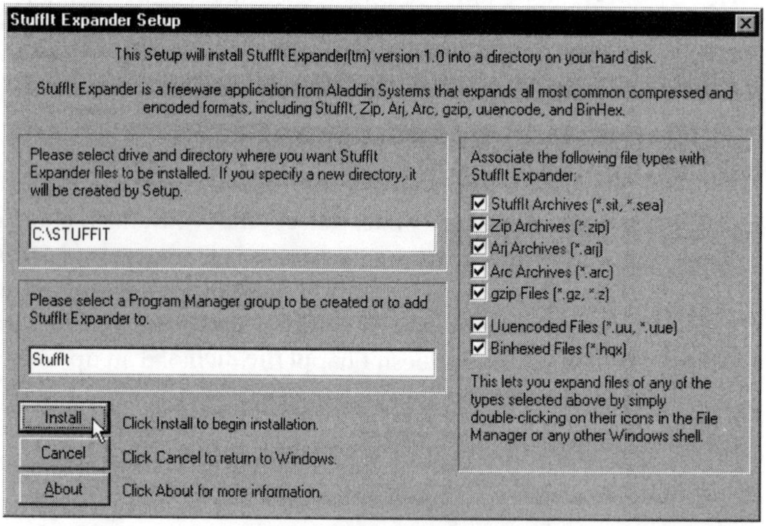

3. You will briefly see the message "Setup is copying files," and before you know it, you will see "Setup is complete." That's all there is to it.

NOTE NOTE NOTE NOTE NOTE NOTE NOTE NOTE NOTE NOTE NOTE NOTE NOTE NOTE NOTE

StuffIt Expander can also open zip archives, but it cannot zip up files or compress files by any other means. It is strictly a decompression utility.

After you install StuffIt Expander, give it a try on some compressed files with these steps:

1. Start StuffIt Expander by selecting Start ➢ Programs ➢ StuffIt ➢ StuffIt Expander.
2. You can expand a variety of compressed file formats by using one of these options:
   - Drag the compressed file from Explorer or My Computer directly into the StuffIt Expander window and drop it.
   - Select File ➢ Expand or click the Expand button on the left end of the StuffIt Expander toolbar. In the Expand dialog box, navigate through your folders to the location of the compressed file, highlight it, and click OK.
3. StuffIt Expander will automatically expand every file in the compressed file into a folder, which it creates and which has the same name as the original compressed file (or a truncated version of the name). When expansion is complete, you can close the program by selecting File ➢ Exit or by clicking the Exit button on the right end of the StuffIt Expander toolbar.

StuffIt Expander expands files into the same folder as the compressed file, unless you specify a different destination file with the Options ➢ Destination command. For more information on StuffIt Expander's options, select Help ➢ Help Index to read the help files. StuffIt Expander even has a Help ➢ Using Help command that leads to the Windows Help Topic on how to use online help files, so there's no excuse for not looking something up.

NOTE NOTE NOTE NOTE NOTE NOTE NOTE NOTE NOTE NOTE NOTE NOTE NOTE NOTE NOTE

Mac users can also download the ZipIt shareware program so they can send `.zip` **archives to the Windows world. ZipIt can be found at** `http://www.awa.com/softlock/zipit/`.

Shareware.com

SKILL 10

A good "one-stop-shopping" place to go to download the latest version of software available free on the Net is c|net's Shareware.com site (see Figure 10.9).

The Shareware.com site will offer automatic links to recent arrivals and popular downloads, but you can search for any program by name. Just type the name (or part of it) in the search box, specify your operating system (Windows, Macintosh, etc.), and click the Search button. Shareware.com result pages contain links to various files (including duplicates at different sites) matching your search terms. Select a file name to download a file.

FIGURE 10.9: Finding software is a breeze at Shareware.com.

HOW SHAREWARE WORKS

Shareware is software that's distributed for free (sometimes in a limited or *lite* format) on a trial basis. If you like the software and want to continue to use it beyond its trial period, it is your responsibility to register and pay for it. Sometimes you will gain access to additional features (or prevent the program from expiring entirely), printed documentation, or technical support.

continued

Software distributed absolutely free is called *freeware*. Programmers who make freeware either derive personal satisfaction from the adoption and use of their handiwork or benefit financially from the reputation that accrues to the developer of a popular program. Software that reminds you to register all the time is often called *nagware*.

Here are two good shareware sites for owners of both Windows and Macintosh computers: `http://www.tucows.com` (the ultimate collection of Windows Software) and INFO-MAC HyperArchive ROOT, at `http://hyperarchive.lcs.mit.edu/HyperArchive/HyperArchive.html` (a bonanza of Macintosh programs).

Looking for People on the Internet

In Skill 5, *Advanced E-mail Tricks,* I mentioned that there are a few ways to look for people's e-mail addresses. Now that you have the hang of using a Web browser to search, I will point you to a useful site for looking for people.

Using WhoWhere?

The best site to use to look for e-mail addresses is WhoWhere? To try it out, point your browser to `http://www.whowhere.com/`.

Type a name in the Enter Person's Name box. If you know an organization that the person you're looking for might be listed with, type the organization's name in the second box (but that's optional). Then click the Search WhoWhere? button.

Other people-search sites find nothing for *Christian Crumlish,* but WhoWhere? finds me with no trouble (see Figure 10.10).

TIP TIP TIP TIP TIP TIP TIP TIP TIP TIP TIP TIP TIP TIP TIP TIP TIP TIP TIP TIP TIP TIP TIP TIP TIP

Yet another site you can use to look for e-mail addresses is called Four11 (point your browser to `http://www.four11.com/`**). To look for companies, try Big Book at** `http://www.bigbook.com/`**.**

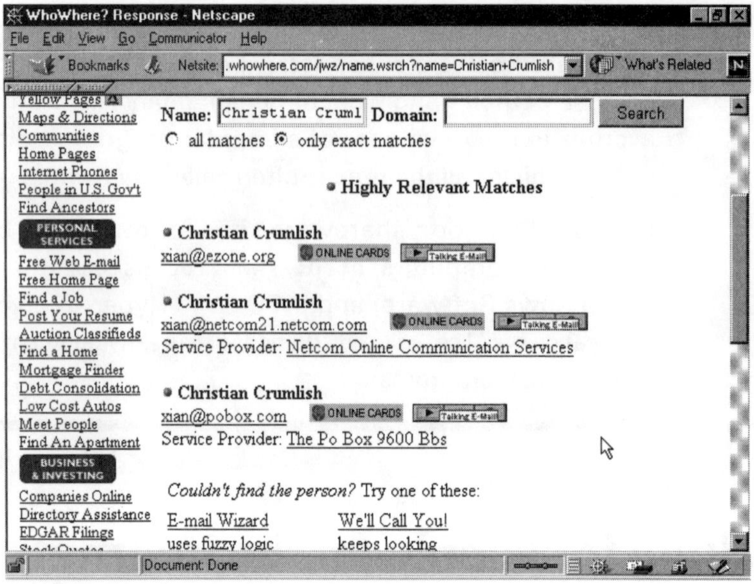

FIGURE 10.10: A WhoWhere? search: I just entered my name—no organization—and it found me.

Searching off the Web

Because the Web doesn't constitute the entire Internet, there are some Internet resources that don't show up when you're searching for Web sites. Fortunately, there are search engines and gateways out there that specialize in finding information in these other non-Web media.

WARNING WARNING WARNING WARNING WARNING WARNING WARNING WARNING

Some of the non-Web resources can be even flakier than the Web when you're trying to make a connection, especially during the business day in the continental U.S.A. If you have trouble getting through, try, try again (and then give up and try a couple of hours later).

Searching Usenet

Usenet and related newsgroups are the public discussion bulletin boards of the Internet. Because articles posted to Usenet expire after several weeks or months (depending on the news server), there's no way to search everything that's ever been posted there, but it is possible to search all the posts made recently.

NOTE NOTE NOTE NOTE NOTE NOTE NOTE NOTE NOTE NOTE NOTE NOTE NOTE NOTE NOTE NOTE

Subscribing to and reading Usenet newsgroups (as opposed to searching them) is covered in Skill 13, *Joining Usenet Newsgroups*.

Probably the best Usenet search engine is DejaNews at `http://www.dejanews.com/`. To find articles through DejaNews, type one or more keywords in the Quick Search For box and click the Find button. (For more complicated searches, click the Power Search icon.) DejaNews will give you a list of articles containing your keywords, with links to the text of the articles themselves and to the author of each article (see Figure 10.11). Clicking on the article's subject takes you to the article's contents. Clicking on the author takes you to a "profile" of the author that includes statistics about the author's Usenet posting habits.

TIP TIP TIP TIP TIP TIP TIP TIP TIP TIP TIP TIP TIP TIP TIP TIP TIP TIP TIP TIP TIP TIP TIP TIP TIP TIP TIP

The AltaVista search site also has a Usenet search option that scans some 16,000 newsgroups for your search terms. To use it, go to `http://altavista.digital.com/`. In the first search screen, click the Usenet in the Search textbox. The other option in this box is the Web, which is selected by default.

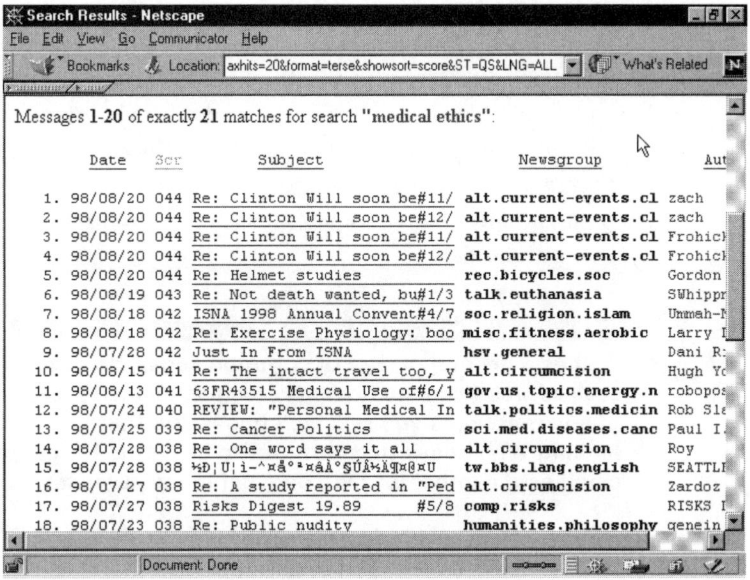

FIGURE 10.11: DejaNews has found many articles containing the keywords *medical ethics*.

Buying Things Online

As electronic commerce becomes more and more commonplace, you may find yourself searching for and purchasing products online. Aside from software, some of which you can actually obtain over the Internet, other purchases are "fulfilled" in traditional ways (by mail, courier, and so on), much like catalog sales.

Perhaps the biggest remaining bugaboo holding back the inevitable tide of online commerce is the question of security. How can you safely transmit something delicate like your credit card information over an open, public network such as the Internet? There are several different answers to this question, but no single universal model exists yet for online credit purchases.

One way to look at it is to compare it to handing your credit card to a waiter without worrying that someone in the kitchen might jot down your number and expiration date. The difference is that text data transmitted over the Internet could lie around on drives and backup disks indefinitely and individuals so inclined could probably hunt for likely information long after the fact.

Some online businesses have invested in secure Web servers that, when coupled with savvy Web browsers, initiate an encrypted "secure" connection, thereby preserving the secrecy of your private information. For that matter, most browsers will inform you *any* time you send information on a form to a nonsecure server, just in case the information in the form might be sensitive.

Other companies skirt the entire issue for now, offering alternative verification methods using 800 numbers or the like. This is an adequate approach for the time being, because it relies on more dependable existing methods of checking credit card info, but it takes away a good deal of the convenience of shopping online by adding those extra steps. Another approach some businesses take is to have you set up an account (and choose from various payment methods) the first time you make a purchase.

WARNING WARNING WARNING WARNING WARNING WARNING WARNING WARNING

Just as a general matter of common sense, do not send private information, such as credit card numbers via regular, unencrypted e-mail, and be suspicious of any messages you receive suggesting that you do so. Beware of official-looking Web pages that turn out to be fronts for people who just want your credit card number for their own nefarious purposes.

In addition to the matter of security, you may also have legitimate concerns about your privacy. Of course, these issues are not limited to the Internet. Any time you use a credit card or automatic-teller (debit) card you are leaving an electronic "paper trail" tracking your spending habits. The issue is similar on the Net.

Beyond the basic transaction information any store would naturally expect to track, some online businesses will also request or require that you fill out a questionnaire before completing your purchase. Your answers on such a form will become part of a customer database that may then find its way into the hands of other businesses.

If you're concerned about limiting your exposure when spending money on the Net, refuse to fill out such questionnaires whenever possible and refuse to be put on mailing lists or to have your registration information "made available" to other entities—again, whenever possible.

Having addressed all the potential negatives of online shopping, I'd like to avoid giving too negative or scary an impression. I've bought a number of real-world objects and services online and have not had a problem yet.

At most "store" sites, such as Compact Disc Connection (`http://www.cdconnection.com/`), you can search or browse your way to the merchandise you want and then add it to a shopping basket (essentially a list of items you wish to buy), to be "rung up" all at once when you're finished shopping. You repeat this process as often as you wish, and then proceed to an order page or area where you can buy the items you selected (see Figure 10.12).

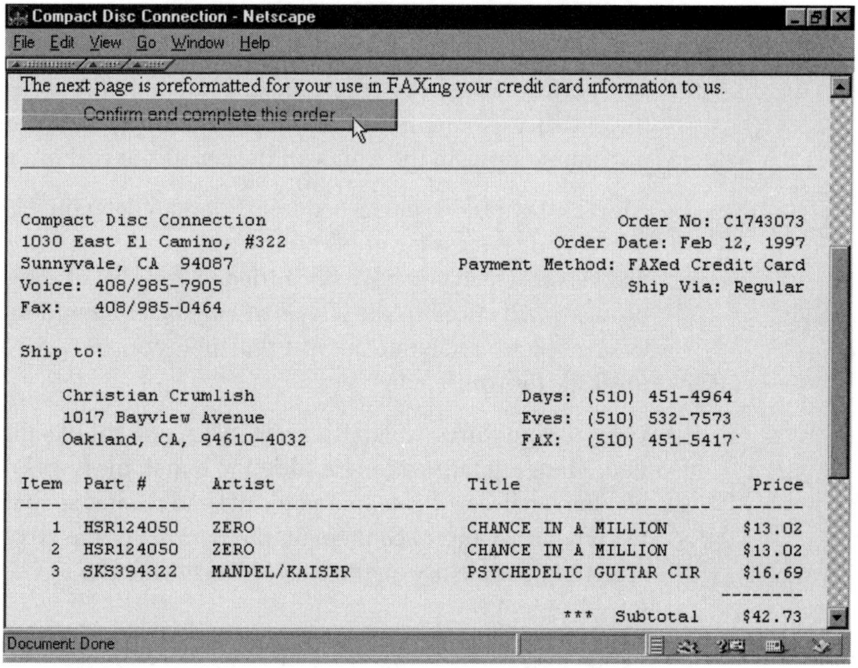

FIGURE 10.12: Buying some CDs at CD Connection

Security Features

These days, everybody is more security conscious as they browse and conduct business on the Internet and the Web. The current Web browsers include security provisions that warn you when you are about to transmit unsecured information over the Internet or when you are about to accept a downloaded file. You then have an option to cancel the transmission or proceed anyway.

The upcoming or just-arrived versions of these browsers (Netscape Navigator 4.5 and Microsoft Internet Explorer 4) have additional security features that give you more control over how security is implemented in your Internet and Web transactions.

Here are some of the new security options you may encounter or you may wish to implement:

- **Encryption** You now have the option of encrypting your messages, Web pages, and transactions by scrambling the transmissions with a special code that can only be unraveled by the intended recipient who has the decrypting information.

- **Certificates** Companies can develop security certificates, which are chunks of encrypted code that can be appended to Web sites, Webcasting channels, or Java applets and ActiveX scripts (small programs that accompany Web sites and perform interactive or animated functions). You can choose to accept the certificate, which means that, in the future, your browser will accept transmissions from the source of the certificate without warning you.

- **Alerts** Your browser can send you alerts when you are connecting to a site or receiving a message or Webcast from an address that has no security provisions (or which you have not added to your list of acceptable sources). The browser will check to see if a certificate is registered for the source of the transmission. If not, the browser will alert you and ask for your permission to let the transmission proceed.

- **Digital Signatures** Signatures are also code chunks that uniquely identify you. These signatures can be added to e-mail messages or they can be part of a Personal Certificate that you can send to sites so that you can be admitted when you approach them on the Internet or the Web. So far, few sites are screening people out on the basis of certificates.

NOTE NOTE NOTE NOTE NOTE NOTE NOTE NOTE NOTE NOTE NOTE NOTE NOTE NOTE NOTE

Think of security settings as a gatekeeper for your computer. You give the gatekeeper a list of "guests" who are allowed in without question, as well as instructions about not admitting guests who arrive without an invitation (the certificate). When the gatekeeper is approached by visitors who are not on the list and who do not have invitations, it calls you (or alerts you) to find out whether you want them to be let in.

Checking Your Security Settings

It will probably take some time before you are comfortable with all your security options and with determining what level of security is appropriate for your transactions. You can examine and modify the security setting features of Netscape Navigator 4.5 and Microsoft Internet Explorer 4 with the steps described next.

Netscape

When you are in any Netscape Communicator component, you can check security by selecting Communicator ➢ Security Info. This displays the Security window, shown next. If you are in a Messenger window looking at a message, the Security Info will let you know whether the message was encrypted or digitally signed.

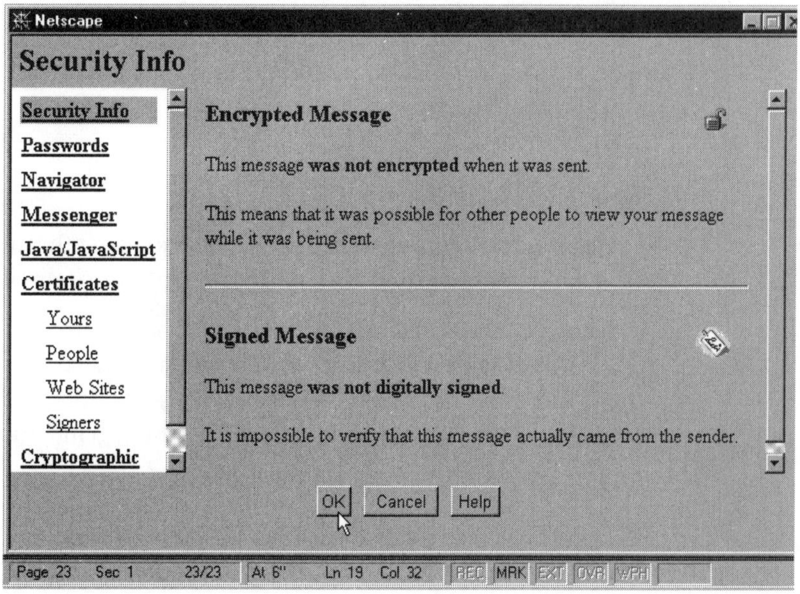

Netscape Communicator's Security Info window includes a pane on the left side where you can access other security features by clicking on them. These features are summarized here:

- **Passwords** Select this option to assign a password to your copy of Communicator and to direct Communicator about how often and under what circumstances to ask you for your password.
- **Navigator** Use these settings to instruct Navigator when to issue warnings and when to check for certificates. Your choices for warnings are:
    - Before entering an encrypted site
    - Prior to leaving an encrypted site
    - Before viewing a page of mixed encrypted and unencrypted information
    - In advance of sending unencrypted information to a site
- **Messenger** The settings in your e-mail component can be adjusted to direct Messenger when to encrypt or digitally sign your outgoing messages.
- **Java/JavaScript** This feature lists programs you have approved for downloading with a Web page, as well as those that are expressly forbidden. You can update this list by clicking the Remove, View Certificate, or Edit Privileges buttons.
- **Certificates** Here is where you can check the list of acceptable certificates, including yours (for sending out to others), other people's, and Web sites. You can View, Verify, and Edit these certificates by clicking the appropriate buttons.

Microsoft Internet Explorer

All of Internet Explorer's security options are accessed through various tabs in the Options dialog box, reached via the View ➢ Options command and described here:

- **Security Tab** Click the Security Tab to set Security Levels for different Security Zones, which include Trusted Sites, Restricted Sites, the Internet, and a Local Intranet. The Security Levels—High, Medium, Low, and Custom—are explained on the tab. See this tab in Figure 10.13.

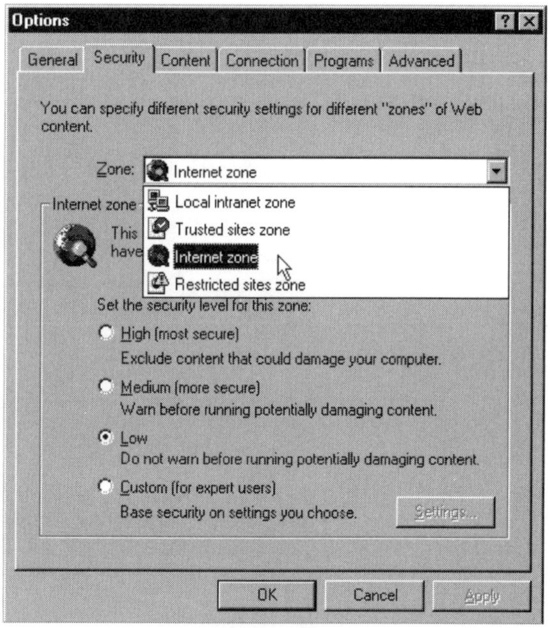

FIGURE 10.13: Microsoft Internet Explorer's Security tab in the Options dialog box

NOTE NOTE NOTE NOTE NOTE NOTE NOTE NOTE NOTE NOTE NOTE NOTE NOTE NOTE NOTE

The Low Security Level setting is a good choice if you are not purchasing much online and are not downloading files, but are just cruising around to check out what's on the Web. The higher the security level specified, the more alerts and annoying messages you will receive as you browse the Web.

- **Content Tab** This tab contains information on certificates you have accepted in the Certificates area, and on your own personal information and how secure it should be in the Personal Information area. Click the Personal, Sites, or Publishers buttons in the Certificates area to view or delete any of the listed certificates. This tab is shown in the top half of Figure 10.14.
- **Advanced Tab** Click this tab to change the security actions Internet Explorer will take during certain operations. Scroll down to the Security settings in the large window to see what is checked. You can check additional settings or uncheck those that do not seem appropriate for you. This tab is shown in the bottom half of Figure 10.14.

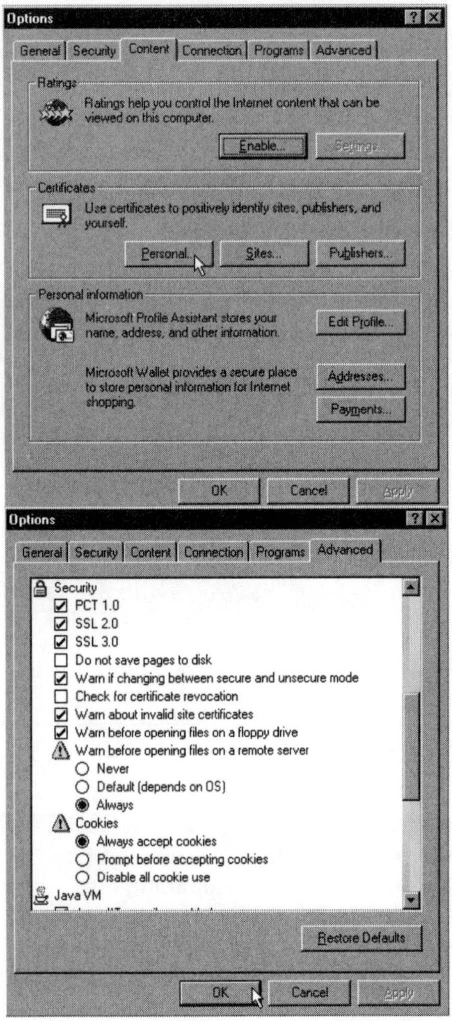

FIGURE 10.14: Microsoft Internet Explorers Option dialog box also has additional security settings on the Content and Advanced tabs.

At this point, not very many Web sites or companies have certificates, digital signatures, passwords, alerts, and all of the other trappings of a secure online society. However, as more and more users congregate on the Internet, the need for security features may grow. Right now you should familiarize yourself with security problems and solutions, such as anti-virus software, certificates, and encryption, and be prepared to take action when necessary.

Are You Experienced?

Now you can...

- ☑ find sites on the Web by searching directories such as Yahoo!
- ☑ refine your searches with topics, keywords, and search engine features
- ☑ protect your system and files with anti-virus software and security settings
- ☑ download files from Web sites
- ☑ download freeware and shareware compression utilities
- ☑ use compression programs to decompress files from the Internet
- ☑ discover people's Web addresses with online directories
- ☑ find articles through Usenet
- ☑ purchase items online while preserving security and privacy

SKILL 11

WORKING WITH MULTIMEDIA

- **Installing media viewers**
- **Setting up helper applications**
- **Installing browser plug-ins**
- **Exploring popular media formats**
- **Using specialized Web browsers**
- **Viewing multimedia files with Microsoft Internet Explorer and Netscape Navigator**

Part of the fun of the Internet and the Web is that there are a lot of different media out there to explore. What do I mean by media? Well, the most basic medium is text. The next most common media are various forms of pictures. Beyond that, media available on the Internet include sounds, movie clips, animations, and even more elaborate formats combining the basic media in all sorts of different ways. We still haven't reached a point where your computer is going to be as flashy as a television, and I'm not sure we'll ever get to that point. For one thing, the snazzier the medium, the bigger the files. For example, even the smallest picture file is bigger than most text documents you find on the Internet. These bulky files can bring your system to a processing and playback standstill, unless you have a fast connection, a very powerful processor, and lots of free memory.

To actually see, hear, or otherwise experience these media, you need a computer equipped with the right hardware (such as a sound card, enough memory to make movies play smoothly, a big enough hard drive to store large-format files, and so on) and you need software installed on your computer, either as part of a Web browser or as a stand-alone program that can interpret and display—or just "play"—the various media file formats. If you can put together all the ingredients, then you can start to experience the Internet as the world's largest CD-ROM, with new content appearing online daily.

Every Web browser can at least download files. So if you can get a stand-alone program to interpret a multimedia file you've downloaded, then you can experience that medium even without a sophisticated Web browser. In this lesson, I'll show you the various ways to handle these media, depending on the flexibility of your browser.

What's New with Multimedia?

The biggest handicap to multimedia development on the Web has been bandwidth limitations—people connecting to the Net via modems just can't be expected to wait long enough for huge media files to download. *Bandwidth* is the capacity of the communication lines transmitting data back and forth between the Internet and your computer. When you use a modem, your telephone line is transferring the data, and this can result in slow loading of Web pages or playback of video and audio clips. If you cruise the Internet from a network connection at work, your bandwidth capacity is greater, but network traffic is also heavier because many people may be using the network simultaneously. Any of these factors (line capacity, traffic, modem speed) can interfere with smooth browsing.

Another problem has been that most multimedia extensions to the standard Web format (HTML) have required that the user install a special piece of software into the Web browser. This has meant taking a side-trip from the site offering the media content to the Web site of the manufacturer of the plug-in. Any time someone leaves a site, there's some chance she'll never come back, as the siren call of tangential sites attracts her further and further from the original activity.

Fortunately, the latest version of one major Web browser, Microsoft Internet Explorer, already incorporates a more automatic process for downloading and installing plug-ins, and the other major browser, Netscape is likely to follow. This is similar to promises that upcoming Web browsers and other Internet tools will update themselves from time to time (or on request) automatically, by connecting to the software publisher's site, downloading patches or new setup files, and incorporating them into the existing package.

Downloading and Installing Applications

In Skill 10, *Finding Stuff on the Web and the Net,* I told you how to download a file using a Web browser. To experience almost any medium, you first have to download a large file. Depending on your browser, the file will be displayed inside the browser window; the browser will automatically start up a program that can display the file, and the file will appear outside the browser; or, at minimum, the browser will store the file on your computer where you can open it yourself using the right program.

The type of program that you launch separately to display a file is called a *viewer* or *player* program. If your browser can automatically start an external program whenever it needs to display certain types of files, then the program is referred to as a *helper application,* because it helps the browser with this extra job. The type of program that becomes part of the browser and enables the browser to display a file within the browser window is called a *plug-in* (or, in some programs, an *add-in*). I'll cover all three variations in the upcoming sections.

At Web sites that offer multimedia files, you will often find additional hypertext links to sites from which you can download the appropriate player software. Usually you can simply follow these links to the Web site housing the software, read the installation instructions, and download the correct program for your type of computer. You can often choose to automatically open and install the software as soon as it is downloaded (in fact, some programs can begin the installation process before the entire package is completely downloaded). Occasionally, you may still have to use a Setup or Install program to get the installation started.

NOTE NOTE NOTE NOTE NOTE NOTE NOTE NOTE NOTE NOTE NOTE NOTE NOTE NOTE

Your employment prospects will improve if you understand how sound, graphics, and video files work on the Web and how Web page design can accommodate system limitations while still looking good. Add a Web page to your portfolio—one that works whether the sound, graphics, or video features are turned on or off, so that people with any type of computer and connection can use it. (See Skill 19 for more information on how to make a Web page.)

Different Ways to View Media

As I just suggested, there are different ways to view various media files depending on the type of browser you have, the media formats you're working with, and the additional software you install. Here's a quick rundown of the different approaches.

TIP TIP TIP TIP TIP TIP TIP TIP TIP TIP TIP TIP TIP TIP TIP TIP TIP TIP TIP TIP TIP TIP TIP TIP TIP

Don't be put off by the use of the word *viewer* to describe multimedia player applications. Because the first media (after text) to be widely distributed were picture (image) formats, the viewer terminology took hold and is now used even for media, such as sounds, that you can't actually see.

Viewers and Players

A viewer program is one that can be used to view or play a specific type of file. (Even the ones used to play sounds, for example, are still referred to as viewers in browser instructions, so viewers and players are different names for the same thing.) Even with a character-based browser like the Unix program Lynx, you can still download files. It's true that you'll then have to get the file from your Unix account to your desktop computer, but when that's done you can "play" the file you downloaded if you have the appropriate software (such as Sound Recorder for Windows) installed on your computer. This approach will also work with browsers, such as AOL's, that are not equipped to launch external programs automatically.

The trick, then, is finding the appropriate viewer program to display the media files you download. As I mentioned in the "Downloading and Installing Applications" section, this is usually a matter of following the suggestions from the Web site where you found the original file. Other places you can look for files are mentioned in Skill 10, *Finding Stuff on the Web and the Net*.

Helper Applications

Netscape Navigator and other browsers based on that graphical model have the ability to launch external programs—called *helper applications*—when a nonstandard file format is selected. Helper applications will let your browser open files in formats it could not otherwise handle, such as a Sun audio file. They do, however, have to be "taught" where to look for the helper application. You can either do this in advance, by entering the Options or Preferences area of the browser and looking for the Helper Applications (or Helper Apps) section, or you can attempt to download a media file and then, when the browser tells you it doesn't recognize the file format, you can educate it about which viewer to use with that type of file. You do this simply by typing in the path and file name for the correct program, or by clicking a Browse button and rummaging around on your hard disk for the program you need. After that, your browser will automatically launch the right helper application whenever you select that type of media file again.

Plug-Ins

The most sophisticated way to work with multimedia files is to plug special add-on software directly into a browser. Such a program, usually called a *plug-in*, is an application that works in tandem with another program (often a browser), enhancing its features as if you had taken a piece of hardware and added it to your computer to give it more features.

With plug-ins installed, a browser can then display an unusual format *in-line*, meaning inside the browser window, instead of launching an external program to display the file.

Compressed Files and "Streaming Media"

One of the strategies used to address bandwidth limitations is to compress files as much as possible, most often using widely accepted compression standards. This might mean converting media files, such as images, to file formats that have data compression built right in (pictures on the Web are all stored in compressed formats) or it might mean compressing the original files with a zip or StuffIt type program, and requiring that the recipient decompress it himself. (The unzip or StuffIt Expander programs are always available as freeware and shareware. See Skill 10, *Finding Stuff on the Web and the Net*, for more on downloading and installing programs.)

NOTE NOTE NOTE NOTE NOTE NOTE NOTE NOTE NOTE NOTE NOTE NOTE NOTE NOTE NOTE NOTE

Despite all our efforts, competition for bandwidth may well always be a problem—even when we someday have virtual-reality meeting rooms, we will probably be complaining about them being "jiggly" or something like that.

A second approach to distributing long-format media (such as movies, radio, music, and the like) across limited bandwidths is to use a *streaming* format, meaning a format that sends the information in a continuous stream (with some clever innovations to deal with the flux and discontinuities of the Internet), enabling the receiver or playback device to start playing the media content without waiting for the entire file to finish downloading.

NOTE NOTE NOTE NOTE NOTE NOTE NOTE NOTE NOTE NOTE NOTE NOTE NOTE NOTE NOTE NOTE

Streamed media formats are not saved on your hard disk in the browser's *cache* (special memory that stores files for quicker access). The browser has to access the streaming media from the Web site itself, which slows down playback. Static media files can be saved in cache memory, which makes them an easier and faster format for browsers to use.

The first plug-in to popularize a streaming media format was Progressive Networks' RealAudio (and now RealPlayer, which plays movies as well). Microsoft inevitably countered with TrueSound (which failed) and more recently, MediaPlayer, which challenges both RealAudio and Apple's thus-far dominant QuickTime format. Streaming media should continue to evolve and interact with dynamic, interactive HTML and Webcasting (see Skill 12, *Push and the Desktop Web*, for more on Webcasting and "push" media).

Types of Media

The multimedia world on the Internet is still in a sort of "Wild West" phase, with many competing formats for the various types of media. In this section, I'll describe some of the media you'll encounter and clarify how the different file formats are used to get those media onto your screen.

TIP TIP TIP TIP TIP TIP TIP TIP TIP TIP TIP TIP TIP TIP TIP TIP TIP TIP TIP TIP TIP TIP TIP TIP TIP

For more (or more up-to-date) information on multimedia file formats available on the Net, check out `http://www.iics-sf.org/` (the San Francisco Bay Area chapter of the International Interactive Communications Society). This site has links to other multimedia resources.

Pictures

The first graphical Web browser, Mosaic, could only display one picture format when it first appeared—CompuServe's *GIF* (Graphic Interchange Format), which is a compressed file format. The other major picture format is called *JPEG* (named for the Joint Photographics Experts Group that designed the format). Mosaic, at first, could only display JPEG files in a helper application. When Netscape Navigator came along, it sported in-line JPEGs, which most browsers can now also handle. In-line JPEG files load right along with the Web page they are on without the need to launch an additional helper application.

Some GIFs are *interlaced*, which makes them appear to load faster on your screen. GIFs can also have transparent backgrounds, which accounts for the illusion of images with irregular (non-rectangular) edges. The images actually do have square edges, but their transparent background makes their content appear to float on the page.

NOTE NOTE NOTE NOTE NOTE NOTE NOTE NOTE NOTE NOTE NOTE NOTE NOTE NOTE NOTE

Using GIF files or the most current version of the JPEG format (progressive JPEGs) can be beneficial because, as they load on the page, the images appear to be gradually filled or drawn in. This activity may hold the attention of your average impatient Web browser who does not want to sit and stare at a static page, waiting for the graphics to appear. At least with GIF files, the viewer can watch the images slowly filling in and coming into focus. The older formats of JPEG files did not load in the same manner.

JPEGs can be compressed to much smaller file sizes than equivalent GIFs, but the more they are "squished," the worse the quality of the image becomes.

NOTE NOTE NOTE NOTE NOTE NOTE NOTE NOTE NOTE NOTE NOTE NOTE NOTE NOTE NOTE

The newest graphics format coming down the pike is *PNG* (which some say stands for "Png's Not Gif"). PNG combines some of the best features of GIF and JPEG formats in an open standard. MS Internet Explorer 4 and Netscape Communicator and its Navigator 4 browser can display PNGs.

Sounds and Music

There are many different sound file formats available on the Net. The most common of these include Microsoft's *WAV* (wave) format, perhaps the most widespread; the Macintosh *AIFF* format; and the Unix (originally NeXT) *AU* format. Many Web sites offer sounds in more than one format, in order to make it easier for each user to download a file format native to their type of computer.

Other sound formats include *MIDI* (Musical Instrument Digital Interface); the Amiga *SND* format; the *VOC* format for the SoundBlaster sound card; and *MP2* or *MPA*, which are MPEG sound formats. (*MPEG* is a movie format named after the Motion Picture Experts Group, but movies, of course, often also include sounds, so the MPEG standard specifies a sound format as well.)

After a while, you'll start to recognize what programs you'll need to view or play files by the (usually) three-letter extension following a file name. This will tell you whether it is a movie, a sound file, a picture, or something else, and what method of compression—if any—was used on it. Some of the more common file compression suffixes are `.zip`, `.hqz`, `.Z`, `.gz`, `.sit`, `.sea`, `.exe`, and `.tar`. For more on compression, see Skill 10, *Finding Stuff on the Web and the Net*.

A new approach to sound files (and, eventually, for movie files as well) is *streaming*. Streaming is when files are sent a little at a time and start playing almost immediately. This model differs from those in which an entire file is sent and then starts playing only after it has been completely downloaded. The most popular streaming format these days is *RealPlayer* or *RealAudio*. The tools needed to create and listen to such sounds are made by a company called Progressive Networks. This format allows sounds to be broadcast something like they are in radio. In fact, the National Public Radio Web site uses the RealAudio format to broadcast some of their reports over the Internet (see Figure 11.1).

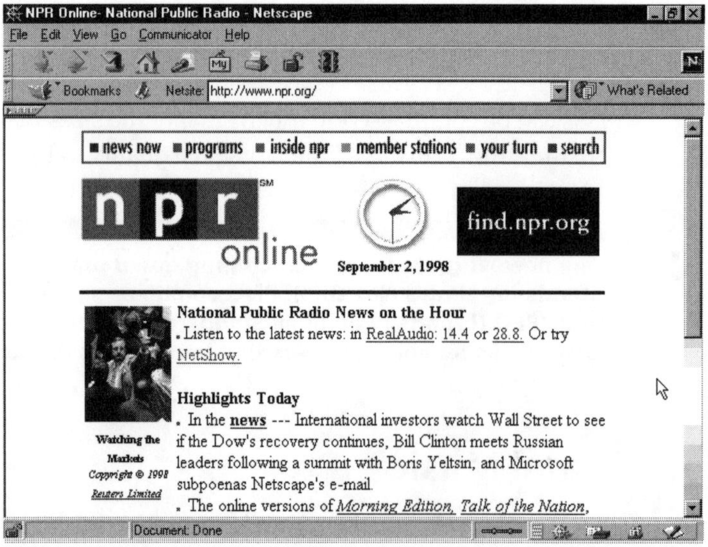

FIGURE 11.1: NPR's Web site offers current broadcasts in RealAudio format.

NOTE NOTE NOTE NOTE NOTE NOTE NOTE NOTE NOTE NOTE NOTE NOTE NOTE NOTE NOTE

Microsoft Internet Explorer can now handle *in-line* sounds, which will automatically start playing as soon as you arrive at a page (if you have the right sound software installed, of course), whether you like it or not!

Movies and Animations

As with sounds and pictures, there are various competing movie and animation formats available on the Net. Technically, the difference between a movie and an animation is that movies use video or film images (variations on photographic technology), while animations use drawn illustrations. With computer art tools being what they are, this distinction will probably fade eventually. A lot of computer art these days starts off as photography and is then manipulated into something entirely different.

Probably the most widespread movie format is the MPEG (Motion Pictures Experts Group) format, a compressed format. Another popular format is *QuickTime,* which started off on the Macintosh platform but can now be displayed on most computers. QuickTime files usually have a `.qt` or `.mov` extension.

A third common movie format, native to the Windows platform, is *AVI.* There are also streaming movie formats, such as Progressive Networks' RealPlayer. Webcasting's "push" model offers yet another alternative method for sending video-style content to a viewer's screen. (See Skill 12, *Push and the Desktop Web,* for more on push technology and Webcasting.)

3-D Environments

The future of the Net may be glimpsed in the still-evolving 3-D formats with which real or imaginary spaces are depicted in perspective, and the user has the ability to move (walk or fly) around, viewing the space from multiple angles.

The most common format for 3-D worlds on the Web is called *VRML,* which stands for Virtual Reality Modeling Language. VRML is still an evolving standard, and there are several competing implementations of it out there, including a version of QuickTime called, naturally enough, *QuickTime VR*. VRML files usually have a `.wrl` extension.

One of the future goals of VRML developers is to create worlds in which many users can meet and interact, as if in person. The present state of VRML development, however, involves users downloading copies of 3-D environments and then moving around in them all by themselves.

Figure 11.2 shows a VRML art gallery at `http://www.construct.net/`, designed by Michael Gough and curated by Annette Loudon, a Web artist.

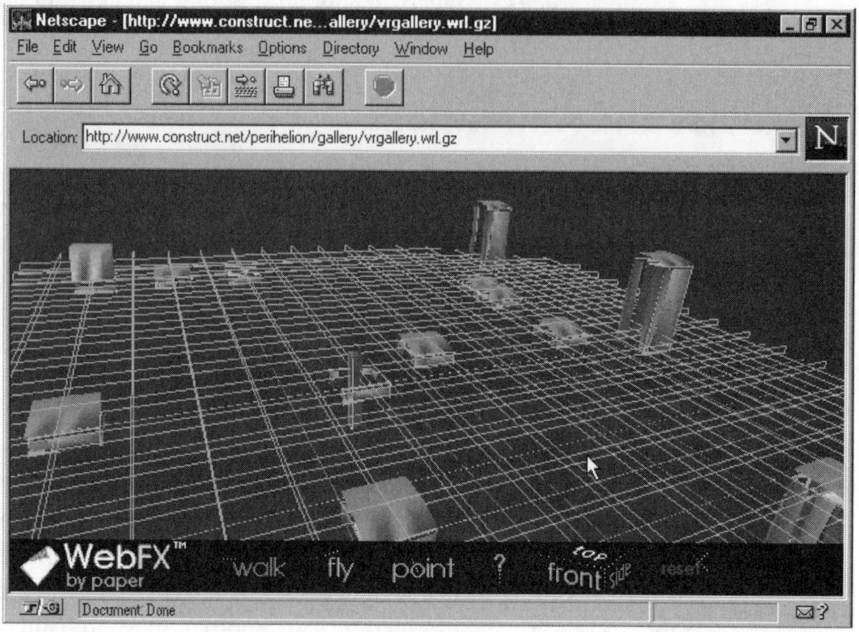

FIGURE 11.2: Construct's sample VRML art gallery

> **TIP** To see the gallery space shown in Figure 11.2, your browser may have to decompress files compressed with Gzip, a variant in the zip family of file compression software. See Skill 10, *Finding Stuff on the Web and the Net*, for more on compressed file formats.

There are also some special browsers out there, such as one called WebFX, designed specifically for viewing and moving through 3-D spaces. (For more on this, see the "A Few Words about Specialized Browsers" sidebar later in this lesson.)

> **TIP** To find info on VRML browsers, builders, tools, documentation, and sample VRML worlds, check out `http://www.sdsc.-edu/vrml` or `http://www.vrml.org/`.

Document/Mixed-Media Formats

Aside from the familiar HTML format and plain text (`.txt`) files, which browsers can easily display, there are some document file formats intended to give designers and publishers more control over the precise look of a document. HTML is quite flexible but HTML documents look different in every browser because they have to use whatever fonts are built into the user's computer, and they even change their shape and layout depending on the size and shape of the browser window. For artists, publishers, and designers trained in the world of print publishing, most of these compromises are unacceptable.

The most popular document format is Adobe's *PDF* (Portable Document Format). The external helper application for viewing PDF files is called Adobe Acrobat. The Netscape plug-in that performs the same function is called Adobe Amber. Visit `http://www.adobe.com/` for more information on the PDF format.

Another document format that requires special viewers is Postscript, which can be used for both text and images. Postscript files usually have a `.ps` extension.

Interactive Programs and Multimedia Presentations

The next wave of special media formats for the Web will involve interactive programs or demonstrations, running either in separate applications or in the browser window. Macromedia makes a product called Director that enables artists to assemble movies, animations, pictures, sounds, and interactive elements (such as clickable buttons and other user-influenced choices) into a single, self-running application. The Director plug-in is known as Shockwave. Shockwave now has a Flash format designed specifically for the Web. Flash enables smooth interactive performance over an Internet connection in a streamable format using very compact vector graphics. Designers rave about Flash. See `http://www.macromedia.com/software/flash/` for more about this format.

The other popular application-development format for the Web is Sun's Java programming language, a variant of C++. With a special Java-savvy browser such as HotJava, Netscape Navigator 3 and higher (or earlier versions of Navigator with a Java plug-in), or Microsoft Internet Explorer 3 and higher, users can interact with fully operational programs inside of the browser window.

Staying Informed about the Latest Advances

There are new viewers and new file formats coming out on the Net all the time. It's literally impossible for me to make this lesson be fully up-to-date by the time you read it! As with any Internet software, you will have to do a little work if you want to stay up-to-date with the latest developments. Your best bet is to visit your browser's home page (most browsers have a logo button near the upper-right corner of the window to take you there automatically) from time to time and read the announcements to see if any new capabilities or plug-ins have been announced.

TIP

Netscape Navigator automatically provides you with a link to its Plug-In Finder page if you connect with a file format that Navigator does not support. You can also visit Netscape's Plug-In page by selecting Help ➢ About Plug-Ins in the Navigator or Communicator menu. The help document will show you which plug-ins are preinstalled in Communicator and Navigator. If you click on the "click here" link at the top of the document, you will be taken to the plug-in page (`http://home.netscape.com/plugins/index.html` at the time of this writing).

A Few Words about Specialized Browsers

One way to experience some of the latest multimedia offerings on the Web, even without customizing your browser, is to obtain a specialized browser designed to display one or more of the multimedia formats. In the long run, as general-purpose browsers become more flexible, this may no longer be a useful option, but for now, if you have the type of access that allows you to install and run your own browser, you can download a program such as Sun's HotJava browser (`http://www.javasoft.com/`). There are actually quite a few stand-alone VRML browsers, such as Cosmo (http://cosmosoftware.com/), 3Space Assistant (`ftp://ftp.sd.tgs.com/3SpaceAssistant/X86/`) and Pueblo (`ftp://ftp.chaco.com/pueblo/`) to name a few.

Multimedia for Specific Browsers

As in the earlier lessons in this book, I'll finish up by running through many of the most popular Web browsers to tell you what alternatives you have (setting up helper applications or adding plug-ins) to increase the capabilities at your disposal and what media can be viewed with them.

Microsoft Internet Explorer

NOTE NOTE NOTE NOTE NOTE NOTE NOTE NOTE NOTE NOTE NOTE NOTE NOTE NOTE NOTE

"Add-in" is the Microsoft term for plug-in type software.

Internet Explorer automates the add-in (plug-in) process quite nicely. If you visit a site with a media format that your browser does not yet "know," (such as the short Shockwave clip available via the "shocked house" link at `http://www.attraction.org/`), Internet Explorer will automatically connect to the media-format maker's Web site and offer to download and install the appropriate add-in.

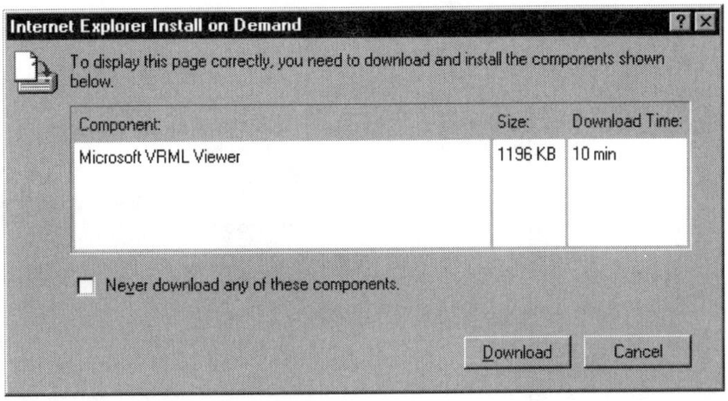

There is no way to manually install an add-in to Internet Explorer. You may have to restart your computer once the add-in has been installed.

Internet Explorer can display GIFs and JPEGs in-line. It can also play any of the standard Microsoft file formats (such as the AVI movie format, the WAV sound format, and so on), and it comes with the ability to play RealAudio sound files.

Netscape Navigator

One way to tell Navigator about a helper application is to start downloading an "unknown" file type and then, when Navigator balks and the Unknown File Type dialog box pops up, tell it what program to view the file with by clicking on the Pick App button and following the instructions that appear.

You can also plan ahead by assigning file types to specific Helper applications with these steps:

1. Open Netscape Navigator and Communicator by double-clicking the Netscape Communicator desktop shortcut or by selecting Start ➢ Programs ➢ Netscape Communicator ➢ Netscape Navigator.
2. Select Edit ➢ Preferences, and click the Navigator ➢ Applications item in the Category box at the left (see Figure 11.3).

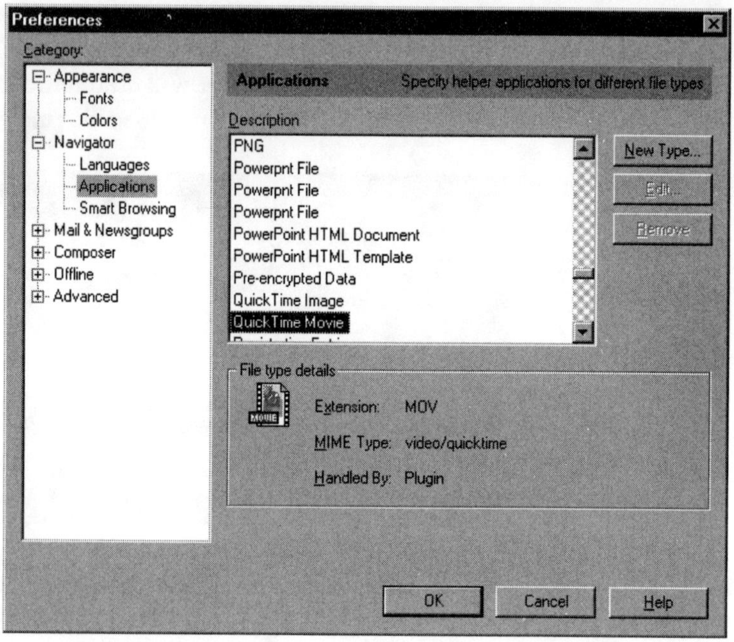

FIGURE 11.3: Navigator's Preferences dialog box with Applications selected

3. Select a file type in the large list box at the top of the dialog box and click the Edit button.
4. In the Handled By area, choose the application you want to use when opening this type of file. Either type the path for the application in the Application

text box, or click the Browse button and find the application and its path in your folders. Click Open to copy the path into the Application textbox.

5. Click OK to close the Edit Type dialog box, then click OK again to close Preferences.

NOTE

In Navigator, select Options ➢ General Preferences and click the Helpers tab in the Preferences dialog box. Select the Launch the Application button in the Action area near the bottom of the dialog box, and then either type the path and file name of the helper application that can display the file type or click the Browse button to hunt around on your hard disk for the program you want. Then click OK.

To set up a plug-in for Navigator, click the puzzle-piece "plug-in required" icon when you see it on a Web page. When the Plugin Not Loaded dialog box appears, click Get the Plugin. This takes you to Netscape's Plug-in Finder page, where you can download the plug-in you need.

WARNING

Plug-ins installed for Navigator 3 will not automatically work with 4 or 4.5, nor will they be installed as far as Netscape Communicator is concerned. When you download plug-ins, save the setup files in a set-aside "Install" folder. Then, when you upgrade to a new version of Netscape, re-install the plug-ins, directing them to your new browser.

Install the plug-in as instructed. Navigator will do the rest. Navigator can display GIFs, JPEGs, and PNGs in-line (versions before Navigator 4 can't display PNGs), as well as animated GIFs—GIF files that contain multiple frames and instructions on how to show them. Navigator also has a built-in Java interpreter that can be set up to use an almost unlimited number of helper applications. There are already many plug-ins for Navigator on the Net, and more are always on the way.

NOTE

Netscape does not yet automatically download and install plug-ins the way Microsoft Internet Explorer tries to.

Are You Experienced?

Now you can...

- ☑ **work with sound and video files on Web pages**
- ☑ **use plug-ins, add-ins, and helper applications to view, listen to, or play multimedia**
- ☑ **discover the 3-D virtual reality aspects of the Web**
- ☑ **investigate how portable document formats can control online document appearance**
- ☑ **visit Web sites dedicated to research on multimedia and file formats to see what's new**

SKILL 12

PUSH AND THE DESKTOP WEB

- **Defining push technology and Webcasting**
- **Discovering Web content with Microsoft Internet Explorer subscriptions**
- **Tuning in to the Web with PointCast and Microsoft Active Channels**
- **Establishing an Active Desktop in Windows**

This lesson could also be called "pushin' the desktop Web," since it's not entirely clear that the world is crying out for *push*, live desktops, or Web/desktop integration, but the newest generation of Web browsers incorporates all of these things.

At first, it's not even clear why content "pushed" or Webcast to your computer has anything to do with a live or active desktop. The connection is that the people behind these new technologies (or rather, old technologies in a new form) would like to have access to your desktop. The integration of the Web browser with the day-to-day computer desktop will permit the establishment of little Web windows on your screen, showing HTML (Web document) content, news ticker tapes, Java applications, dynamic HTML (shifting content), and so on.

One potential advantage of this emerging technology is the time you could save by having a Webcasting program automatically access your favorite Web sites and store them on your hard drive for you. Instead of dozing off in front of your computer as Web pages load at glacial speed, you can be off doing something else, returning later to peruse the latest update in real time rather than "Web time."

But first, let's go back to this latest of hype metaphors, *push*.

The Push Metaphor

First of all, "push" is a synonym for "Webcasting." Both terms refer to media content that appears to be "broadcast" from a Web site to the user's desktop or browser window. I say the content appears to be broadcast because it is generally downloaded ahead of time and then displayed when needed, and the user needs to preselect the "channels" she wishes to see in this medium so that up-to-date content is available on demand.

The first example of push broadcasting to become popular on the Internet was PointCast (mentioned in Skill 8, *Navigating the Web*). The latest version of PointCast (version 2.5) incorporates up-to-date features competitive with the newest offering from Microsoft, Internet Explorer's Active Channels.

The ultimate motivation behind the push hype is to find a way to make money on the Internet, which is the goal of most business people setting up shop online. One potentially successful model everyone is trying to recreate is based on TV programming and advertising. The content is free, paid for by a steady stream of advertisements. This method works best when the viewer is passive (a couch or mouse potato). It may turn out that the Web is too interactive for TV-type projects to work. The conventional Web browsing situation is frustrating to aspiring Web media moguls because the Web audience is still very independent, quirky, and unpredictable. On the Web, people don't always sit still for "a message from our sponsors." Nevertheless, many companies have flocked to the Web to try and tap into its large following of prospective consumers.

This urge to beam information to a passive audience is converging as technology advances. The latest Web applications have streamlined conventional Internet tasks. Browser technology seems to be headed toward total automation of Internet access, searching, and downloading functions. Ultimately all this is expected to lead to the development of intelligent agents that can be "wound up" and sent off to go browse the Internet and report back, all without direct supervision. Still, that world of intelligent agents is a ways off. Under the fancy interfaces, the push model is still closer to that of announcement mailing lists (where you subscribe to the list and receive content updates, which you direct your software to check for periodically). These mailing lists are described in Skill 7, *Signing Up for Mailing Lists*.

For the most part, the content being pushed to you (remember, only things you specifically request or subscribe to will come) will still be Web content, although the standards are evolving toward something called dynamic HTML, which will permit more fluid content changes. Some of the push technologies are open and permit anyone to develop or view content, whereas others are proprietary. It remains to be seen whether push will be dominated by slick media outfits, like the TV medium it's patterned after, or whether it will permit the same kind of grass-roots ("public access"-style) content development that the Web itself has nurtured.

Push Tools

Undoubtedly, additional push receiver programs will appear on the Web if this model succeeds. (The tools used to develop channels and content are experimental and difficult to use at present.) At the moment there are two major tools out there: PointCast, and Microsoft Internet Explorer with its Active Channels push feature.

Microsoft Internet Explorer

Internet Explorer 3 has no push component, but Internet Explorer 4 provides push content through its Favorites ➢ Subscriptions feature and its Active Channels. As with Netscape's What's New feature (the command found on a menu in the Bookmarks window—not the lame "best of the Net" pages at the Netscape Web site), Microsoft Internet Explorer 4's new Smart Favorites feature notifies you when one of your favorite sites has changed. When a site is updated, the favorite item will appear on the menu with a red "gleam" (after your browser has had a chance to check your favorites).

NOTE NOTE NOTE NOTE NOTE NOTE NOTE NOTE NOTE NOTE NOTE NOTE NOTE NOTE NOTE

Favorites will also appear on your Start menu if you install the ambitious Shell Extensions portion of Internet Explorer (for Windows users only).

To further automate and "pushify" this process, Internet Explorer provides a new feature called Subscriptions. Ostensibly, Subscriptions are used to automatically download Web content (on a regular, scheduled basis, or when a targeted site changes) for later off-line browsing. The same feature, however, can also be used to subscribe to special "channels" that provide push content that conforms to an open standard (that is, it can be provided by Microsoft software, PointCast content-creation tools, or other third-party products).

The shell-integration module of Internet Explorer provides the slickest push vehicle, the Active Desktop (which I'll discuss in the last section of this lesson).

Microsoft Active Channels

Internet Explorer 4's most TV-like feature is the Channel Bar, which appears on your desktop when you have the Active Desktop feature in play. Each block on the Channel Bar leads to a content provider, such as Warner Brothers, Disney, or MSNBC, or to a content category, such as News & Technology or Lifestyle & Travel. Inside the categories are additional content providers. For example, the News & Technology category has channels for c|net, ZDNet (the online home of the Ziff-Davis family of computer magazines), the New York Times, and other Web sites of interest.

Previewing and Subscribing to Active Channels

You can use the Internet Explorer Channel Bar and the Active Channel Viewer to get a sneak peak at channels before subscribing to them. Then you can decide whether to subscribe to them, and if you do, you can add them to your subscription list. Here's how to do it:

1. Click on any channel to open the Active Channel Viewer (see Figure 12.1), which connects to the Web to find the site you selected in the Channel Bar. If you click on one of the categories, the Viewer displays the channels for that category. Click on one of the channels in the Viewer to get to that site.

TIP

You can also display the Viewer and learn more about it by clicking the View Channels button (the one that looks like a satellite dish) in the taskbar near the Start button. You will see the Active Channel Viewer window and a short guide to this feature, as shown in Figure 12.1.

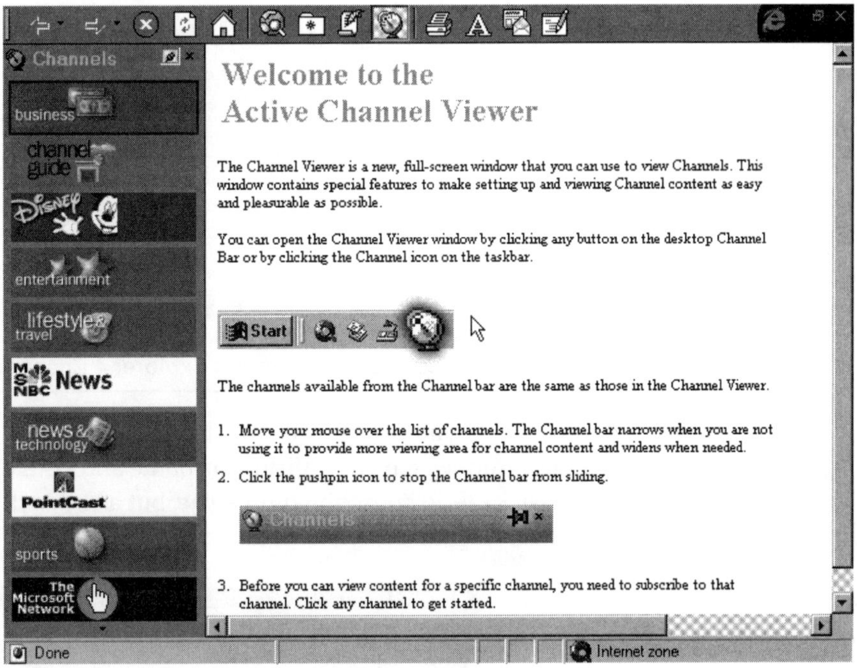

FIGURE 12.1: The Active Channel viewer window in Microsoft Internet Explorer

2. If you would like to get a preview of the listed channels before subscribing, click the Channel Guide in the Channel Bar. Internet Explorer 4 will connect to the Internet and take you to the site corresponding to that channel. You will see an online presentation about the site and then you can decide if you would like to be a subscriber. The Channel Guide window is shown in Figure 12.2.

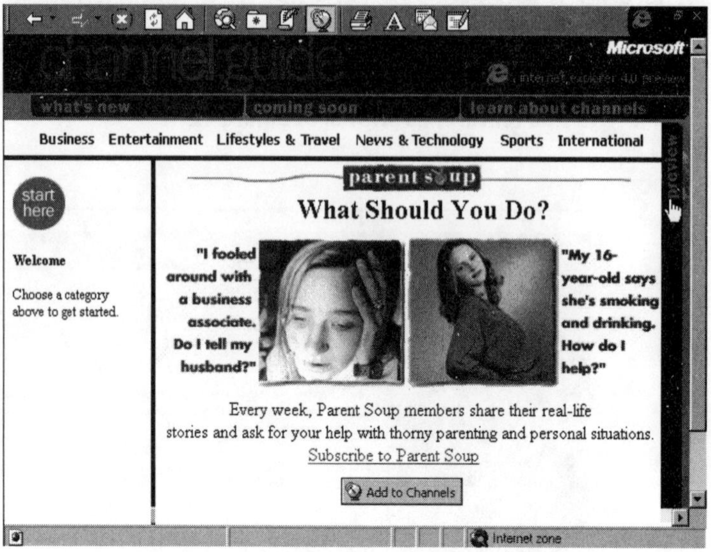

FIGURE 12.2: The Microsoft Internet Explorer 4 Channel Guide Window

3. If you like what you see, click the Add to Channels button. You will see the Subscribe window, which confirms the name and URL of your subscription. You can click OK to subscribe right away, but a better choice would be to choose the Customize button, as described next.

Subscribing with the Channel Subscription Wizard

If you do want to customize your channel subscription by specifying how often your Web site is updated and how much of the site is downloaded to your hard drive, use these steps:

1. Click the Customize button, which leads to the first screen of the Channel Subscription Wizard, which guides you through the subscription process. The first question the Wizard asks is whether you would like to make this channel into a screen saver. Select Yes to add it to the Channel Screen Saver feature, or No to leave it out, and then click the Next button.
2. The next Wizard screen is important, because it asks how you wish to be alerted to changes in your channel. Internet Explorer will add a red star to the channel's icon in the Favorites ➢ Channels list, but you can also be notified by e-mail. If you click Yes, the Change Address button becomes active. Click that button if you want to be notified at an address other than the one the Wizard has. Click the Next button to move on.
3. The next Wizard screen asks how you want the channel to be updated. Your options are AutoSchedule, Custom Schedule, or Manually. Choose one of these options:
   - **AutoSchedule** is fine if you are connected to a network, but if you are using a modem, you might like the options in Custom Schedule.
   - If you select the **Manually** option, your channels will be updated only when you select Favorites ➢ Subscriptions ➢ Update All.
   - Choose **Custom Schedule** to specify an exact time interval for when you want updates to occur.
4. If you select Custom Schedule, click the Next button. Otherwise click the Finish button and then click OK.
5. When you choose Custom Schedule in the Wizard screen and click the Next button, the schedule window appears. Your choices are Daily, Weekly, or Monthly for updates, but you can click the New or Edit button to further refine these intervals. If your channel is quite active, you will probably want daily updates, while a site with less going on could be updated less frequently. Click the Finish button, then click OK to complete the subscription.

Internet Explorer adds the channel to your list immediately, then transports you to a special channel page for that Web site. These channel pages can be fairly complex, with many linking pages, so be sure that you have adequate space on your hard drive for them, as described in the next section, "Changing Active Channel Settings." Your channel will not actually be downloaded to your hard drive until its scheduled time (set during the subscription process).

You will see your new subscription in the Favorites ➢ Channels list. When you point to the channel, its subpages appear in a submenu. If you point to a channel in the Favorites list that you haven't subscribed to, you will not see any subpages listed.

TIP TIP TIP TIP TIP TIP TIP TIP TIP TIP TIP TIP TIP TIP TIP TIP TIP TIP TIP TIP TIP TIP TIP TIP TIP TIP

To delete a subscription, select Favorites ➢ Subscriptions ➢ Manage Subscriptions. In the Subscriptions window, highlight the channel to be deleted and press the Delete key, or right-click on the channel and select Delete from the shortcut menu. You can find out more information about your channels in the Subscriptions window by selecting View ➢ Details and looking in the Last Update, Next Update, and Size (K) columns.

Changing Active Channel Settings

To change any of the settings you selected in the Channel Subscription Wizard, use these steps:

1. Open the Subscriptions window in Internet Explorer by selecting Favorites ➢ Subscriptions ➢ Manage Subscriptions.
2. Right-click on a channel in the list of channels you subscribe to and select Properties from the shortcut menu.
3. In the Internet Explorer Updates Properties dialog box, click the Receiving tab to change notification procedures, or downloading methods.
4. Click the Advanced button in the Downloading area of the Receiving tab to reach a very important dialog box, Advanced Download Options.
5. In the Preferences area, you can specify a maximum download size in kilobytes (K) per update to avoid crowding your hard drive. Even better, you can screen out certain Web page items to speed up download times (and reduce file sizes) in the Items to Download area. For example, deselecting the Sound and Video checkbox (or leaving it blank) will keep these potentially huge files from being downloaded on your channel. The text and images will still be there. Similarly, leaving the ActiveX Controls and Java Applets box unchecked will save space and time, too, though these files are sometimes needed for certain interactive features on a Web page.

6. Click OK when you are finished with the Advanced options. You can also change the downloading schedule on the Schedule tab.
7. When you are all done, click OK and your channel's properties will be changed.

PointCast

You can download the latest version of PointCast from `http://www.pointcast.com/`. The setup is painfully easy (everything is explained carefully and it's difficult to go wrong). You can always change your configuration later too.

PointCast can be set to update its information according to a schedule and you can also update any particular channel of information by selecting it. (PointCast uses the open standard that Microsoft is promoting, so you can see channels designed for Internet Explorer 4.)

A new feature in PointCast 2.5 is the news ticker (a digital ticker tape) that appears at the bottom of the screen and contains headlines for breaking news stories (see Figure 12.3). Click the small weird icon (3 lines in a black and white box) in the upper-left corner of the ticker and choose Hide Ticker if you don't want it there.

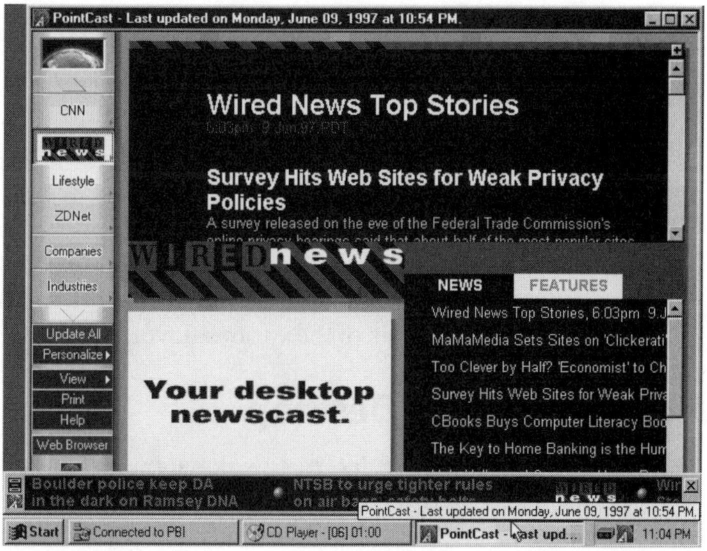

FIGURE 12.3: PointCast is friendly and easy to use.

PointCast is still perhaps most popular in its screensaver mode, where it takes control of your screen when you leave your computer idle for a while and cycles through its current batch of headlines (and ads), whether you watch or not.

Will the Browser Take Over the Desktop?

"Convergence" is a favorite buzzword you'll hear on the lips of cyberpundits and telecommunications magnates. It usually translates into the merging of existing media formats or the formation of corporate monopolies. You get the Internet over your TV, television shows on your computer screen, e-mail in your microwave, etc. Currently, the personal computer world is attempting a convergence baby step: merging the desktop and the Web. What does this mean? Right now you look at the Web through your Web browser, which appears as a window on your desktop. So what's the big deal?

People who work on computer interfaces think that the Web-browser interface is proving easier and more intuitive than the famous, Macintosh-popularized, graphical user interface (folders, windows, lots of double-clicking). If that's so, they reasoned, then perhaps the computer desktop should look like a Web site, and you should be able to browse it by clicking on hyperlinks. Also, maybe it shouldn't make a difference if you're looking at your local disks (through the desktop or the browser) or a remote Web site (again through the desktop or the browser). As usual, the problem is that corporate jockeying begets lots of competing, inconsistent approaches.

For instance, Microsoft is merging its Windows 95 Explorer interface and its Internet Explorer 4 interface (making it possible to put Web pages on your desktop); while Netscape is inviting you to browse your computer from within their suite of programs, making it possible to overlay Webtops on top of your operating system's desktop, whether it be Windows 90-something, the MacOS or whatever comes next, or one of the various flavors of Unix.

Microsoft's Active Desktop

If you install Microsoft Internet Explorer 4 with its Shell Extension, then you're getting a taste of what convergence is all about. The Explorer is reconfigured to look more like, to function more like, and actually to become a part of Internet Explorer (or vice versa). Icons now have blue underlined titles and single-clicking opens or launches documents (this can take some getting used to). Additionally, it's very easy now to place a Web document on your desktop. Just right-click on a blank portion of the desktop, choose Properties, and then click the new Web tab in your Display Properties dialog box. There you can customize what (if any) Web documents appear on your desktop.

TIP TIP TIP TIP TIP TIP TIP TIP TIP TIP TIP TIP TIP TIP TIP TIP TIP TIP TIP TIP TIP TIP TIP TIP TIP

To turn off the Active Desktop and to suspend display of pushed or other Web browser content on your desktop, just right-click on the desktop, select Properties, and click the Web tab in the Display Properties dialog box. Then, check the Disable All Web-Related Content in My Desktop box.

Are You Experienced?

Now you can...

- ☑ find interesting push channels on the Web and subscribe to them
- ☑ use channel bars and drawers to manage your subscriptions
- ☑ use preview features to evaluate content before subscribing
- ☑ specify schedules for updating channels
- ☑ conserve hard disk space by limiting the size of scheduled channel downloads
- ☑ set up your subscription to notify you immediately when content changes
- ☑ load active channels onto your desktop for continuous updates

PART IV

Conducting Group Discussions

The Internet can be a solitary place, and it may feel slightly unreal as you skim from Web site to Web site. For many people, though, the whole focus of the Internet is interaction with other people, and there are numerous ways (in addition to mailing lists) to participate in and even initiate group discussions.

Skill 13 explains the vast Usenet newsgroup system, a network of electronic bulletin boards with continuing discussions on almost any topic of interest. Skill 14 deals with a more immediate form of communication, chat (or IRC). Skill 15 covers the more collegial, collaborative forms of live group discussion, using conferencing software on the Internet or on more private intranets.

SKILL 13

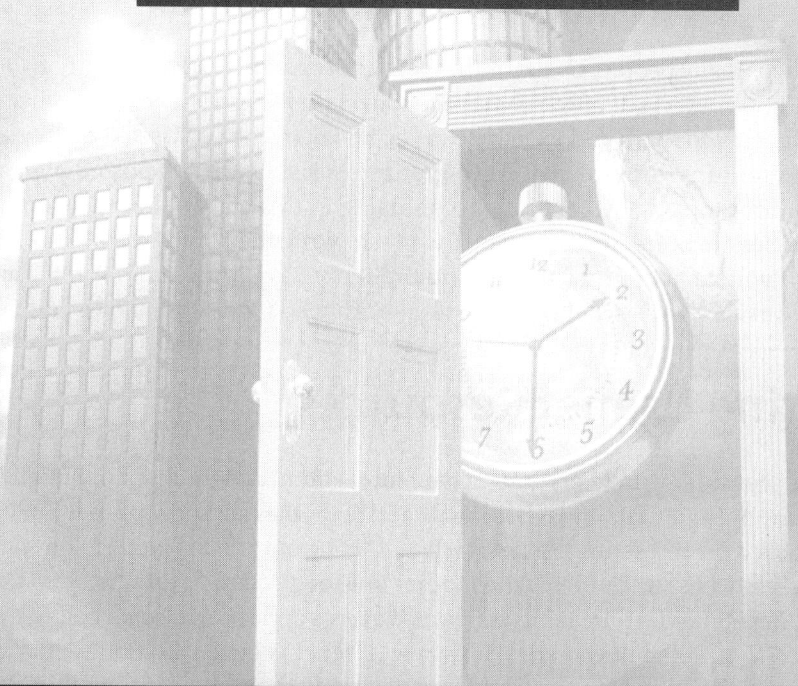

JOINING USENET NEWSGROUPS

- **Understanding Usenet newsgroups**
- **Preparing your newsreader**
- **Reading and replying to articles**
- **Posting and crossposting**
- **Filtering out bozos**
- **Reading news with online services**
- **Reading news with Microsoft Outlook Express, Netscape Messenger, NewsWatcher, and News Xpress**

For many people, Usenet *is* the Net. *Usenet* is a network of other networks, BBSs, and computers, all of which have made bilateral agreements with other members of Usenet to share and exchange news. So what's news? Usenet is divided up into newsgroups (topic areas). Newsgroups consist of articles posted by readers and contributors. The word *news* is confusing in this context because Usenet news articles are posted by whomever wants to write them, not by a staff of reporters.

If you have Internet access, you probably have access to Usenet. This lesson discusses what Usenet is and how you can read (and write) news yourself.

Discovering Usenet Resources

As soon as I log in to my Internet account, I immediately check my mail. After that, I compulsively run my newsreader and skim the newsgroups that I'm currently hooked on. In a sense, Usenet is where I "hang out" on the Net. I'm on some mailing lists as well, but Usenet is the mother lode of discussion groups.

Sometimes fast-breaking real-world events appear on Usenet before they appear on TV or in the newspaper; however, Usenet is generally not the information source "of record" in the way some newspapers are. Look for tabloid-style gossip in `talk.rumors` or among the `alt.fan` groups (such as the tasteless `alt.fan.oj.drive-faster` group created during the high-profile murder trial of the former football star).

People post about what they find interesting; however, if you post to a newsgroup looking for information, you might be told to "go to a library" to look it up for yourself. Every newsgroup sees its share of posts that begin with something like "I'm writing a high-school paper on …" and end with "… please reply to me by private e-mail, since I don't read this group."

WARNING

It's been said that the fastest way to get information on Usenet is to post incorrect information because people will immediately post to correct you or flood your e-mail Inbox with the correct information. I don't recommend this. People out there skimming the newsgroups might see only your erroneous post and none of the corrections, but this gives you an idea of the culture of Usenet.

On the other hand, there are plenty of *wizards* out there who believe there's no such thing as a dumb question and who are willing to share their knowledge with anyone who asks.

Some Newsgroups Are Mailing Lists, Too

Some Usenet newsgroups, particularly those that evolved from mailing lists, maintain a gateway with a list, so that all posts to the newsgroup or the list are shared between both. Even if you don't have Usenet access, you should still be able to join lists that share posts with Usenet newsgroups. See Skill 7, *Signing Up for Mailing Lists,* for more on lists, and later in this lesson I'll explain how to post to Usenet through e-mail.

One Way Not to Look Like a Newbie

Not that there's anything wrong with looking like a newbie, but here's one way not to give yourself away (besides not confusing Usenet and the Internet): Call a newsgroup a newsgroup. Don't call it a forum, a board , a bboard, a SIG, an echo, a file, a conference, a list (well, except for the ones that are also lists), an America Online folder, or a Prodigy folder.

On the other hand, who cares if you do, besides Usenet snobs?

Where Everybody Knows Your Signature

Usenet has been called the biggest bulletin board in the world. It can be more entertaining than television (hard to imagine?). I think of it as an enormous magazine rack, filled with magazines, each of which has infinitely long letters-to-the-editor pages and no articles.

WARNING WARNING WARNING WARNING WARNING WARNING WARNING WARNING

Usenet is also an anarchy—with rules. Nobody reigns from above, but the entire community is knit together through customs, traditions, and netiquette. More and more, this culture is coming under attack, most recently by greedy advertisers who deliberately misinterpret the acceptable use of the medium. If you are interested in Usenet, take some time to familiarize yourself with the existing culture so that you can become a net.citizen (or netizen) and not one of the net.barbarians beating down the gates.

Usenet has also been referred to as a huge writing project, and enthusiasts claim that we are now involved in a renaissance of the written word, as a direct result of e-mail and Usenet communication.

Fundamentally, Usenet is a way to share information. Many newsgroups that are technically not part of the Usenet hierarchy flow through the same servers (computers that store and share news) and are passed along as part of the newsfeed (electronic mail pouch, often just referred to as the *feed*) from computer to computer not unlike other long-distance carriers traveling on AT&T wires.

Your provider is not obliged to supply you with a full newsfeed. Many networks carry an incomplete feed, usually more because of disk-storage limitations than corporate censorship, though some of the more controversial `alt` groups certainly experience a limited distribution because of their topics. Many system administrators refuse to carry *binaries*, which generally contain huge posts, each post part of a large *binary file* (a program, image, or other special-format file—as opposed to a text file). This refusal is as much because of the enormous storage requirements as because of the pornographic nature of some of those files.

Most providers do carry all of the newsgroups in the Usenet hierarchy proper, as there are complicated plebiscite mechanisms in place to limit the proliferation of new newsgroups. In the `alt` hierarchy, however, pranksters create joke newsgroups every week, some of which are probably carried only by those providers that carry everything. Though these groups may wither on the vine from disuse, old `alt` groups never die.

What Is a Newsgroup?

So what exactly is a newsgroup? A newsgroup is an area for posting articles on a given topic. The topic names are arranged hierarchically, which means everything branches off from the main hierarchies the same way that files are associated with directories in a directory tree, or with subfolders and folders (a familiar image to Mac users who work in the Finder and Windows users who work in File Manager or Explorer). This hierarchical organization helps people look for and find newsgroups of interest in a systematic way. This means, for example, that there's no newsgroup called `nintendo`, nor is there one called `rec.nintendo`, but there is one called `rec.games.nintendo`.

There are seven official Usenet hierarchies: `comp`, `misc`, `news`, `rec`, `sci`, `soc`, and `talk`, and numerous "unofficial" ones (some of which are listed in Table 13.1).

TABLE 13.1: Newsgroup Hierarchies

Newsgroup Hierarchy	Meaning
comp	Computers—from the extremely technical, to help for beginners, to geek wars between Mac enthusiasts and Amiga diehards
misc	Miscellaneous—anything that doesn't fit into the other hierarchies
news	News—information about Usenet itself, discussion of new newsgroups, advice for Usenet
rec	Recreation—games, sports, music, entertainment, etc.
sci	Science—discussions of research, developments, techniques, policy
soc	Social—both in the sense of socializing and in the sense of talking about society
talk	Talk—some think this hierarchy should be called "argue"; these newsgroups house some of the eternally polarized debates, such as those on gun control and abortion
alt	Alternative—topics that don't fit into the mainstream newsgroups
bitnet	Bitnet listservs—for newsgroups gated to bitnet listservs
bionet	Biologists and biology
biz	Business—advertising explicitly acceptable
gnu	Free Software Project
k12	Education—grade-school students, teachers, parents, etc.
local hierarchies	Geographical regions—examples include, ca for California, uk for United Kingdom, and de for Germany (Deutschland)

why.group.names.look.weird

Newsgroup names are in the form of two or more words or abbreviations, separated by periods. Figure 13.1 shows the start of the full list of newsgroups that you can subscribe to and a window with the group that my friend Nick subscribes to. The other window shows what new newsgroups have been created since Nick last logged in.

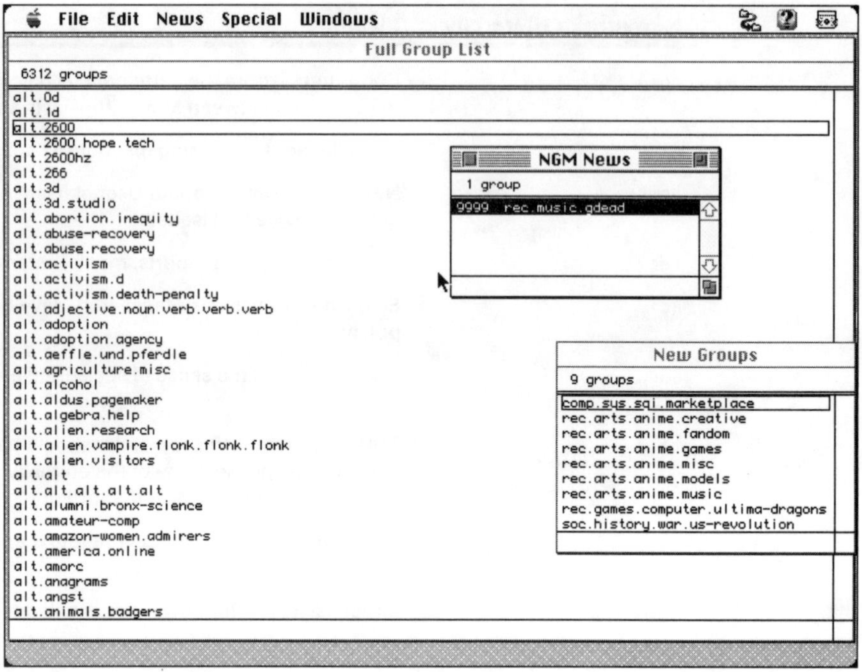

FIGURE 13.1: My friend Nick (who captured this screen for me) subscribes to this group, which focuses on the music of a band still popular despite the loss of its key performer. (What's shown is a window in the Mac NewsWatcher program.) Notice how the newsgroups' names provide a way to organize the groups into hierarchies.

NOTE NOTE NOTE NOTE NOTE NOTE NOTE NOTE NOTE NOTE NOTE NOTE NOTE NOTE NOTE

So how do you pronounce these names? Remember, you pronounce a period as "dot," so that `comp.sys.mac.games` **is pronounced "comp-dot-sys-dot-mac-dot-games." While that's the traditional pronunciation, many people drop the "dots"; for instance, they would pronounce that newsgroup's name "comp-sys-mac-games." Regulars in a newsgroup often refer to the group by its initials—"c.s.m.g" or "csmg" or "CSMG," for example.** Soc**—one of the seven major newsgroup hierarchies—can be pronounced "soak" or "soash."**

The words between the dots correspond to directories on the machines (usually Unix computers) that store the Usenet postings. If more than one word is needed to describe something, the two words are joined by hyphens, not periods. There can be at most fifteen characters between two periods.

Newsgroup Names Are Not Always Obvious

Unfortunately, the hierarchical system does not always help you find the newsgroup you're looking for. For instance, the jazz newsgroup is called `rec.music.bluenote`—look for the perennial "rap is not music" flame war there. Likewise, you'd never know that the newsgroup `alt.fan.warlord` is devoted to reposting and spoofing monstrous signatures from other Usenet newsgroups, especially those with ASCII art such as enormous swords, crude Bart Simpsons, and maps of Australia with Perth pointed out on them. (Read that newsgroup to find out what "tab damage" is.) Sometimes you have to ask around a bit.

Especially in the `alt` hierarchy, sometimes two or more newsgroups will cover the same topics but have slightly different names. There's `alt.coffee`, `alt.food.coffee`, and `alt.drugs.caffeine`. (Newsgroup purists hate to see a specific word like coffee as a first-level hierarchical distinction, but coffee lovers know that coffee is a basic element of life, like music or sex.) A similar debate surrounded the formation of the newsgroups named `alt.philosophy.zen`, `alt.religion.zen`, and `alt.zen`.

What Kinds of Groups Are Out There?

This is just a brief sampling of the sorts of topics that are discussed on Usenet. There are over 20,000 newsgroups, and more are created all the time.

There are newsgroups on art, entertainment, writing, just about every hobby you can imagine, games, sports, sex, politics, pets, science, school, computers, television shows, music, theater, cooking, want ads, religion, net.personalities, and so on.

Because most of the original Usenet readers were scientists, researchers, or computer programmers, the range of topics available on Usenet is still skewed toward techie interests, even among recreational topics. There are at least seven newsgroups devoted to some aspect of Star Trek, including one called `alt.sex.fetish.startrek`. The `misc.writing` newsgroup leans heavily toward science fiction and fantasy writing. And, of course, there are entire hierarchies devoted to computers and science.

If you can't find a newsgroup on the specific topic you're interested in, look for a more general newsgroup whose topic would include yours. Then post to that group about the subject you're interested in. Someone may point you toward a mailing list. Or you'll start a series of threads about your subject. If the interest is high enough, you can look into creating a splinter newsgroup for your particular interest. There is a long-standing procedure for broaching this topic on the Net. You start with a *request for discussion*—of course, there's an acronym for that too, *RFD*—and work up to a *call for votes* (*CFV*).

What Is an Article?

An article, also called a post, is a message sent to a newsgroup. Posts are very similar to e-mail messages, although the header information at the top is different. An article can be posted apropos of nothing or as a reply to a previous post. A series of articles and replies is called a *thread*.

Eventually articles expire, meaning they are deleted from the directory in which they are stored. The expiration date governing how long articles survive after they are posted varies from site to site. On my system, articles expire after two weeks. When you start reading a newsgroup for the first time, your newsreader program might tell you that it's "skipping unavailable articles" or something like that. This means that some of the posted articles have expired, at least at the point where you are accessing them.

You can also cancel your own articles after you post them (though you can't cancel anyone else's). This won't prevent some people from seeing the canceled article in the meantime, because some machines will already have propagated it beyond your network's server. Eventually, it will disappear from cyberspace, but the cancel message has to follow the thread of the original post.

Common Acronyms

Inevitably, as you start reading Usenet newsgroups, you'll notice certain acronyms showing up in posts. Most of these have come about as a way to save typing, although others were invented as jokes or to sow confusion. Some are used as disclaimers. You'll often see *IMHO* (*in my humble opinion*) attached to comments that are anything but. I'm waiting for *IMOO* (*in my obsequious opinion*) and *IMUO* (*in my unctuous opinion*) and a host of others, but I haven't seen them yet. Table 13.2 contains a brief and arbitrary listing of some common acronyms.

TABLE 13.2: Common Acronyms

Acronym	What It Stands For
BTW	By the way
FAQ	Frequently asked questions
FOAF	Friend of a friend
FQA	Frequently questioned acronyms
FUQ	Frequently unanswered questions
FWIW	For what it's worth
IMO	In my opinion
IMHO	In my humble opinion
IMNSHO	In my not-so-humble opinion
LOL	Laughing out loud
MOTAS	Member of the appropriate sex
MOTOS	Member of the opposite sex
MOTSS	Member of the same sex
ROTFL	Rolling on the floor laughing
SO	Significant other
UL	Urban legend
WRT	With respect to
YMMV	Your mileage may vary

What Is a Newsreader?

A *newsreader* is a program you run to read Usenet news. With any newsreader you can:

- See which newsgroups are available
- Subscribe to newsgroups
- Read articles in a newsgroup
- Post articles to a newsgroup

There are many popular newsreader programs. Later in this lesson I'll explain basic newsreading principles and then explain the details of using a couple of the more popular newsreaders. I'll also show you how to use a Web browser as a newsreader.

TIP TIP TIP TIP TIP TIP TIP TIP TIP TIP TIP TIP TIP TIP TIP TIP TIP TIP TIP TIP TIP TIP TIP TIP TIP

Remember when you're reading Usenet that not everyone else is seeing the exact same things that you are seeing. Other readers may be getting their feed more slowly or their articles in a different order. They may be reading a newsreader with a different number of characters per line or with different keyboard shortcuts from yours. Try not to jump to conclusions about your audience's environment (for example, telling someone to "click the Next button if you don't like what I'm saying" is meaningless for people using newsreaders that don't have that button).

Conducting Yourself in a Usenet Public Forum

While not completely public, Usenet is essentially a public forum, and you should view anything you post in the same way you would view being published. Your words may be noted or ignored by thousands or hundreds of thousands of readers. Anything you write will be available to strangers anywhere in the world. Some people say you should never post anything to the Net that you wouldn't want to see on the front page of a newspaper.

WARNING WARNING WARNING WARNING WARNING WARNING WARNING WARNING

For the same reason, you probably should not put your telephone number in your signature file or in your posts in general. While strangers still might be able to figure out your phone number if you give your name and address, or by tracking down your account or looking you up in the membership directory of your online service, at least you will not seem to be inviting people to call.

Semi-anonymity on the Net

You will never see the vast majority of people whose posts you read on the Net, which creates a veil of semi-anonymity. Because of this, people fly off the handle more easily, misunderstandings proliferate, and people simply behave in ways that would be much more difficult, if not impossible, in face-to-face encounters.

Some of the users you have contact with may be quite young and not used to conducting themselves in adult society. Bear that in mind and try to ignore the occasional vicious, unprovoked attack.

NOTE NOTE NOTE NOTE NOTE NOTE NOTE NOTE NOTE NOTE NOTE NOTE NOTE NOTE NOTE

This semi-anonymity I speak of should not be confused with true anonymity, which can be used to disguise the origins of a post or e-mail message.

Unfortunately, this same semi-anonymity makes it possible for losers to harass females (or anyone with a female-sounding name) on the Net. For this reason, some women may prefer to use a genderless login instead of their real name when posting.

TIP TIP TIP TIP TIP TIP TIP TIP TIP TIP TIP TIP TIP TIP TIP TIP TIP TIP TIP TIP TIP TIP TIP TIP TIP

If you want to truly protect your privacy while still being able to post to Usenet groups, consider obtaining a second e-mail/Internet account with an independent vendor. You can assign a pseudonym to this account instead of your real name, and no one reading your posts will be able to tell where you work, as is often the case when you use your work-related e-mail address. People often rent post office boxes for the same reason.

How People Identify You on Usenet

There are three ways people can identify you on Usenet. The first is by your e-mail address, or at least the login part of it before the @ sign. The second is by your real name, which will appear in the author column of the article listing in a newsreader (although some put the e-mail address there). Third, people will see your signature file, if you have one, attached to the end of your posts.

Be a Good Netizen

Try to get yourself up to speed before you start contributing to Usenet. Read the newsgroups you're interested in for a while to get caught up and avoid posting something that's been repeated so often it's become nearly a mantra in that group.

Also, read the newsgroup's FAQ before jumping in. One of the purposes of a frequently-asked-questions list is to save people the trouble of answering the same few questions over and over to the end of time. A newsgroup's FAQ will be posted to the newsgroup on a regular basis, anywhere from every two weeks to every two months. FAQs are built and maintained by volunteers, just like every other institutional aspect of Usenet.

Newsreading Basics

Here are the basic things you'll do with any newsreader:

- Prepare the newsreader and set up a reading list
- Start the newsreader
- Select a newsgroup to read
- Select articles to read
- Browse the articles:
    - Read articles
    - Save articles
- Respond to articles
- Start a new thread
- Quit the newsreader
- Get help when you need it

Also, you'll want to know a few more advanced features, such as how to *cross-post* (post an article to more than one newsgroup at a time), and how to filter out bozos (although not all newsreaders can do this for you).

TIP TIP TIP TIP TIP TIP TIP TIP TIP TIP TIP TIP TIP TIP TIP TIP TIP TIP TIP TIP TIP TIP TIP TIP TIP

You can also search Usenet newsgroups with some Web search engines, such as DejaNews, as explained in Skill 10, *Finding Stuff on the Web and the Net*. Another Web site you can use to search Usenet is called the NetNews Overview Index at `http://harvest.cs.colorado.edu/Harvest/brokers/Usenet/query.html`.

Preparing the Newsreader

Before your newsreader can pick up and sort out new articles for you, it has to know where to look. This means you have to do a little setup on your newsreader, which is somewhat analogous to the sort of information you put into a mail program so it knows where to look. There are two categories of information you have to supply: the name of the news server you have access to, and your identity.

Obviously, you can't be expected to know the name of the news server off the top of your head. Your provider will have to supply it for you (and probably did in your original information package). In some cases, such as with online services, you don't have to do this, as all the appropriate information is automatically supplied. As for your identity, this is exactly the same information that was needed by your e-mail program: you supply your "real name," your e-mail address, and the address of the mail server that handles your outgoing mail so you have the option of replying directly (by e-mail) to the poster of a newsgroup post. You can look this information up in the Preferences or Options dialog box of your e-mail program. (See Skill 4, *E-mail Basics,* for more about setting up and using mail programs.)

Also, the first time you run your newsreader, it doesn't know what you want to read about. Fly fishing or macrobiotic cooking? Urban legends or international conspiracies? So you're stuck with a massive all-or-nothing problem. Some newsreaders start you off with a subscription to every single newsgroup, leaving it up to you to unsubscribe from the ones you don't want to read.

NOTE NOTE NOTE NOTE NOTE NOTE NOTE NOTE NOTE NOTE NOTE NOTE NOTE NOTE NOTE

The process of subscribing to or unsubscribing from newsgroups is instantaneous and completely reversible. Your list of newsgroups will most likely shrink and grow with your changing interests. You'll realize that you never read certain groups and will most likely unsubscribe from them. You'll hear about new ones, or go looking for ones on a new subject, and add them.

Other newsreaders start you off without subscribing you to any newsgroups. You then browse through a list and add the newsgroups that interest you. I think this is the better approach. If a newsreader starts you off with no groups, you'll be asked if you want to download an up-to-date list of groups. Say yes, but then go have lunch or something, because it will take a while. When the list is complete, you can usually search for and subscribe to groups by entering keywords to find the groups you want.

TIP TIP TIP TIP TIP TIP TIP TIP TIP TIP TIP TIP TIP TIP TIP TIP TIP TIP TIP TIP TIP TIP TIP TIP TIP

In newsreaders that subscribe you to every group automatically, you're best off finding the `.newsrc` file (or whatever it's called in your program) and editing it, changing every colon (indicating a subscribed group) to an exclamation point (indicating an unsubscribed one).

Responding to Articles

There are two ways to reply to someone's post. One way is to post a follow-up article, including some or none of the previous post, and appending your comments. The other way is to send e-mail directly to the poster to discuss the post further. You have to decide whether your follow-up is appropriate for the entire newsgroup (the thousands of invisible readers) or just for the one person whose ideas caught your fancy.

WARNING WARNING WARNING WARNING WARNING WARNING WARNING WARNING

If somebody's post angers you, think twice before dashing off a reply, especially if you intend to post the reply to the entire group. It is easy to take people's writings in a spirit different from the intent of the writer. Most disagreements can be worked out more easily in private e-mail than in gladiatorial contests in front of the rest of the group. Angry, insulting posts are called *flames*.

When you post a response to an article, your post becomes part of the thread of the original article. Usually, you keep the same subject line, although you can edit it if you like. As with replying by e-mail, you also have the choice of including the text of the preceding article or not.

If you include text from the article you're responding to, be sure to trim it down to the minimum amount of text necessary to give the context of your reply. It's just as bad form to quote an entire long message followed by your own short reply as it is to post a reply without any context at all (so that the meaning of your reply is lost).

When replying, some newsreaders will give you a last chance to change your mind and not post. Some will even try to convince you not to, to save the resources of the Net.

TIP TIP TIP TIP TIP TIP TIP TIP TIP TIP TIP TIP TIP TIP TIP TIP TIP TIP TIP TIP TIP TIP TIP TIP TIP

If you're using a newsreader that doesn't handle word-wrapping for you, keep your lines down to 75 characters each (or 80 at the most). Many people, probably including you, can only get 80 characters on the screen at once, and any more will wrap to the next line and look bizarre. I recommend 75 instead of 80 so people can quote you without starting the bad-wrap problem.

When you reply to the author of an article by e-mail, you also have the option, in most newsreaders, to quote the text of the post you're responding to. Your newsreader will then allow you to write and edit an e-mail message as usual, placing you into some sort of text editor. When you are done, exit from the text editor if necessary and then send the response.

> NOTE
>
> **Not everyone's postings point back to their e-mail addresses properly. Sometimes, when you try to reply to a post via e-mail, the message "bounces." If so, it's probably not your fault.**

Ignoring Flamers and Trolls

Arguments that rage on for a while or that become more and more incoherent or ad hominem are called *flame wars*. After you've been on the Net for a while you'll recognize flame wars in the making and learn how to avoid them. They might be entertaining at first, but they follow such regular patterns that they inevitably become boring.

Some people enjoy flaming and causing flame wars, so they post deliberately inflammatory articles designed to incite others. Such posts are called *flame bait*. Often the instigator will drop out of the conversation and watch how long the fire rages on its own. You'll also learn to recognize flame bait after awhile. By then, other newbies will be taking up the gauntlet every time it's thrown down.

A more subtle net.pastime than flame-baiting is called *trolling*. To troll is to deliberately post information so egregiously incorrect that most people will see that it's a joke. However, those with a strong desire to correct people and go on record with the right information will post follow-ups insisting that Bing Crosby and David Crosby are not actually father and son. (Everyone knows that David Crosby's father is Bill Cosby.)

Starting a New Thread

In any newsreader, there will be a separate command for posting a new article without any reference to previous posts. Use this command for starting a new thread, although it may grow no longer than your one post. (Even interesting posts do not always evoke follow-ups or e-mail replies.)

Crossposting

You can post an article to more than one newsgroup—if it is relevant to all of them. This is better than posting the same article more than once, because it will be stored only in one place even though it will be available to all the newsgroups it is posted to.

If you follow up someone else's article, be sure to check which newsgroups your reply is going to and edit the line (or the Follow-up line) if necessary. Look out for pranksters who've directed follow-ups to `*.test` newsgroups. Newsgroups such as `misc.test`, `alt.test`, and so on, exist so that you can test the propagation of articles that you post through your newsreader. If you post to them (on purpose or accidentally), automated Unix programs called *daemons* will send you e-mail verifying that your posts are getting through. Your mailbox can easily overflow as daemons from around the world send you electronic postcards.

NOTE NOTE NOTE NOTE NOTE NOTE NOTE NOTE NOTE NOTE NOTE NOTE NOTE NOTE NOTE

Articles can also have a Follow-up line that specifies different newsgroups from the ones originally posted to.

Killing and Autoselecting

Not all newsreaders allow you to kill or autoselect posts automatically, but the best ones do. The file of automatic commands that gets created when you do this is called a *killfile*, because most people use them to filter out unwanted posts, not to automatically select their favorite topics and authors. Killfiles are sometimes called "bozo filters" because they allow you to filter out some of the bozos who fill newsgroups with their bleatings. Autoselecting is also sometimes called "watching a thread."

Reading News with Specific Newsreaders

The main distinction worth noting between newsreaders is whether they are *threaded* or *unthreaded*. Because they allow you to follow conversations from post to reply to follow-up, threaded newsreaders are better than unthreaded ones. Unthreaded newsreaders don't keep track of which posts are related to which. You have to figure this out from the context of the post or from the quoted text at the beginnings of some of them.

Another distinction is between *offline* newsreaders and *online* newsreaders. Offline newsreaders download all the current articles in all the newsgroups you subscribe to and then log off. You can browse through the downloaded articles at your leisure without running up your phone bill or connect-time charges. Then you can compose articles and replies, and log in again to send your posts. Still, offline newsreaders function more or less the same way online newsreaders do, from your perspective.

You can read news with the programs that come with either of the two major Web browsers (Netscape Messenger or Microsoft Outlook Express), or you can use a stand-alone newsreader. I'll also cover NewsWatcher for the Macintosh and News Xpress for Windows. I'll tell you where to get those programs (they're free!) and I'll also name a couple of others and tell you where to get them so you can choose the right program for you.

Microsoft Outlook Express

Microsoft Internet Explorer comes with a mail and news program called Outlook Express. (See Skill 6, *E-mail Programs*, for a discussion of the e-mail features of Outlook Express.)

Subscribing to Newsgroups with Outlook Express

These are the steps for subscribing to newsgroups in the Windows version of Outlook Express (the steps will be slightly different in the Mac version):

1. Start Outlook Express by double-clicking its icon, by choosing it from the Start menu, or by entering `news:`*`URL`* into the Internet Explorer address box (substituting the address for *URL*, of course).
2. To subscribe to newsgroups, click the Newsgroups button and wait for the entire group list to be displayed in the dialog box that appears.
3. You can type a keyword in the box to limit the groups that are displayed. Then highlight any group you want to subscribe to and click the Subscribe button.
4. Click the Subscribed tab on the dialog box to show just your subscribed groups. Click the Go To button to start reading the selected group or click OK to save the additions to your subscription list.

Reading Newsgroup Articles with Outlook Express

Reading newsgroup articles with the News feature in Outlook Express is easy, and you also have options for following article threads and reviewing articles by looking at their headers.

To read articles with Outlook Express, follow these steps:

1. To select a newsgroup, double-click on its name in the left frame, under the name of your news server (see Figure 13.2).

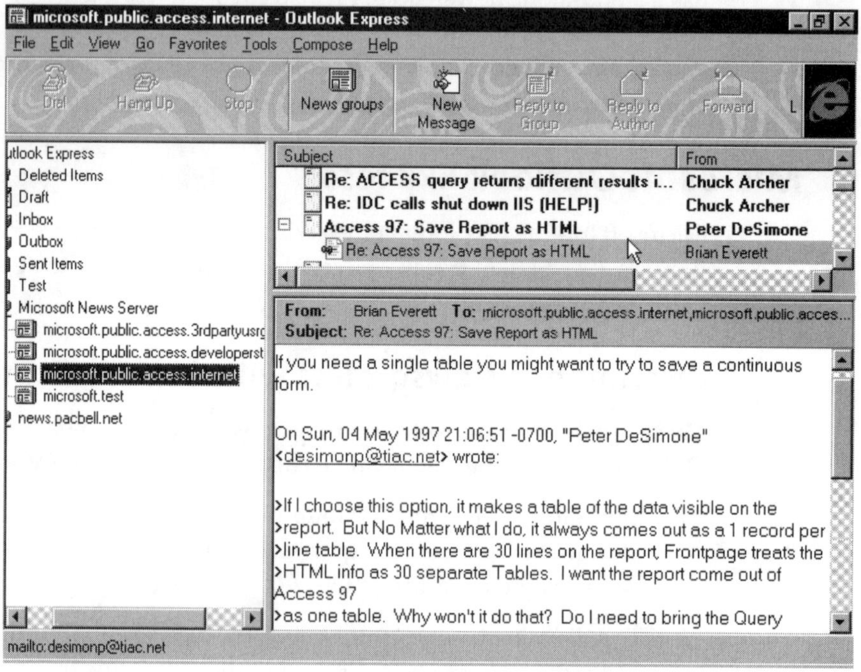

FIGURE 13.2: An article displayed in Outlook Express

2. Articles are threaded (listed by topic), if possible. Threads appear as folder icons. Double-click on a thread title to display all the articles in the thread.
3. To read an article, double-click on its subject. The article will appear in the lower-right frame.
4. To quit Outlook Express, select File ➢ Exit.

Managing Newsgroup Articles with Outlook Express

Outlook Express supplies additional options for managing your newsgroup articles. You can mark articles as unread to save them for later review. You can also respond to articles with e-mail replies to the article's author, replies posted to the entire newsgroup, or new messages (or articles) posted to the group.

Here are some of the things you can do:

- To mark an article as unread, select Edit ➢ Mark as Unread.
- To mark all articles as read, select Edit ➢ Mark All as Read.
- If you want to reply to an article by e-mail, click Reply to Author. Outlook Express will open a new message window addressed to the author of the article. Use these steps to compose the reply:
    1. Click in the message area and type your reply.
    2. Cut as much of the quoted article as possible, retaining enough to preserve context.
    3. When you're done, click the Send button.
- To post a reply to the newsgroup, click the Reply to Group button. Outlook Express will open a new message window, where you can use one or both of these options:
    - To crosspost to more than one newsgroup, type additional newsgroup names, separated by commas, in the Newsgroups box at the top of the window.
    - Type your message (reduce the quoted material as much as possible but leave enough for appropriate context) and then click the Send button.
- When you want to post a new message to the newsgroup, click the New Message button. Outlook Express will open a new message window with the name of the current newsgroup already entered and all the other boxes blank. Here's how to complete the posting:
    1. Type a subject in the Subject box.
    2. Type (or paste from the clipboard with Ctrl+V) your article in the message area.
    3. Click the Send button.

As usual, to quit Outlook Express after any of these options, select File ➢ Exit.

Filtering Newsgroup Articles with Outlook Express

You can filter out messages you don't want to see using Outlook Express's simple Newsgroup Filter feature. You can screen out messages according to size, author, subject, or date sent. Here are the steps for building a filter:

1. Select Tools ➢ Newsgroup Filters.
2. In the Group Filters dialog box, click Add to display the Properties dialog box.
3. Specify the criteria (such as specific authors or subjects) to describe articles you don't want to see.
4. When you are done, click OK and then OK again.

Outlook Express's Help menu has standard Windows-style help as well as links to Microsoft's Web site (for updates, bug fixes, etc.).

NOTE NOTE NOTE NOTE NOTE NOTE NOTE NOTE NOTE NOTE NOTE NOTE NOTE NOTE NOTE

Outlook Express can work as an offline newsreader, but it does not have an autoselect (filtering) feature.

Netscape Messenger

Netscape Communicator includes an all-in-one e-mail and discussion program called Netscape Messenger (which you've already seen in the e-mail skills in this book). I'll explain how to use Netscape Messenger to read Usenet newsgroups in this section.

Netscape Messenger lumps together e-mail, newsgroups, and local discussion groups. You can get into newsgroups by selecting Communicator ➢ Messenger or, if you're already reading mail in Messenger, you can simply choose a news server (instead of the mail server).

Subscribing to Newsgroups with Netscape Messenger

Netscape Messenger supports newsgroup subscription lists and even allows you to search by keyword for new groups to add to your subscription list. Here are the steps:

1. To subscribe to a newsgroup, select File ➢ Subscribe to Discussion Groups.

2. Click the Search for a Group tab to search for a keyword (type it in the Search For box and then click Search Now).
3. Then select any group you want to subscribe to and click the Subscribe button.
4. Click the New Groups tab on the dialog box to show only a list of new groups that you have just subscribed to.
5. Click OK to save the additions to your subscription list.

TIP TIP TIP TIP TIP TIP TIP TIP TIP TIP TIP TIP TIP TIP TIP TIP TIP TIP TIP TIP TIP TIP TIP TIP TIP

If your news server is not yet set up, the Mail & Discussion Groups Wizard dialog box will appear to walk you through the process of setting up a news server.

Reading Newsgroup Articles with Netscape Messenger

Opening Netscape Messenger for reading newsgroup articles and posts is an easy operation. Follow these steps:

1. Start Netscape Communicator by double-clicking its icon or selecting Start ➢ Programs ➢ Netscape ➢ Netscape Communicator.
2. If you are already in a Netscape Communicator component, select Communicator ➢ Messenger or click the Read Newsgroups button on the Component Bar.
3. Double-click on a newsgroup to start reading it in the Message Center window.
4. You can also follow article threads:
   - Article headers will appear in the upper frame (or upper-right frame). Articles are threaded (listed by topic), if possible. Threads appear as folder icons. Click on a thread title to display all the articles in the thread.
   - To read an article, click on its subject. The article will appear in the lower frame (see Figure 13.3).

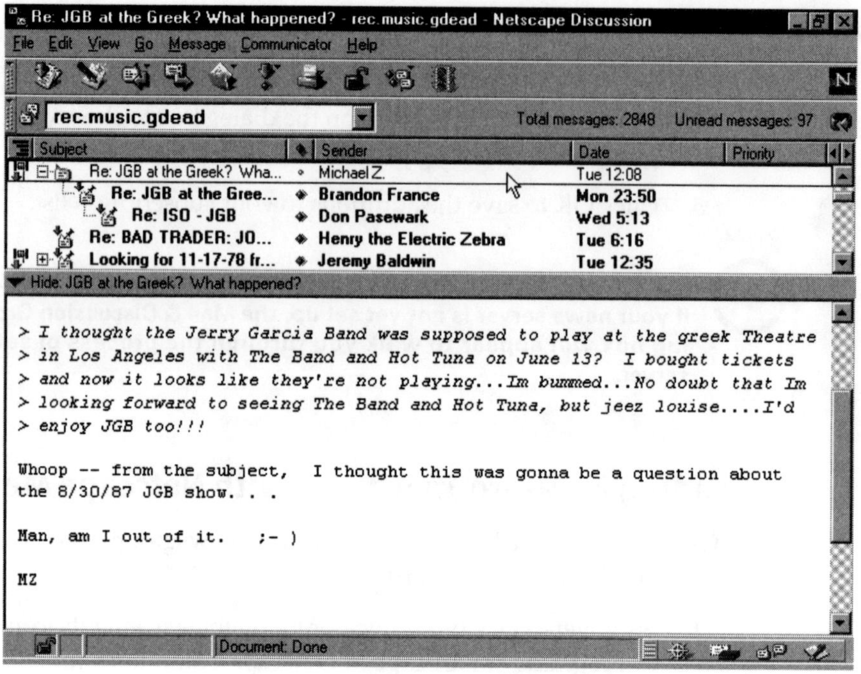

FIGURE 13.3: An article displayed in Netscape Messenger

Managing Newsgroup Articles with Netscape Messenger

Your options for handling newsgroup articles include marking specific articles as unread, saving them for later reading, responding to articles or messages with e-mail, and posting original comments of your own. Here are the details on these options:

- To mark an article as unread, select Message ➢ Mark ➢ As Unread or click the Mark Messages button and select As Unread.
- To mark all articles as read, select Message ➢ Mark ➢ All Read, or click the Mark Messages button and select All Read, or press Shift+C.

- If you want to reply to an article, click the Reply to Message button, and follow these steps:
    1. On the menu that drops down, select the recipient (Sender, Sender and All Recipients, Group, or Sender and the Group). Netscape will open a new message window.
    2. Click in the message area and type your reply. Cut as much of the quoted article as possible, retaining enough to preserve context.
    3. When you're done, click the Send button.

- When you want to post a new message to the newsgroup, click the New Message button (or press Ctrl+N). Netscape will open a new message window with the name of the current newsgroup already entered and all the other boxes blank. Complete the new message as follows:
    1. Type a subject in the Subject box and type your article in the message area.
    2. Then click the Send button.

NOTE NOTE NOTE NOTE NOTE NOTE NOTE NOTE NOTE NOTE NOTE NOTE NOTE NOTE NOTE

Netscape Messenger can also function as an offline newsreader.

NewsWatcher

NewsWatcher

NewsWatcher is the most popular Macintosh newsreader. You can download it (for free) from `ftp://ftp.acns.nwu.edu/pub/newswatcher/`. NewsWatcher may be shipped to you as a compressed file; double-click the icon you receive to unpack it. When it is ready to run, it will look like the icon shown here.

NOTE NOTE NOTE NOTE NOTE NOTE NOTE NOTE NOTE NOTE NOTE NOTE NOTE NOTE NOTE

Another popular Macintosh newsreader is Nuntius, found at `ftp://ftp.cit.cornell.edu/pub/mac/comm/test/Nuntius-archive-mirror/`.

Subscribing to Newsgroups with NewsWatcher

Run NewsWatcher by double-clicking its icon. When it first starts up, it will read the full list of newsgroups from whatever server you instructed it to connect to (under File ➢ Preferences). This may take a few moments.

NOTE NOTE NOTE NOTE NOTE NOTE NOTE NOTE NOTE NOTE NOTE NOTE NOTE NOTE NOTE

Users of Internet Config (freeware) should check that option in Preferences (Miscellaneous) because NewsWatcher can obtain connection settings from Internet Config.

NewsWatcher will check for any new newsgroups that have been created since your last session and then will display a dialog box listing them. If this is your first session, it will simply display the full list of newsgroups on your server, in a window marked Untitled. This resembles what NewsWatcher calls a User Group List window, which will have fewer newsgroups than the full list. You start with no subscribed groups, so the User Group List window starts out empty.

To subscribe to a group, select it and complete the subscription with either of these options:

- Copy-and-paste (or drag-and-drop) the group into your User Group List window.
- Click on it and select Subscribe under the Special menu.

TIP TIP TIP TIP TIP TIP TIP TIP TIP TIP TIP TIP TIP TIP TIP TIP TIP TIP TIP TIP TIP TIP TIP TIP TIP TIP TIP

You don't have to subscribe to any groups the first time you run the program if you don't want to. You can always subscribe to groups later.

To unsubscribe from a group, select it in your User Group List window and use one of these options:

- Press the Delete key.
- Choose Special ➢ Unsubscribe.
- Drag the group to the trashcan icon.

After subscribing to your initial groups, close the Full Group List window. Now the only window on your screen is your untitled User Group List window. (To show the Full Group List again, select Show Full Group List under the Windows menu.)

Use the File ➢ Save command to save your modified User Group List, giving it a name like "My Newsgroups."

To look for other newsgroups, simply choose Windows ➢ Show Full Group List to call up the window with a list of all the newsgroups available.

Reading Newsgroup Articles with NewsWatcher

To start reading a newsgroup, double-click on it. This will open a new window with a list of the articles displayed. You can arrange or resize the windows easily, as you can with all Macintosh applications.

Articles are threaded (listed by topic), if possible. To jump from thread to thread, select News ➢ Next Thread. To jump to the next newsgroup in your list, choose News ➢ Next Group. Double-clicking on an article opens it up in a new window (see Figure 13.4).

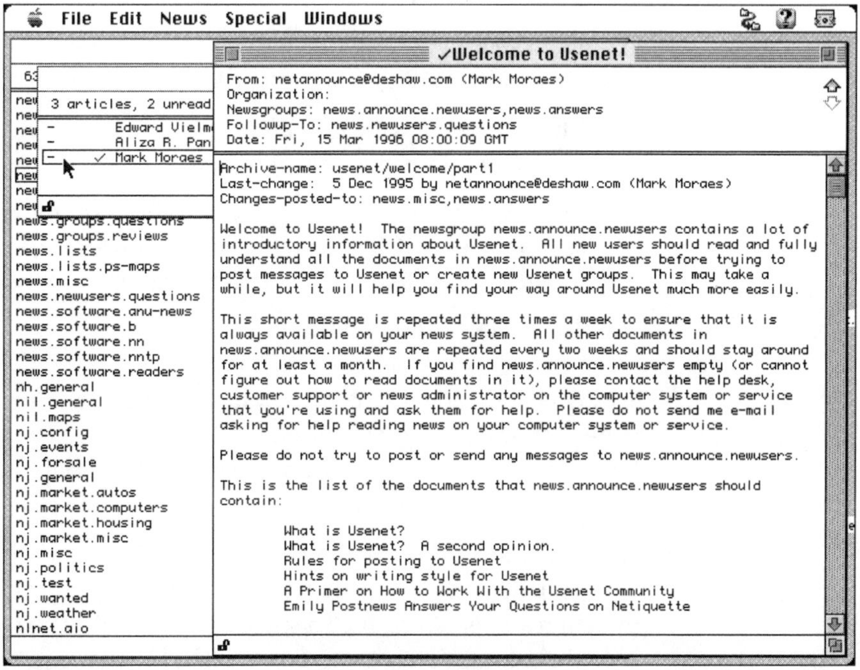

FIGURE 13.4: An article displayed in NewsWatcher. Notice the list of articles in one window and the list of newsgroups in the other, behind the front window.

Managing Newsgroup Articles with NewsWatcher

NewsWatcher supplies many of the same options for managing newsgroup articles, postings, and messages as are found in programs that you have to pay for. Here's what you can do with newsgroup articles after you review them:

- To mark an article as unread, select News ➢ Mark Unread (or press Command+U).
- To mark all of the articles as read, click on the first article and drag down to the last article to select all of the articles. Then, choose the News ➢ Mark Others Read command.
- To reply to an article, click the Reply button. NewsWatcher will open a new message window. Follow these steps to create the reply:
    1. Click in the message area and type your reply. Cut as much of the quoted article as possible, retaining enough to preserve context.
    2. When you're done, choose whether you want the message to be sent as private e-mail, a post to the entire group, or a message to yourself, by choosing among the three icons at the top of the window.
    3. Then click the Send button.
- To crosspost to more than one newsgroup, type additional newsgroup names, separated by commas, on the Newsgroups line at the top of the window. Type your message (reduce the quoted material as much as possible, but leave enough for appropriate context) and then click the Send button.
- To post a new message to the newsgroup, select News ➢ New Message. NewsWatcher will open a new window with the name of the current newsgroup already entered. Type a subject in the Subject box and type your article in the message area, then click the Send button.

To quit NewsWatcher, select File ➢ Quit.

TIP TIP TIP TIP TIP TIP TIP TIP TIP TIP TIP TIP TIP TIP TIP TIP TIP TIP TIP TIP TIP TIP TIP TIP TIP

NewsWatcher has excellent online help available—try downloading its 151-page manual or other help files from `ftp://ftp.acns.nwu.edu/pub/newswatcher/helpers/`.

News Xpress

Nx

News Xpress is an excellent—and free—Windows newsreader. You can download it from `ftp://ftp.hk.super.net/pub/windows/Winsock-Utilities/`. Look for a file name that starts with `nx` and ends with `.zip`, such as `nx10b4-p.zip`, and download that file. The higher numbered files are the more recent.

> TIP
>
> **Other popular, free Windows newsreaders are Free Agent** (`http://www.forteinc.com/agent/`) **and WinVN** (`ftp://ftp.ksc.nasa.gov/pub/win3/winvn`).

Subscribing to Newsgroups with News Xpress

Even though it is an absolutely free newsreader program, News Xpress still has plenty of options for subscribing to newsgroups. Here's how to subscribe:

1. Run News Xpress by double-clicking its icon.
2. News Xpress will check for any new newsgroups that have been created since your last session and then display a Newsgroups dialog box listing them. After clicking the checkbox to the left of any groups that you want to add to your subscription list, click the Subscribe button. Then click Close.
3. To subscribe to existing groups, select View ➢ All Groups (or press Ctrl+G) and wait for the entire group list to be displayed. Then select any group you want to subscribe to and select Group ➢ Subscribe (or press Ctrl+S).
4. Select View ➢ All Groups (or press Ctrl+G) again to show only a list of subscribed groups.

> TIP
>
> **You can limit the newsgroups shown to those that match a keyword or even a few characters by typing the word (or characters) into the Filter box at the bottom of the window.**

Reading Newsgroup Articles with News Xpress

News Xpress uses the quick, simple, double-click method to access most of its features, including article threads. Here's how to read newsgroups:

1. To start reading a newsgroup, double-click on its name. This will open up a new window with articles displayed. The old window will still be there, but behind the new one.
2. Select options on the Window menu to bring a different window to the front or to arrange all the windows.
3. Articles are threaded (listed by topic), if possible. Threads appear as folder icons. Double-click on a thread title to display all the articles in the thread.
4. To read an article, double-click on its subject. The article will appear in a new window (see Figure 13.5).
5. To quit News Xpress, close the article window and select File ➢ Exit.

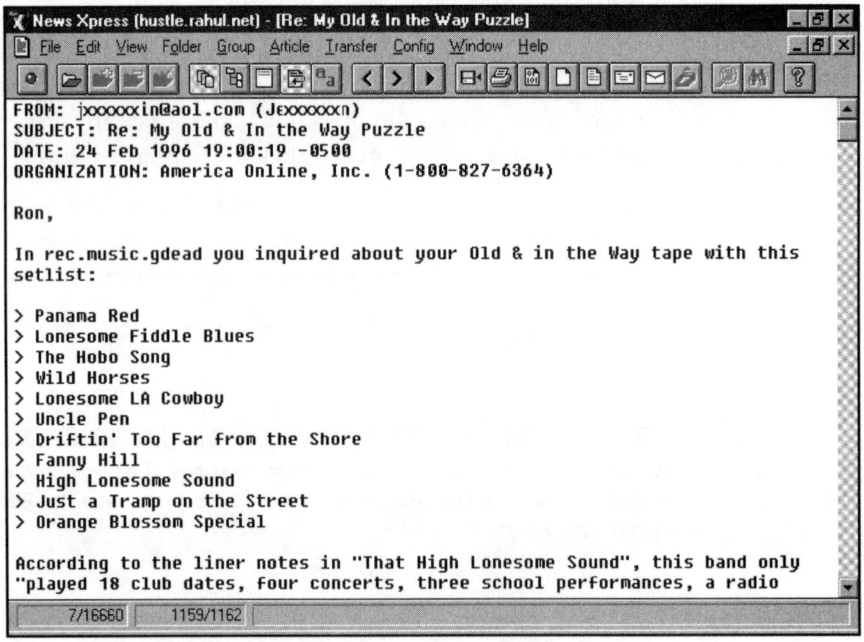

FIGURE 13.5: An article displayed in News Xpress

Managing Newsgroup Articles with News Xpress

As with most of the other newsreader programs available for free or for a price, News Xpress provides features for replying to articles, posting responses, and marking articles as unread.

- To mark an article as unread, select Article ➢ Mark Unread (or press Ctrl+U).
- To mark all articles as read, click the Catch Up button.
- If you want to reply to an article by e-mail, select it and click the Reply button, or select Article ➢ Reply. News Xpress will open a new message window, which you can fill in with the following steps:
    1. Click in the message area and type your reply.
    2. Cut as much of the quoted article as possible, retaining enough to preserve context.
    3. When you're done, click the Send button.
- To post a reply to the newsgroup, click the Follow Up button, or select Article ➢ Follow Up. News Xpress will open a new message window. Fill out the message with these options:
    - To crosspost to more than one newsgroup, type additional newsgroup names, separated by commas, in the Newsgroups box at the top of the window.
    - Type your message (reduce the quoted material as much as possible but leave enough for appropriate context) and then click the Send button, or use File ➢ Send.
- When you want to post a new message to the newsgroup, click the Post button. News Xpress will open a new message window with the name of the current newsgroup already entered and all the other boxes blank. Type a subject in the Subject box and type your article in the message area. Then click the Send button.

News Xpress's Help features are minimal—what do you want for free? Select Help ➢ Topics to see what there is.

NOTE NOTE NOTE NOTE NOTE NOTE NOTE NOTE NOTE NOTE NOTE NOTE NOTE NOTE NOTE

News Xpress has no provisions for killing or autoselecting authors, articles, or threads.

Are You Experienced?

Now you can. . .

- ☑ search for interesting newsgroups
- ☑ understand the logic behind newsgroup names
- ☑ browse newsgroup articles and save only what you need
- ☑ respond to articles, messages, and postings with polite, concise replies
- ☑ subscribe to newsgroups and manage articles from multiple sources
- ☑ use newsgroup acronyms with flair
- ☑ follow newsgroup article threads through related conversations
- ☑ tap into Usenet resources with a variety of methods and programs

SKILL 14

CHATTING (AND IRC)

- **Chatting with Irc**
- **Chatting with Ircle**
- **Chatting with mIRC**

So far we've covered e-mail, mailing lists, and newsgroups, but there's still one other way to communicate with people over the Internet. If you're in the mood for immediate communication, rather than tag games in e-mail or mass-market publication on Usenet, then you can look for people with similar interests and chat with them in real time.

Back at the office, you can use similar technologies to work with colleagues across an intranet, to schedule virtual meetings, and to coordinate your calendars.

Live Chatting

There's been chatting on the Internet since Unix users were able to page each other using the `talk` *`username@address`* command. Unlike e-mail, chatting takes place "live" in what Internet folks call *realtime*, meaning both people participate at the same time. The formal terms elucidating the difference between chat and e-mail are *synchronous* and *asynchronous*.

Chat is synchronous (happening for all participants at the same time) and e-mail is asynchronous (taking place variously at different times). Telephones are synchronous, answering machines are asynchronous, beepers are synchronous, and voice mail is asynchronous. U.S. Mail is totally asynchronous.

TIP TIP TIP TIP TIP TIP TIP TIP TIP TIP TIP TIP TIP TIP TIP TIP TIP TIP TIP TIP TIP TIP TIP TIP TIP

I prefer e-mail to chat because I like considering and editing my replies in writing and responding when the time is best for me.

The original talk protocol only provided for one-on-one conversations. It was followed by a chat protocol that permitted many people to converse with each other at once. Finally, IRC (Internet relay chat) provided for multiple channels ("rooms") where completely separate conversations, all potentially many-to-many, became available to anyone on the Internet.

The IRC protocol remains the underlying basis for other forms of real-time communication (such as voice or video conferencing).The standard chat interface, with a big dialog window, a narrow list of participants, and a command-line at the bottom for typing your responses, continues to be used in many real-time collaboration tools.

WARNING WARNING WARNING WARNING WARNING WARNING WARNING WARNING

This is also where the mass media go hunting for stories of "computer sex." That's because the immediacy and near-anonymity of this medium lead many an adolescent (or perpetual adolescent) to cruise chat channels hoping to talk dirty. Watch out if you have a female-sounding login or "real name."

Chatting is a form of immediate communication. With a chat program, you join conversations, and whatever you type appears on the screen of everyone else who's participating in or listening in on the conversation (you can also direct messages to specific people). It's not unlike talking over the telephone with teletype machines. However, with too many people involved, conversations can degenerate into what net.folk call *noise* (when so much chatter is going on that the topic gets buried in the blizzard of messages). With the right number of people, a sort of conversation or debate can take place.

IRC—The Internet's Chat Protocol

IRC works because a series of IRC servers band together in a network to share channels of communication, like communicating with everyone on a single radio frequency. If you connect to one server in such a network, you have access to all the channels and all the users connected to any of the servers on that network.

There are two major networks of IRC servers: EFNet, the traditional network, and the Undernet, a smaller, more community-oriented alternative network. Most basic information provided in IRC client programs covers EFNet. For more on the Undernet, see `http://www.servers.undernet.org` or look at the Undernet IRC FAQ at `http://www.rahul.net/dholmes/irc/ufaq1.html` and `http://www.rahul.net/dholmes/irc/ufaq2.html`.

The first time you run an IRC client, you might have to select a server to connect to (or it might automatically select one for you). After that, you'll connect whenever you start the program. The next step is to list what channels (conversation "rooms") are available out there and choose one to join (or decide that none look interesting enough and start your own).

NOTE NOTE NOTE NOTE NOTE NOTE NOTE NOTE NOTE NOTE NOTE NOTE NOTE NOTE NOTE

Some conversations are kept open by what are called *'bots*. These are robotic participants in the conversation. Some of them are not bad conversationalists, compared with a lot of real people.

Then you join a channel. You'll be able to see who else is on the same chat channel, and you'll see what everyone types (except for their private communications).

> TIP
> **Some conversations are invitation only. This means someone in the conversation has to give you a password or invite you to join.**

You can type messages to the entire channel or send private messages (called *whispering*) to individuals. When you're done, you quit the channel and then the program.

For more information about IRC, see the following documents on the Web:

- IRC FAQ (`http://www.irchelp.org`)
- IRC Servers List (`http://www.funet.fi/pub/unix/irc/docs/servers.txt`)

Other Real-Time Amusements

There are also games out there that you can play against other people on the Net in real time—everything from simple board games to MUDs (Multiple User Domain/Dungeon), which are huge role-playing text games with a large number of participants—supposedly they're very addictive. These games usually involve telnetting to some other system. Ask around on Usenet in the `rec.games` hierarchy for specific host sites and ongoing games. (See Skill 18, *Getting around with FTP and Telnet*, for more on Telnet, and Skill 13, *Joining Usenet Newsgroups,* for more on Usenet.)

There are also two new multimedia communications technologies that are somewhat similar to IRC—Internet Phone and CU-SeeMe. Internet Phone enables anyone with a microphone, speaker, and sound card in their computer to talk to other people on the Internet. CU-SeeMe enables anyone with a video camera, and enough memory in their computer to play video images, to see other people on the Internet.

For more information about Internet Phone, see the Internet Phone User Directory (`http://www.pulver.com/iphone/`). For more information about CU-SeeMe, see its Web page (`http://www.cuseeme.com/`).

Chatting with Specific IRC Programs

I can't explain every chat program out there, but I want to cover some of the most popular ones. We'll discuss Irc, Ircle, and mIRC. Irc is a Unix program, Ircle is a Macintosh program, and mIRC is a Windows program. If your provider does not offer an IRC or chat program, you can telnet to a host that does. Skill 18, *Getting around with FTP and Telnet*, explains Telnet.

Chatting with Irc

To run Irc in the Unix environment, use the following steps, which outline the Unix commands you need:

1. Type **irc** at the Unix prompt and press Enter. If this command is not recognized, try typing **chat** at the prompt and pressing Enter. The program called Chat is older than Irc and has been replaced on most systems, but if it's all you've got, give it a try.

TIP

People will also be able to see your "real name" (or whatever you've set it to with `chfn`**) with the** `/who` **command. If you don't want them to see your real name, you have to type setenv ircname *"nickname"* at the Unix prompt, inserting whatever nickname you want to be known by, and press Enter. (You can also put this command in any of your startup files, such as** `.login`, `.profile`, **or** `.cshrc`.**)**

2. The program will start and tell you if your login conflicts with any other one currently on the system. If so, you'll have to change your IRC *nick* (short for nickname). You may want to change it anyway. To do so type **/nick *new-nickname*** at the IRC prompt, inserting whatever new nickname you want to use. (All IRC commands start with the / symbol.)

After logging on to IRC, use the options described in the next three sections to hold an Irc conversation.

See What's Going On Use the `/list` command to see what conversations are in progress. Conversation names all start with the # symbol. You can narrow your search by specifying the minimum and maximum number of participants you want in the groups the `/list` command displays. For example, type **/list -min 3 -max 4** and press Enter.

Join a Conversation To join a conversation, type **/join *#conversation***. Type **/who *#conversation*** to get a list of who else is in on the conversation.

Your End of the Conversation To talk to the whole group, just type whatever you wish to say and press Enter (see Figure 14.1).

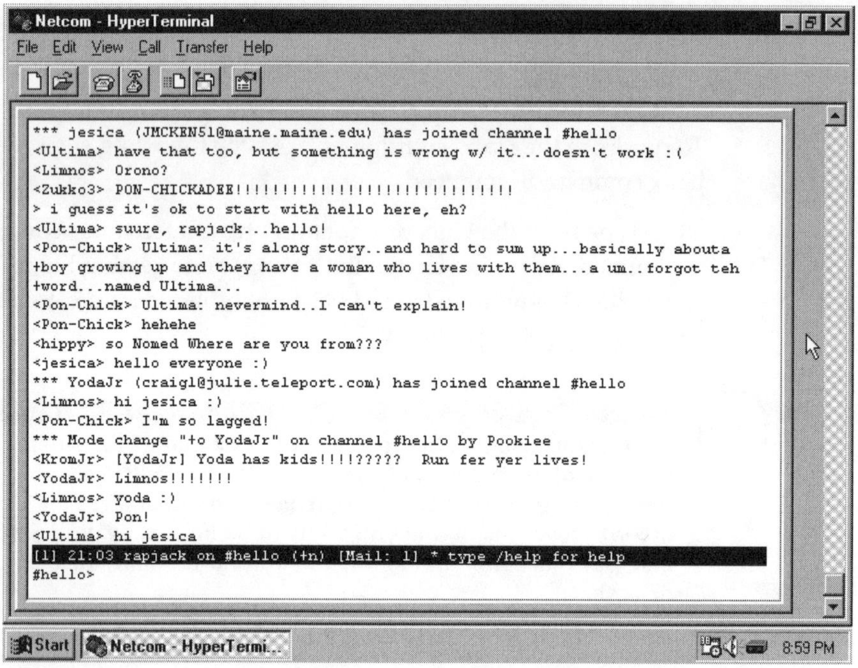

FIGURE 14.1: Talking on IRC in Unix

If you want to send a message to just one person, type ***/their-nick your-message***, inserting the recipient's nickname and whatever you want to say.

When you're ready to leave the conversation, type **/join 0**. To quit Irc, type **/quit**.

At any point, you can get help by typing **/help** and pressing Enter. People will usually help you out if you just ask questions.

Chatting with Ircle

ircle3.0b

Ircle updates the basic IRC command line environment for mouse-based Macintosh users. To obtain Ircle, point your Macintosh Web browser to the official Ircle home page (`http://alf8.speech.cs.cmu.edu/ircle/`) and download the latest version.

Ircle is modeled on all the other easy-to-use programs designed for the Macintosh. The following steps will get you started in Mac chatting:

1. To run Ircle, double-click its icon. The program will open.
2. To start a chat session, choose File ➢ Open Connection, which will connect you to whatever server is selected. To change the server—or your name, nickname, or password—select File ➢ Preferences.
3. After Ircle connects to the IRC server, the program will tell you if your login conflicts with any other one currently on the system. If so, you'll have to change your Ircle nickname, in File ➢ Preferences ➢ StartUp. You may want to change it anyway to be anonymous.

Now that you are connected, use the instructions in the following sections on Ircle to explore the chat possibilities.

See What's Going On To see what conversations are in progress, select the Commands ➢ List to see a list of conversations. You can specify a minimum and maximum number of participants you want in the Channel Specifications dialog box that pops up. Conversation names all start with the # symbol.

Join a Conversation To join a conversation, select Commands ➢ Join, then type in the name of the channel you wish to join, preceded by a #, or just select the channel in the Channel List window and click the Join button.

To get a list of who else is "on," choose Commands ➢ Who, or select Windows ➢ User to open the small window marked Userlist. The name of the conversation will appear in the title bar at the top of the Userlist window, with the names of the participants in the box below.

Your End of the Conversation To talk to the whole group, just type what you wish to say, as if it were a command, in the Inputline window and press Enter (see Figure 14.2).

If you want to send a message to one person, type ***/their-nick your-message***, inserting the person's nickname and the message you want to send.

To leave the conversation, just close the window or select File ➢ Close Connection if you want to leave the server. To quit Ircle, select File ➢ Quit.

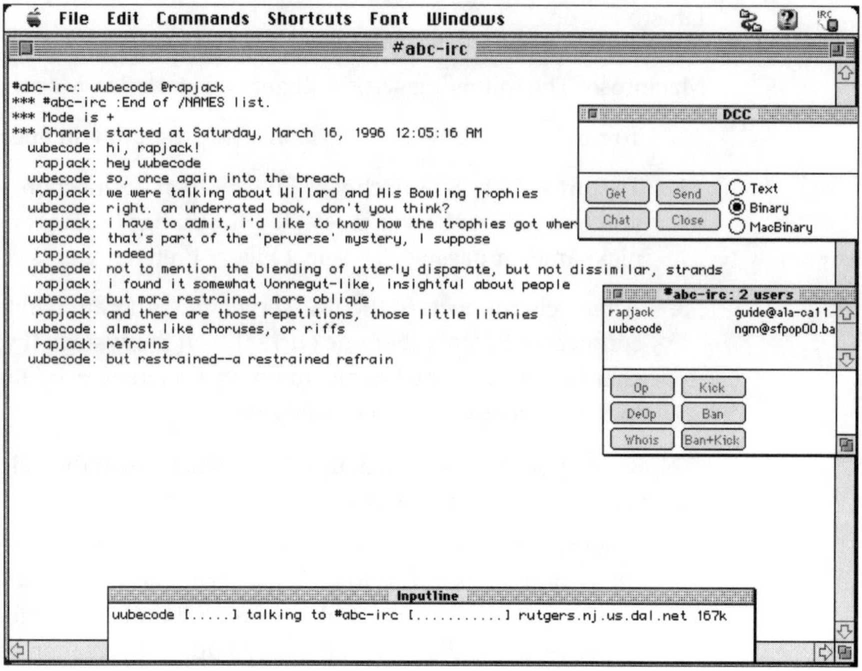

FIGURE 14.2: Talking on IRC in Ircle

Ircle has an extensive array of help documents at its Web site. There is also an entire Web page devoted to help—go to `http://www.aloha.net/sputnik/irclehelp.html`.

Again, it does not matter whether you are chatting with IRC or Ircle when you need help. In general, the people you are chatting with will help you out if you just ask questions.

Chatting with mIRC

mIRC is the Windows version of an IRC chat program, and it takes advantage of some Windows features to make chatting a little easier. To obtain mIRC, point your Web browser at `ftp://cs-ftp.bu.edu/irc/clients/pc/windows` and click on the mIRC file to download it.

Use the following steps to connect with mIRC and begin your chat session:

1. To run mIRC, double-click its icon. The program will start.
2. Click the Connect button to connect to a server.
3. mIRC will tell you if your login conflicts with any other one currently on the system. If so, you'll have to change your mIRC nick. mIRC will prompt you with the beginning of the command (`/nick` followed by a space). Just type the new nickname you want and press Enter.

TIP

To change your nick at another time, right-click anywhere, select Other from the menu that pops up, and then click Nickname. Type your new nick in the dialog box that appears and press Enter.

After you have logged in and established your username, you can work with the commands described in the next three sections to join conversations.

See What's Going On To see what conversations are in progress, right-click anywhere, then choose Other ➢ List Channel. Conversation names all start with the # symbol. Just as in the other chat programs, you can narrow your search by specifying the minimum and maximum number of participants in the groups displayed. Do this by typing the `/list` command directly (for example, type **/list -min 3 -max 4**) and pressing Enter. mIRC will list the available channels in a new window.

Join a Conversation To join a conversation, double-click on the name of the channel you want to join. A new window will open for that channel.

If you want to get a list of who else is "on," right-click on the channel name in the list window and select List Users.

Your End of the Conversation Click on the @server line in the right pane of the chat channel window if you want to talk to the whole group. Type what you want to say in the main window and press Enter (see Figure 14.3).

To send a message to one person, double-click on that person's nick in the right pane of the channel window. From then on, everything you type will go to only that person. Click on the @server line again to start talking to everybody.

When you are ready to leave the conversation, just close the channel window. To quit mIRC, select File ➢ Exit.

At any point, you can get help by selecting Help ➢ Contents.

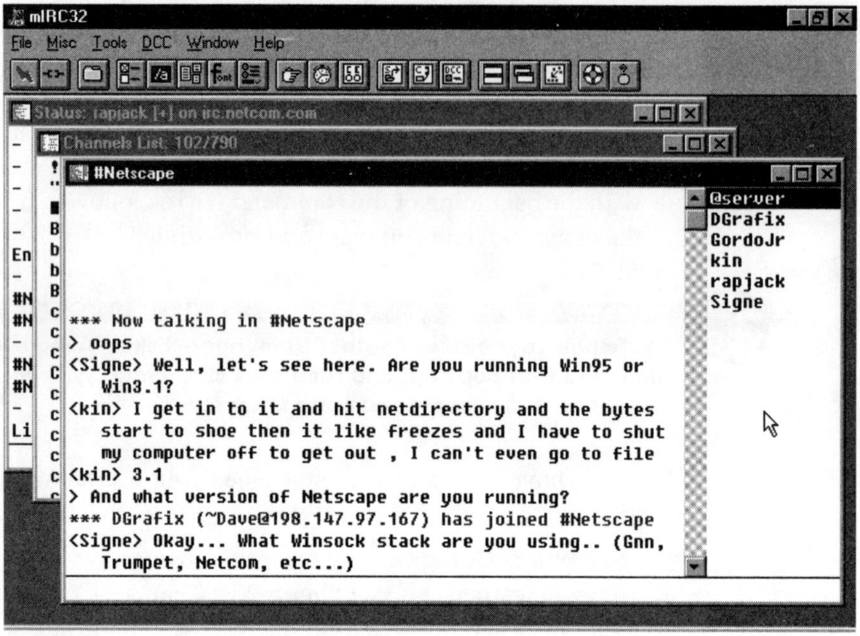

FIGURE 14.3: Talking on IRC in mIRC for Windows

Other Ways to Chat

New chat formats are constantly appearing on the Net. Not all of them are compatible with IRC. Here's a brief look at a few alternatives.

Chatting at Online Services

AOL, CompuServe, and other online services have their own IRC equivalent, usually referred to as chat rooms. The concept is the same, but these conversations are not open to anyone on the Internet—only to members of the specific online service.

Though not IRC-based, online-service chat rooms use the same familiar chat interface (dialogue, participant, and entry windows).

Web Chatting with Java Apps

Most Web sites that feature chatting based on Java applications are in fact IRC-compatible and usually offer equivalent access via standard IRC programs. Two examples of such sites are HotWired's Talk.com (`http://www.talk.com/`) and Talk City (`http://www.talkcity.com/`), shown in Figure 14.4.

FIGURE 14.4: You can participate in IRC-based chats with a Java app at Talk City.

Proprietary Chat Environments and 3-D Worlds

Both VRML (an Internet 3-D virtual-reality standard) and proprietary 3-D or visual chat sites (where you appear as an "avatar," a character you choose from a menu, and interact in an imaginary, but visible, space), require souped-up multimedia computers, but may give a hint of how real-time communication might work in the future. See `http://www.vrml.org` for more about VRML.

Are You Experienced?

Now you can...

- ☑ download IRC chat programs
- ☑ chat with Internet users on Macintosh, Unix, or Windows computers
- ☑ find out where to get help while chatting

SKILL 15

CONFERENCING AND COLLABORATING

- Holding conferences with Netscape Conference and Microsoft NetMeeting
- Working with others on an intranet
- Using whiteboards to share images
- Sharing applications with Microsoft NetMeeting

An extension of the IRC-type chatting you learned about in Skill 14 is *multiple-party conferencing*. Both of the major Web browsers offer tools to facilitate this form of collaboration. These tools can also be used to work with colleagues across an intranet, to schedule virtual meetings, and to coordinate your calendars.

Conferencing and Collaborating over the Internet (or an Intranet)

So how can your business or enterprise make use of real-time communication on the Internet (or, yes, an int*ra*net)? Well, if you and your colleagues have the right sort of conferencing and collaboration software installed (generally, you both have to have the same kind of software), then you can schedule "virtual meetings" and include people who work at home, colleagues in satellite offices, and so on. With some tools, you can even work together on the same document over a Net connection.

What's an Int*ra*net?

You may have encountered an explanation of the term *intranet* already in the book, but if not, here goes: A few years back, people used the word *internet* (with a lowercase *i*) to mean any small network running on the same protocols that the big-*I Internet* runs on (namely TCP/IP and the other so-called Internet protocols). When the idea of running an enterprise's in-house network on Internet protocols started to take hold last year, the alternative term *intranet* came into use (though it's still too close to Internet and probably confuses more people than it helps). Lately, I've started to see the term *extranet* used to describe a small, private network connecting secure, remote sites over the public Internet.

The advantage, by the way, behind all the hype about intranets, is that tools for browsing Internet and Web-style resources are already cheap and plentiful, and most workers have already trained themselves to use some of them. The drawback is that all the old proprietary network systems had their own highly sophisticated tools, and some people will be taking a step back if they go to an all-intranet/extranet approach.

Workflow and Whiteboards

The basic function of a conferencing program is to enable real-time chatting (usually written, but sometimes with sound or video as well, hardware willing), much like IRC, but most such programs also offer collaboration tools or modules as well. The most sophisticated sort of collaboration involves sharing documents remotely and even working on them together with a remote colleague. Most programs include a *whiteboard*—the electronic equivalent of the real thing you see in corporate meetings every day. These whiteboards have brought illegible handwriting into the world of computers (see Figure 15.1); but they do permit the sort of jotting and diagram drawing that's not possible with typewriter characters.

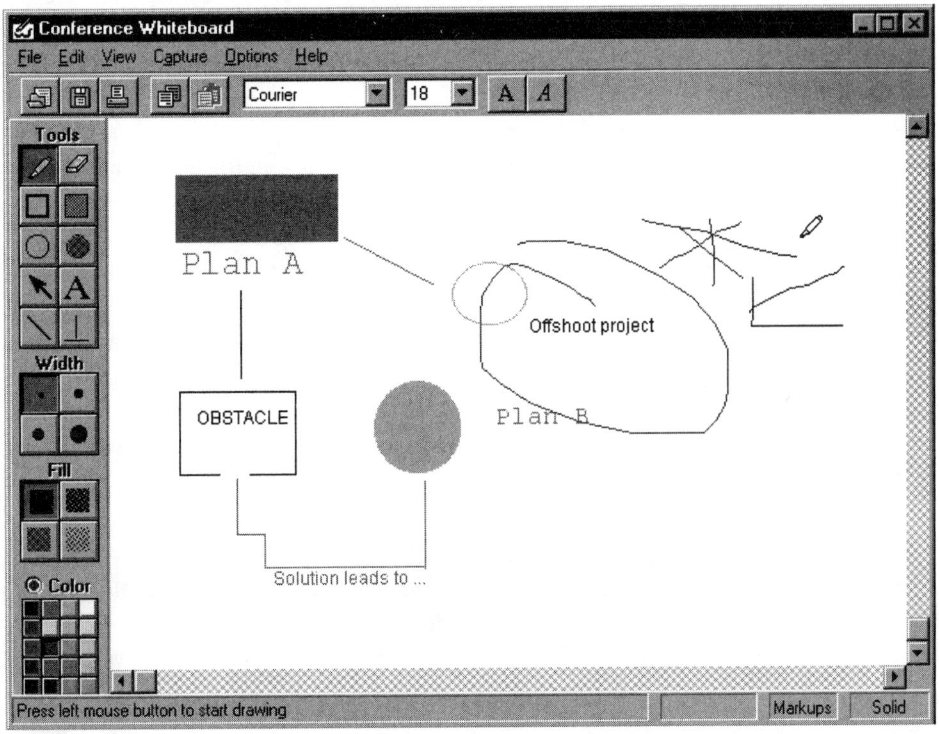

FIGURE 15.1: A whiteboard can sometimes come in handy, after you master its features.

Conferencing Programs

The two main contenders in the conferencing field right now are the programs built into Microsoft Internet Explorer 4 (NetMeeting) and Netscape Communicator 4 (Netscape Conference). NetMeeting has more features (most notably, it enables users to share an application, even if only one of them has the program installed), but Netscape Conference is compatible with more platforms (Macintosh, Unix, and so on, in addition to the various flavors of Windows).

Microsoft NetMeeting

Designed to integrate with Internet Explorer (you can download it for free, either as part of Microsoft Internet Explorer 4 or separately), NetMeeting has a very full set of features (including chat, audio using a microphone, video, file transfers, whiteboard, and application-sharing) and a surprisingly easy interface to use. It also walks you through the setup the first time you use it, with one of Microsoft's familiar wizard routines.

The biggest drawback to NetMeeting is that it's only available for Windows at this time. It uses its own type of server, but you can access public servers at Microsoft (listed in the Options dialog box). Initiating any of the several parts of the program (such as sending or receiving a file) is a matter of using the menus (or, frequently, the toolbars).

Connecting to people is a matter of choosing them from the general directory (they have to be connected and running NetMeeting to show up) or from your personalized Speed Dial list. Applications can be shared in a View Only mode (in which only one person can make changes) or Group Effort mode (in which anyone can mess with the document). Figure 15.2 shows a NetMeeting call.

NOTE NOTE NOTE NOTE NOTE NOTE NOTE NOTE NOTE NOTE NOTE NOTE NOTE NOTE NOTE

Remember, in order for everyone at the online meeting to participate, they must all have Microsoft NetMeeting installed on their computers. Otherwise, these special features will not work.

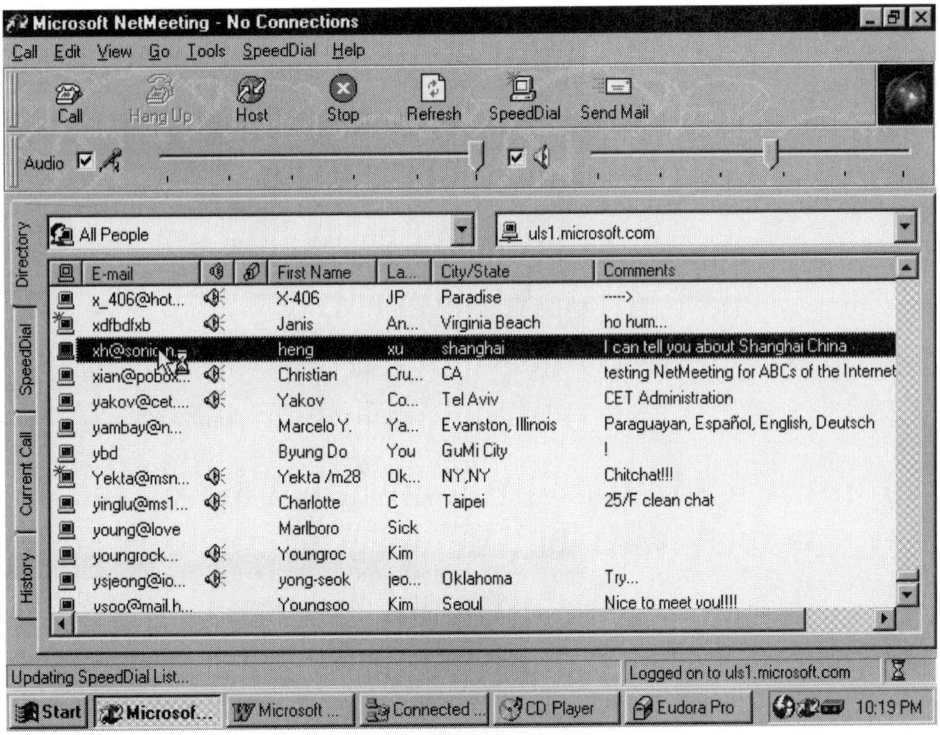

FIGURE 15.2: NetMeeting is not too much trickier than a standard IRC program, with a few extra features (and some different lingo—they're not channels here, they're *calls*).

Installing Microsoft NetMeeting

Before you can use Microsoft NetMeeting, you will need to install it with a series of wizard screens or dialog boxes. The wizards ask you for various settings and information about yourself. Here are the steps for installing NetMeeting:

1. Double-click NetMeeting's desktop icon or select Start ➢ Programs ➢ Microsoft NetMeeting. You will see an introductory screen about NetMeeting, which you should read before clicking the Next button.

2. The second NetMeeting screen asks you which directory server you want to use. A `microsoft.com` server is selected by default, but you can choose an alternate server from the list. You can always change servers later. Click Next when done.

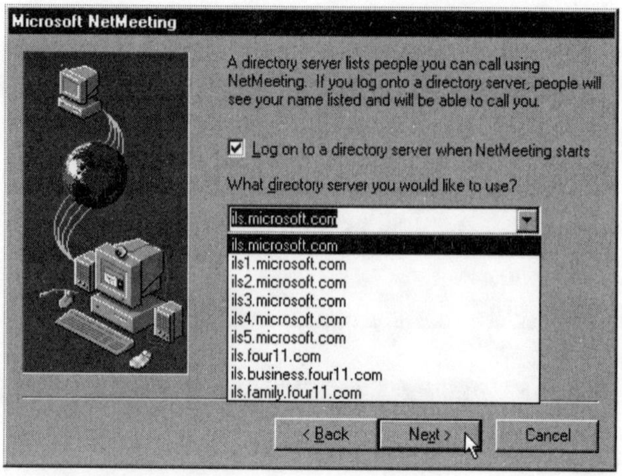

3. Enter your e-mail information on the next NetMeeting screen, then click Next.

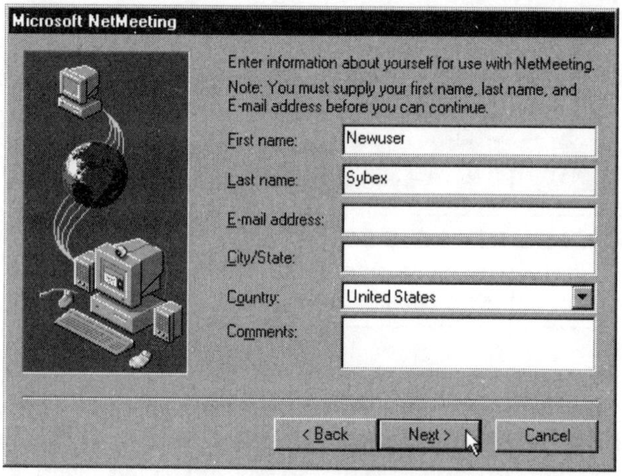

4. The next screen asks you to categorize your NetMeeting activity for personal or business use, and to indicate whether it will be suitable for all ages or for adults only. Check the appropriate boxes and click Next.
5. You will see the Audio Tuning Wizard screen, which tests your sound equipment and software for communicating with your microphone in NetMeeting. Close all sound software and click Next to begin.

6. The second audio screen asks you to specify your communications connection from these options: 14,400 bps modem; 28,800 bps modem; 56,600 bps modem; ISDN; or Local Area Network. Check one of the connection boxes and click Next.

7. On the third audio screen, you should have your microphone plugged in to your computer and be ready to speak. Click the Start Recording button and talk into the microphone clearly and slowly for about 30 seconds. Click the Next button when the audio wizard tells you the tuning is complete. You can calibrate your sound system again later by selecting Tools ➢ Audio Tuning Wizard from within NetMeeting.

8. Click the Finish button on the final screen to complete the installation. You will see a message telling you that the installation was a success.

Setting Up Your NetMeeting Identity

After you have installed NetMeeting with the Microsoft NetMeeting Setup Wizard, you can always return to the Options feature to change your personal information or modify technical settings, such as audio and video characteristics, or how you want SpeedDial to work. Simply start NetMeeting by choosing Start ➢ Programs ➢ NetMeeting. In the main NetMeeting window, select Tools ➢ Options to display the Options dialog box. Use any of the following choices to alter the way NetMeeting works for you.

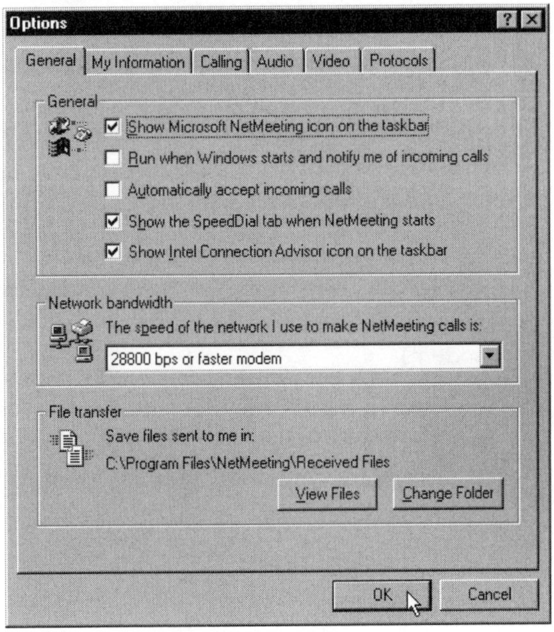

- On the **General** tab, select different option buttons in the General area to change the way NetMeeting loads and how NetMeeting accepts incoming calls. You can also change your connection type in the Network Bandwidth area, and you can change where files sent to you by others during NetMeeting sessions are stored.
- Use the **My Information** tab to alter the personal information you entered during NetMeeting setup.
- The **Calling** tab contains settings for your SpeedDial functions and identifies which server you log on to when NetMeeting starts. You can set new SpeedDial entries to be created automatically for every person you call and for people who call you, or you can restrict SpeedDial entry creation to only those that are approved by you.
- Select the **Audio**, **Video**, or **Protocols** tabs to modify technical settings for your sound, video, and network connections. For example, you can direct NetMeeting to send and receive video in small, medium, or large image sizes. You can also choose to sacrifice video quality for faster transmission.

Chatting with Microsoft NetMeeting

Even though Microsoft NetMeeting supports some fairly high-end conferencing features, such as video and audio communications, you may find that you need to revert to chat sessions when your network or modem becomes overloaded with all the data passing back and forth. NetMeeting's video and audio links can only be set up between two people (you and the receiver) anyway, so the chat service can open up communications among more than two participants. The chat feature cannot be used while you are sharing applications (collaborating), but it can be used when the whiteboard feature is in use.

Here's how NetMeeting Chat can be used:

1. Start Microsoft NetMeeting by selecting Start ➢ Programs ➢ Microsoft NetMeeting. The main NetMeeting screen will appear and you will be prompted to log on to your Internet service provider (if you are using a modem).
2. Click the Call button in the NetMeeting toolbar, or select Call ➢ New Call from the menu. In the New Call dialog box, type in the Internet address, e-mail address, or modem phone number of the person you wish to call. Then click the Call button.

TIP TIP TIP TIP TIP TIP TIP TIP TIP TIP TIP TIP TIP TIP TIP TIP TIP TIP TIP TIP TIP TIP TIP TIP TIP

If you have added SpeedDial numbers (with Call ➢ Create SpeedDial), you can double-click on any entry in the SpeedDial tab of the main NetMeeting window to begin a call to that number or address. You can also double-click on any entry in the Directory tab, which lists the addresses or numbers of everyone listed in the directory of the server you are logged on to. Check the server's name in the Server list box above the directory to see which one is active. If you have made calls before, you can also double-click on entries in the History tab to call people who you have called in previous sessions.

3. If your call cannot be completed, you will be asked if you wish to leave an e-mail message instead. Click Yes to have NetMeeting display a message window addressed to the person you tried to call. Type your message, then click Send.

NOTE NOTE NOTE NOTE NOTE NOTE NOTE NOTE NOTE NOTE NOTE NOTE NOTE NOTE NOTE

People may not be available for various reasons when you try to call them. They may be engaged in another meeting or call, they may be screening calls, or they may not wish to be disturbed. You can use the Accept or Ignore options to deal with calls coming in to you, and you can select Call ➢ Do Not Disturb on the NetMeeting menu if you do not want to be interrupted by calls.

4. If the person you called is available and is accepting calls, their name and other particulars will appear in the list in the Current Call tab. After you have established connections with everyone you want to include in your chat, select Tools ➢ Chat in the NetMeeting menu, or click the Chat button in the NetMeeting toolbar. The Chat window will appear.

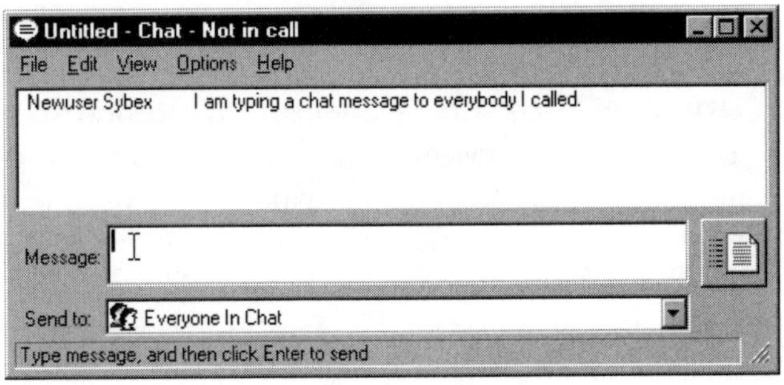

5. Type your message in the smaller Message box and press Enter when you are ready to send it. You can send the message to Everyone in Chat, or you can select one person to send it to (known as *whispering*) from the Send To list box. The chat messages from all the participants are displayed in the large window. You can change how the chat comments are formatted with this procedure:
   - Select Options ➢ Chat Format to access the Chat Format dialog box. Choose options in the Information Display area and in the Message Format area to change how the chat messages appear in the chat window.

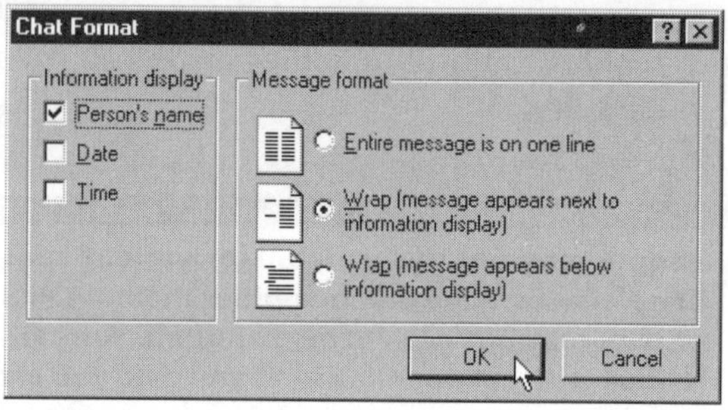

6. When you are finished chatting, select File ➢ Exit. You will be asked if you wish to save the current chat session as a list of messages. If you would like to preserve a particularly good session, select Yes and type in a name and choose a location in the Save As dialog box.
7. Select Call ➢ Hang Up to end the session. If people at your chat session have set up their own audio, video, or chat connections with other people, they can continue conversing among themselves after you disconnect.

Using the Microsoft NetMeeting Whiteboard

The Microsoft NetMeeting whiteboard is another feature that can be shared among all of the meeting participants, not just one. You can draw things on the whiteboard during your meeting, or you can prepare whiteboards ahead of time and present them to people in the meeting in a slide show format. If you do not lock the white-board image against further input, your participants can make their own marks on the whiteboard. Here are some of the basic whiteboard steps to get you started:

1. Start NetMeeting and call up participants as explained in Steps 1 through 4 in the previous section, "Chatting with Microsoft NetMeeting." Select the

Current Call tab in the NetMeeting window and click the Whiteboard button in the NetMeeting toolbar or select Tools ➢ Whiteboard. You will see the Whiteboard window and a large, blank white canvas on which you can scribble, draw, or write.

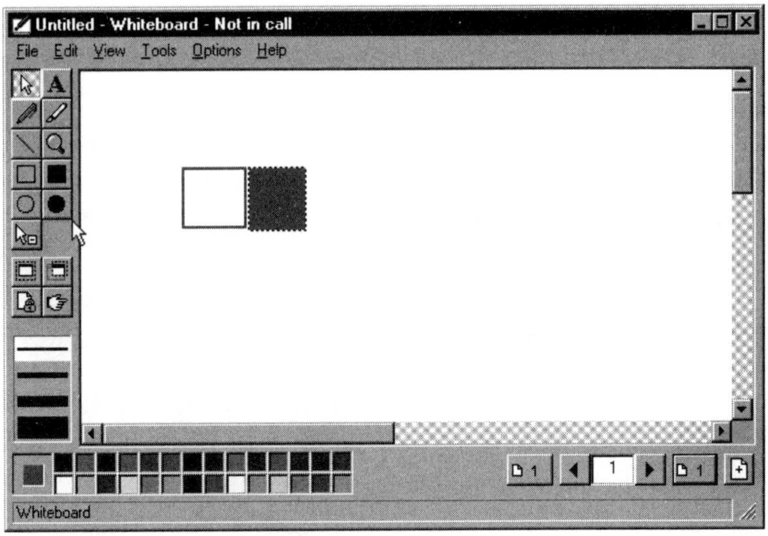

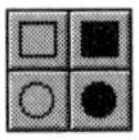

2. Start creating a whiteboard presentation using the graphics tools in the palette to the left of the whiteboard. Clicking the Rectangle, Filled Rectangle, Ellipse, or Filled Ellipse button turns your pointer into a crosshair tool. Click on the work area and drag out a shape based on the tool you selected. Select a different color from the palette at the bottom of the whiteboard to change the newly drawn item's color.

3. Use any of these options to further enhance your presentation:

   - Click the Remote Pointer button to place a hand-shaped pointer on the whiteboard. You can click on this pointer and drag the pointing hand around on the whiteboard to indicate various features.

   - Click the Lock Contents button to prevent the whiteboard from being accessed by other meeting participants.

   - Select the Highlighter button to change the mouse pointer into a yellow highlighter that you can swipe across various whiteboard elements for emphasis. Change the thickness of the line by choosing Options ➢ Line Width and checking a line of a thinner or thicker width.

- Click the Select Window or Select Area button to access a very cool feature, a screen capture tool. If you use Select Window, the next window you click on will be pasted into your whiteboard. This could be handy for copying a Web page frame or menu into your whiteboard to show your collaborators how your own Web page could look. Use the Select Area button to drag a rectangle around any portion of the screen, which will be pasted into the whiteboard when you release the mouse button.
- Select the Text button, which has a large "A" on it, to turn your mouse pointer into an insertion point. Click with the mouse anywhere on the whiteboard and start typing. You can change the color of the font with the color palette, and you can change the Font Name and Font Size with the corresponding buttons on the Whiteboard toolbar.

4. When you have completed your whiteboard session, you can print the whiteboard with File ➢ Print, or you can save the whiteboard as a file with a `.wht` extension with File ➢ Save. Select File ➢ Exit to leave the whiteboard function and return to the NetMeeting main window.

Collaborating with Shared Applications

NetMeeting also allows you to open another application and show meeting participants the files and operations from this application, even if they don't have the application themselves. Even better, you can direct NetMeeting to let participants collaborate with you by actually using the application (instead of just viewing it while you use it). Use the following steps to start collaborating with NetMeeting:

1. Start NetMeeting and call up participants as explained in Steps 1 through 4 of the "Chatting with Microsoft NetMeeting" section. Select the Current Call tab in the NetMeeting window and open the application that you wish to either show to other participants or have them work with.
2. Click the Share button on the NetMeeting toolbar, or select Tools ➢ Share Application and select the application you want to show to the others.
3. Work with the application as you normally would, by opening files, editing the contents, and so on. Other meeting participants will be able to follow along as you perform application tasks.
4. After you have shown participants how to use the application, you may want them to try to use it, too. Click the Collaborate button or select Tools ➢ Start Collaborating to begin the collaborative effort. Anyone who wants to

work with the application must also click the Collaborate button on their toolbar, then double-click in the application that everyone is sharing. Only one person at a time can use the application. If things get confusing, the person showing the application can click the Collaborate button again to end the application sharing.

5. When everyone is done working with the application, save any new or revised files that you wish to keep and close the application. If anyone at the meeting wants a copy of a file resulting from the collaboration, select Tools ➢ File Transfer ➢ Send File, or drag the file onto that person's entry in the Current Call list.
6. Select Call ➢ Hang Up to end the session.

Netscape Conference

Netscape Conference is an integral part of Netscape Communicator 4 (there is no equivalent for Netscape Navigator 3). It lacks some of the advanced features of Microsoft NetMeeting (specifically, video and application sharing), but it runs on many more computer platforms. These two programs use different protocols, so people cannot communicate with each other unless they are both using the same tool. One other drawback to Conference is that it only permits one-on-one conversation (more like the old talk protocol than IRC).

As with Microsoft NetMeeting, Netscape Conference setup is guided by an easy-to-use wizard the first time. You can select names from a public server or from your own address book. Transferring files and jotting on the whiteboard are also easy to figure out. Conference's one unique feature is a holdover from the old Netscape Chat product, something now called Collaborative Web Browsing (some of the Java-based talk Web sites have the same sort of thing). It enables a pair of people to browse the Web together, with one person taking the lead. Figure 15.3 shows me trying to set up a call.

Installing Netscape Conference

Be sure to close all programs and have your microphone handy prior to beginning your Netscape Conference installation. Conference setup is easy because Netscape uses help screens, very similar to the wizards used in the Microsoft NetMeeting setup, to lead you through the process. Here are the procedures involved:

1. Select Start ➢ Programs ➢ Netscape Communicator ➢ Netscape Conference or select Communicator ➢ Conference from any component menu.

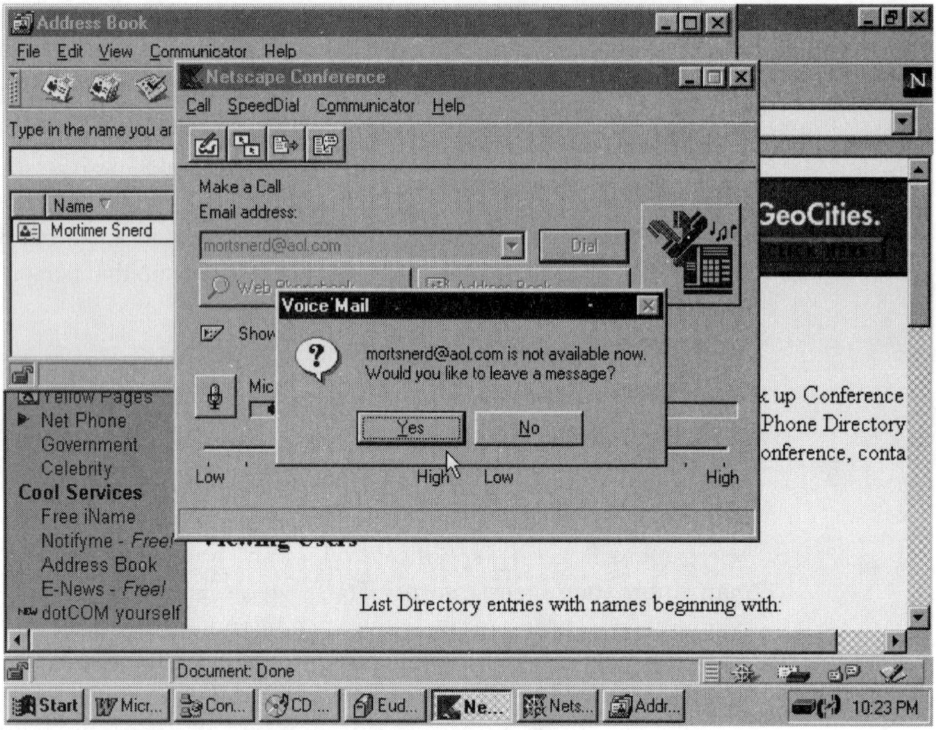

FIGURE 15.3: Netscape Conference works only for one-on-one chats.

2. Read the Welcome to Netscape Conference screen then click the Next button to move along.
3. In the About the Netscape Conference Setup Wizard screen, read about the information you should have available, get this information together, then click Next. You need your e-mail address, the network connection you are using, and other details for your business card form, which serves as a calling card during conferencing.
4. The next screen you see is the Setting Up Your Business Card screen, shown on the next page. Type in your name, e-mail information, and business facts, such as your company and your title. Include the name of the file containing your photo if you would like to include one. (You can include any image file here, such as a logo, or a photo of someone surfing, for example.) Click the File Folder navigation button next to the Photo textbox to point Netscape to the location of this photo, if necessary. Click Next when you're ready to proceed.

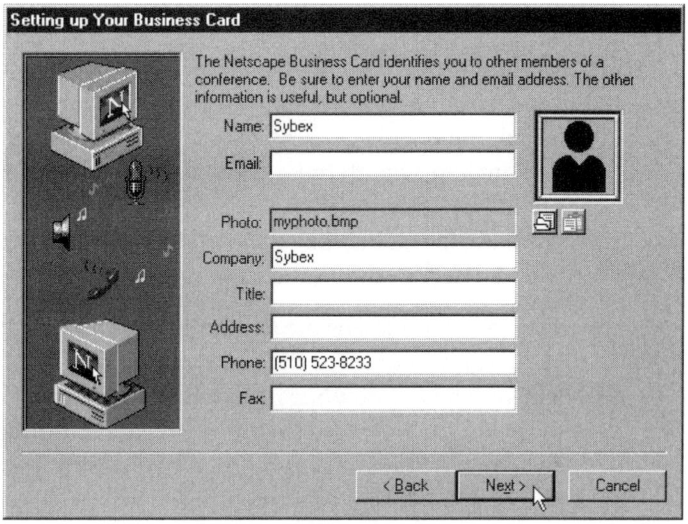

5. You will see the Setting Up Your Directory Preferences screen, shown below. Netscape supplies a default e-mail call server and a default Web phonebook, both of which you can change if you like by clicking the drop-down list boxes next to DLS Server and Phonebook URL. Click Next when you are done.

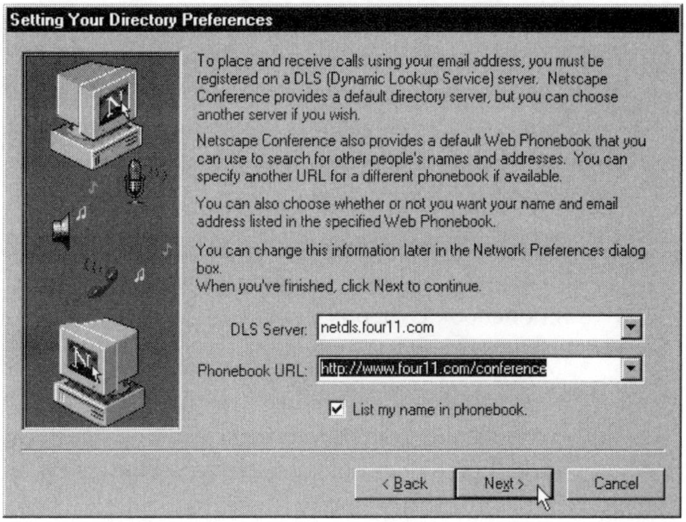

6. In the Specify Your Network Type window, choose one of the connection options: 14,400 bps modem; 28,800 bps modem; ISDN; or LAN (local-area

network). If you have a 56,600 bps modem, use the 28,800 bps modem choice. Click Next to continue.

7. The Detecting Your Sound Card window contains autodetect choices for your microphone and speakers, which were made by the installation program. If you are happy with these choices, select Next; otherwise, change the microphone specification in the Record, Transmit Your Voice area and change the speakers in the Playback, Hear Others' Voices area. You can change these settings later in the Audio Preferences dialog box.
8. The next two screens are the Testing Audio Levels screens. You can tune out background noise for the test by adjusting the slide control on the Silence Sensor. Speak into your microphone in a normal voice for 10 to 20 seconds, then click on Next to go to the second audio testing screen. You can also postpone this whole process by clicking the Skip button, and calibrating your equipment later in Netscape Conference's Call window.
9. Click Next in the Setup Complete Screen to finish the installation and start Netscape Conference.

Setting Up Your Conference Identity

Netscape Conference has flexibility for changing user information and technical settings similar to that provided by Microsoft NetMeeting. All of the user, network, and audio information you specified when you installed Conference can be modified later to fit your needs as they change. All you have to do is start Conference by double-clicking its desktop icon or by selecting Start ➢ Programs ➢ Netscape Communicator ➢ Netscape Conference, then select Call ➢ Preferences in the Netscape Conference window. Choose from any of the following options to adjust settings to fit your situation.

- Use the **Network** tab to change your network connection information. Type in a new conference server or phonebook in the DLS Server text box or in the Phonebook URL box.
- Modify any of the information on the **Business Card** tab (shown on the next page), such as your name, e-mail address, or other particulars. Click the Load Bitmap button to browse through your image files for a suitable representation (it does not have to be an actual photo of you!). All of this information is available to other Netscape Conference users during a call.

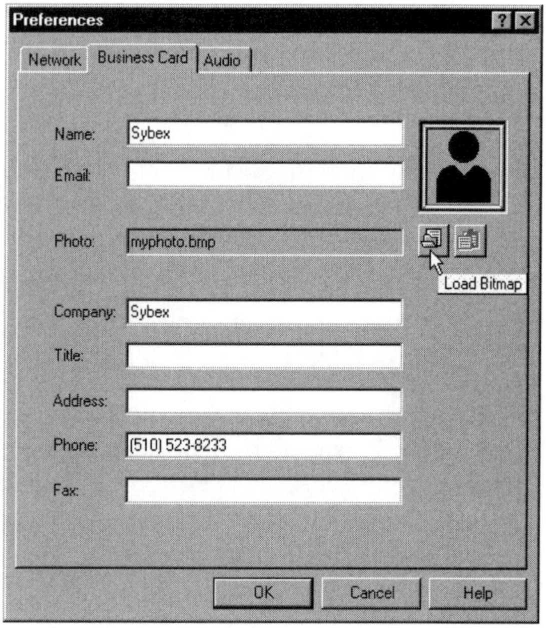

SKILL 15

- Change audio settings on the **Audio** tab, including what type of device is being used for recording (your microphone) and playback (your speakers). There are additional settings that audio fanatics may wish to tamper with in the Compression area and on the Advanced button in Echo Suppression, but the default choices will probably be fine for most users.

Chatting with Netscape Conference

Netscape's chat tool is great for conducting conversations with more than one person, especially for those who do not have the requisite audio equipment to use voice communications. Netscape Chat is less of a drain on system resources, too. You can also print out and save a record of your chat session for future reference. Here are the steps to begin chatting:

1. Start Conference by selecting Start ➢ Programs ➢ Netscape Communicator ➢ Netscape Conference, or if you are already in another Communicator component, select Communicator ➢ Conference. You will see the Netscape Conference window (see Figure 15.3, a couple of pages back).
2. Type in the e-mail address or Internet address of the person you wish to contact in the E-mail Address textbox. You can also click the Web Phonebook or Address Book buttons to search for the address.

3. Click the Dial button when ready. You will see a status display as the call is placed and, if there is no answer, you will be asked if you wish to leave a message. If the call connects, the other person's Business Card logo or other image will appear to the right in the Conference window.

4. Click the Microphone button to begin an audio conversation with one person; otherwise, call other participants until you have everyone for your chat session.

5. Click the Chat button in the Conference toolbar to start your chat session. You will see the Conference Text Chat window, where you can type messages, paste in material from the Clipboard, or import files to send to other participants.

6. Type messages into the Personal Note Pad area of the Conference Text Chat window. When you have finished typing, press Ctrl+Enter, and click the Send button, or select File ➢ Post Note Pad to send your message to other chatters. The log of the chat session is recorded in the Log File area of the Conference Text Chat window.

7. You can also click the Include button or select File ➢ Include to browse for files with the Include File into Pad dialog box. Select the file you want to add and click Open. The contents of the file will be pasted into the Personal Note Pad window. Delete any parts of the file you do not need before sending it to others.

8. Select File ➢ Close to close the Conference Text Chat window. You can save or print the chat session prior to closing by selecting File ➢ Save or File ➢ Print.

9. Select Call ➢ Hang Up in the Netscape Conference menu to disconnect from the chat session.

Using the Netscape Conference Whiteboard

The Netscape Conference whiteboard, shown earlier in Figure 15.1, is a good tool for sharing images and diagrams with other users. The Conference whiteboard can be used by Macintosh and Unix users as well as Windows users. The white-board can also work with a variety of image file formats, including `.jpeg` (Macs only), `.gif`, `.tif`, `.bmp`, and some Unix image file formats.

The conference whiteboard operates much like Microsoft NetMeeting's whiteboard. These procedures give you a basic outline of how to use the whiteboard in Netscape Conference:

1. Start Conference and call up participants as explained in Steps 1 through 4 in the "Chatting with Netscape Conference" section. Click the Whiteboard button to open the Conference Whiteboard window.

2. Click the Open File button in the Conference Whiteboard toolbar, or select File ➢ Open to browse through your image files in the Open dialog box and select a file to place on the whiteboard. Click the Open button in the Open dialog box when you are ready.
3. Work with any of the following tools to add more features to your whiteboard presentation:

   - Click the Rectangle, Filled Rectangle, Ellipse, or Filled Ellipse button to turn your pointer into a crosshair drawing tool. Click on the work area and drag out a shape based on the tool you selected. Select a different color from the palette on the lower left side of the whiteboard to change the newly drawn item's color.

   - Click the Pointer button to place an arrow-shaped pointer on the whiteboard. You can click on this pointer and drag it around on the whiteboard to indicate various features.
   - Select the Text button, which has a large "A" on it, to turn your mouse pointer into an insertion point. Click with the mouse anywhere on the whiteboard and start typing. You can change the color of the font with the color palette, and you can change the Font Name and Font Size with the corresponding buttons on the Whiteboard toolbar.
   - Select Capture ➢ Window, Capture ➢ Desktop, or Capture ➢ Region to activate the screen capture tool. If you use Capture ➢ Window, the next window you click on will be pasted into your whiteboard. Capture ➢ Desktop will do the same for your entire desktop. Use the Capture ➢ Region command to drag a rectangle around any portion of the screen, which will be pasted into the whiteboard when you release the mouse button.

TIP TIP TIP TIP TIP TIP TIP TIP TIP TIP TIP TIP TIP TIP TIP TIP TIP TIP TIP TIP TIP TIP TIP TIP TIP TIP TIP TIP TIP

If you have pasted, captured, or imported an image into the Conference Whiteboard, your canvas consists of two layers—the Image layer and the Markup layer. This is great because you can doodle freehand on top of your image with the Freehand Line tool, remove all of the scribblings with Options ➢ Erase Markups, and start over with the original image restored. To take everything off the whiteboard, use Edit ➢ Clear Whiteboard.

4. When you have completed your whiteboard session, you can print the whiteboard with File ➢ Print, or you can save the whiteboard as a file with a `.bmp`, `.jpg`, or `.tif` extension with File ➢ Save. Select File ➢ Close to leave the whiteboard function and return to the Conference main window.

Other Netscape Conference Features

Netscape Conference does not have the collaborative shared applications feature of Microsoft NetMeeting, but it does have robust Collaborative Browsing and File Transfer functions. The Collaborative Browsing feature allows two users to browse the Web together, with one taking the lead. File Transfer is another way to send files to users during a chat session or voice call.

Here are the steps for using Collaborative Browsing:

1. Start Conference and call up participants as explained in Steps 1 through 4 in the "Chatting with Netscape Conference" section. Click the Collaborative Browsing button to open the Collaborative Browsing dialog box.
2. Click the Start Browsing button to begin the joint session. Conference will open Netscape Navigator and let the other person know that they have been invited to join your browsing session. Make sure the Control the Browsers box is checked in the Leading area of the Collaborative Browsing dialog box.
3. Click the Sync Browsers button to make sure that you and your browsing companion are starting with the same Web page.
4. Click the Stop Browsing button to end the session.
5. Exit from Navigator and select Call ➢ Hang Up in the Netscape Conference menu to end the connection.

To use the File Transfer feature, follow these steps:

1. Start Conference and call up participants as explained in Steps 1 through 4 in the "Chatting with Netscape Conference" section. Click the File Exchange button during an audio session to send files.
2. In the Conference File Exchange window, select File ➢ Add to Send List or click the Open button to select files from the Add File to Send List window.
3. Before you send the file, choose any of these options to compress files (they will be automatically decompressed at the other end) or to change the file format so that different computer systems can still use them.
   - Select Options ➢ Compress to compress the files before sending.
   - Select Options ➢ ASCII to convert files into a text format that can be used by most computers.
   - Select Options ➢ Binary to send files in a format that can be used by Macintosh computers.

Is Wednesday Good for You?

One of the hardest parts of arranging meetings, whether they're face to face or virtual, is figuring out the best time when everybody (or nearly everybody) is available. There are various tools available for coordinating schedules and registering meeting dates in a centrally accessible database. As usual, each solution requires that everyone involved be using the same system—your company or organization will have to make a decision (and probably someone will just tell you) about what system to use. There are products that work with the major Web browsers (at least the latest versions of them): Netscape Calendar (it comes only with the Professional version of Netscape Communicator 4) and Microsoft Outlook.

There are also long-standing groupware programs that address this same issue, such as GroupWise. No matter what system gets put in place on your intranet, you'll use the software much the way you would a traditional organizer or personal information manager (logging addresses, phone calls, notes, meeting dates, and so on), as shown in Figure 15.4.

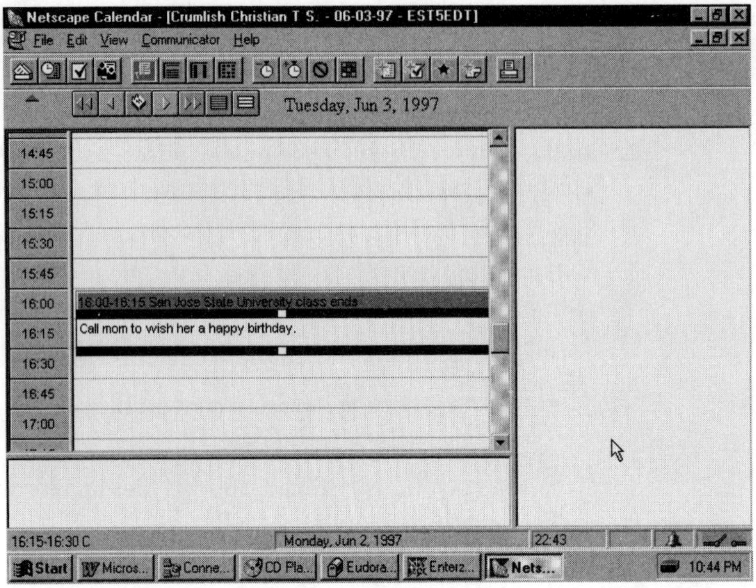

FIGURE 15.4: You can use Netscape Calendar to keep track of your schedule and coordinate open times for meetings.

Are You Experienced?

Now you can...

- ☑ share documents, images, and applications over the Internet or an intranet
- ☑ collaborate with others via a whiteboard or chat session
- ☑ set up an online meeting and interact with all the participants
- ☑ use your communications programs to call others, leave messages, or send meeting invitations
- ☑ send files to other online users in a format they can use

PART V

Alternative Approaches to the Net

The first four Parts of this book cover the most common approaches to the Internet. Part V describes some of the other tools you can use to access the Net.

Skill 16 discusses America Online, the single most popular Internet access provider, which comes complete with its own unified interface. Skill 17 touches on the other popular online services (CompuServe and MSN), Web-based free e-mail accounts, and WebTV, which allows you to access the Internet without using a computer. Skill 18 explains some of the more technical and "old-fashioned" Internet methods, FTP (File Transfer Protocol) and Telnet. Lastly, Skill 19 shows you how to add your own page to the Web.

SKILL 16

ACCESSING THE INTERNET WITH AOL

- **Starting AOL**
- **E-mailing via AOL**
- **Web browsing via AOL**
- **FTP with AOL**
- **Newsgroups with AOL**
- **AOL chatting**
- **AOL for the whole family**

America Online (also known as AOL) is the most popular online service today. If you use it to get on the Net, then you can stay within one familiar program the whole time, which you may find comforting. If you're not an AOL user, you can skip this lesson. (If you use another online service, such as CompuServe or MSN, or if you're using Web-based e-mail, such as Juno or Hotmail.com, or if you've got WebTV, see Skill 17.)

Connecting to AOL

Start your America Online program by double-clicking the America Online icon on your desktop, or by selecting Start ➢ America Online in Windows 95 or 98. (If you are using an earlier version of Windows, you can create a shortcut and drag it out onto your desktop, where you can then double-click it to start your application. On a Macintosh computer, you can put an alias on your desktop, on your launcher, or on the Apple menu and start AOL that way.)

Type your password and press Enter to connect to AOL.

Using E-mail via AOL

AOL has an easy-to-use e-mail interface, both for sending mail to other members of the service as well as for sending Internet mail. When you log in, the Welcome screen will alert you if you have new mail.

Reading E-mail

To read your new mail, click the You Have Mail icon. (At any time, you can also click the Read Mail button on the main toolbar.) Then follow these steps:

1. Double-click the subject of a message in the New Mail tab of the Mailbox dialog box (see Figure 16.1).
2. Read the message and close the window when you're done. Once you've read a message, AOL moves it to the Old Mail dialog box.
3. To read an old message, select the Old Mail tab of the Mailbox dialog box. As with new mail, double-click the subject of any message you want to read.
4. AOL also keeps copies of outgoing messages. To read them, select the Sent Mail tab.
5. Close all open dialog boxes when you're done.

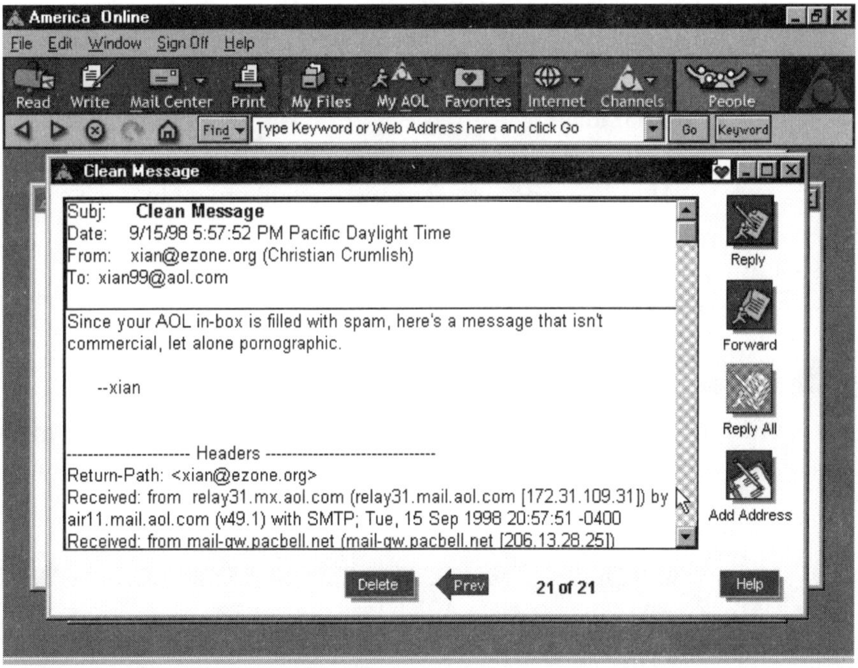

FIGURE 16.1: America Online's e-mail program is very easy to learn.

Sending E-mail

Here's how to create e-mail with America Online:

1. Compose an e-mail message by clicking the Write button in the main toolbar.
2. Type the recipient's address (if they're on AOL you can just use their *screen name,* which is what AOL calls a username) in the Write Mail window.
3. Press Tab twice and type a subject line.

4. Press Tab again to get to the message area and type your message.
5. When you're done, click either the Send Now or the Send Later button.

TIP TIP TIP TIP TIP TIP TIP TIP TIP TIP TIP TIP TIP TIP TIP TIP TIP TIP TIP TIP TIP TIP TIP TIP TIP

America Online lets you compose messages offline; then you can log in and send them in something called Automatic AOL (formerly known as a Flash Session), so you're not tying up your phone line while racking your brains over what to write.

After you send some e-mail, you will probably receive some return messages, which you can open and read.

Essential E-mail

Reply

Reply All

To reply to an open message, click the Reply button (or click Reply All to send your reply to all the recipients of the original message). This opens up a new mail window just like the kind you get when you send a new message.

To delete a message, select it and then click the Delete button at the bottom of the dialog box.

WARNING WARNING WARNING WARNING WARNING WARNING WARNING WARNING

You can't undelete AOL e-mail messages.

Forward

You can forward America Online mail to another address by clicking the Forward button in the message window.

To send mail to multiple addresses, just type the addresses in the To box, separated by commas, or press Tab and type some of the addresses in the Cc box.

Filing E-Mail Messages

If your old mail starts piling up and you have trouble finding important messages, you may want to learn how to file your messages. Follow these steps to create a new folder for filing messages:

1. Select My Files ➢ Personal Filing Cabinet.
2. In the dialog box that appears, select the Mail folder and then click Add Folder.

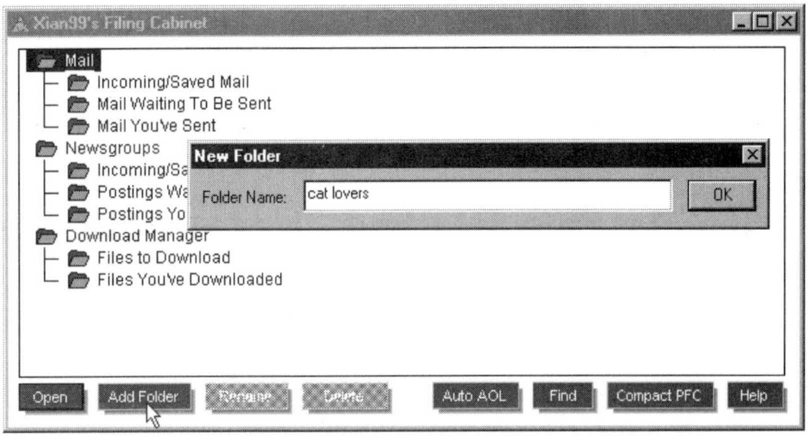

3. Type a name for the new folder and click OK.

To file a message in any of your folders, select its subject in a mail window and drag it to whichever folder you want.

Attaching Files to AOL Messages

To send an attached file with an e-mail message, follow these steps:

1. While in the Write Mail window, click the Attachments button.
2. In the Attachments dialog box that appears, click the Attach button (yes, it seems kind of redundant to me, too).
3. Select a file in the Attach File dialog box that appears (this looks just like the typical Open dialog box you see in any normal program) and then click OK.
4. Repeat steps 2 and 3 for any additional files you'd like to attach (or go on to the next step).
5. Click OK again.

TIP TIP TIP TIP TIP TIP TIP TIP TIP TIP TIP TIP TIP TIP TIP TIP TIP TIP TIP TIP TIP TIP TIP TIP TIP

Remember which directory (or folder) contains the file you want to attach to your message, so that you can quickly go there and attach the file without spending a lot of time searching for the attachments.

The file (or files) will be attached using the MIME format. Make sure your recipient's e-mail program can understand that format. You can also receive files sent to you from Internet e-mail addresses—as long as the sender's program can send MIME attachments. Internet file formats are discussed in Skill 10, *Finding Stuff on the Web and the Net*.

Downloading Attached Files from AOL Messages

When you receive a message with an attached file, two buttons will appear at the bottom of the message window: Download File and Download Later. Use one of these two options, depending on your plans:

- Click Download File to download the file immediately (the message will also give you a rough estimate of how long the download should take).
- Click Download Later to leave the file waiting until you're ready to download it.

Using the AOL Address Book

AOL provides you with an address book for managing your e-mail addresses. To add an address to it, use these procedures:

1. Select Mail ➢ Address Book.
2. In the Address Book window that appears, click the New Person or New Group button.
3. Enter the e-mail address (or addresses) and any additional information you want.
4. Click OK to add the name to the address book.

Once you've entered some addresses, it's easy to use your address book to send a new message using these steps:

Address Book

1. In the Write Mail dialog box, click the Address Book button.
2. Choose a name and its associated e-mail address and then click the To button.
3. Click OK to insert the corresponding address into the To box.

NOTE

AOL's mail program does not include a spell checker or a way to attach signatures to outgoing messages.

Getting to the Web via AOL

AOL's built-in Web browser is a licensed version of Microsoft Internet Explorer. The easiest way to launch the browser is to click the Go to the Web icon in the Welcome dialog box (or choose Internet ➢ Go to the Web). You can also type a URL into the address box near the top of the AOL window.

Figure 16.2 shows the AOL home page that comes up automatically when you connect to the Web without specifying a particular site.

FIGURE 16.2: America Online's browser starts you off at the AOL home page.

SKILL 16

Using Netscape Navigator with AOL

To run Netscape Navigator with AOL, first download the entire Communicator suite (go to keyword Netscape by selecting Go To ➢ Keyword ➢ Netscape) and install it. Then simply connect via AOL and double-click the Communicator icon on your desktop or select Start ➢ Programs ➢ Netscape Communicator ➢ Netscape Navigator. Navigator will use the AOL connection to show you the Web.

WARNING WARNING WARNING WARNING WARNING WARNING WARNING WARNING

Before you download files or programs from the Internet, invest in some anti-virus software for your computer and learn how to use it. Make sure the anti-virus program is turned on before you start your downloads. You can also use the anti-virus software to scan files downloaded from the Web before you got the anti-virus program or to scan files someone gave you on a floppy disk or other removable media. If the software finds a virus in your files, it can usually repair them and can even remove the virus from your hard drive in some cases.

TIP TIP TIP TIP TIP TIP TIP TIP TIP TIP TIP TIP TIP TIP TIP TIP TIP TIP TIP TIP TIP TIP TIP TIP TIP

You can also download an external version of Microsoft Internet Explorer from `http://www.microsoft.com/ie/` **(via the AOL Web browser) and install it to use with AOL. See Skill 10, *Finding Stuff on the Web and the Net*, for information on downloading files from the Web.**

Reading Usenet News with AOL

AOL offers access to newsgroups in much the same way that it offers access to its own local bulletin boards. Because AOL is an all-in-one package, you don't have to do any technical setup to begin reading news. You start by choosing newsgroups to read.

TIP TIP TIP TIP TIP TIP TIP TIP TIP TIP TIP TIP TIP TIP TIP TIP TIP TIP TIP TIP TIP TIP TIP TIP TIP

For more on Usenet newsgroups, see Skill 13.

1. To get to the newsgroups, click Internet ➢ Newsgroups in the toolbar. This will display the Newsgroups dialog box (see Figure 16.3).

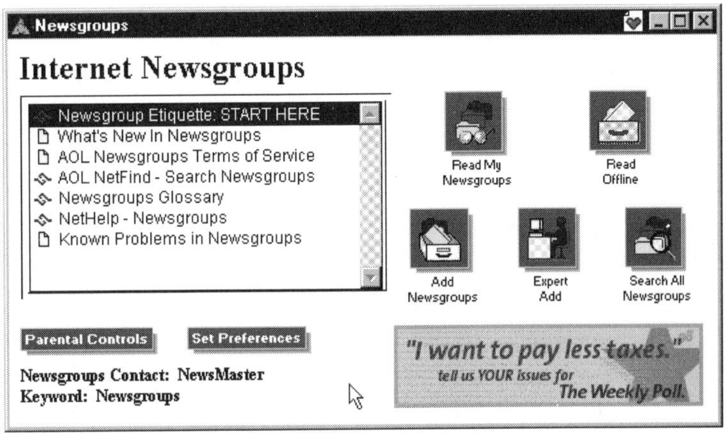

FIGURE 16.3: AOL's Newsgroups dialog box

2. To add newsgroups to your subscription list, click the Add Newsgroups button in the Newsgroups dialog box. This brings up the Add Newsgroups—Categories dialog box. Newsgroups are listed by plain English descriptions as well as by their top-level hierarchies.

SKILL 16

TIP

The Add Newsgroups button gives you access to a selected number of newsgroups. You can also click the Expert Add button to add any group if you know its exact name.

3. Double-click a category to see the subchoices associated with it. Repeat this process until you've zeroed in on a specific group. So, for example, to find your way to the `news.announce.newusers` newsgroup, you'd first choose the `news.*` choice, and then the `news.announce` choice, and finally the spelled-out Explanatory Postings for New Users choice.

TIP

If you'd prefer to see the Internet names of the newsgroups, click the Internet Names button above the list.

4. When you arrive at a group you want to read, click the Add button to subscribe to it or click the List Subjects button to immediately see its contents.
5. When you are finished adding or reviewing newsgroups, close all of the newsgroup windows by clicking the close box in the upper-right corner of each window (or the upper-left if you're using a Mac).

AOL Chat Rooms

AOL is famous for its chat rooms, which essentially are live, running conversations (similar to IRC, as discussed in Skill 14). Some chat rooms are created for specific topics. Others are created on the spur of the moment, just to be sociable.

If you're looking for someone to chat with live, click People ➢ Find a Chat.

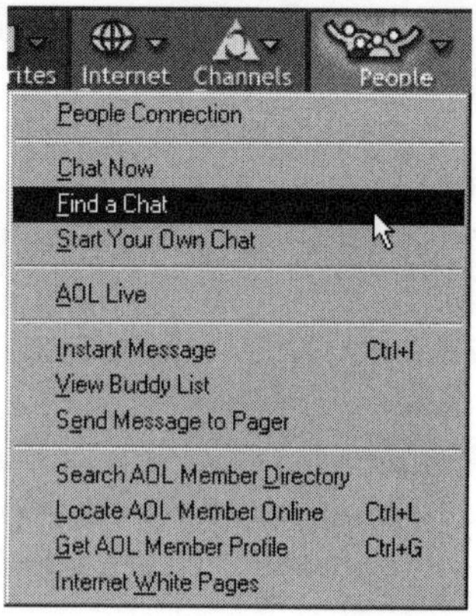

This will bring up the Find a Chat dialog box, which makes it easy to select an ongoing chat by topic or to start your own chat. Click the word "help" in the lower-right corner of the dialog box if you're not sure what to do (see Figure 16.4).

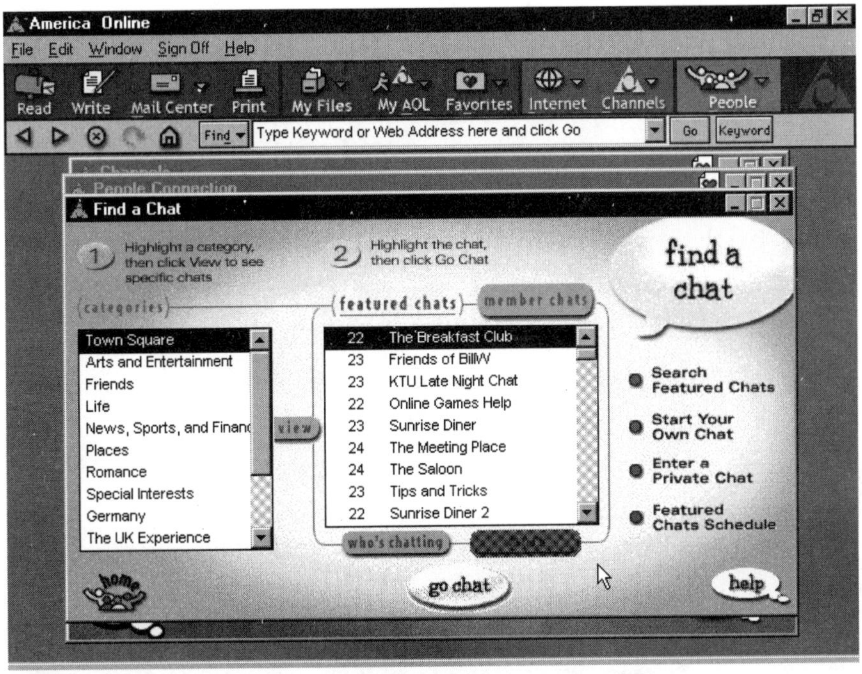

FIGURE 16.4: For some people, AOL is an all-night bull session.

Transferring Files with AOL

Folks with ordinary Internet connections will have to wait till Skill 18 to learn how to transfer files using FTP (File Transfer Protocol), but AOL's all-in-one interface makes downloading files a snap. (The e-mail section of this lesson also tells you how to attach files to e-mail messages.)

TIP TIP TIP TIP TIP TIP TIP TIP TIP TIP TIP TIP TIP TIP TIP TIP TIP TIP TIP TIP TIP TIP TIP TIP TIP

See Skill 10, *Finding Stuff on the Web and the Net,* for more about what types of programs and other files are available

To look for files or software to download, select Internet ➢ FTP (File Transfer).

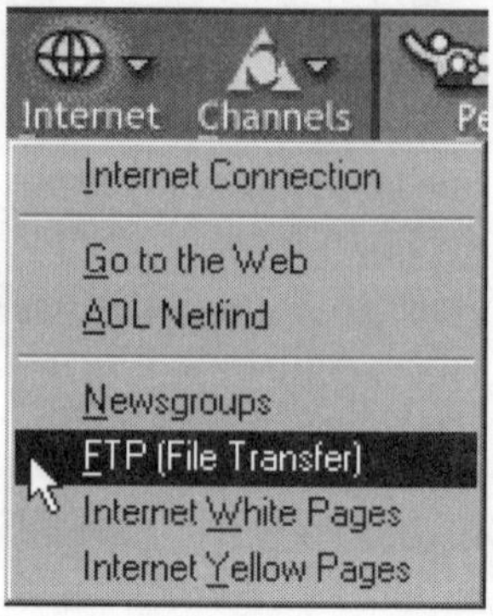

AOL's FTP—File Transfer Protocol dialog box appears (see Figure 16.5). It explains exactly what FTP is and makes file transfers as simple as choosing from a dialog box. Be sure to check out the Best of FTP folder, where AOL makes available the most popular shareware and other files for rapid download.

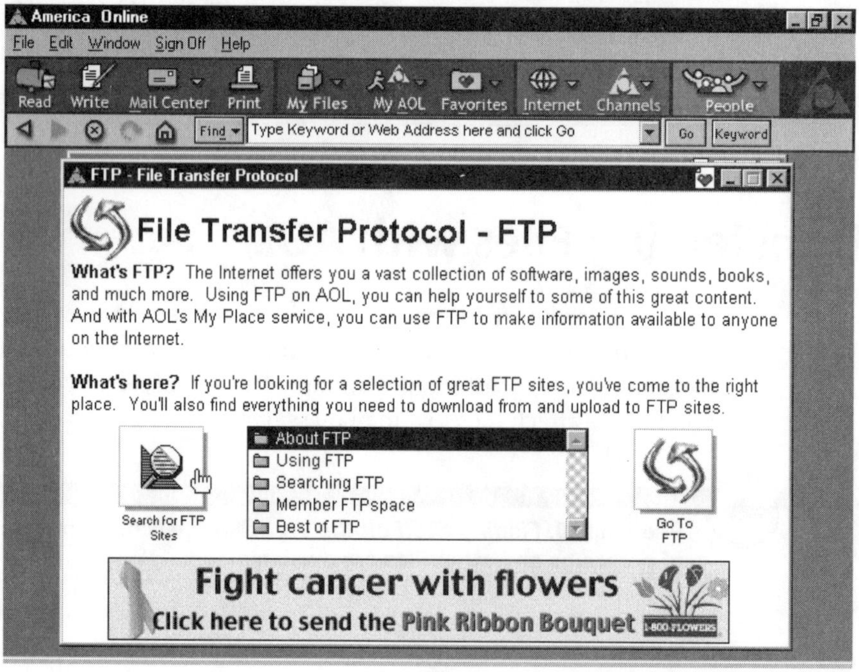

FIGURE 16.5: AOL makes FTP as easy as opening files with an Open dialog box.

AOL for Your Family

Skill 3 discussed how your entire family can make safe and healthy use of the Internet. Since AOL is an all-in-one interface, it has its own set of parental controls that enable you to decide what your children will and won't be permitted to do with the software (and what they will and won't be exposed to from the outside world). You can jump to the Parental Controls dialog box from many different vantage points within AOL. The easiest link is directly from the Welcome dialog box, or you can just type **Parental Controls** in the Keyword box just below the toolbar and click Go (or press Enter) from anywhere in AOL.

The Parental Controls dialog box gives you an overview of the features you can control (see Figure 16.6). The first step you'll want to take is to create separate screen names for each child in your family who might use AOL. Then you can establish rules for your child or children, fine-tuning them if necessary for a range of ages and levels of maturity.

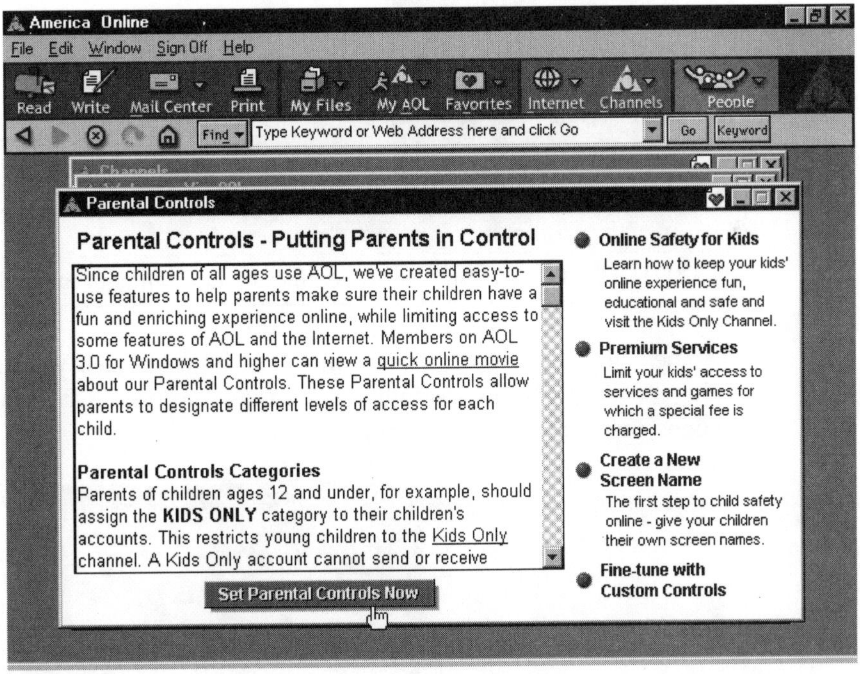

FIGURE 16.6: AOL's Parental Controls dialog box explains how you may limit your child's exposure on the Internet.

When you're ready, click Set Parental Controls Now. This brings up another Parental Controls dialog box. Start by indicating the age-range of the screen name whose access you're customizing (see Figure 16.7).

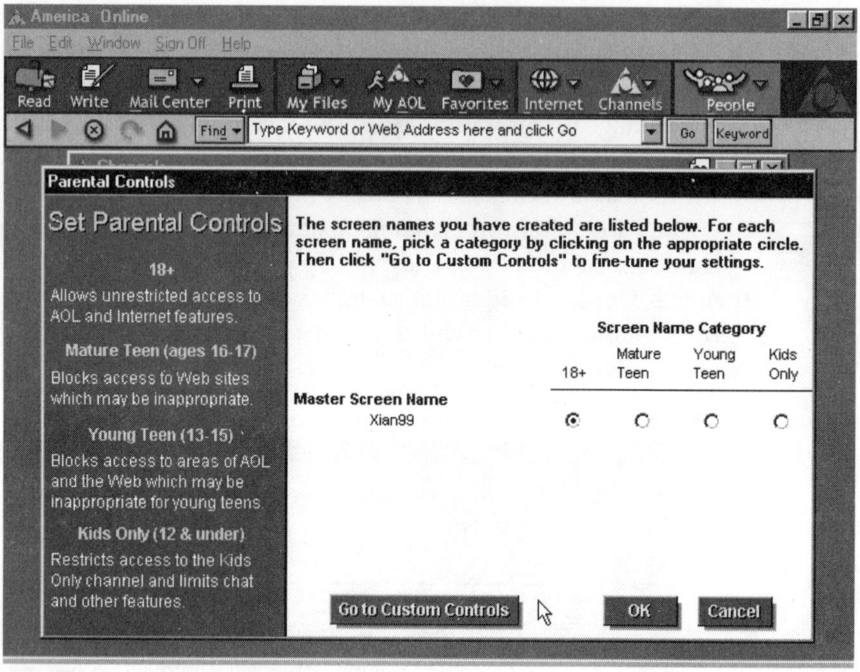

FIGURE 16.7: Start by indicating the age-range of the child in question.

Then click the Go to Custom Controls button. AOL lets you know you won't be charged (unless you have a window to a premium service open) for the time you spend fine-tuning your parental controls.

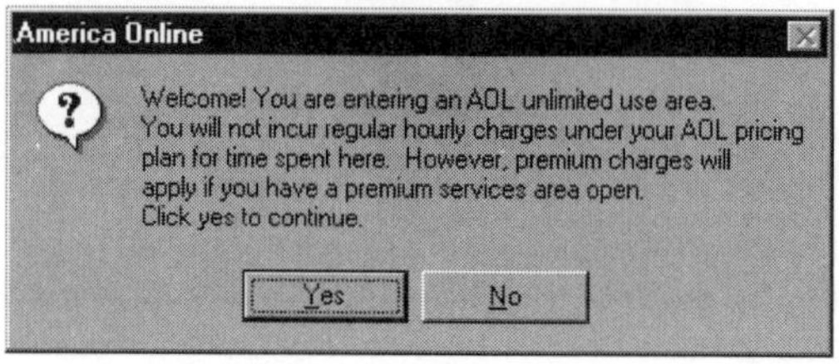

When you click Yes, the Custom Controls dialog box comes up, indicating six areas you can control (Chat, Instant Messages, Downloading, Web, Mail, and

Newsgroups). If you click on any of these categories, an explanation appears in the text box to the right (see Figure 16.8).

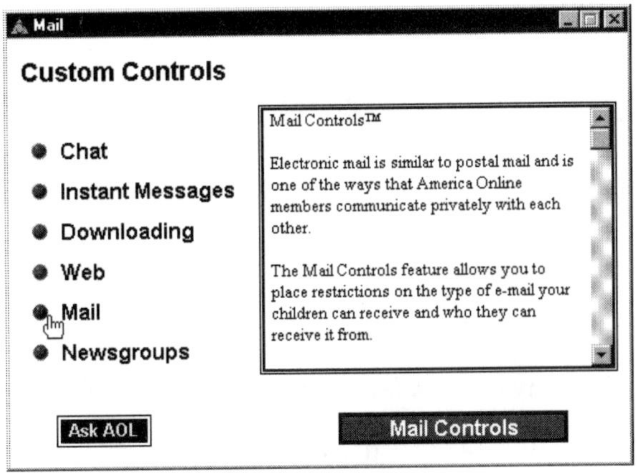

FIGURE 16.8: Choose a category to control.

Click the red button below the text area (it changes depending on which category you've selected; in our example it reads "Mail Controls") to bring up a dialog box that you can use to fine-tune your controls in that category. Figure 16.9 shows the range of possibilities in the Mail Controls dialog box. If you check Block E-mail with Pictures or Attached Files, for example, you can be sure no one will be sending your child any pornography!

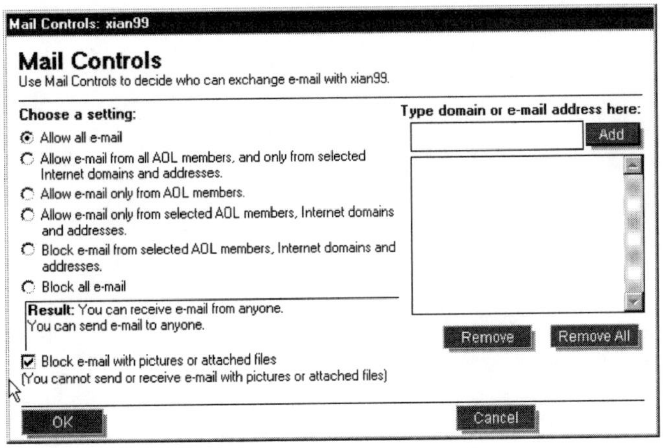

FIGURE 16.9: The Mail Controls dialog box gives you fine-tuning control over the mail your child may send or receive.

Repeat the process for each of the categories you're concerned about. Remember, though, that there's no substitute for discussing these important issues with your children, just as you tell them how to behave and who they may speak with in public.

Are You Experienced?

Now you can...

- ☑ log in to AOL
- ☑ send and receive e-mail in AOL
- ☑ browse the Web from AOL
- ☑ read newsgroups with AOL
- ☑ enter AOL chat rooms for live conversations
- ☑ transfer files with AOL
- ☑ customize AOL for your entire family

SKILL 17

OTHER ONLINE SERVICES, WEBTV, AND FREE WEB-BASED E-MAIL

- **The other big online services (CompuServe and MSN)**
- **Free Web-based e-mail accounts**
- **WebTV (Internet for couch potatoes)**

This book assumes that you'll connect to the Internet the way most people do, with a computer, a modem or network, an Internet service provider (ISP), and Web browser and e-mail software. There are, however, alternative approaches. One such approach, America Online, is discussed in the previous lesson, but AOL is not the only online service (just the most popular). There are two other online services with high profiles: CompuServe and MSN (the Microsoft Network). Last year, AOL bought CompuServe, but so far, they've kept it a separate service. MSN wouldn't ordinarily be considered a contender, but—Justice Department or no—any product backed by Microsoft is automatically in the running for industry leader, no matter how many times MS has to retool and rerelease the product before they get it right.

Another all-in-one solution to Internet access is Web-based free e-mail. With this approach, you can still get an ISP or take advantage of public or work access to the Internet, but you don't maintain e-mail software of your own and you don't keep your e-mail messages in any one place. Instead, you use a Web interface to read and send mail from any computer with a Web connection. These e-mail accounts are free because they are supported by advertisements (as are most free services on the Web).

A third alternative does away with the presumption that you must have a computer to communicate on the Internet. We're already seeing the first generation of television/Internet set-top boxes. I'll briefly discuss how this approach compares to the "traditional" method (if anything so relatively young can be said to have traditions).

Other Online Services

There are other online services besides the few discussed in this book (Prodigy, for example), but CompuServe and MSN will serve to illustrate the two remaining models for these services. Like AOL, CompuServe offers an all-in-one interface. The current incarnation of the Microsoft Network, however, is designed to integrate smoothly with the Web, with Windows, and with Microsoft's other software, making it in many ways more like a standard ISP, except with a lot of paid-for content.

CompuServe

CompuServe is the second-most popular online service (after America Online). To use the steps detailed below, first open CompuServe. In Windows 95 or 98, select Start ➢ Programs ➢ CompuServe ➢ CompuServe Information Manager.

Creating CompuServe Messages and Checking E-mail

To send and read e-mail using CompuServe, follow these steps:

1. First click the Mail Center button.
2. This brings up the Mail Center window with its Read tab selected, showing your incoming messages (see Figure 17.1).

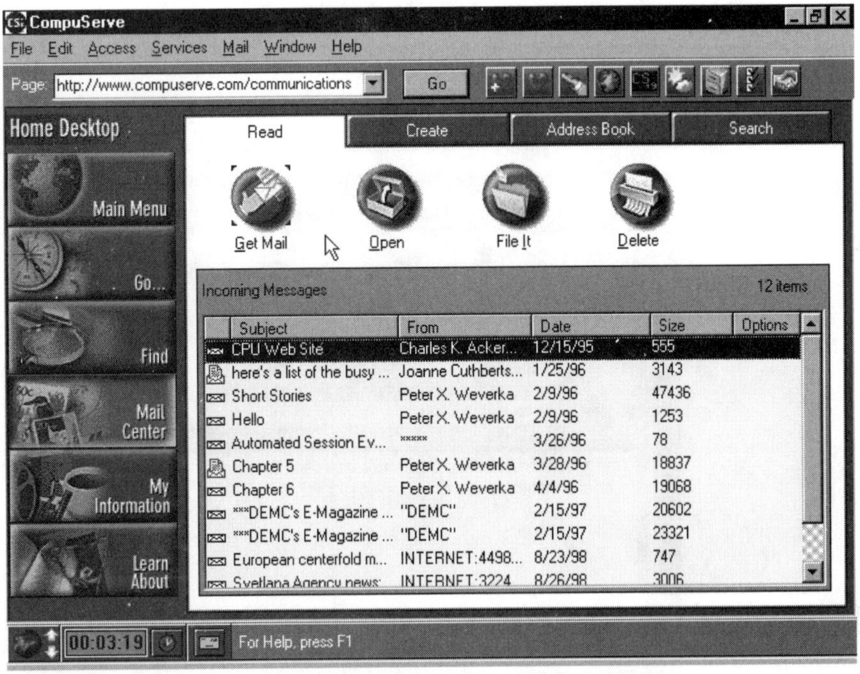

FIGURE 17.1: CompuServe's mail interface is simple to use and understand.

3. To get your new mail on CompuServe, click the Get Mail button.

4. Double-click on a message to read it. To reply to a message, click the Reply button at the top of the message window. To delete a message, click the Delete button and then click Yes.

WARNING WARNING WARNING WARNING WARNING WARNING WARNING WARNING

CompuServe e-mail messages cannot be undeleted.

To send a message, follow these steps:

1. Click the New button.
2. Type the recipient's name, press Tab, type the e-mail address, press Tab again, type a subject, and press Tab yet again.
3. Write your message (see Figure 17.2).
4. Click the Send or Send Later button when you are finished writing.

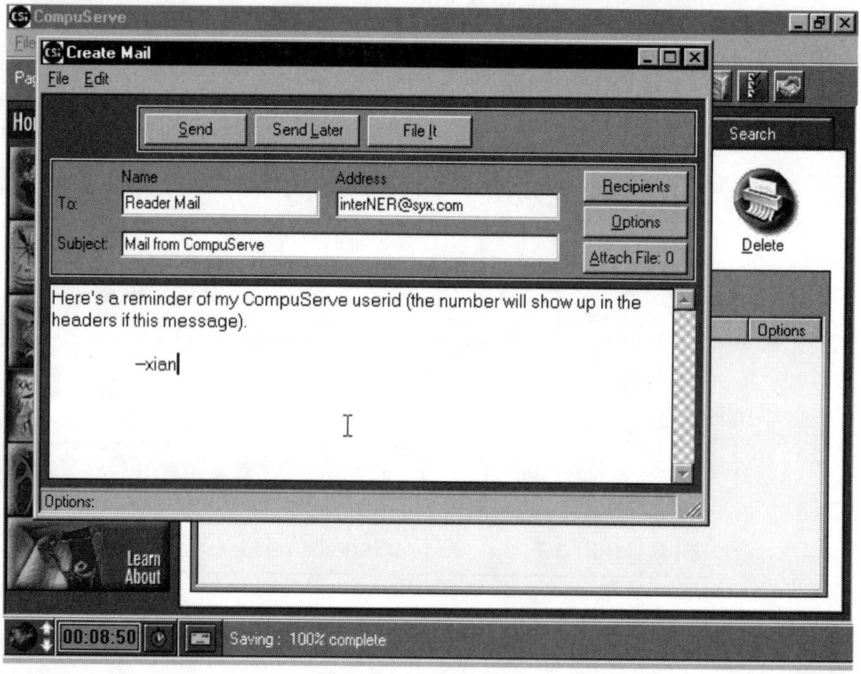

FIGURE 17.2: With CompuServe, click the Send button to send the message immediately or click the Send Later button to store the message until you disconnect.

TIP TIP TIP TIP TIP TIP TIP TIP TIP TIP TIP TIP TIP TIP TIP TIP TIP TIP TIP TIP TIP TIP TIP TIP TIP TIP TIP

CompuServe lets you compose any number of messages offline and put them in your Out Basket to send later. You can then use the Mail ➢ Send/Receive All Mail command to send and receive all your mail as quickly as possible so you can get back offline.

Sending and Forwarding CompuServe Messages

CompuServe's e-mail has simple instructions for performing the usual e-mail functions:

- To forward mail to another recipient, click the Forward button in the Read Mail window, then proceed as you would with a normal message.
- To send mail to more than one recipient, simply type the recipient addresses in the To line, separated by semicolons.

Attaching Files to CompuServe Messages

Use CompuServe's File Attachment feature to include files with your messages. If you have written long memos or reports in your word processing program, you can reuse them by attaching the file to a short message.

1. Create the message as usual and then click the Attach File button.
2. Select a file from the Open dialog box that appears and then click OK twice (CompuServe always makes you confirm everything).
3. Type your message and then click the Send or Send Later button.

Using Your CompuServe Address Book

CompuServe includes an address book where you can store the names and e-mail addresses of your colleagues and friends. To add an address from an existing message to your address book, click the Address button in the Read Mail window. In the Add to Address Book dialog box that appears, select the address and click the Add button.

At any other time, you can add an address to your address book with these steps:

1. Click the Address Book tab of the Mail Center window.
2. Click the Add Entry button.
3. Choose Individual Address or Group Mailing List, enter the address(es), and click OK twice.

To add an address from your address book to a new message, click the Recipients button in the Create Mail window. In the Message Recipients dialog box that appears, click the Address Book button, select recipients, and click OK twice.

> **TIP**
>
> **CompuServe does not currently have a spell checker or a way of attaching signature blocks to mail messages.**

If you want more information about CompuServe's mail feature, type Mail Center in the Page box (like a browser's address box) at the top of the window, and click the Go button.

The Web via CompuServe

Internet

CompuServe comes with a built-in edition of Microsoft Internet Explorer (though it's also possible to run an external browser, such as Netscape, once you're connected). The new CompuServe interface seamlessly switches to the Web browser when you enter a Web address in the Page box. You can also click the Internet button on the Main Menu. Figure 17.3 shows the CompuServe home page that comes up automatically when you click the Internet button on the main menu.

Changing to a Different Browser in CompuServe

You can choose an external Web browser or change the CompuServe default browser by using these procedures (after the browser is installed):

1. Select Access ➢ Preferences and click the General tab on the Preferences dialog box.
2. Click the Use External Internet Browser checkbox. CompuServe will use the browser listed in the Internet browser box (which will be Internet Explorer, if you haven't tampered with it yet).
3. To select a different browser, click the Select button, make your way to the browser you want (look for Netscape under `c:\Program Files\Netscape \Communicator\Program`; look for Internet Explorer under `c:\Program`

`Files\Microsoft Internet` or `c:\Program Files\Plus!`), select it, and click OK.

4. Then click OK again to close the Preferences dialog box.

The next time you click the Internet button in the main menu or enter a URL in the Page box, CompuServe will launch your chosen browser.

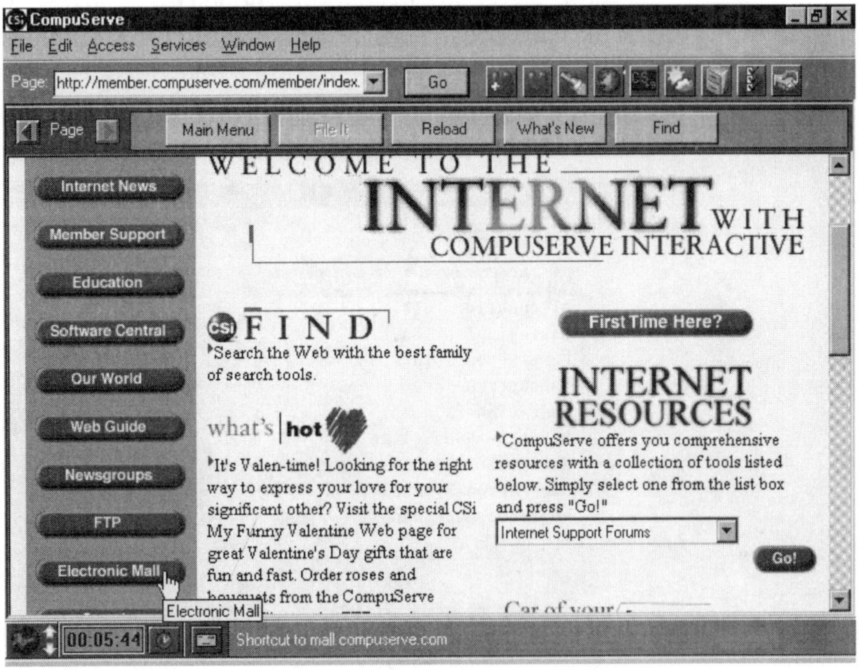

FIGURE 17.3: The Internet Explorer browser built into CompuServe's slick new interface starts you off at this CompuServe home page.

Usenet via CompuServe

Access to newsgroups is built into CompuServe software. You don't need any technical setup to start reading news. All you have to do is choose the newsgroups to read. It's also possible to read news in CompuServe with another external newsreader.

NOTE NOTE NOTE NOTE NOTE NOTE NOTE NOTE NOTE NOTE NOTE NOTE NOTE NOTE

Usenet is explained in detail in Skill 13, *Joining Usenet Newsgroups*.

Subscribing to Usenet Newsgroups with CompuServe

Follow these steps to access Usenet newsgroups and read the postings with CompuServe:

1. To subscribe to newsgroups with CompuServe, type **CIM Reader** in the Page box and click the Go button. The Usenet Newsgroups dialog box will appear.
2. To add newsgroups to your subscription list, choose Subscribe to Newsgroups in the dialog box and click the Select button. This brings up the Subscribe to Newsgroups dialog box. Newsgroups are listed by plain English descriptions as well as by their top-level hierarchies (see Figure 17.4).

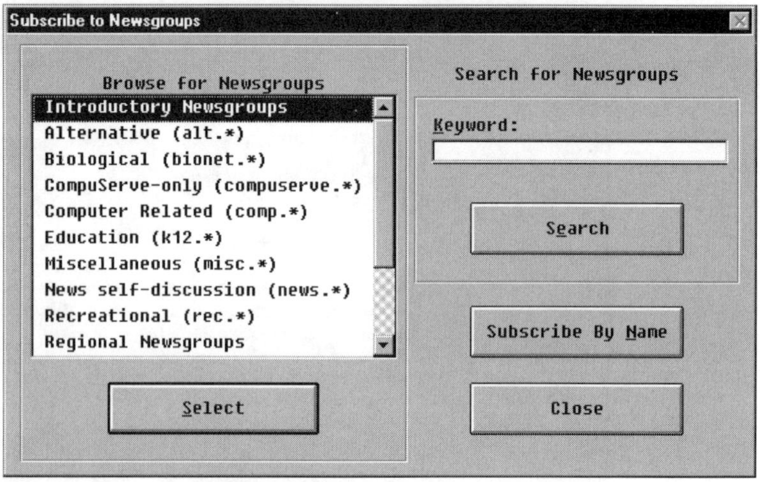

FIGURE 17.4: CompuServe's Subscribe to Newsgroups dialog box

TIP

You can also type a keyword in the Keyword box to search for newsgroups containing that word.

3. Double-click on a category to see the newsgroups in it. To subscribe to a newsgroup, click the checkbox next to the name of a group, click the Subscribe button, and then click OK in the dialog box that appears.

4. When you are done selecting groups in a category, click the Cancel button. Repeat the process with other categories if you wish.

5. Click the Close button in the Subscribe to Newsgroups dialog box when you are done choosing categories.

TIP

To subscribe to a group directly (if you know its exact name), click the Subscribe by Name button, type the name, and press Enter.

Reading Newsgroup Articles with CompuServe

After you have subscribed to some interesting newsgroups, you can open CompuServe, log on, and immediately read some newsgroup articles with these simple steps:

1. To go directly to your subscribed newsgroups, choose Access Your Usenet Newsgroups in the Usenet Newsgroups dialog box, and then click the Select button.

2. To see the articles in a newsgroup you've subscribed to, click the Browse button in the bottom-left corner of the Access Newsgroup dialog box.

3. To read an article, double-click on its subject or select it and then click the Get button (see Figure 17.5). Scroll through the message area in the window that appears.

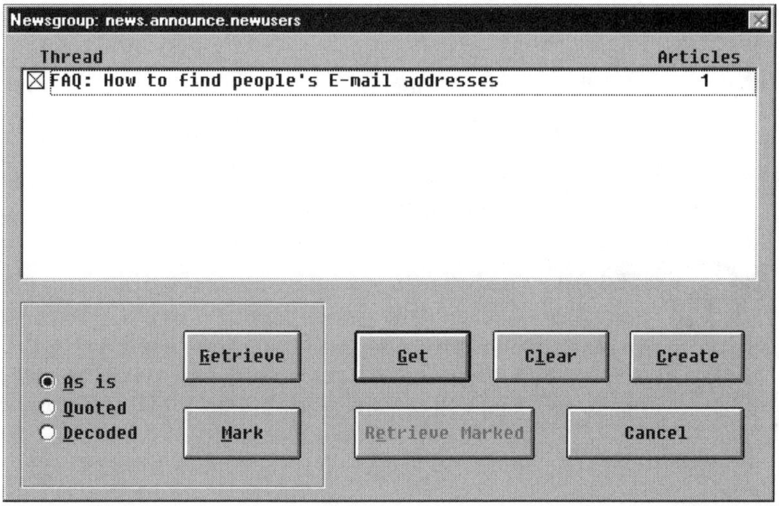

FIGURE 17.5: Choose an article to read in a Newsgroup dialog box and then click the Get button.

4. Use these options to view articles and threads:
   - To read the next article in a thread, click the > button under Article.
   - To jump to the next thread and read it, click the > button under Thread.
   - To save an article so you can re-read it later, click the Hold button.
5. Click the Leave button when you're ready to quit reading news.

TIP TIP TIP TIP TIP TIP TIP TIP TIP TIP TIP TIP TIP TIP TIP TIP TIP TIP TIP TIP TIP TIP TIP TIP TIP

You can mark a number of articles and then get them all at once.

Responding to Newsgroup Articles with CompuServe

Sometimes you will be inspired to compose a reply or to post another related newsgroup article in response to one of particular interest to you. Here are the steps for making your response:

1. If you want to reply to an article, first select and copy (Ctrl+C or Command+C) the portion of the article you wish to quote.
2. Then click the Reply button. CompuServe will create a new message window for you with the selected portion of the original article already included for context.
3. Uncheck the Send via E-mail option if you don't want to send your reply directly to the original sender, and check the Post to Newsgroup(s) option to post your reply. By default, CompuServe will check off the current newsgroup's name in the Newsgroups' area, but you can select any of your subscribed newsgroups. If you select more than one, your article will be crossposted to all of the selected groups.
4. Write your reply, making it clear that you are quoting an earlier message, and then click the Send button.

TIP TIP TIP TIP TIP TIP TIP TIP TIP TIP TIP TIP TIP TIP TIP TIP TIP TIP TIP TIP TIP TIP TIP TIP TIP

Remember, you can always write your responses offline in a word processing or text editing program, then copy the response to the clipboard with the Ctrl+C (or Command+C) command and paste it into your CompuServe response when you are online with the Ctrl+V (or Command+V) command.

If you have some important news items on a relevant subject that you want to post to a specific newsgroup, use these procedures for posting:

1. To post a new article to a newsgroup, click the Create button in the main Newsgroup dialog box. (If you've got an article window blocking the original Newsgroup dialog box, click its Cancel button first.)
2. Type a subject in the subject box.
3. After typing your article, click the Send button.

To get help, click the ? button on the toolbar.

NOTE NOTE NOTE NOTE NOTE NOTE NOTE NOTE NOTE NOTE NOTE NOTE NOTE NOTE NOTE

CompuServe has no provision for filtering out unwanted authors or article threads.

MSN (Microsoft Network)

About a year after its debut, MSN retooled itself as a Web-based online service. When you connect to MSN, you automatically have a PPP connection you can use to run any Internet program, including any browser you wish. (See Appendix A for more on PPP and other types of connections). More importantly, the new MSN interface is a specially adapted version of Internet Explorer, which is now being used as more than just a Web browser. Some buttons in this interface are directly linked to Web sites. To go directly to one of these predefined Web addresses, move the mouse pointer to the address box to open it up and click on the name of the page you want to jump to (see Figure 17.6). Once connected to MSN, you can also run any Web browser (such as Netscape Navigator) through the MSN connection, but (naturally) MSN content is designed to look and work best with Microsoft's Web browser, Internet Explorer (discussed in Skill 9, *Web Browsers*).

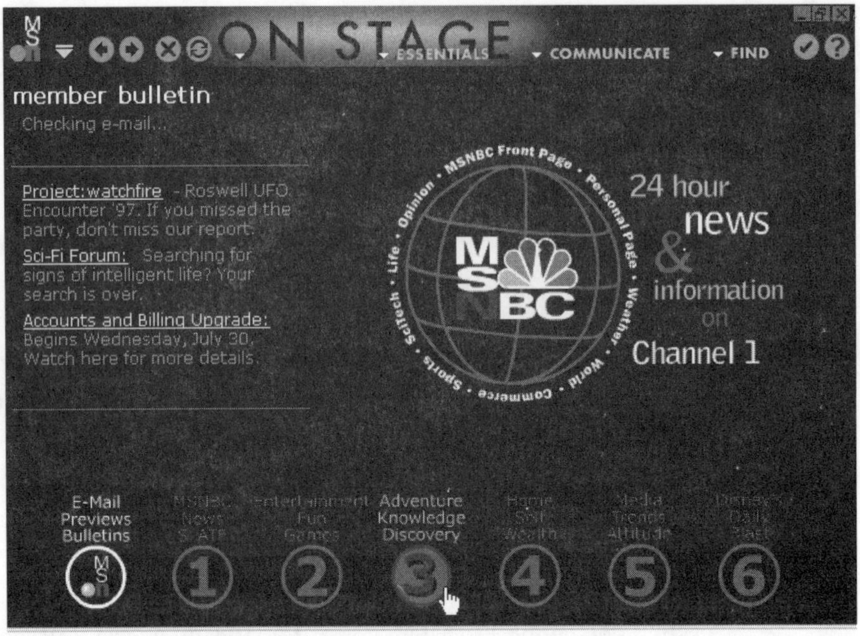

FIGURE 17.6: MSN's On Stage page cycles through its content channels, or you can simply click one of the links across the bottom of the page

If you're a Windows user (and most MSN customers are) your mail will work with whatever default e-mail program you're using. Microsoft Exchange (formerly Microsoft Mail) came with Windows 95. Microsoft Outlook 97 (a lot like Exchange, but with other groupware capabilities) comes with Office 97. Microsoft Outlook Express accompanies Microsoft Internet Explorer 4 and provides e-mail functions without the calendar, scheduler, and contact manager. You can download the Microsoft Outlook Express program from the Web. All these, as well as third-party programs such as Qualcomm's Eudora and Pegasus Mail, can send and receive your MSN mail for you.

NOTE NOTE NOTE NOTE NOTE NOTE NOTE NOTE NOTE NOTE NOTE NOTE NOTE NOTE NOTE

See Skill 6, *E-mail Programs*, for more on how to use Outlook Express as your mail program.

If you get your Internet access from MSN, then you'll read newsgroups with whichever newsreader Microsoft was giving out at the time you signed up (or you can use any newsreader you like as long as you tell it the correct news server to check for your feed). Most likely you'll be using Outlook Express (or one of its earlier incarnations, such as Microsoft Internet News).

NOTE NOTE NOTE NOTE NOTE NOTE NOTE NOTE NOTE NOTE NOTE NOTE NOTE NOTE NOTE

See Skill 13, *Joining Usenet Newsgroups*, for more on how to use Outlook Express to read Usenet newsgroups.

Microsoft has tried to give a common look and feel to MSN, Internet Explorer's Active Channels, and Windows 98's Active Desktop. There's no inherent association between these things. Internet Explorer by default starts at an MSN page, but you can change that. You can also view those same pages with another Web browser. Active Channels and the Active Desktop can only appear via Internet Explorer or Windows 98, but the content for such channels can be created by anyone. If you use MSN, you may find it convenient to have the Active Desktop turned on or to subscribe to Active Channels (see Skill 12, *Push and the Desktop Web*).

Free Web-Based E-mail

The versatility of the Web made it almost inevitable that developers would eventually come up with Web-based e-mail accounts. This form of e-mail eliminates the need for a stand-alone e-mail program, and allows you to check your mail from anyone's Internet connection just by surfing to the Web site for your e-mail host. Web-based e-mail accounts are typically free and supported by advertising built into the Web-mail interface.

These sorts of free accounts can function well as a second address, or as an address to give with Usenet postings, so that your primary mail address does not become a target of spam (see Skill 21 for more on dealing with spam).

For any of these services, all you have to do is visit the host site and fill out a few forms to set up your own account. Read the forms you fill out carefully, as you'll most likely be given the option of turning down commercial solicitations, updates, and "special offers."

One of the first free Web-mail services to appear was called HotMail. It has become so popular that Internet Explorer's Internet Start page now offers a direct link to the HotMail home page. Figure 17.7 shows the HotMail home page, where you can sign up or log in (if you're already signed up).

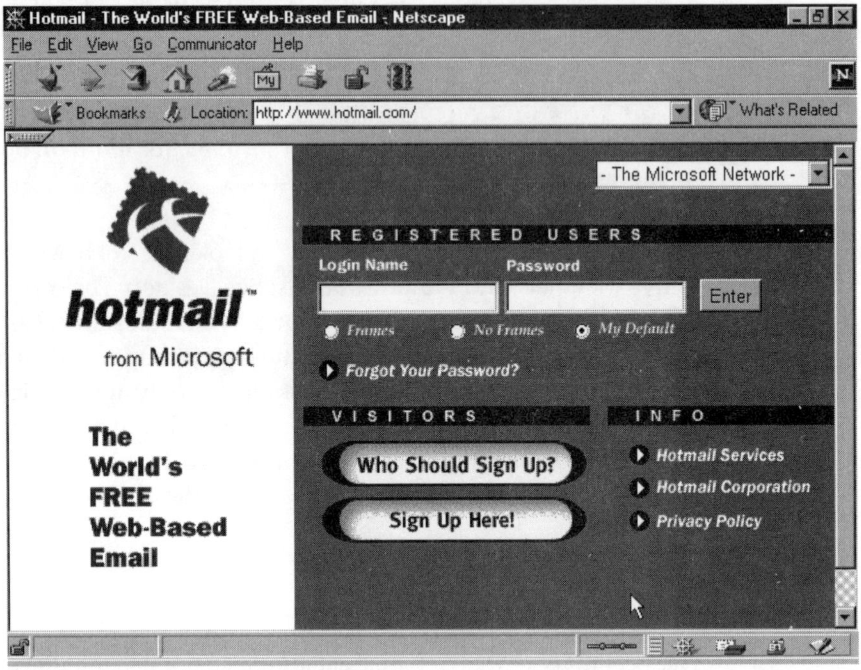

FIGURE 17.7: HotMail is the original Web-based free e-mail service.

NOTE

Another service that's been around nearly as long as Hotmail is Juno.com (`http://www.juno.com/`).

To compete with Microsoft, Netscape offers a link to its own free e-mail service, WebMail, directly from the NetCenter home page. Once you fill out the sign-up forms (including accepting or rejecting a range of custom content called In-Box Direct), you can send and receive mail through the WebMail interface (see Figure 17.8). Your e-mail address will be the *`username`* you choose `@netscape.net`.

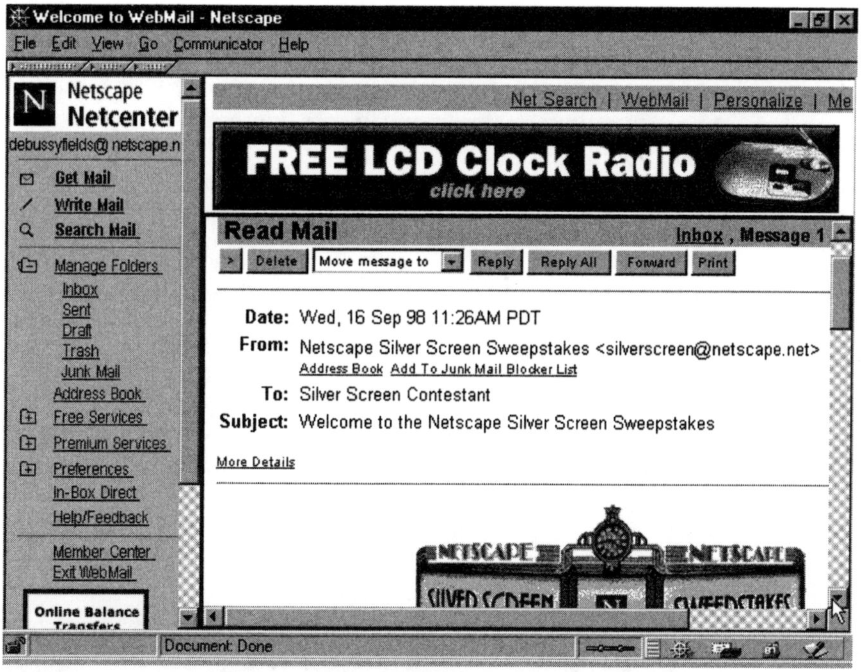

FIGURE 17.8: There's already some mail in the Inbox of my new `debussy-field@netscape.net` free WebMail account.

All the so-called portal Web sites now offer some form of free e-mail these days (for example, see the Yahoo! Mail link on the Yahoo! home page). Another search site that offers free mail is Deja News (the Usenet search site). As part of the trend toward customizable sites named My This and My That, your e-mail address with free Deja News e-mail is `your-username@my-dejanews.com`. This address serves a double purpose, permitting you to post messages to Usenet groups through the Deja News Web site without exposing your main e-mail address (or any other address) to spam. Deja News promises to filter spam out of the replies you receive to your free account.

Look Ma, No Computer (WebTV)

The Internet started as a network of computer networks, mostly on university campuses, military installations, and other research centers, but in the intervening years it's become something of a panglobal network used for just about every purpose you can think of. Now there's a way to participate in the Net without even owning a computer. All the pundits in the technology biz foresee a great "convergence" coming someday, a convergence of all media, or more particularly of TV and computers. What form this synthesis will actually take is anybody's guess, presuming it does come to pass (just because it's possible—and it is—doesn't mean it will happen).

In some ways the process has already begun. Not too long ago, several companies put out a new product called an Internet set-top box, a unit that can plug into an ordinary television and an ordinary phone jack, and—with a special keyboard and remote—enable a TV to display e-mail and Web content. At the same time, the same folks introduced a new service provider, WebTV, to provide Internet access and custom content for this new interface.

This doesn't just mean Web access without a computer. The service also ties in traditional television programming, so that viewers can actually look up related information on the Net while watching ordinary TV. If you think maybe you'd rather do your Web surfing on a couch, clicking on a large screen from a cross the room, then check out the WebTV Web site (on someone else's computer, presumably), shown in Figure 17.9.

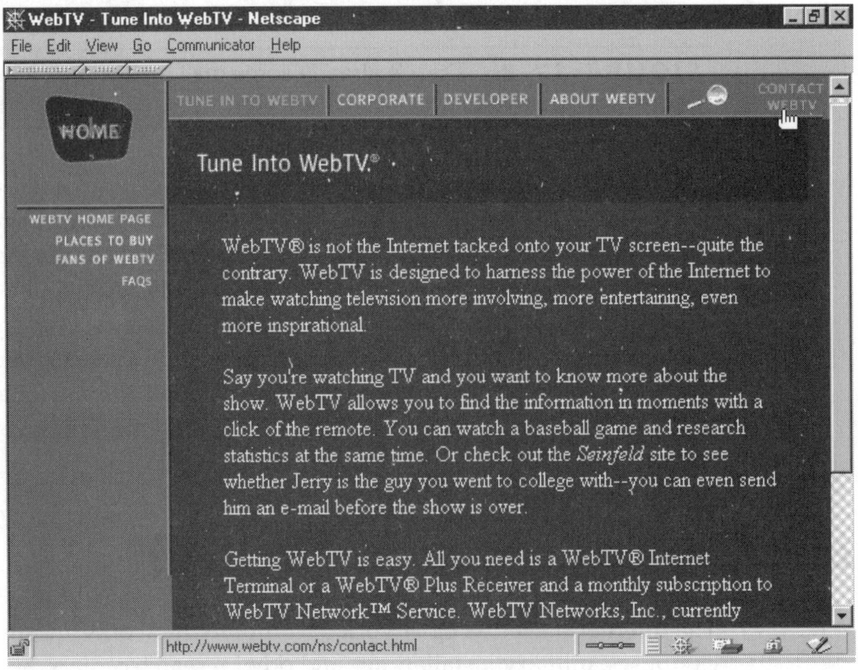

FIGURE 17.9: WebTV makes it possible to be an Internet geek without bothering to become a computer nerd first.

Are You Experienced?

Now you can...

- ☑ use the Internet via CompuServe
- ☑ use your mail, news, and Web programs with MSN
- ☑ establish a free Web-based e-mail account
- ☑ connect to the Internet without a computer

SKILL 18

GETTING AROUND WITH FTP AND TELNET

- Downloading files to your computer
- Finding FTP sites
- Using FTP with e-mail
- Using FTP with Web browsers (Netscape Navigator and Internet Explorer)
- Exploring stand-alone FTP programs (Fetch and WS_FTP)
- Finding a Telnet program
- Telnetting from your Web browser

Before the World Wide Web was invented, there were already ways to grab files from around the Net and connect to other computers. Nowadays, most people never look beyond e-mail and the Web, but there are still useful resources accessible via older protocols, such as FTP (*File Transfer Protocol*) and Telnet (a remote login, usually to Unix computers). Think of these methods as alternative ways of accessing the Net. Also, if you eventually set up an intranet or create a site on the Web, you may end up using FTP at least part of the time to get your files "out there," or to bring them back "in" to edit them. Telnet use is becoming a little more rare, but if you ever have to connect to Unix machines (and a lot of the computers on the Internet run Unix, not Windows or the MacOS), Telnet will come in handy. On the other hand, feel free to skip this chapter if you don't think these methods will prove useful to you.

NOTE NOTE NOTE NOTE NOTE NOTE NOTE NOTE NOTE NOTE NOTE NOTE NOTE NOTE NOTE

You've already learned a little bit about FTP, such as how to download files from an FTP site with a Web browser, in Skill 10, *Finding Stuff on the Web and Net,* and Skill 11, *Working with Multimedia.*

FTP—The File Transfer Protocol

You can send files attached to e-mail, but this is inefficient and wastes resources if the files are large. Instead, there's *FTP* (File Transfer Protocol), a method of retrieving files from (and sending files to) other computers on the Net.

Ideally, FTP will be built into the Windows and Mac operating systems some day (as it already is for Unix), so that managing files on the Internet will be as easy as managing files on your own computer. For now, though, you have to use FTP with either a special program designed for that purpose or with a Web browser.

You may also hear references to *anonymous FTP*. Most of the time when you'll use FTP, you'll use it anonymously, at public FTP sites. This means you log in as *anonymous* and give your e-mail address as a password. If you use FTP to transfer files from a machine that you are authorized to access, then you won't do it anonymously. You'll log in as yourself and give your password.

What's New with FTP?

In just a few years, FTP has gone from a "techie" protocol you had to learn Unix to master to a file-transfer method as easy to manage as a Web browser. The next step in the evolution of FTP is its direct incorporation into programs and computer operating systems. Already, programs like Microsoft Office 97 have the ability to open files from or save files to FTP sites (see Figure 18.1). Upcoming browser releases promise to turn FTP into a standard desktop operation, and it's a good bet that the next major upgrades of Windows and the MacOS will incorporate FTP capabilities directly into the interface, making it almost indistinguishable from moving files from one folder to another or from your hard drive to a Zip disk.

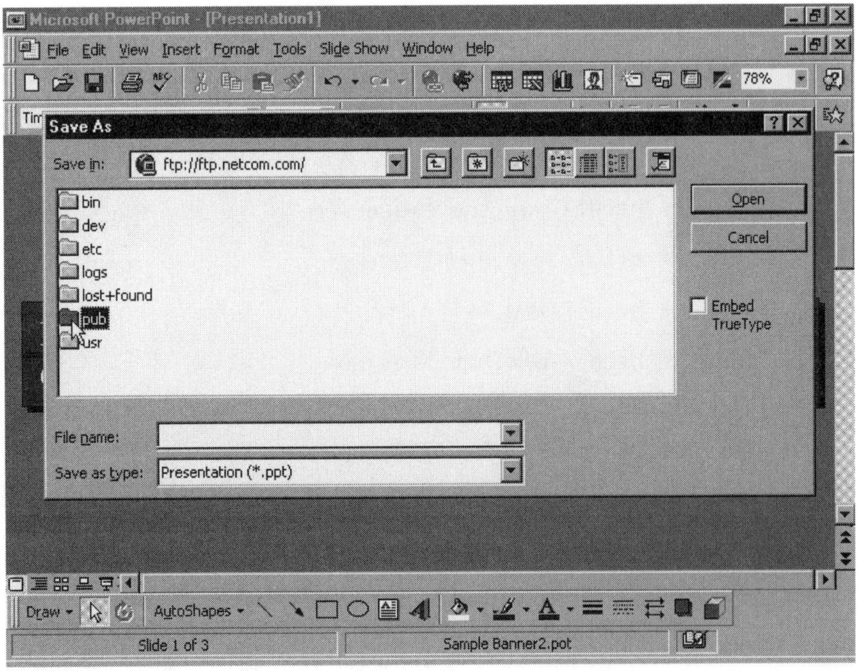

FIGURE 18.1: You can transfer an Office document to an FTP site simply by saving it there.

It's also getting easier to find FTP sites on the Net. Since they're not technically part of the Web (although you *can* connect to FTP sites with a Web browser), FTP archives have not always been "findable" at Web search sites. The Archie legacy system was the only way to find sites and files. More recently, Web sites have appeared that specifically offer to search FTP sites for file names, as I'll explain in the next section.

NOTE NOTE NOTE NOTE NOTE NOTE NOTE NOTE NOTE NOTE NOTE NOTE NOTE NOTE NOTE

Even though you can download many files via the Web now, it is still a good idea to learn how to perform FTP downloads because you may be asked to do just that in the workplace. Many companies store documents and other files on FTP sites, and you can often get access to these sites through reciprocal agreements with other businesses. Some FTP sites are used as repositories for Web content files, too.

Finding FTP Sites

If you're looking for files to download from FTP sites, try searching at any of these Web sites:

- `http://www.shareware.com/`
- `http://www.download.com/`
- `http://www.filez.com/`
- `http://www.hotfiles.com/`

You can still look for files the old ways too. Say you're reading a Usenet newsgroup (see Skill 13, *Joining Usenet Newsgroups*) and you wonder if the old posts you never got to see are archived anywhere. You post your question and someone e-mails you to tell you that, indeed, the archive is available by anonymous FTP at `archive.big-u.edu`. You cut the address and paste it into a text file and then check out the FTP site with your FTP program. That's one way to find out about sites.

There's also an anonymous FTP FAQ and a huge, alphabetically organized set of FTP site lists (16 in all) posted regularly to `comp.answers`,`news.newusers.questions`, and many other Usenet newsgroups.

To have any or all of these documents mailed to you, send an e-mail message (with no subject) to `mail-server@rtfm.mit.edu`. Include in it one (or both) of the following lines:

- **`send usenet-by-group/news.answers/FTP-list/faq`**
- **`send usenet/news.answers/FTP-list/sitelist/part1`** through **`send usenet/news.answers/FTP-list/sitelist/part11`**

These same files are also available via (what else?) anonymous FTP from `rtfm.mit.edu`. Look in the `/pub/usenet-by-group/news.answers/FTP-list/sitelist` directory for the 11 site list files, and the `/pub/usenet/news.answers/FTP-list/faq` directory for the FAQ.

TIP TIP TIP TIP TIP TIP TIP TIP TIP TIP TIP TIP TIP TIP TIP TIP TIP TIP TIP TIP TIP TIP TIP TIP TIP

More often than not, you'll find your way to an FTP site through your Web browser. Since you'll just be clicking on links, you may not even realize that you're connecting to an FTP site when you do this.

Many of the largest, most popular FTP archives have mirror sites, which are other FTP sites that maintain the exact same files (updated regularly) to reduce the load on the primary site. Use a relatively local mirror site whenever you can.

Connecting with FTP

The typical FTP session starts when you run the FTP program and connect to an FTP site. Depending on the program you have, you'll either enter your login information before connecting or you'll be prompted to do it after you connect. If you're using a Web browser to connect to an anonymous site, the browser will prompt you to log in. These general steps illustrate a typical FTP session:

1. Start your FTP software or Web browser by double-clicking the program's desktop shortcut or by using the Start ➢ Programs menu.
2. Connect to an FTP site.
3. If you are asked for a username or userID, type **anonymous** and press Enter. Then type your e-mail address when you are asked for a password, and press Enter. This will put you at an FTP prompt.

TIP TIP TIP TIP TIP TIP TIP TIP TIP TIP TIP TIP TIP TIP TIP TIP TIP TIP TIP TIP TIP TIP TIP TIP TIP

Popular sites such as RTFM at MIT are often busy. It's best to do your file transfers during off-peak hours, such as at night or on the weekends, to minimize the load on the FTP site.

WARNING WARNING WARNING WARNING WARNING WARNING WARNING WARNING

When logging into an FTP site as *anonymous*, never enter your real password. This is a security breach, as your password will appear in a log file that many people can read. If you do this by mistake, immediately change your password.

4. Now view the file lists and hunt through the directory structure for the files you want. If you're not sure where to start looking at the FTP site, start off by looking for a `pub` directory. If there is one, open it and work your way through the subdirectories.
5. If the files you want to transfer are not simple text files (if they're programs, for example), specify *binary* in the FTP program before doing the transfers. When you find the files you want, transfer them with the Get command (or the Multiple Get command, to transfer several at once).
6. Quit the FTP program when you are done transferring files and browsing directories.

NOTE

When you are using FTP or Web software, you might connect to a Unix machine or to another type of computer on the Net in your quest for FTP sites. Fortunately, you won't have to know all the different commands they require. You only need to know the commands for your FTP program or Web browser. The program will then translate your requests into whatever format the host computer requires.

FTP with Your Web Browser

You've already seen (in Skill 10, *Finding Stuff on the Web and the Net*, and Skill 11, *Working with Multimedia*) how to download files from FTP sites with a Web browser (it usually involves just clicking on a link). If you want to go directly to an FTP site, you can type its address in the browser's address box, starting with `ftp://`, for example, `ftp://rtfm.mit.edu/pub/usenet-by-group`.

With older browsers, you could only connect anonymously, and you could only receive files, not upload them. However, with most new browsers, you can connect with a username by preceding the FTP address with the username and an @ sign. For example, to log in to the FTP site for my magazine, I connect to `ftp://xian@ezone.org`.

The commands for sending files to sites vary from program to program. I'll show you how to use FTP with the two main Web browsers: Microsoft Internet Explorer and Netscape Navigator.

FTP with Internet Explorer

Microsoft Internet Explorer's FTP interface is based on the ordinary Windows Explorer folders and windows, which makes remote file access as easy as poking around the folders on your own computer. Follow these simple steps to make an FTP connection with Internet Explorer:

1. Activate Internet Explorer by clicking its desktop shortcut or by selecting Start ➢ Programs ➢ Internet Explorer ➢ Internet Explorer.
2. Connect to a site directly by entering its address in the Address box (such as `ftp://ftp.microsoft.com` or `ftp://`*`your-username`*`:`*`your-password`*`@ftp.`*`your-ISP`*`.com`). (See Figure 18.2.)

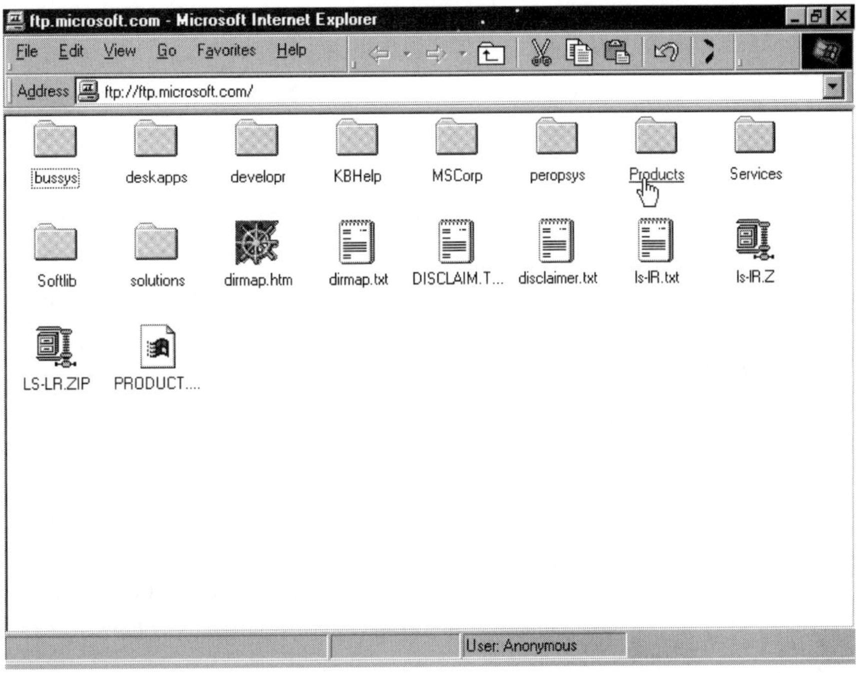

FIGURE 18.2: If you don't look in the address box, your FTP connection with Internet Explorer may seem like just another folder on your desktop.

3. To navigate the FTP site, click folder icons to open subdirectories.

4. Click on files to download them. (Internet Explorer will display files on your screen if it can; to prevent this, you can right-click or click-and-hold and select Save Target As.)
   - To send files to a site (where you have permission to upload), simply drag a file into the browser window and click Yes to upload it.
5. Exit Internet Explorer by selecting File ➢ Close. You will be prompted to disconnect from your Internet service provider.

FTP with Netscape Navigator

Netscape Navigator's FTP features are similar to Internet Explorer's. Access files and folders by double-clicking underlined text (indicating an active link) or file folder icons. The steps listed here will walk you through the process:

1. Launch Navigator by clicking the Communicator desktop shortcut or by selecting Start ➢ Programs ➢ Netscape Communicator ➢ Netscape Navigator.
2. Connect to a site directly by entering its address in the Location box (such as `ftp://ftp2.netscape.com` or `ftp://`*`your-username`*`@ftp.`*`your-ISP`*`.com`). For a private account, you'll also have to enter a password.
3. To navigate the FTP site, click folder icons to open subdirectories.
4. Click on files to download them. (Netscape will display files on your screen if it can; to prevent this, you can right-click, or click-and-hold, and select Save Link As.)
5. To send files to a site, use one of these procedures:
   - Find your way to a folder where you have permission to upload files (usually your own account or one for which you have a private username). Then select File ➢ Upload File. Choose the file you want to send in the Open dialog box that appears and then click OK.
   - You can also simply drag a file into the browser window and click Yes to upload it (see Figure 18.3).

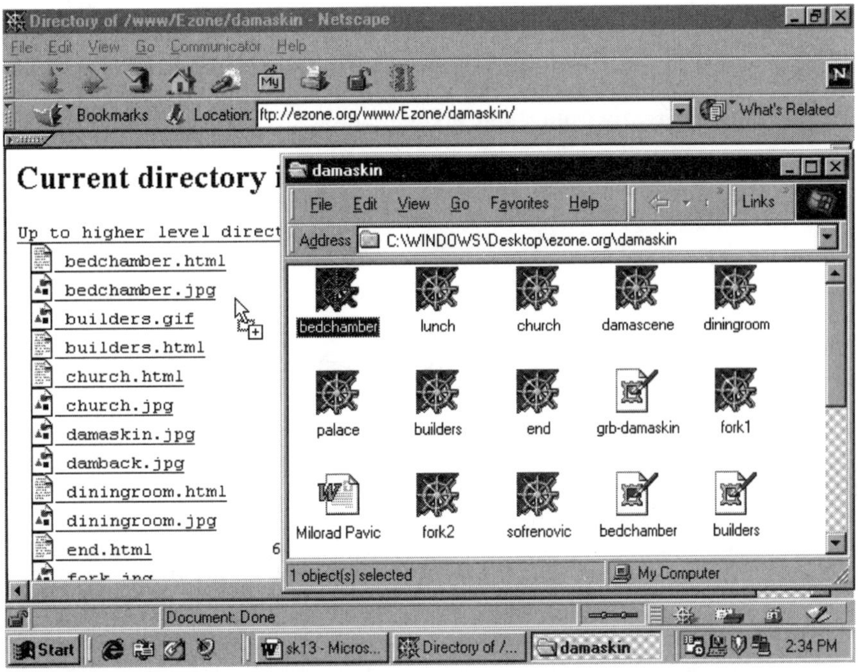

FIGURE 18.3: You can click on a file and drag it onto an FTP directory for uploading with Netscape Navigator.

WARNING WARNING WARNING WARNING WARNING WARNING WARNING WARNING

Netscape doesn't do a great job of uploading text files from one type of computer to another. Better FTP programs handle text (ASCII) and nontext (binary) files differently.

Specific FTP Programs

Before going on to discuss Telnet, I'll explain the details of a couple of specific FTP programs. If you use a Macintosh, you'll want to use Fetch. Fetch is an easy-to-use FTP client for the Mac. If you're stuck in a Unix shell, you'll want to use Ftp or its slightly improved cousin Ncftp. If you're using Windows, then WS_FTP is probably your best bet for FTP (although those weaned on Unix FTP may prefer the DOS-style FTP program that comes with Windows these days).

TIP

Most online services, such as AOL and CompuServe, offer FTP, but they generally also maintain their own archives of the most popular files and programs from the Net, and you may find it faster and easier to download them directly from those archives.

Fetch

On Macintoshes, the standard file-transfer program is called Fetch. You can obtain Fetch from `http://www.dartmouth.edu/pages/softdev/fetch.html`. Fetch is simple to use and has a number of valuable features for getting around in FTP sites and obtaining files of different types. The procedures for using Fetch will be familiar to you if you have used other FTP programs for Macintosh or Windows environments. These steps will get you started:

Fetch

1. Double-click the Fetch icon, which brings up the Open Connection dialog box (see Figure 18.4).
2. If you don't want the default host, type a new one in the Host box.
3. Enter your password in the password window and enter a directory if you know the one you're headed for. (If you don't, just leave it blank.) Then click OK.
4. Once you're connected to the host, you can navigate to the directory structure by clicking the folder icons, just as with any Macintosh program.

NOTE

In Fetch 3 the Open Connection dialog box has become the New Connection box, but the FTP methods remain basically the same.

5. Click the Binary radio button to specify a binary file, or leave Automatic clicked to let the program figure it out.
6. Highlight the file or files you want and click the Get File button to get them (see Figure 18.5).
7. To send files you can just drag and drop them into the Fetch window.
8. When you are done, select File ➢ Quit.

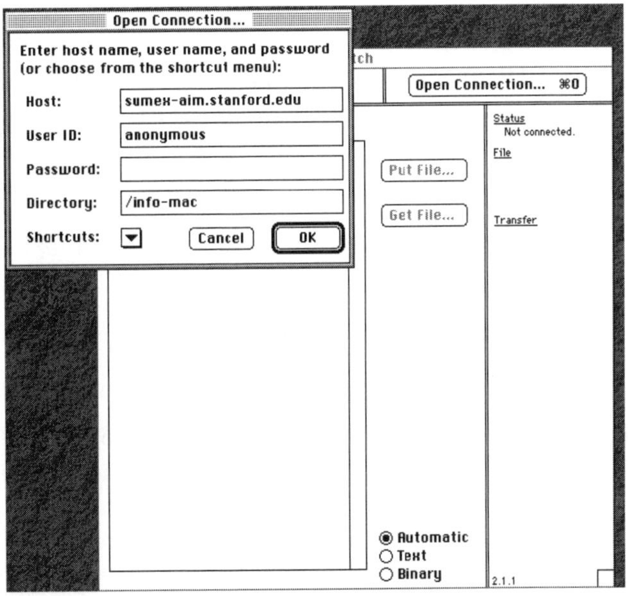

FIGURE 18.4: The Open Connection dialog box in Fetch

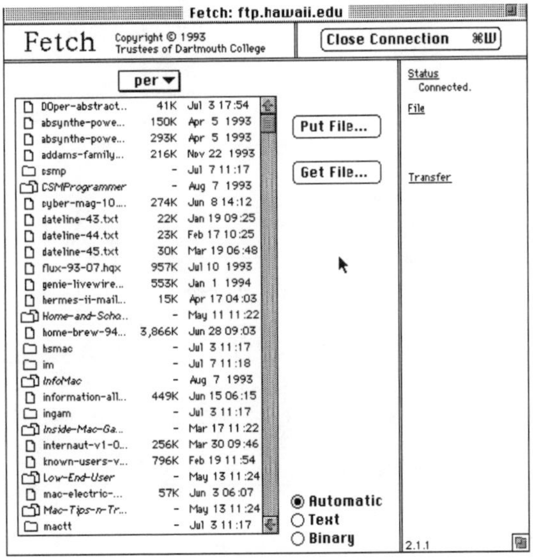

FIGURE 18.5: The Macintosh interface makes fetching files simple.

WS_FTP

A good FTP client for Windows is WS_FTP (`ftp://129.29.64.246/pub/msdos/`). WS_FTP is shareware and makes fair use of visual commands and point-and-click buttons to bring you the world of FTP. For guidance on using WS_FTP, work through the following steps:

1. Start WS_FTP by double-clicking the WS_FTP desktop shortcut.
2. The Session Profile dialog box pops up. If you don't want the default host, type a new one.
3. Enter your login name and password in the Remote Host box.
4. Enter a directory if you know the one you're headed for. Then click OK.
5. Once you've connected to the host, WS_FTP will show you the contents of your own computer in the left two panes and the contents of the remote host in the right two (see Figure 18.6). The top panes show directories and the bottom ones show files. Click the Binary radio button to specify a binary file.

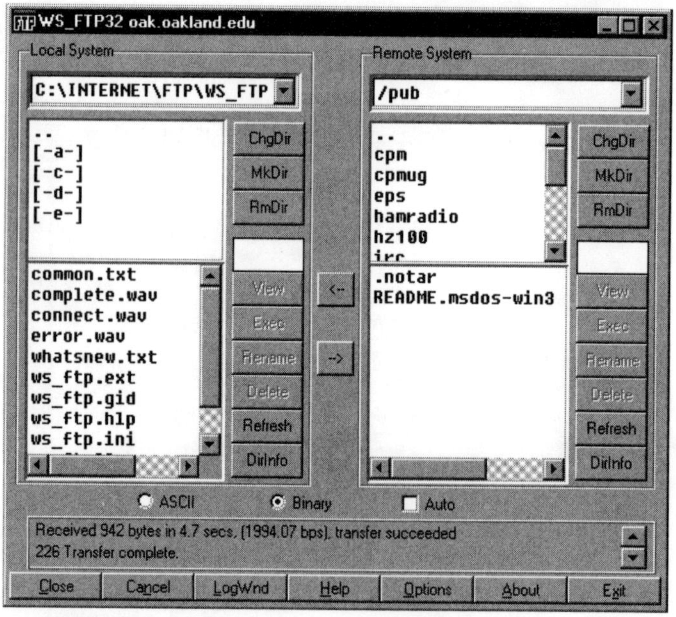

FIGURE 18.6: WS_FTP gives you an easy way to get around a remote computer and retrieve files from it.

6. Highlight the file or files you want and click the "<–" button between the Local System and Remote System areas to transfer the files.
7. To send files, you can just drag and drop them into the WS_FTP window, or highlight a file or group of files and click the "–>" button between the Local System and Remote System areas. When you are done, click the Exit button on the far right at the bottom of the window to close WS_FTP.

Probing the Internet with Telnet

One aspect of the interconnectedness of the Net is that you can log in to other machines on the Internet directly from your own computer. With Telnet, you can log in to any Unix-style computer or network for which you have a password, as well as thousands of public sites where passwords are not required. You would not be able to work on these Unix systems without Telnet, which turns your Windows or Macintosh computer into a remote terminal that is compatible with computers outside of the personal computer universe.

Many university and public libraries now make their catalogs available by Telnet, as do countless other repositories of useful information. Of course, as with so many other Internet resources, you need to know where to go to take advantage of these public sites. Unfortunately, there's no comprehensive index or guide to available Telnet sites. In general, you have to ask around and collect remote login sites just as you do with FTP sites.

TIP

If you have a Unix account, you can even Telnet to your own service provider and log in to your own account, even if you're already logged in there! This is actually more useful when you are borrowing someone else's computer and want to log in to your own account to, say, check your e-mail.

After you have started your Telnet program, you need to open an Internet connection and log in to the site with the steps described here:

1. Type **telnet** and press Enter at the Unix prompt.
2. This will put you at a `telnet>` prompt. Then type **open** ***host-sitename*** and press Enter.
3. Logging in with Telnet is the same as logging in to any computer system. You type your username and press Enter.
4. Then you type a password and press Enter.

TIP TIP TIP TIP TIP TIP TIP TIP TIP TIP TIP TIP TIP TIP TIP TIP TIP TIP TIP TIP TIP TIP TIP TIP TIP TIP

For public sites, you might have to log in under some special name, and either you won't be asked for a password or you'll be able to just press Enter when asked for a password.

In Figure 18.7, I'm Telnetting from my Unix shell account to California State University's Advanced Technology Information Network to get information about California agriculture. The Telnet site is `caticsuf.cati.csufresno.edu`, and the username that I log in with is `public`.

```
{netcom2:4} telnet caticsuf.cati.csufresno.edu
Trying...
Connected to caticsuf.cati.csufresno.edu.
Escape character is '^]'.

SunOS UNIX (caticsuf)

login: public
```

FIGURE 18.7: Logging in to the Advanced Technology Information Network via Telnet

The site doesn't ask for a password. Instead, a screen full of welcoming information appears.

From this point on, you're on your own. Depending on where you've Telnetted to, you'll be either at a Unix prompt or, more likely, at the main menu of some information program. There are many such programs and each one works differently, but don't worry. They'll all prompt you, and they're designed for laypeople. Generally, you can press Enter to accept defaults until you're given a menu of information. Then you have to make some choices.

Logging out from a Telnet session is generally a matter of typing **bye** or **exit** or **logout** at a prompt, pressing **q** (for quit), or choosing the appropriate menu choice from within an information program. Telnet will sign you off with "Connection closed by foreign host."

Finding a Telnet Program

Windows 95/98, Windows NT, and Windows 3.11 for Workgroups come with a perfectly fine Telnet client program called, as you might expect, Telnet (the filename is `Telnet.exe`, and it is located in the Windows directory or folder on your hard drive). Unix also has a Telnet program built-in. To run it, just type **telnet** ***sitename*** at the Unix prompt and press Enter. For the Macintosh, you can download an excellent Telnet client program called NCSA Telnet (`http://www.ncsa.uiuc.edu/SDG/Software/Brochure/MacDownSoft.html#MacTelnet`).

Telnetting from Your Web Browser

Links to Telnet sites can be embedded into Web pages. When you select such a link, your browser will attempt to launch your Telnet program to connect to the site. It will fail, though, if you've never told your browser where your Telnet program is. Solving this problem involves going to the Options or Preferences dialog box, choosing the Apps (or Applications, or Supporting Applications—not to be confused with Helper Applications) tab or Apps area of the dialog box, and then entering the path and file name of your Telnet program in the Telnet box.

In earlier versions of Netscape Navigator for Windows, for instance, you have to perform the fairly convoluted action of choosing Options ➢ General Preferences, choosing the Apps tab, clicking in the Telnet box, typing **telnet**, and then clicking OK. However, Netscape Communicator has bypassed this requirement and automatically launches the Telnet program when needed.

TIP TIP TIP TIP TIP TIP TIP TIP TIP TIP TIP TIP TIP TIP TIP TIP TIP TIP TIP TIP TIP TIP TIP TIP TIP

If you're not sure of the exact path or file name of your Telnet program, you can click the Browse button to hunt around on your hard disk for it.

Are You Experienced?

Now you can...

- ☑ **explore FTP sites with Web browsers or FTP programs**
- ☑ **find files on FTP sites by clicking on folders or directories**
- ☑ **specify different file formats with FTP software**
- ☑ **download files from FTP sites**
- ☑ **use a variety of FTP programs**
- ☑ **access non-Windows information sources with Telnet**

SKILL 19

MAKING A HOME PAGE OR WEB SITE

- **Finding and saving a home page template**
- **Understanding a little HTML**
- **Editing an HTML document**
- **Adding pictures and links to a page**
- **Previewing a home page**
- **Finding a home for your page**
- **Making Web documents without learning HTML**
- **Maintaining a Web site**

This is the sort of bonus lesson that brings everything together. You've now learned all you need to know to function on the Internet and explore the resources that are out there. The next step is to put your own information up on the Net. You already know how to contribute to mailing lists and Usenet newsgroups—it's as simple as sending a message to the right address. Publishing your own home page can be a little trickier.

Why would you want your own home page? Well, it's a little like putting up a flag in cyberspace. One that says, "Here I am." A home page can be as simple as a yearbook entry with a few images, some facts about you and perhaps your family (and maybe your pets), and a list of your favorite Web sites; or it can be as complicated as a full-service front end for a company or organization. Telling you all the ins and outs of making an elaborate Web site would take another whole book, but I can recommend an easy way to put together a simple home page and point you to a few other alternatives as well.

For those of you in search of new employment opportunities, a home page can be used to present your professional image online. While many employers limit their Internet and Web recruitment programs to specific employment sites and search services, it's still a good idea to have your own online presence separate from the recruiting posts. For one thing, you have complete control over how your Web page looks and what its content is, which will make you stand out from those who just submitted an online résumé to a job listing. You can also add work samples to the page, such as examples of your writing or artwork, a list of your publications with excerpts, and so on.

When the time comes to make your Web creations public, you'll need to find a host and to start thinking of the material you've created collectively as a "Web site," which means, among other things, that you've got to be willing to keep the information in it up to date.

In the early parts of this lesson, I'll explain how HTML works and how you can create Web pages from scratch, but you should feel free to skim over that material if you'd rather use Web site software that does the HTML coding for you. I discuss several of these later in the lesson in the "Web Editing Tools" section.

TIP

You can include information and terms specific to your profession on your Web page. Employers in your field who are searching for special skills will find you when their search engine locks on to those specialized keywords.

A Quick-and-Dirty Home Page

If you just want to stake a small claim in Webspace and you're not (yet) contemplating an elaborate Web site empire, I'll point out a few free or low-cost approaches to throwing up a "straw mat" Web page in no time flat. If you simply want your name out there, a picture or two, some of your favorite links, and a "mail to" link for anyone who wants to send you e-mail, then try one of the services I mention in this section. (However, if you want to plunge directly into HTML formatting, hyperlinking, and Web site design, feel free to skip ahead to the next section, "Creating a Web Page.")

Before you go knocking on doors, check with your current Internet service provider to see if they offer Web site hosting as one of their services. You may be entitled to a small patch of their server as part of your account (as long as your traffic stays low), usually with an address such as `http://www.`*`myprovider`*`.com/~`*`myusername`* or `http://www.`*`isp`*`.com/users/`*`myusername`*.

At the moment, I can name three free home page sites you can check out (there are sure to be more as time goes on)—GeoCities, Tripod, and Angelfire, at the following URLs:

```
http://www.geocities.com/
http://www.tripod.com/
http://www.angelfire.com/
```

Some of these sites are also Web guides or even potential communities (check out Firefly at `http://www.firefly.com/`). Sites that are primarily guides sometimes offer free home pages as well (such as `http://www.suite101.com/`). You can also search for other hosts that offer free home pages at `http://www.free-homepage.com/freewp.htm`.

TIP

Try searching for "free home page" at any search engine (see Skill 10, *Finding Stuff on the Web and the Net,* for more on searching) to find out about the latest, newest services to appear.

If you set up your home page at one of these services, then your Web address will be a branch of their address, and they'll effectively be your "landlords" on the Web. A lot of public sites organize their home pages by interest group or categories. Take some time to check out the neighborhood you're moving into.

GeoCities, for example, is a thriving community. I'm in the process of setting up an *atelier* space in the LeftBank area of Paris at GeoCities. The specific address is `http://www.geocities.com/Paris/LeftBank/4964/` (see Figure 19.1).

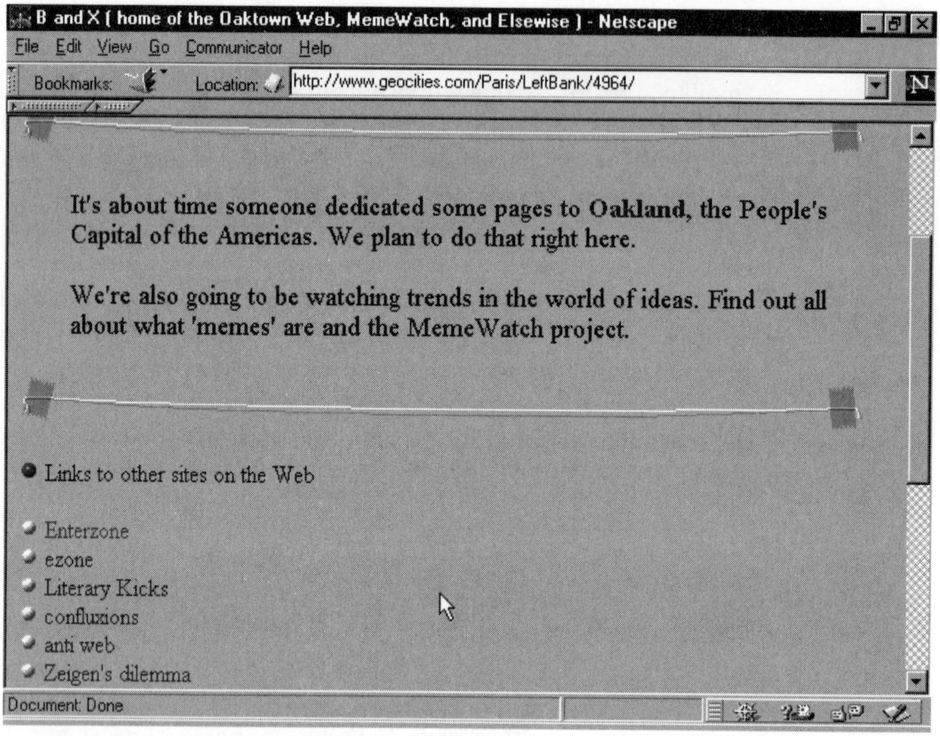

FIGURE 19.1: I slapped together this home page in about an hour (OK, a day, if you count procrastination).

GeoCities offers free home pages, organized as cities and famous neighborhoods. The idea is to form communities of like-minded people. To hunt for the right neighborhood, check the GeoCities Neighborhood Directory (`http://www.geocities.com/neighborhoods/`). Once you find the neighborhood you want, search for a vacant address (the instructions are straightforward if you just click Join on the main neighborhood page, and then Yes), and then apply for the address you want. Fill out a form (including your current e-mail address), and GeoCities will send you the password (allow up to a day) and some basic instructions, including the advice to change your password right away and register your interests and any real-world geographical location connections you'd like to make. (For instance, my Left Bank pages will feature a site devoted to Oakland, California, my home town.)

You can start moving in right away. If you can create your own pages (discussed in the next section of this lesson), you can use GeoCities' EZ Upload feature (or regular FTP, as discussed in Skill 18, *Getting Around with FTP and Telnet*), to send your files from your computer to your new home page address. Otherwise, you can use one of the three HTML editor forms provided at the GeoCities File Manager page (`http://www.geocities.com/members/tools/file_manager.html`), not to be confused with the Windows 3.1 File Manager. More basic information is available at the Homestead page (`http://www.geocities.com/members/tools/homestead.html`).

You get two megabytes of disk storage free with your basic account—possibly more if you can show that your page is a credit to the community.

Creating a Web Page

To build a coherent Web (or intranet) site, you have to have an overall organizational plan for the site. In the end, though, the project comes down to creating the individual Web pages. You may have existing documents you need to convert to HTML, but most likely you'll be creating the basic pages for the site from scratch. You can do this easily either in a simple text editor or by using one of the many Web publishing tools available. No matter how you go about it, the same basic issues prevail.

First you have to create a blank page (or start a new page from an existing template). Then you have to add basic content, usually text. Don't forget to budget some time to do the necessary writing (or some cash to pay the writer)!

Basic Formatting

Once the text is in place, you need to format it to give your site a glossy (and consistent) look. You also have to make some basic color decisions (about the page's background, text, and visited and unvisited links). If you create pages from a standard template, you can make site-wide color-scheme decisions in the template and then not have to repeat them for each document.

Text formatting on the Web is still fairly limited compared with the state-of-the-art in word processing, at least without getting into gimmicky tricks that may not work in other browsers. You can assign heading levels, separate sections of text, make tables, add emphasis to selections, make block quotations, and use some other basic formats.

Understanding HTML

HTML, or Hypertext Markup Language, is a simple way to mark the text in your Web page file with different formatting codes. These codes are enclosed in angle brackets, and are referred to as *tags*. As an example, <H1> marks the beginning of a Level 1 heading.

If you're not a programmer, right now you might be planning to skip this section because any mention of coding suggests something way too technical for the average person. However, adding HTML coding to your text is much easier than writing a computer program. If you have some experience with word processing, you will understand how to use HTML immediately.

NOTE NOTE NOTE NOTE NOTE NOTE NOTE NOTE NOTE NOTE NOTE NOTE NOTE NOTE NOTE

At the end of this lesson, I'll explain how you can use a WYSIWYG ("What You See Is What You Get") Web editor to create Web documents without learning HTML first.

For example, when you make text bold in your word processor, you highlight the text and click the Bold button in the toolbar. If you are using a Web page program, you will be doing the same thing. Even if you are manually adding HTML codes in a text editor program, all you do to make text bold is type this HTML tag, <B>, followed by the text you want bold, and another tag, </B>, so that your line appears as

```
<B>this is bold text</B>
```

NOTE NOTE NOTE NOTE NOTE NOTE NOTE NOTE NOTE NOTE NOTE NOTE NOTE NOTE NOTE

The first tag tells the Web browser program where the special formatting starts. For instance, you would place the <B> tag for *begin bold text* at the beginning of the text you want to appear as bold. The tag with the slash (/) in it tells the browser where to stop the special formatting, so your </B> tag for *end bold text* goes right after the last character you want bold.

You can also *nest* the HTML tags, meaning that you use one set of tags inside the other, to make text both bold and italic, for instance. All you have to remember is to keep the tags together, and not alternate one tag with the other. Your Web browser will be confused if it does not find the tag pairs where it expects to see them. Here is an example of a nested group of HTML tags:

```
<B> Overall, we are using bold text for this sentence,
however, one part of the sentence <I>is also italic</I>.
The italic effect only lasts for a few words.</B>
```

NOTE

If you have Web publishing software, such as Microsoft FrontPage or Netscape Composer, you do not have to worry about HTML codes and nesting codes because your application will take care of that for you. However, it is still a good idea to learn a little about HTML to fine-tune your Web page.

There are HTML tags for all manner of effects, including font color, bulleted or numbered lists, different heading levels, and more. The latest versions of word processing programs, such as Microsoft Word and Corel WordPerfect, have HTML editing features built right in. Check your word processing program to see if it has any Web publishing templates—preformatted documents you can use to create your Web page. You may not want to use the canned format of the template, but you can view the source code and play around with it to change the page to fit your aesthetics.

Table 19.1 presents a list of basic text tags to get you started. These tags have been around since the first version of HTML came out. We are now up to HTML 4, but tags added in later versions of HTML will not display properly in browsers designed around the earlier HTML versions. Keep your viewers in mind when you add fancy formatting to your page, and be aware that many will not have the latest version of your favorite browser.

TABLE 19.1: Basic HTML Tags

Tag	What the Tag Does
Structure Tags	
<!— ... —>	Creates a comment (not visible on the page, but visible for anyone viewing the source code)
<HTML> ... </HTML>	Indicates the start and end of the entire HTML document
<HEAD> ... </HEAD>	Denotes the header information in the HTML document
<BODY> ... </BODY>	Encloses the body (text and tags) of the entire HTML document
<META name="*keywords*" content="*your own keywords*">	Notifies Web search engines about the contents of the page or site so that people searching for your page will find it
Text Function Tags	
<TITLE> ... </TITLE>	Denotes the title of the document, which will appear in the list of Web search results

TABLE 19.1 CONTINUED: Basic HTML Tags

Tag	What the Tag Does
	Text Function Tags
<H1> ... </H1> to <H6> ... </H6>	Encloses headings 1 through 6, with Heading 1 being the largest and 6 the smallest
<P> ... </P>	Indicates that the enclosed text is a basic paragraph
<OL> ... </OL>	Encloses an ordered (numbered) list
<UL> ... </UL>	Encloses an unordered (bulleted) list
<LI>	Denotes a list item for either type of list
	Formatting Tags
<B> ... </B>	Encloses bold text, you can also use <STRONG> ... </STRONG>
<I> ... </I>	Marks italic text, you can also use <EM> ... </EM> (for emphasis)
<U> ... </U>	Denotes underlined text
<TT> ... </TT>	Indicates monospaced text, good for user instructions, explaining computer messages
<CITE> ... </CITE>	Signifies book, film, or other title citations with italics
<CODE> ... </CODE>	Identifies source code using a monospaced font
<HR>	Inserts an embossed horizontal rule
 	Preserves a line break, prevents short lines, such as addresses, from wrapping as one line
<BLOCKQUOTE> ... </BLOCKQUOTE>	Encloses long quotes or citations in a different font or indented margins
<ADDRESS> ... </ADDRESS>	Denotes an address block with information about the Web page, its author, and last update
	Link and Image Tags
<A HREF="*URL*">Click Here</A>	Anchor tag defining a Web address or file link for the "Click Here" hypertext
<IMG SRC="*filename*.gif">	Inserts the image whose file name appears in the tag
<ALT="*Text describing image*">	Displays text instead of an image for browsers not displaying images
<A HREF="URL"><IMG SRC="*filename*.gif">	Links the URL or filename referenced to a Web page image

TABLE 19.1 CONTINUED: Basic HTML Tags

Tag	What the Tag Does
	Advanced HTML Tags
<IMG SRC="*filename*.gif" ➥ALIGN=left>	Aligns image to the left, can also use right, top, middle, or bottom
<TABLE> ... </TABLE>	Defines the beginning and end of a table and all its contents
<TABLE BORDER> ... </TABLE>	Displays a table with a border
<CAPTION> ... </CAPTION>	Adds a table title to the top of the table
<TR> ... </TR>	Denotes table rows, each one marked separately, can also use ALIGN within these tags
<TD> ... </TD>	Marks table cells within rows, you can also use ALIGN within these tags
<TH> ... </TH>	Encloses cell headings (usually columns) for the table, can also use ALIGN within these tags

NOTE

Find out more about HTML and Web publishing with one of Sybex's Web publishing books, such as *HTML 4.0: No experience required, FrontPage 98: No experience required,* or *Web by Design: The Complete Guide.*

Inserting Pictures

Whenever possible, you should add illustrations to your Web pages, to make them more attractive to the eye and communicate more clearly. Inserting images into pages is very easy with most Web editors, and it's not too terribly hard even if you're working with raw HTML. You can align an image with the left or right edge of the page (or table cell) and have text wrap around it.

SKILL 19

The simplest HTML reference to an image just places it in your document and includes the image's filename, so that the browser knows which image file to display. Here is the tag for a basic image:

```
<IMG SRC=imagefilename.gif>
```

NOTE NOTE NOTE NOTE NOTE NOTE NOTE NOTE NOTE NOTE NOTE NOTE NOTE NOTE NOTE

Pictures on the Web have to be in GIF or JPEG format, but other formats, such as PICT, BMP, and TIF can be converted to either of those formats by a variety of image-manipulation programs (from the expensive, professional tool, PhotoShop, to the shareware tool, Lview Pro). You might find it easier to ask your favorite graphics whiz to do this for you. Copy graphic files to the same directory (or folder) that the Web page document is saved in. Also, did you notice that the image file tag does not have an end tag? Not that the people who invented HTML are trying to confuse you or anything, but there are some other tags like this, too. You probably spotted them in Table 19.1.

Image file tagging can get much more involved, of course. You can set up image files as links to other Web pages, either within your own Web document or out on the Web itself. Some HTML experts call images with hyperlinks *image maps*. You can even divide an image up into different areas and have each area serve as a link to somewhere else (it's best to use a larger image for this). You can put small images in your Web page, and, if viewers would like to see a larger, more detailed version of that image that takes longer to load, they can click on the small image. These small pictures are called *thumbnails*.

If the image you put in your Web document is serving some purpose other than decoration, you might want to specify an alternative to the image, to help people who have turned off the automatic display of images on their browser to speed up Web page loading. They will not see the image, but will see a brief description of the image to let them know what they are missing. Here is how you tag the text that will take the image's place in text-only displays:

```
<IMG SRC=imagefilename.gif> <ALT="A picture of some importance">
```

Buttons, Borders, and Lines

Images are not the only graphical elements in a Web page. You can add lots of character to your page through judicious use of buttons, borders, and horizontal lines. Buttons are small icon-like squares, circles, or other shapes that can be used to highlight bulleted lists. Buttons with active links can act as jump points to send people to other parts of your home page, or to a secondary Web page. A portion of the Greenbelt Alliance's Web page, shown in Figure 19.2, makes good use of buttons that symbolize the pages they are linked with.

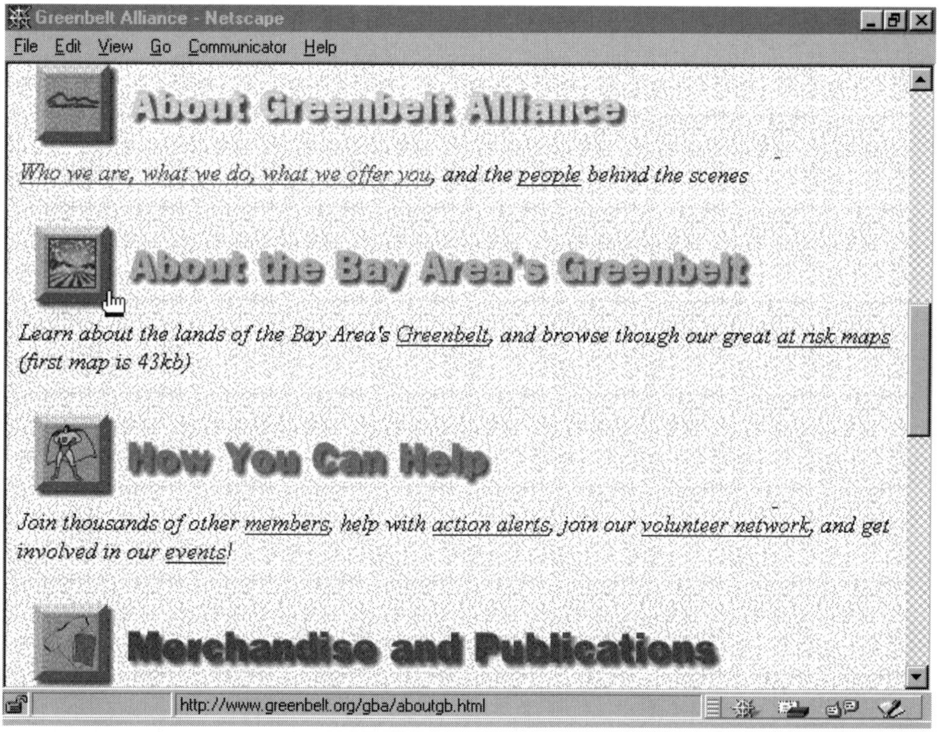

FIGURE 19.2: A Web page that effectively uses buttons

You can find Web buttons in clip-art collections, download them from the Web, or make your own using your own images and an image editing program. To add any button to your Web page, you must give the button's image file a name and store it in your Web page folder. The HTML tag information will look similar to the tags I described a little earlier in this section.

Borders and horizontal lines (or *rules*, as they are sometimes called) are also great ways to add visual interest to your page without going to a lot of trouble. You can obtain borders from clip-art collections or make your own. One colorful border, or a series of related borders, can be used to separate various portions of your page. Include the same border at the top of each page in your site, for stylistic consistency, or experiment with different borders that complement each other. Border image files are referenced (tagged) on your Web page in the same way as other files.

You can also make horizontal rules out of thin borders (referenced in the same way as other image files), or you can use HTML's `<HR>` tag, which adds an embossed horizontal line across the page.

Linking Pages Together

The essence of a Web site is that the individual pages are connected with hyperlinks. You can insert links into a document and then create the pages you're linking to, or you can create all your pages without links, and then add the links afterward (the latter approach works better with Web publishing programs, most of which can make links and track the linked documents automatically). You can also add external links from any of your pages to other sites on the Web or other resources on the Internet).

The link tag is a pair of tags, `<A>` and `</A>`, with the `<A>` part of the pair containing the actual link address—the address to which the person clicking on the link will be sent. The `<A>` stands for *anchor*, and it is the spot on the Web page where the user will click to get to the linked document. Anchors can be text, such as "Click Here" or "Click Anchor." Anchors can also be buttons or other images. If you are using an image for an anchor, you will need to reference the image file name in between the `<A>` and `</A>` pair.

Here are examples of how to add links to your page:

Link	What It Does
`<A HREF="LinkFileName.type">` `Click this anchor</A>`	Sends the user to the file, Web page, or Web address when they click on the *Click this anchor* text. (Substitute your own filename or address for the *LinkFileName.type* place-holder. Substitute your own anchor text for the *Click this anchor* place-holder.)
`<A HREF="LinkFileName.type">` `<IMG SRC="LinkImage.gif"></A>`	Sends the user to the file, Web page, or Web address when they click on the image or button named in the *LinkImage.gif*. (Substitute your own filename or address for the *LinkFileName.type* place-holder. Substitute your own image file name for the *LinkImage.gif* place-holder.)

Links As Navigation Aids

There is a lot more you can do with links and with the images and text you use as anchors for the links, but you will have to do more research and experimentation on your own to learn about the details. Keep in mind that links can also be used to help the people browsing your Web page. For example, when they get to the bottom of a fairly long page (which can be more than one screenful of information), it would be nice to include a link that they can click on to return to the top of the page. Similarly, you can include links at the bottom of each page that your viewers can click on to go to any other page in your Web site, without having to get there in a linear fashion. Home page links at the top, bottom, or other noticeable area of your secondary pages are great for people who wish to return to your main page immediately.

But those are finishing touches. For now you can rely on the Forward, Back, and Home buttons in your browser software to help people get around your Web site. You can always add more links and navigational aids to your pages after you build the basic components. Most sites on the Web are constantly being updated and nobody minds if you load a primitive Web page to start with and continue refining and improving it as you develop stronger skills. You can even download "Under Construction" images to put on your page to let people know that it is a work in progress and that they should return to it later to see what has changed.

Getting Noticed on the Web

There are a few tricks you can pull to make sure that people searching for your page will find it. Once their search engine finds it, you can work some more formatting magic to control how the description of your page is displayed in the listed search results. Here are the basic adjustments you can make to your page:

- **Write a good, descriptive document title** The text between the `<TITLE>` ... `</TITLE>` tags in the `<HEAD>` ... `</HEAD>` area at the top of the document will appear in the listed search results. People scanning a list of Web pages may decide to click on an address based on this title. Some search programs also rank your page higher in the search results if terms specified by the person conducting the search match words in your title.

- **Include a META tag with keywords** META tags can also be added high up in your Web document between the `<HEAD>` ... `</HEAD>` tags, right after the `TITLE` tags. Some search programs will also rank your page higher in the search results if terms in your META tags match those specified by the person searching. To add keywords this way, use this META tag: `<META name="keywords" content="`*`relevant terms for your page`*`">`.
- **Add a META tag with a brief description** When your page appears in a list of search results, the search program displays whatever is between the `TITLE` tags as the title and includes a few lines from the body of your HTML document as the description. Write your own brief description that best describes your site and will appeal to people searching for what you have to offer. Enclose this description in the following META tag, and the search program will display your description instead: `<META name="description" content="`*`Some compelling words about your page`*`">`
- **Update your home page and its linked pages on a regular basis** Search programs display the date that the page was last modified in the search results and some searchers limit their searches to only the most recently updated material. If your home page has not been modified as recently as some of the other pages, that older date will appear in the search results and may discourage people from clicking on your address.

Learning More about HTML

If you want to learn more about HTML and Web-page creation, visit any of these destinations:

- Creating Net Sites at `http://www.netscape.com/assist/net_sites/`
- Introduction to HTML at `http://www.cwru.edu/help/introHTML/`
- HTML Help at `http://www.htmlhelp.com/`

Web Editing Tools

You can evaluate Web page editors based on whether they take a raw-HTML or WYSIWYG approach, and on how well they handle the following tasks:

- Text formatting (and lists)
- Images
- Links
- Tables
- Forms
- Frames
- Multimedia objects
- Previewing the page or showing HTML

For instance, the rugged individualist approach, using a text editor like Notepad or SimpleText and typing all the tags yourself, would have no special shortcuts for formatting, pictures, links, tables, forms, frames, or multimedia, but you could easily preview your pages by dragging them into your Web browser window.

HTML editors, such as WebEdit for Windows or BBEdit for the Mac (with HTML add-ins) do give you shortcuts for most basic tags, including formatting, pictures, links, tables, and frames. A rudimentary WYSIWYG editor such as Microsoft Word 97 has toolbar buttons and dialog boxes to automate formatting and ease the insertion of images, links, tables, and forms (at least the front-end part of forms), if not frames or multimedia objects, and it can show you the underlying HTML just fine if you want to see it. (It makes pretty ugly HTML though: hard to read and computer-dumb, with lots of redundancies.)

NOTE NOTE NOTE NOTE NOTE NOTE NOTE NOTE NOTE NOTE NOTE NOTE NOTE NOTE NOTE

WYSIWYG (pronounced whizzy-whig) stands for What You See Is What You Get, as opposed to what I call WYSIHTML, which stands for What You See Is HTML. WYSIWYG denotes a word processor-style HTML editor, which shows a formatted page-layout view, instead of raw text and interspersed tags or codes.

Now, on to the real Web page editors.

Adobe PageMill

For Mac users, PageMill is the hands down, most popular, hands off (no HTML knowledge required) Web editor. It came out first, it's from venerable old Adobe (the software company that markets and updates PageMaker desktop publishing software), and it's about as easy to use as PageMaker has always been. If you have a Mac and you want to get going quickly, but don't want to learn HTML, download a trial version of PageMill from the Adobe Web site (`http://www.adobe.com/`)—it works but it can't save the pages—and buy it if you like it. Adobe recently came out with a version for Windows users, too. You can get the demo version from Adobe's site. Figure 19.3 shows a page from my 'zine, *Enterzone*, partly completed in PageMill.

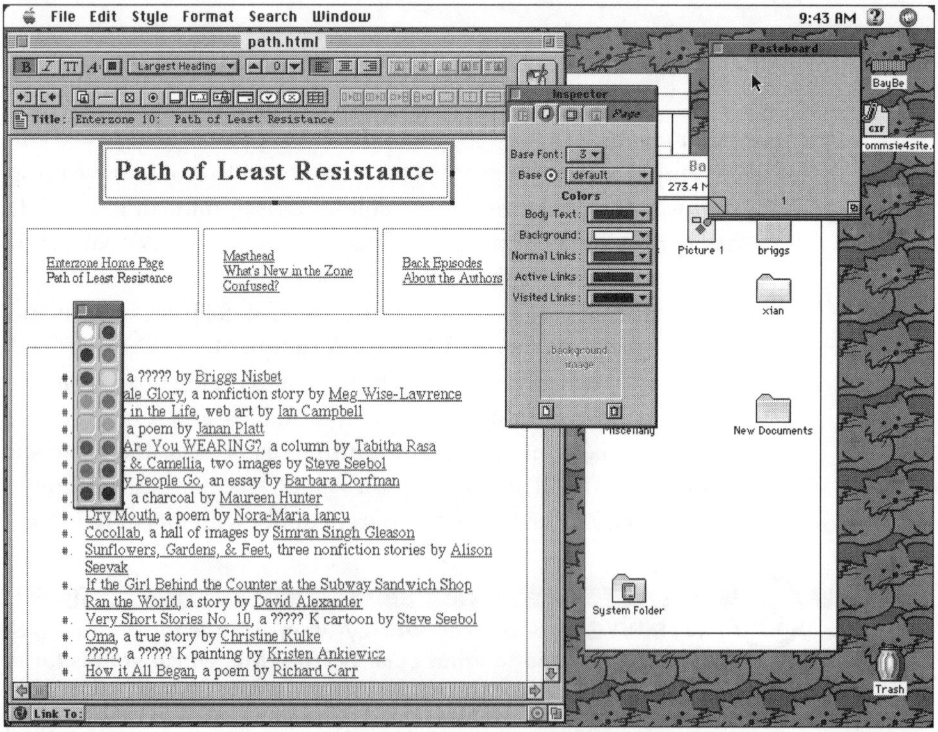

FIGURE 19.3: PageMill makes it easy to edit and format Web pages.

PageMill has a good HTML view available as well, if you need to tweak something (see Figure 19.4).

> **NOTE** I can't prove this, but I suspect this program is named after Page Mill road in the Palo Alto, California, area near Adobe's headquarters. (A man named Page once owned a mill up that road, but that's another story.)

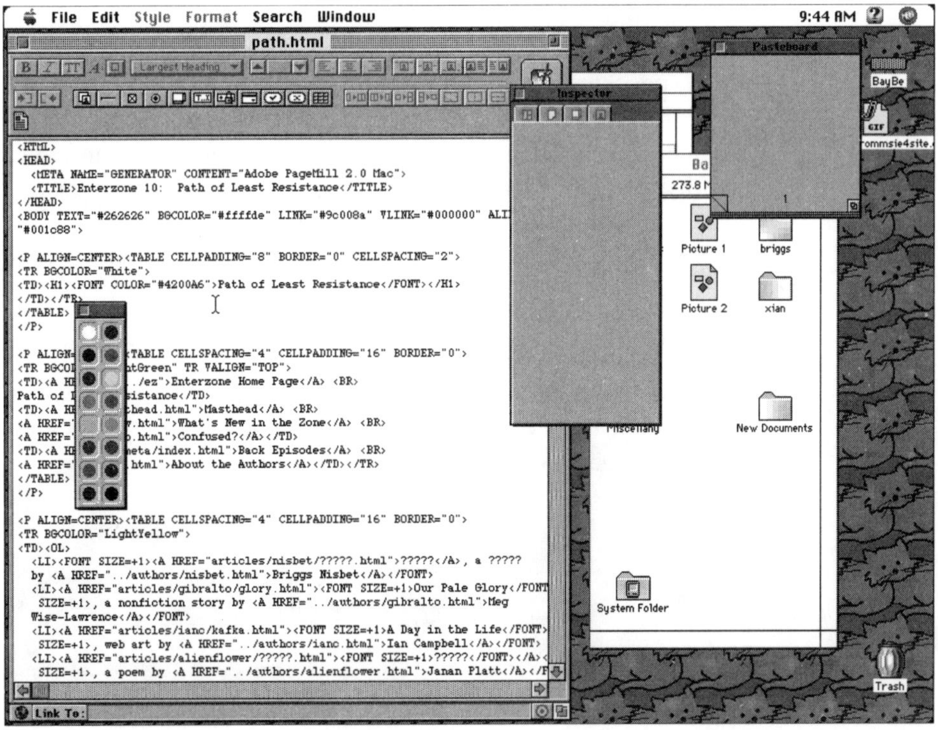

FIGURE 19.4: PageMill's HTML view

Microsoft FrontPage Express

Microsoft FrontPage Express is a very simple WYSIWYG Web editor that works something like Microsoft WordPad (which itself is sort of a cross between Microsoft Notepad and Microsoft Word). You can start up FrontPage Express and create a document from scratch, or you can use it to open existing Web documents on your computer or on the Web itself. If you are browsing the Web with Microsoft Internet Explorer and you click the Edit button, Microsoft FrontPage will start up on your machine (if you have it installed) and a copy of the page you were viewing will be opened in it. If you don't have FrontPage, then FrontPage Express will start up instead.

NOTE NOTE NOTE NOTE NOTE NOTE NOTE NOTE NOTE NOTE NOTE NOTE NOTE NOTE NOTE

Microsoft FrontPage is discussed in the next section, "Building a Web Site."

FrontPage Express is a good introduction to the world of Web publishing, because it includes a Personal Home Page Wizard that gets you started on your home page. FrontPage Express includes some of the features of FrontPage, which is a full-featured Web publishing package. You can start your publishing efforts with FrontPage Express, which comes with Microsoft Internet Explorer 4, then graduate to FrontPage or another commercial program after you master all of the basic procedures and want to learn more.

Here are the steps for creating a starter home page with FrontPage Express:

1. Start FrontPage Express by selecting Start ➢ Programs ➢ Internet Explorer ➢ FrontPage Express. You will see the FrontPage Express window.
2. Select File ➢ New to display the New Page dialog box. Highlight Personal Home Page Wizard in the Template or Wizard list box and click the OK button (see Figure 19.5).

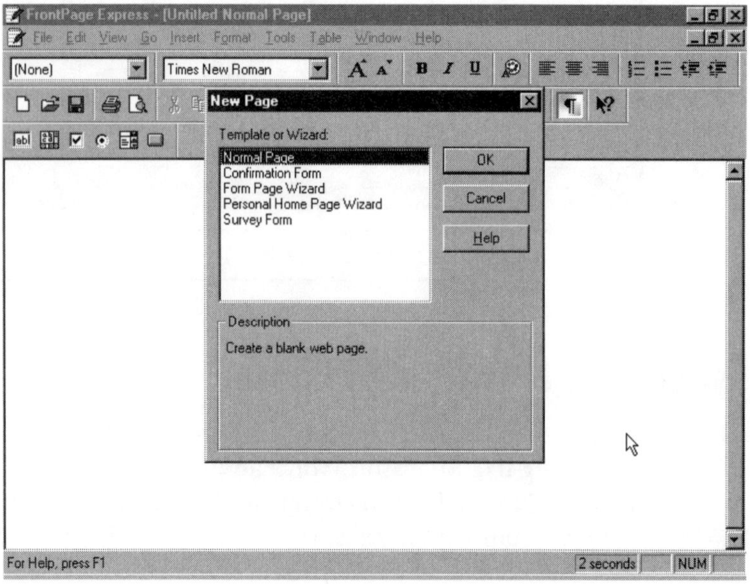

FIGURE 19.5: FrontPage Express offers templates and wizards to help you get started making a home page.

3. The Personal Home Page Wizard appears. Click the checkbox next to each section listed that you want included in your home page, then click the Next button.

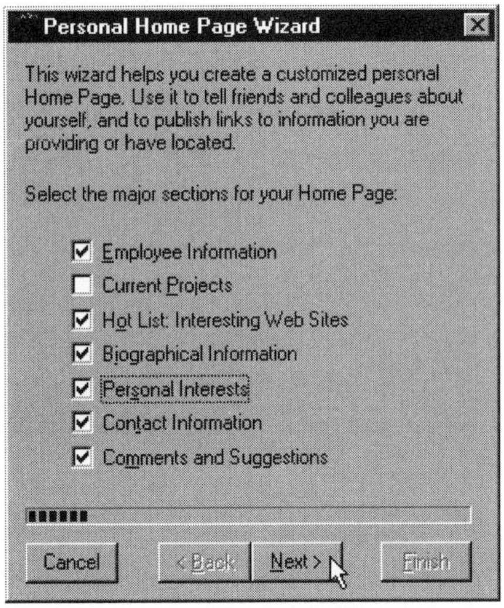

4. Change the name of the Page URL and the Page Title in the appropriate textboxes in the next wizard box. You can use the default URL of `home1.htm` and the default title of "Home Page 1," but you may want something more descriptive. Click the Next button when you're done.

5. Depending on which sections you selected in the first wizard dialog box, you will be prompted to further refine the format of these sections in subsequent wizard boxes. The following bullet items discuss some of the options you may see:

   - **Employment Information** Check the boxes next to the employment information you would like included in the page. If you are making a page for your company intranet, you might want to include all of these options, but for a wider audience, probably the Job Title and Key Responsibilities are sufficient. Click Next when you're done.

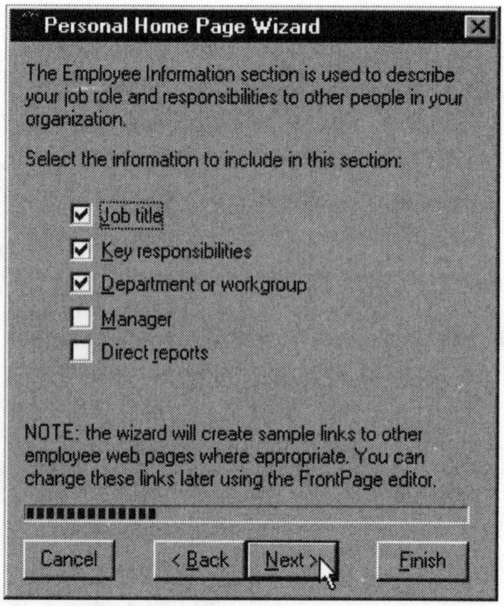

- **Hot List: Interesting Web Sites** Select the list option that's best for your Hot List of Interesting Web Sites, which will provide links to other sites of interest for people visiting your page. The Definition List (Item Plus Description) is preferable, but only if you are willing to write a short sentence or two about each site so that users will know whether they want to click on that link. Click Next when you're ready.
- **Biographical Information** Choose a format for your biography. Select Professional if you are preparing this page to introduce yourself to online employers or people using the organizational intranet; otherwise, select Personal or Academic, then click the Next button.
- **Personal Interests** Type in your interests, such as sports, dancing, volunteer activities, and any subjects you are studying in school or elsewhere. Select a format, such as Bullet List, for presenting these interests, then click Next.
- **Contact Information** Include addresses and phone numbers in the appropriate textboxes so that people can contact you after seeing your page. Click the Next button.

- **Comments and Suggestions** Choose the option that's best for you for obtaining feedback about your page. Your choices are:

  Use Form, Store Results in Data File

  Use Form, Store Results in Web Page

  Use Link, Send E-Mail to This Address

  The e-mail option is the easiest to keep track of, but you will not be able to do as much manipulation of your feedback data. However, you will still be able to collect the names and addresses of people who are interested in you and your Web page.

6. Continue clicking Next after fine-tuning the options you have selected. You will reach a wizard box where you set the order of the sections in your home page. Highlight any section you wish to move and click the Up and Down buttons to relocate it. A convention of many Web pages is to position the Hot List and the Comments and Suggestions near the end of the page. Click Next to move on.

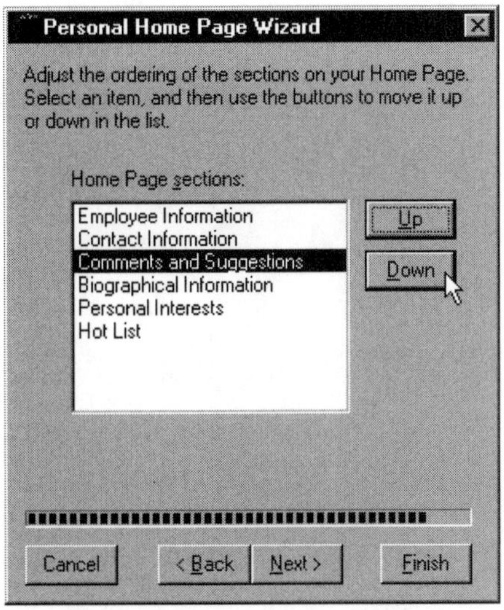

7. Click the Finish button to direct FrontPage Express to design your home page for you. Your plain vanilla page will appear in the FrontPage Express window, where you can begin the lifelong process of decorating and enhancing it.

After you have created your page and added some finesse with font styles, images, and hyperlinks, it is time to save the page and invoke the Web Publishing Wizard, which will take you through the process of publishing your page on the Web. These are the steps you'll follow:

1. With FrontPage Express running and your page open, select File ➢ Save. Change the default Page Title and the Page Location in the respective boxes to more accurately reflect the contents of your page. The Page Location will become your Web address, so check with your company's network administrator or with your service provider to find out the correct address for your page. Click OK.
2. Enter password information in the Enter Network Password dialog box if this applies to you. Click Cancel instead of OK if you are not on a network and do not need a password.
3. Next you'll see the first Web Publishing Wizard screen. Read what the wizard does and collect the information you need about your Web server (the computer where Web pages are stored) from those who know (your network administrators or your service provider). Click Next to continue.

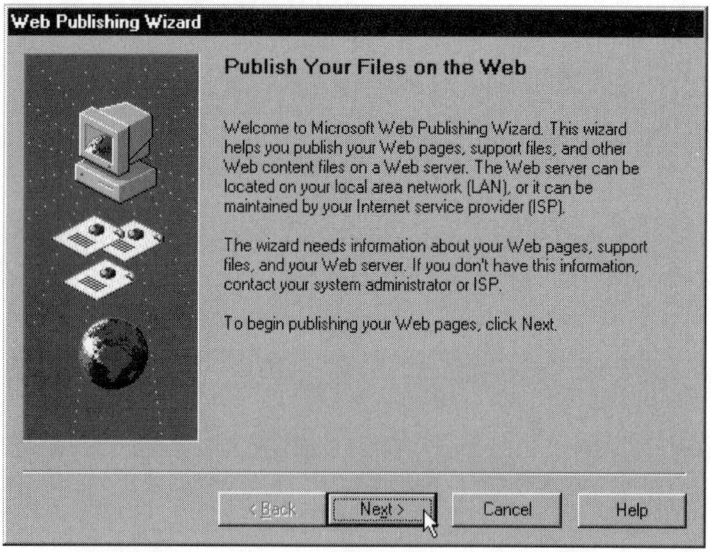

4. In the Name the Web Server window, type the name of your server in the Descriptive Name textbox. This does not have to be the official name of your server, but should be a name you can remember for future publishing, such as *Company Server*. Click Next to proceed.
5. In the Select Service Provider window, highlight your Internet service provider if it appears in the list; otherwise, just click Next to go with the default option, Automatically Select Service Provider.
6. Type the real server name in the Server Name dialog box on the Provide Posting Information screen. Your service provider will have this information, as well as the posting command statement that you need to type into the Posting Command box. Click Next.
7. Click the Finish button in the Publish Your Files window to have the Wizard publish your page.

NOTE NOTE NOTE NOTE NOTE NOTE NOTE NOTE NOTE NOTE NOTE NOTE NOTE NOTE

If you do not have the server information necessary to publish your page, but you want to save it and work on it later, select File > Save As. Click the As File button in the Save As dialog box. Type a name for the page in the Save As File dialog box and browse for a folder to save it in, then click Save. Your page will be saved as a file with an `.htm` extension.

Netscape Composer

Netscape Composer is a marginally improved version of the Netscape Editor module that came as part of the Navigator Gold 2 and 3 packages (for instance, they've added a spell checker). It's an adequate editor and boasts complete integration with the Netscape Communicator 4 package, so you can browse to a page of your own, notice an error, click the edit button, correct the error, click the publish button (warning: requires setup!), and post the page back to your server, error corrected. That can be useful. Figure 19.6 shows my company's home page in Netscape Composer.

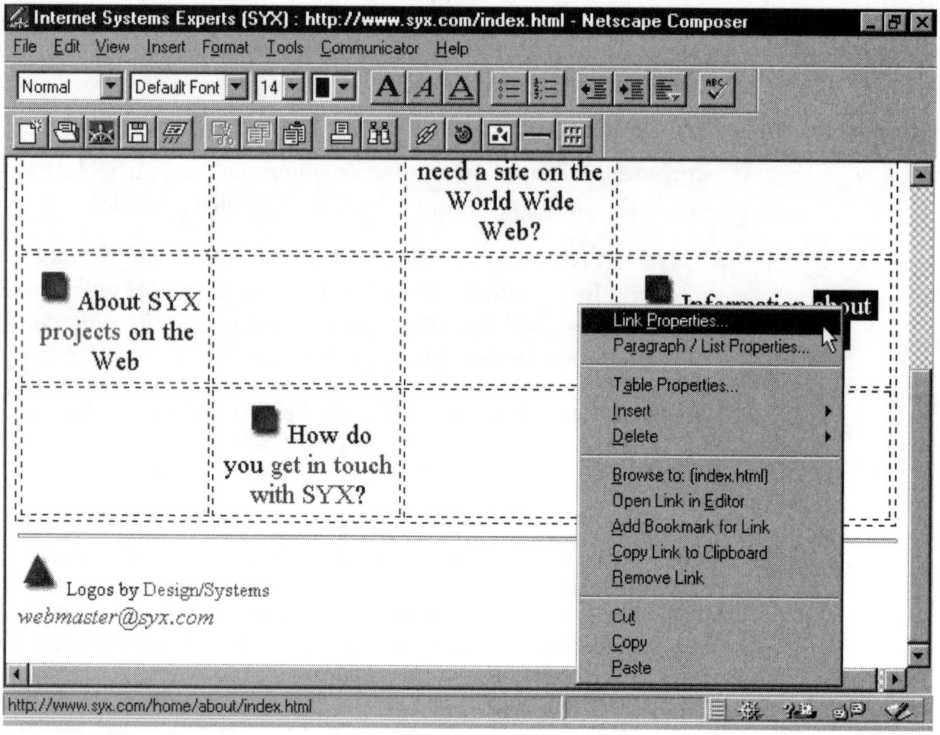

FIGURE 19.6: Composer lags behind the Navigator browser module in terms of features. It can't make frames, for example.

Netscape Composer has a Netscape Page Wizard you can use to create your page by following prompts, in a manner similar to the Personal Home Page Wizard described in the "Microsoft FrontPage Express" section. Unfortunately, the Netscape Wizard is only accessible while you are connected to Netscape's home page on the Web. This means you will have to stay connected while you construct your page, which is fine if you have an online service that doesn't charge for connect time, but not so good if you are watching the clock.

However, the Page Wizard is great because it includes clip art for buttons and rulers, as well as easily-selected color schemes for your page.

NOTE **You can download clip art (rules, buttons, and backgrounds) for your Web page from the Netscape Gold Rush Tool Chest, which is located at** `http://home.netscape.com/assist/net_sites/starter/samples/index.html`**. There are links to this page on both the Netscape Page Wizard and Netscape Web Page Templates pages.**

If you are not worried about how long you are connected to the Internet, here's how to get to the Netscape Page Wizard:

1. Open Composer by selecting Start ➢ Programs ➢ Netscape Communicator ➢ Netscape Composer.
2. In the Composer window, select File ➢ New ➢ Page from Wizard, or click the New button at the far right end of the Composition toolbar, then select the From Page Wizard button in the Create New Page dialog box.
3. Netscape Navigator will launch itself and take you to the Page Wizard address at Netscape's extensive Web site. Scroll through the Netscape Page Wizard information and click Start to begin.

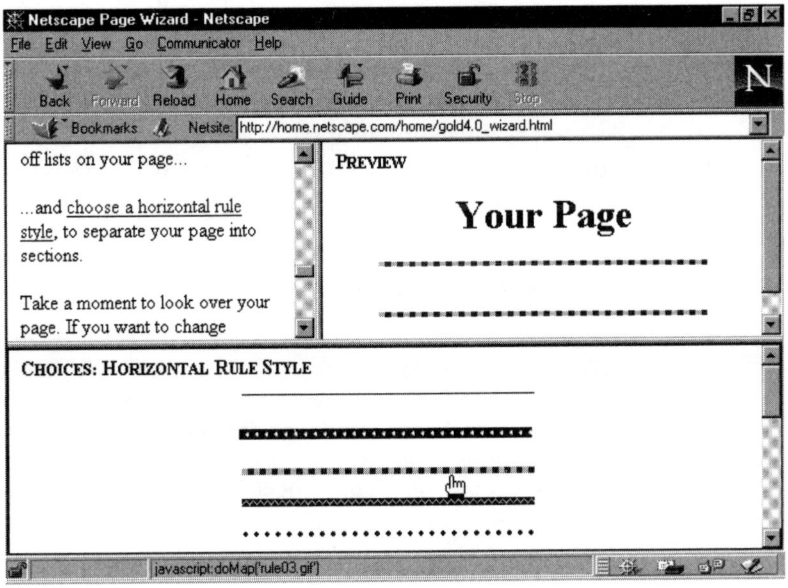

TIP TIP TIP TIP TIP TIP TIP TIP TIP TIP TIP TIP TIP TIP TIP TIP TIP TIP TIP TIP TIP TIP TIP TIP TIP

Write down everything you want on your Web page, save it as a text file or a word processing file, and print it out before using the Page Wizard. You will have all the information right there and you will not spend time thinking about what you want to include while you are online.

You can save a little time by downloading a template from Netscape's site, opening Composer, and saving the template to your hard drive so you can get offline and work with it. Here are the steps for the template approach:

1. Open Composer by selecting Start ➢ Programs ➢ Netscape Communicator ➢ Netscape Composer.
2. In the Composer window, select File ➢ New ➢ Page from Template, or click the New button at the far right end of the Composition toolbar, then select the From Template button in the Create New Page dialog box.
3. In the New Page From Template dialog box, click the Netscape Templates button.
4. Netscape Navigator will launch itself and take you to the Netscape Web Page Templates address at Netscape's Web site. Scroll through the Netscape Web Page Templates information and click My Home Page or Resume to display the template.
5. As soon as the template appears, select File ➢ Edit Page. Netscape Composer will return to the forefront. Click the Save button or select File ➢ Save to save the template on your hard drive.
6. In the Navigator window, select File ➢ Go Offline to end your session. Disconnect from your online service, too.

TIP TIP TIP TIP TIP TIP TIP TIP TIP TIP TIP TIP TIP TIP TIP TIP TIP TIP TIP TIP TIP TIP TIP TIP TIP

If you are trying to limit your connect-time charges, use an existing `.htm` file from your hard drive and save it under a different name so that you can change things in it. For example, you can use your bookmark file, which is located in the Netscape folder on your C: drive (located at `C:\Netscape\Users\`*`YourEmailName`*`\bookmark.htm`.

Improving Your Home Page with Composer

Now that you have your Web page template, here are some of the things you can do to spruce it up:

Text formatting Select any text and click the buttons in the Formatting toolbar to change font size, color, or alignment. Click the Change Style list button on the far left of the Format toolbar to change the text to another HTML style, such as Heading 1, 2, and so on. Choose Format ➢ Font ➢ Other to access the Font dialog box. Change basic font features in the Font Style area. Select Format ➢ Size, Format ➢ Style, or Format ➢ Color to modify these characteristics.

Background Choose Format ➢ Page Colors and Properties and select the Colors and Background tab in the Page Properties dialog box. You can change the background color and the color of text signifying hyperlinks (both the original and clicked-on colors, so your viewers will remember where they have been). Check the Use Image checkbox in the Background Image area and click the Choose File button to point the way to a file that you want to use for your background. Try to use something that is not too grainy and allows people read the text on your page easily.

Hyperlinks Select the Insert Link button on the Composition toolbar or use Insert ➢ Link to reach the Link tab of the Character Properties dialog box. You can add links to your existing page in the Link To area (the wizard already added the basic links within your home page, known as bookmarks, and the template also has some links).

Add images Use the Insert ➢ Image menu to add image files to your page. You can specify how text will wrap around images in the Image tab of the Image Properties dialog box. Click the Alt Text/Low Res button to type in alternative text that will appear when viewers have images turned off in their browsers.

View HTML Select View ➢ Page Source to see the HTML tags which make up your document. If you want to change the tags, you must use Edit ➢ HTML Source. (You must have an HTML Editor to change the tags.)

Building a Web Site

Web editors are all well and good for the laborious task of creating Web documents, but they don't necessarily help out much with the ultimate project of building a coherent site out of its constituent pages. Sure, they might check the links as they exist now, on your computer, but it takes a special program to help you remotely control a site on your server. Such programs can update changed pages regularly and move pages around without you manually retyping all the links to those pages.

These programs are more than Web editors. Since they help out with the site management, they're called Web publishing programs.

Adobe SiteMill

The big brother to Adobe's PageMill, SiteMill makes the process of publishing your locally created pages to the public site a breeze. It finds bad links and corrects links when you rearrange pages. What more could you ask for (maybe for them to finish the Windows version)? Figure 19.7 shows part of the overview of one of my sites in SiteMill. You can download a limited version of SiteMill—it can't publish pages—at the Adobe site (`http://www.adobe.com/`).

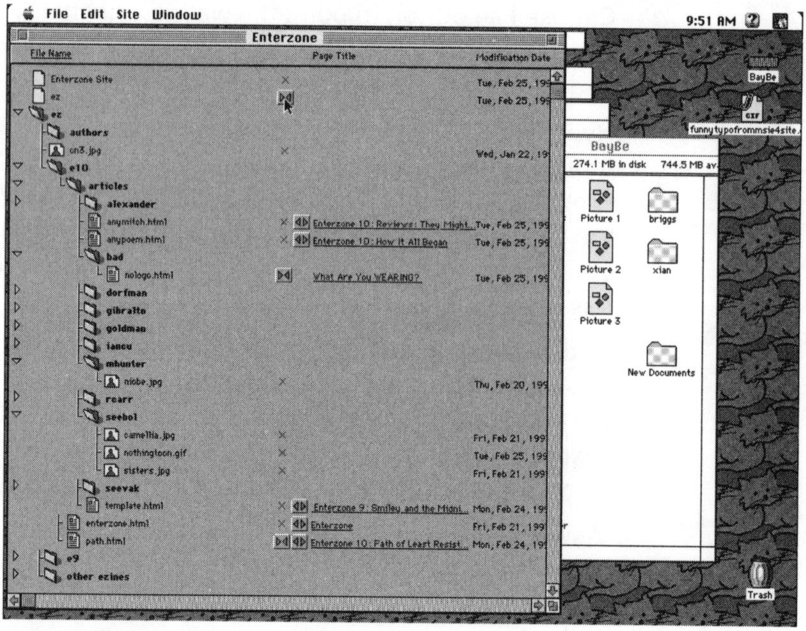

FIGURE 19.7: Here's an overview of a complex hierarchy of Web documents that make up part of my 'zine.

Microsoft FrontPage

Microsoft FrontPage is priced like a basic Web editor but has sophisticated site management and automatic/dynamic content creation. It can be pretty tricky to learn at first. The simple Web editing functions of the Editor module aren't so difficult (see Figure 19.8), and the overview presented by the Explorer module tries to put things in familiar terms (for Windows 95 and 98 users), but the ActiveX handles, objects called *sprites*, and other, even more arcane features might require some trial and error to learn. Consider creating some of the "canned" sites from templates to see examples of how some of FrontPage's features can be used.

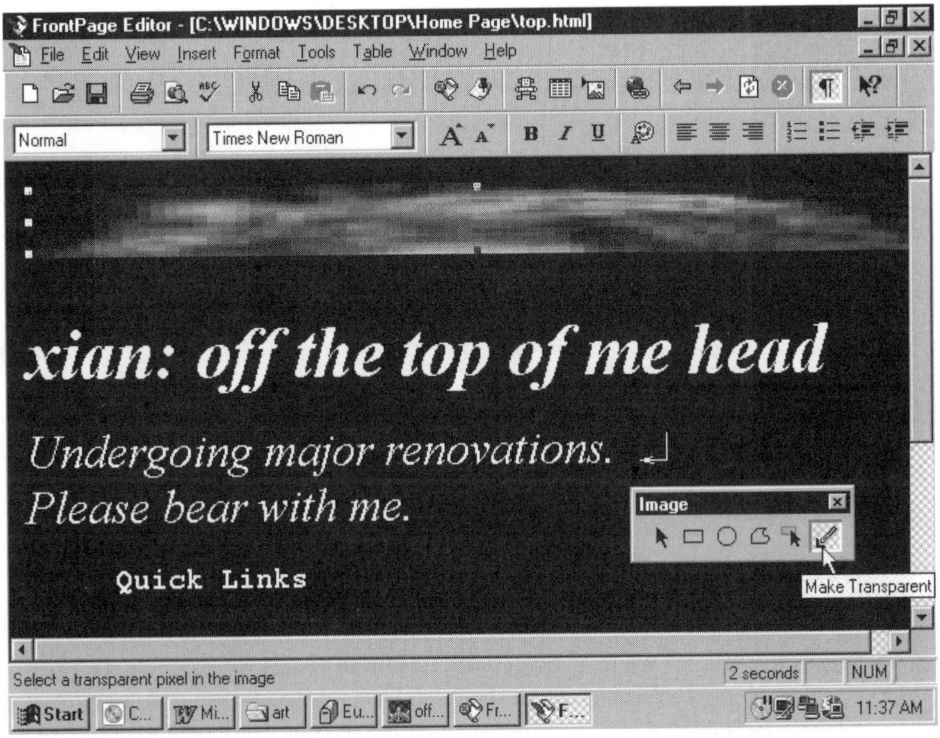

FIGURE 19.8: FrontPage Editor makes laying out Web pages easy (and it writes fairly clean HTML code, too).

Figure 19.9 shows a discussion-oriented Web site, complete with frames and alternative non-frames layouts, as viewed in the FrontPage Explorer.

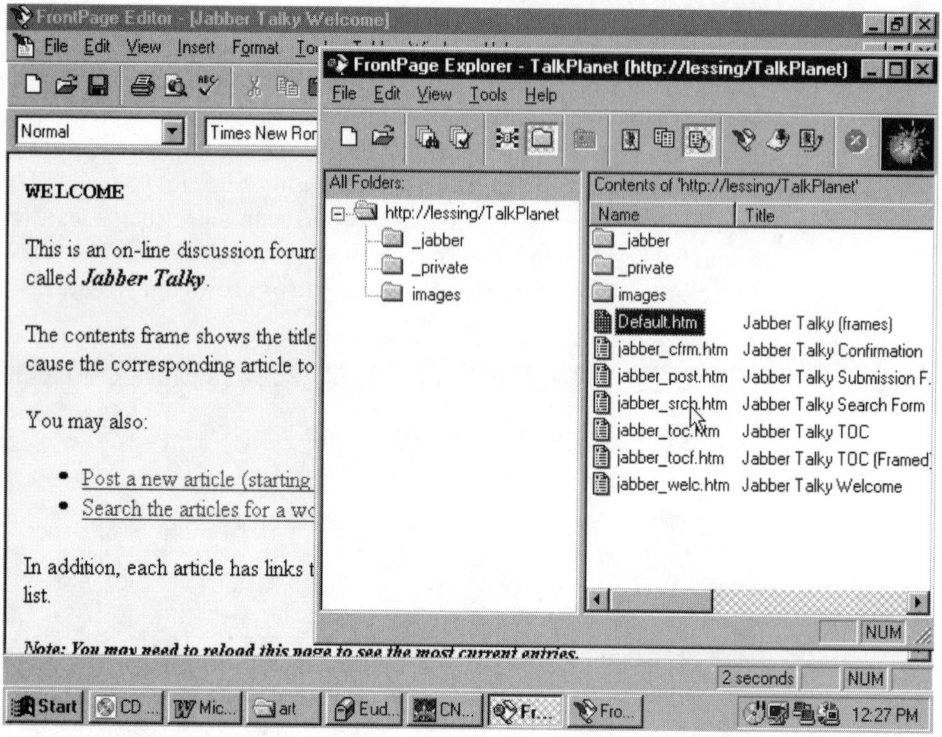

FIGURE 19.9: My straight-out-of-the-template TalkPlanet Web site as viewed in the FrontPage Explorer

NetObjects Fusion

On the Windows side of the street, a lot of busy, dynamic Web sites use NetObjects Fusion to put all the modular pieces together. You can download a test version of Fusion from the NetObjects Web site (`http://www.netobjects.com/`)—it will expire eventually, but you'll have plenty of time to try it out.

NetObjects (everyone calls it that, not Fusion) allows you to design pages in its own format, which it eventually translates to HTML when all the pieces are put together. Figure 19.10 shows a page from Enterzone in NetObjects.

I did have trouble importing an existing site, and I found the interface pretty confusing at first, as anyone but the program's designers probably would.

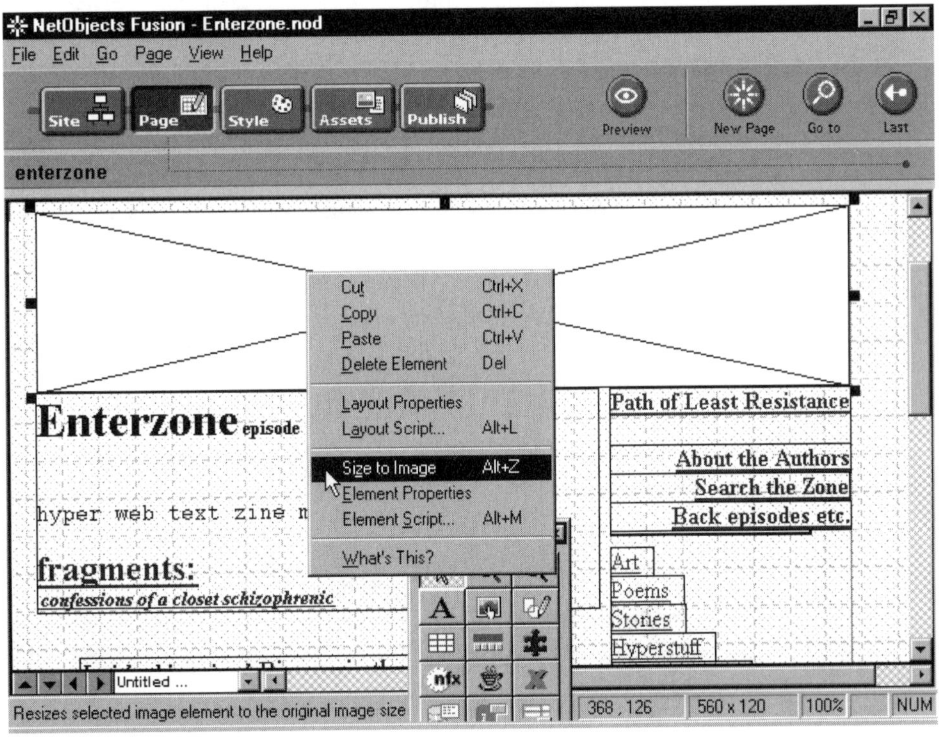

FIGURE 19.10: A recent Enterzone home page as a NetObjects document

Publishing a Site

Publishing a site requires more than just the tools for transferring the files. You need a host to make your files public (or available to your local intranet). Once you find a host for the site and publish it there, you need to promote the site to make sure that the intended audience knows it's there and what's available to entice them to drop by (useful files to download? helpful advice? free information?). Finally, you've got to dig in for the long haul and be prepared to update the site, keep it fresh, and occasionally revise its layout and focus.

Finding a Host

The final question about your home page is where to put it. Many Internet service providers (and some of the online services as well) offer space on their Web servers, up to some quota of disk space (often five megabytes), to all their customers with no extra charge. If your e-mail provider does not offer you access to a Web server, you'll have to find someone else to host your site. Look first at your company or any other affiliations you may have. There are also some free home page hosting sites out there (though they may require that you include an ad for them on your page).

Some providers will ask you to send them your files via e-mail (see Skill 5, *Advanced E-mail Tricks*, for how to send files via e-mail). Others will prefer that you use FTP to upload your files to them (see Skill 18, *Getting Around with FTP and Telnet*, for how to send files via FTP). They will assign you a URL for your home page, often in the format `http://www.`*`theirname`*`.com/~`*`your-username`*, but other variations are possible as well.

Once you get your page (and any associated art files or linked pages) out there on your provider's Web site, then anyone can drop by. E-mail your friends and ask them to visit.

Promoting and Maintaining a Site

If you really want to make your pages public, visit some (or all) of the directory and search sites mentioned in Skill 10, *Finding Stuff on the Web and the Net*, and submit the URL of your page to each of them.

Voilà!

Now you're truly "on the Net."

Are You Experienced?

Now you can...

- ☑ develop content for a personal or professional home page
- ☑ add links, images, and design elements to your page
- ☑ understand the basics of HTML
- ☑ use Microsoft FrontPage Express to create a simple Web page
- ☑ work with Netscape Composer to modify a Web page template
- ☑ compare the features of Adobe PageMill and Microsoft FrontPage Express
- ☑ understand Web site management using Adobe SiteMill, Microsoft FrontPage, or NetObjects Fusion
- ☑ receive feedback from your Web page
- ☑ publish your Web page on a free site, your intranet, or an Internet service provider site
- ☑ maintain your Web page with new content, new links, and a new look

PART VI

Troubleshooting

In the two short lessons in Part VI, I'll address the two most frustrating aspects of Internet use today. Skill 20 deals with flaky and unstable software or hardware setups. These problems plague computer use in general, but technology evolves so quickly on the Internet that software rarely has time to stabilize completely before it's obsolete. I'll tell you what the most common problems are, and what you can do about them.

Skill 21 tries to give you some tools in the daily online battle against spam (unwanted commercial e-mail). There's no sure solution short of censorship, but there are some things you can do to reduce your exposure.

SKILL 20

PROBLEMS WITH CONNECTIONS, PROVIDERS, AND SOFTWARE

- **Recognizing problems**
- **Diagnosing problems**
- **Reconnecting to the Net**
- **Rebooting your machine**
- **Reinstalling your software**

It's nearly impossible for me to anticipate, diagnose, and solve every problem you might have with your computer and the Net in this book format, but I don't want to leave you without any rubrics to fall back on when things stop working. Therefore, this lesson starts by discussing some general approaches to troubleshooting that will help with all but the most unusual problems. Then I'll take you through a slightly more rigorous process for articulating, diagnosing, and (possibly) solving your specific problem. Finally, I'll point out a few online resources that can help you (if you can borrow someone else's Internet access to do the research, that is!).

Sometimes things will just freeze up on you, which could mean there's a problem with the command that you issued, a problem with an Internet server involving the mail server or the newsfeed, or a problem with your provider's network. First try to deal with it yourself. Then ask for help.

General Troubleshooting Tips

You may be surprised by problems you experience with your Internet connection. Some problems, such as busy signals, may be the fault of your service provider. But others are a reflection of the Internet itself—that big, loosely organized bundle of very different computers, spread over an immense amount of territory. So, for example, if your IRC program bumps you off in the middle of a chat session, it might just be the vicissitudes of the Internet in this day and age, and not necessarily the fault of your provider.

NOTE NOTE NOTE NOTE NOTE NOTE NOTE NOTE NOTE NOTE NOTE NOTE NOTE NOTE NOTE

There could also be a problem with your PC, your modem, or the phone lines. If any of these seems to be suffering or if they have conked out, try basic resuscitation procedures—reset the PC or modem, check the phone line, and try dialing again.

Be patient and willing to tinker with things until they work properly for you. Sometimes this means simply quitting an application and starting over. Other times it may mean restarting your computer. As with netiquette, patience will go a long way toward smoothing your travel over the information superhighway.

Stop This Crazy Thing!

When things start going wrong or nothing is happening at all, you sometimes have to interrupt the process by pressing Esc to quit the program that isn't responding (whether it's your e-mail, Web, or news program). Start it again and see if it works this time.

Ultimately, if you can't get your software's or connection's attention, you can always just hang up your modem by quitting the dial-up software. This solution will (eventually) sever the connection to your provider, though it is always better to log out when you can.

Getting Help

Every program you run should have a help system, though admittedly some are more sketchy than others. In Windows or on the Mac, this usually means looking for a Help menu. In Unix, it usually means typing **h** or **?**.

Once you've looked at your software's documentation or help system and have made a good-faith effort to figure things out for yourself, the next step should be to get help from your service provider. Either call them up (they should have given you a phone number for this purpose when you first signed on), or send them e-mail if your mail is working but something else isn't (send it to `info@`*`their-address`* if you don't have a more specific address). Some providers, such as Netcom, also offer technical support through their Web sites.

Articulating the Problem

You may not be able to solve all your own computer problems, but if you can at least articulate the problem and figure out exactly what's going wrong, then your chances of finding a solution will be much greater. Start off by making a statement about what's not working. I'll discuss all the typical complaints I've run into in this section, and for each tell you how to look for the source of the problem. That's the first step.

I Can't Get to This URL

A common problem is not being able to connect to a Web site. At first, it can be hard to tell if the problem is with the site, with your connection to the Internet, with your Internet provider, or with your Web browser software. To diagnose the problem, you should try to connect a second time, check the spelling of the URL, try to connect to other addresses, and try to run other Internet software. If you can connect to other addresses or run basic Internet software, then the problem lies with the Web site itself.

I Can't Get My E-mail

Sometimes you'll tell your e-mail program to go get your mail and it will report back with an error message (usually one that is not helpful at all). This could be a problem with your connection or with your provider. It's unlikely to be a problem with the e-mail software.

Someone Sent Me a File I Can't Read

As discussed in Skill 5, sometimes you will receive e-mail with an attached file that you can't read. There could be several explanations for this. First of all, your mail program and that of the person sending the message have to understand the same encoding methods. Common formats include MIME and Uuencode. If your programs have no common format, you may have to use another method to transfer the files, for example, a public FTP site (as discussed in Skill 18).

Even if you have compatible file-encoding capabilities, your sender still needs to use a file format that you can understand. If you use different word processing programs, for example, the file may come through just fine but you still may not be able to open it. If file format is the problem, see if the sender can convert the file in advance to the format of your software (from WordPerfect to Word, for example) or, failing that, to a fairly common format, such as RTF (Rich Text Format), that most e-mail and word processing programs can understand.

Hello, Internet? (Suddenly, I Can't Connect to Anything)

Often the fault lies not in the specific programs you're running but in your Internet connection itself. The software used to manage these connections is often buggy and can crash or disconnect while telling you that it is still connected. The first thing to try is to disconnect and connect again. It often helps to turn your modem off and on again as well (if you are using a modem). If you determine (in the next section) that something is corrupted in your connection software, you may have to reinstall or replace it.

DNS What?

Web browsers and other Internet tools sometimes report DNS errors, or problems relating to DNS. DNS stands for Domain Name Service and it refers to the system used on the Internet to convert, or "resolve," text-based domain names (such as `www.netcom.com`) to numerical IP addresses. Without the ability to connect to domain name servers and look up domain names, none of your Internet software will function. The problem is, error messages are sometimes just guessing at the source of the problem. If you have a real DNS problem, it may mean that your provider has changed the addresses of its primary and secondary domain name servers and failed to tell you so, or that someone has changed your Internet setup and replaced the old correct DNS addresses with incorrect ones.

Mail Sent to Me Is "Bouncing" (I'm Told)

Sometimes people will tell you (in person or on the phone) that they've tried to send you e-mail but that it came back to them with an error message. When this is happening, it either means that people have your address wrong (spell it for them, slowly) or it could mean that your ISP (Internet service provider) has been having problems staying online 24 hours a day, seven days a week. Make sure you are getting the service you're paying for, or you may have to consider finding a new provider.

I'm Frozen

If your computer completely freezes up (no reaction from the keyboard or mouse), first walk away from it, before you do anything. Sometimes (not often enough), the poor thing has just bogged down in some software equivalent of a maintenance routine or in a seemingly interminable wait for confirmation or a dropped Web connection. If you take a break, stretch your legs, focus your eyes on something distant, you may find the problem has solved itself on your return. If not, try to reconstruct what led to the problem and reboot. If it happens repeatedly, some of your software is probably corrupted (perhaps from an earlier crash?) or you have memory problems.

Things Keep Bombing

Even when you don't lose your whole operating system in one sickening moment, you may still find that your Web browser, your mail program, or even your newsreader may start bombing on you (crashing, failing, quitting unexpectedly) when it had behaved itself up to now. Often this signals it is time to update your software (or reinstall it, at least), and it may be a sign that you are overloading your machine and need more memory.

I'm Getting a Ton of Busy Signals (Or Things Are Painfully Sloooow)

If you never seem to be able to connect, this is your provider's problem. If they can't guarantee you a connection (even at rush hours, after a reasonable number of tries) then they are failing in their basic responsibility to you.

If your connection often seems painfully slow to you, join the club! No, seriously, this could be a problem at the provider end or a problem of expectations. If your software and connection are consistently underperforming their potential, your provider may be able to help go over your configuration with you to find the bottleneck. As discussed in Appendix A, most providers can accommodate a dial-up user with a 56.6 Kbps modem. If you have such a modem and your provider is equipped to handle it *and* you still are not satisfied with the speed of your access, you might want to consider ISDN or one of the more expensive connection solutions, such as a dedicated T1 line. For most uses, though, a 56.6 Kbps modem should be acceptable.

A Different Browser or Mail Program Is Popping Up Now

If you find a different Web browser appearing when you click on links or type URLs in address boxes, or if a different mail program offers to send your messages when you click on "mail to" links at Web sites, then you probably recently installed a new Web browser or other program that took it upon itself to change your associations. Run your preferred software and it will most likely offer to restore itself to the place nearest to your heart.

Diagnosing the Problem

In the previous sections, I sketched some possible explanations for specific problems. To make more than an educated guess, you'll need to do a little experimenting, some testing, and some comparisons. You have to work from the grossest issues (my computer is frozen) to the particulars (I can't connect to this one single Web site).

WARNING WARNING WARNING WARNING WARNING WARNING WARNING WARNING

Don't take error messages too literally or too seriously. They can sometimes be helpful as a diagnostic tool, but they are often way off in their diagnosis of the problem.

Are You on a Network?

If you are on a network, try plugging your computer into a working arrangement and copying the settings from the computer whose address you're borrowing.

TIP TIP TIP TIP TIP TIP TIP TIP TIP TIP TIP TIP TIP TIP TIP TIP TIP TIP TIP TIP TIP TIP TIP TIP TIP

If your network uses a firewall, this could account for why you might not be able to reach some Web sites.

Do You Use a Modem?

If you use a modem, your PC or Mac will have a control panel where you can check the settings against what your provider suggests. You can also look at the modem lights to see if the computer is truly frozen or merely busy uploading or downloading information.

Is It a Hardware Problem?

Don't laugh, but you should always check to make sure that every component of the computer is plugged in nice and snug. You can bump into a computer table and jostle a modem plug loose. The same can happen with the cables that connect a PC to an external modem. If you find a loose connection, you may sometimes have to restart the system to get it recognized again.

Another one that may sound silly (but it happens, believe me): If you use a modem, make sure it's turned on!

Is Your System Crashed?

To figure out if your entire system is frozen, first give it time to settle down in case it's in some program-code tizzy behind the scenes. Then see if you can move the mouse pointer, change what part of the screen is highlighted, or type in a selected text box. If you are getting no response at all, your system has probably crashed and will need to be restarted. If you can click outside a frozen program and get results, then you should be able to shut down the program that's hung up and possibly keep working without further problems. (I'd save all your other work, just to be safe.)

If your software or entire system begins to repeatedly lock up, there may be an inherent conflict (with drivers or extensions, perhaps) between some of your recently updated software. This can be system software, such as a new network driver, or application software, such as an updated Web browser or mail program. Most Web browsers are memory hogs, and some of them *leak* memory, which means that they slowly use up all the available memory on your system until they (or some other program) run into a wall and fold up. Buggy software can be replaced with upgraded (but still, usually, buggy) software, but consider also that if you're always running out of memory, it may be time to add more memory (RAM) to your computer. For Mac users, as a housekeeping measure, be sure to quit programs completely and not just close all their open windows. This will free up some memory.

A program that once worked properly but that crashes all the time now has probably been corrupted in part during some earlier crisis. It will most likely need to be reinstalled to work properly (or upgraded).

Supposedly Connected but Getting No Response?

Sometimes your dial-up software will claim you're connected, but nothing will be happening in any of your Internet programs. This may mean that the dialer or the connection software (TCP/IP stack, if you must know the jargon) may have crashed. It can do so without telling you. Sometimes, you can simply disconnect and then reconnect. If that doesn't work, try quitting the dialer and running it again. If you still get no response, restart your system to flush the crashed program out of memory.

Is It the Host's Problem?

Sometimes the problem is not with your computer, provider, hardware, or even the Internet, but simply with the host of the site you are attempting to visit or contact. If that site is down, you will get an error message through no fault of your own.

Is It a Provider Problem?

If you suspect that your provider is having problems, you can set up your connection software to display a terminal window after connecting. Then you can log in by hand and see whether the connection appears to be made at your provider's end. If you see nothing happening or gibberish or error messages, contact your ISP's technical support line.

Is It a Connection (TCP/IP) Problem?

Problems connecting sometimes yield error messages such as "Unable to resolve domain name" or "Could not open socket." It's not always clear whether the problem is at your end or at the other end. If the error is "Unable to resolve hostname," then the problem is at your end, and someone will have to troubleshoot your connection.

TIP

You can use a terminal program such as HyperTerminal or MicroPhone to see whether the modem is responding and can be dialed at all.

The tools for checking your connection are called Traceroute and Ping (on the Mac, most people use a program called MacTCP Watcher for these purposes). Traceroute is used to define a path, a series of hops, from the Internet address of your computer to that of a host site. So, for example, a Unix or DOS command of

```
traceroute home.netscape.com
```

would yield a series of Internet addresses that you could then individually try to connect to with Ping.

Ping is a program that simply tries to "touch" a target computer and reports back if successful. You can ping another computer to see whether you have any connection at all. You can also ping yourself. The syntax is

```
ping localhost
```

If that yields no reply, then your configuration or hardware is the problem.

Solutions

I wish I could offer more definitive solutions than what I have here, but I hope that these options help you solve your problems.

Some Things Are Out of Your Control

You can't fix every problem. Errors such as "Server not responding" and "Host does not have DNS entry" usually mean that the problem is at the other end. Wait a while before trying to connect again.

Retype the URL

Simple typos can account for failures to connect to Web sites, but your Web browser will report that the site you were trying to reach does not exist at all. Don't be fooled. Check the exact spelling of the site's URL. Does it actually end in `.com` or perhaps `.net` or `.gov` or even `.org`?

Restart Software

Many software problems can be solved by the expediency of saving your work, quitting the program, and then running it again.

Reconnect

After you've been disconnected, first just try to reconnect. Often that solves the problem. If you are being disconnected regularly in the midst of your sessions, then you need to complain to your provider.

Reboot

Occasionally, rebooting the entire system will help a program that has crashed get back up on its feet without tripping over the same old bug.

Reinstall

Sometimes software becomes permanently damaged, often during a crash when the system is not able to clean up after itself as it ordinarily should. When this happens, you can reinstall your connection software, Web browser, or e-mail program (or operating system) from a CD, or in the case of Internet tools, you can frequently download a newer version of the corrupted program from a Web site and take the opportunity to upgrade.

Install New or Different Software

If a program repeatedly causes you problems, consider trying an alternative. There are two or more Web browsers, e-mail programs, newsreaders, and even FTP programs for each type of computer, so you don't have to stick with something that's unacceptably buggy or awkward to use.

Complain to Your Provider

Your provider is charging you for a reliable connection. If you have frequent problems that you can establish are not the fault of your software or your setup, then you have right to complain for better service. You may eventually be forced to find a new provider.

Change an Internet Connection

You don't have to stay with the same provider forever. It's not fun to change your e-mail address (and inform people of this), but you should be prepared to move if need be. You can often pay your old provider to forward mail from your old address to your new address for a set period of time. You might also consider obtaining a permanent forwarding address, such as those offered by `http://www.pobox.com/`, so that you can change your address in the future without ever again having to update anyone.

Make Sure Your Dial-Up Network Settings Are All Correct

It is easy to miss an item. Open up the dialog boxes for TCP, PPP, your modem, and so on, and compare them to the settings suggested by your provider. A mistake may have crept into your configuration.

Online Resources

Obviously, if you can't connect to the Internet, you can't look up any of these resources, but if you end up at work or at home or at a friend's (wherever the problem's *not*), you may find some of these sites helpful.

For troubleshooting TCP/IP networks (Windows users):

```
http://www.halcyon.com/cerelli/kb.htm
http://www.svi.org/pcday/rc_troubleshoot_tcpip.htm
http://www.winfiles.com/connect/ppp.html
```

For Macintosh-specific help, try:

```
http://www.yale.edu/macguide/Trouble/TCP.html
```

For both Mac and Windows (3.1 and beyond) users:

`http://168.31.222.19/Conferences/GETC97/TroubleShooting/First.html`

There's an excellent presentation of TCP/IP troubleshooting at

`http://www.ikan.k12.il.us/pres/controub/sld002.htm`

Another way to get help or answers to your questions is to contact InterNIC. InterNIC is a center funded by the National Science Foundation and founded to help Internet users and people interested in the Net. (*NIC* stands for Network Information Center.)

There are many ways to reach InterNIC with your questions. You can call their hotline at (800) 444-4345 or their regular number at (619) 455-4600. You can fax them at (619) 455-4640. Or you can send them e-mail at `info@is.internic.net`. In addition, they have a Web site (`http://www.internic.net/`). Finally, you can send them regular mail—what people on the Net call *snail mail*—at the following address:

P.O. Box #85608
San Diego, CA 92186-9784

Are You Experienced?

Now you can...

- ☑ define your Internet connection problems
- ☑ diagnose the source of a problem
- ☑ take some basic actions to resolve problems
- ☑ research your problems online

SKILL 21

PROBLEMS WITH SPAM

- What is spam?
- Preventing spam in advance
- Don't bother Removing
- Just delete it!
- Community responses to spam
- Software responses to spam
- Minimizing commercials on AOL

Spam is unsolicited commercial e-mail. It's like junk mail but it shows up in your e-mail box instead. There always seems to be more and more of it, and it threatens to drown out meaningful conversation (it appears in Usenet discussion groups as well).

NOTE NOTE NOTE NOTE NOTE NOTE NOTE NOTE NOTE NOTE NOTE NOTE NOTE NOTE NOTE

Spam is said to get its name from the Vikings whose chanting drowned out the voices of the gits ordering breakfast in the famous Monty Python sketch: "Spam, spam, spam, eggs, bacon, and spam . . ."

The law is perpetually threatening to solve the problem but sometimes aims its gun at our right to express ourselves instead. It's a tough balancing act, trying to limit commercial speech, no matter how unwelcome or crass (or pornographic). For one thing, the Internet transcends ordinary geographical boundaries and areas of jurisdiction. Chances are that users of the Net will have to solve these problems as a community, and that no Big Brother figure is going to be capable, even if willing, to stop unwanted mail or offensive speech.

Just as it's often said that the people who most reliably made fortunes during the Gold Rush were those who sold picks, shovels, or tent stakes, so today is it thought by many that the only people making money off spam are those who sell the software used to spew it into your life.

Minimizing Your Exposure to Spam

By the time you're getting spam, it's too late, in a sense, because your address is already scooped up. It works like this: perhaps you participate in a mailing list, that mailing list's messages are stored in an archive, the archive is available over the Web, and some sleazy little spam mailing-list seller's robot has visited that site and scooped up your address and everything else that looks like an e-mail address so that some other nebbish (Net rubbish) can try to sell you foot cream!

NOTE NOTE NOTE NOTE NOTE NOTE NOTE NOTE NOTE NOTE NOTE NOTE NOTE NOTE NOTE

Usenet is another prime harvesting ground for e-mail addresses.

Spammers buy and sell these mailing lists and then use special multiple-mailing software to instantaneously send their inane messages to every address on the list. They often use a false return address so that the inevitable bounce messages from invalid addresses vanish into the void instead of cluttering up *their* Inboxes. So how can you participate in the public life of the Net without exposing yourself to this constant patter of salestalk?

NOTE NOTE NOTE NOTE NOTE NOTE NOTE NOTE NOTE NOTE NOTE NOTE NOTE NOTE NOTE

Ordinary private or business e-mail correspondence will not usually expose your e-mail address to spammers.

One approach is to maintain multiple addresses. Most importantly, use only one address for public discourse. Perhaps this one can be a free Web-based e-mail account, as discussed in Skill 17. Then keep another for people who know you in person. Some may want to have an even more private address. This all may sound Byzantine to you, but it's easy to filter forward several e-mail addresses to a single account, and then use mail filters to sort out the wheat from the chaff.

The "Remove" Scam

Most spam messages offer to remove you from the sender's mailing list if only you respond, perhaps with the word "Remove" in the header. Boy, if they can get a *response*, particularly one that requires retyping the subject line (something few autoresponding robots will do), then they know they've hooked a live one! You'll be sure to receive a ton more spam, so don't bother communicating with these people. Their discourse is fake.

WARNING WARNING WARNING WARNING WARNING WARNING WARNING WARNING

Never respond directly to a spam message. It only encourages the sender to treat your address as valid.

Delete the Overnight Spam

In the last year I've noticed that I receive most of my spam in the morning. Actually, it has usually been sent in the wee hours of the night, and it shows up in my first batch of mail when I initially check it (usually sometime after I've made the first pot of coffee). This makes it convenient and simple to select it all and delete it in one fell swoop. Sure, I'd rather not have to do it at all, but my main point is that deleting spam is often the least painful response available. Others disagree and follow up each and every spammer and every postmaster at every site that forwarded that message or whose addresses have been hoaxed or spoofed into fake headers. This does drive some spammers off their original hosts but they always seem to land somewhere.

The Spam/Antispam Arms Race

Meanwhile, some bona fide good guys—the folks at Sendmail, Inc. (who make the essential and free Internet utility *sendmail* that is a software backbone of the Internet e-mail system)—are working on methods to detect spam as it courses over the Net. They'll look for certain patterns of words, or consult a constantly updated list of addresses suspected to be sources of spam, and then eliminate the junk before it even arrives at its destination (you). This is very encouraging. However, even the Sendmail folks warn us that they are engaged in something of an arms race and they fully expect the spammers to develop ways of fooling or outwitting their filters. There may never be a single software solution to spam.

NOTE

There are some who believe that spam should not be wiped out summarily, that this would constitute a form of censorship. These are not easy issues to sort out and the rules vary from country to country. Remember that the Internet is not in the United States alone!

Reporting Net Abuse

If you are not satisfied with quietly deleting the ever-growing piles of spam in your Inbox, you can report spam that you receive to the Fight Spam on the Internet! page at `http://spam.abuse.net/` (see Figure 21.1).

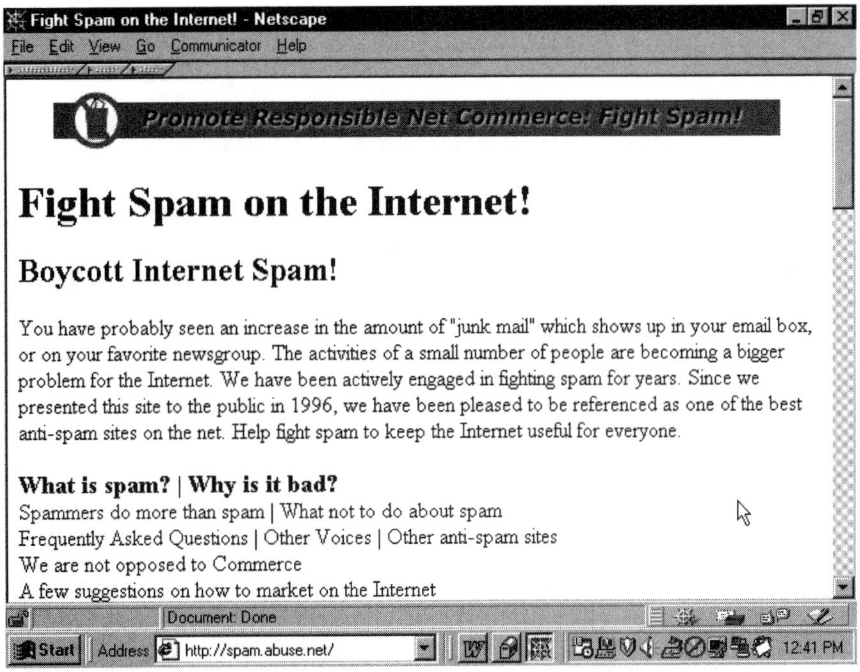

FIGURE 21.1: To connect with other people trying to fight spam, visit this page at `spam.abuse.net`.

Another resource for spam-fighters is Help! I've Been Spammed! at `http://www.stopspam.org/usenet/mmf/faqs/help.html`. Both of these sites use the "neighborhood watch" approach, wherein victims of spam collaborate to build a list of offending e-mail addresses and ISPs. Maybe this is that issue you've been waiting for to get politically active! (Nah.)

Spam Filtering Software

There are programs you can use in conjunction with your e-mail to attempt to sift out and delete spam before you even see it. They work by consulting a constantly updated list of offending addresses at a Web site or by interacting with you as you identify offending messages and patterns yourself. One such program is called Anti-Spam (`http://www.highwind.com/antispam.html`). You can look for others at `http://www.cyberpromo.org/spamfilters.asp` (see Figure 21.2).

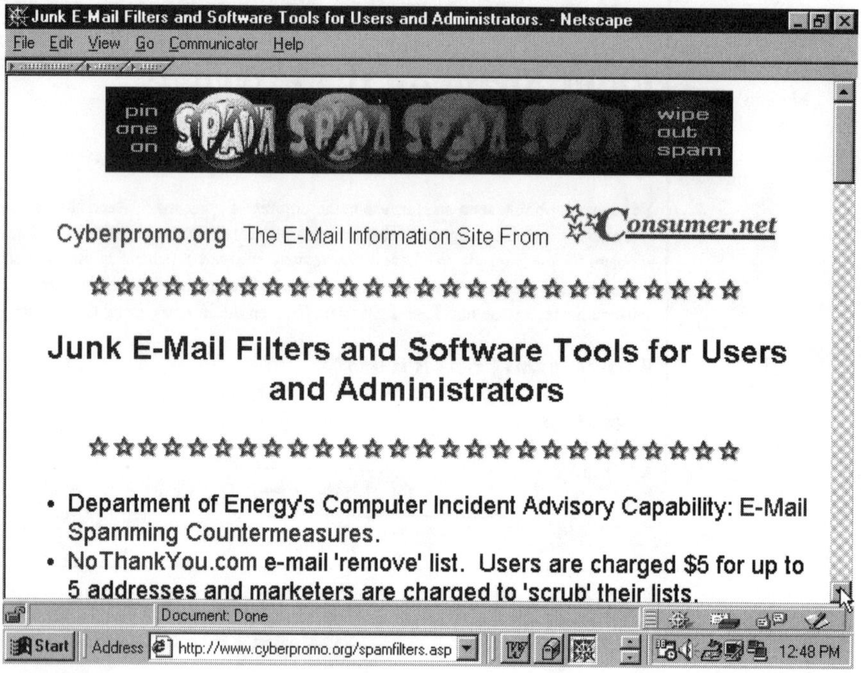

FIGURE 21.2: This site offers a wealth of resources, with just about every filtering method currently available.

AOL-Specific Spambusting

AOL users have to contend with a never-ending onslaught of e-mail spam in addition to the legitimate advertisements and offerings that pop up every time they log in. Fortunately, for you AOL users out there, AOL does offer a way for you to minimize the official commercial offers. First, select My AOL ➢ Preferences ➢ Marketing, and then, in the dialog box that appears (see Figure 21.3), select the various forms of marketing your AOL account may bring you in contact with and, for each one, tell AOL not to bless you with these offers.

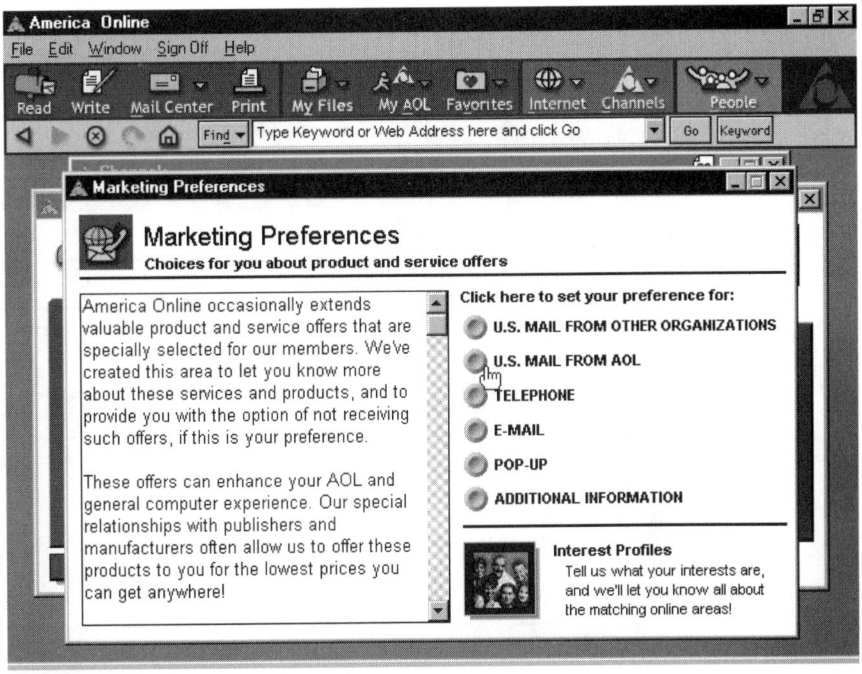

FIGURE 21.3: Unless you say otherwise, AOL might make you commercial offers through any of the methods listed in this dialog box.

For instance, when you select E-mail, AOL will explain that it does not solicit you directly by e-mail—except when it's making a special offer available to you. Choose Continue, and then select No, I Do Not Want to Receive Special Offers from AOL by E-mail in the E-Mail Preference dialog box that appears (see Figure 21.4). Then click OK when AOL confirms the preference setting. Repeat this process for as many other categories as you wish.

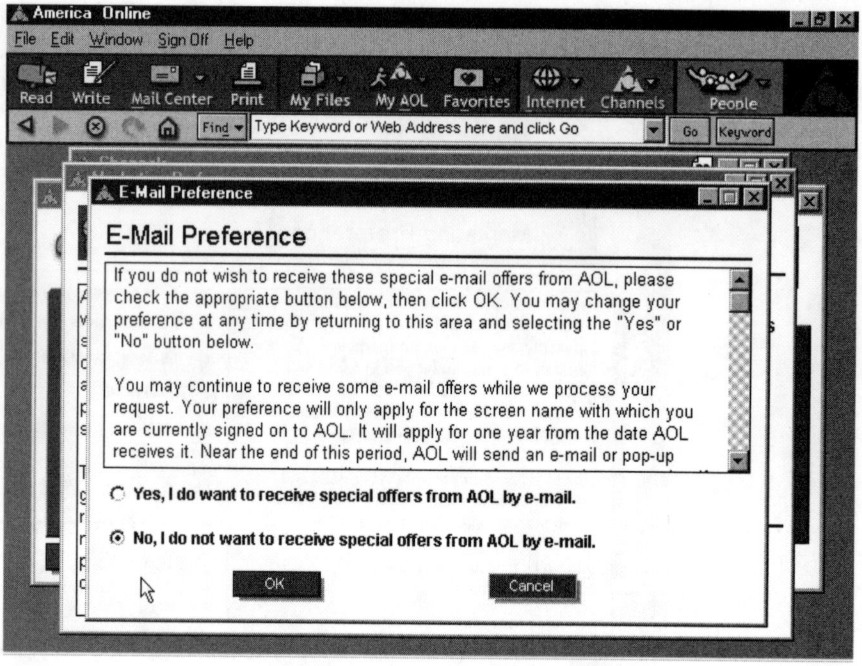

FIGURE 21.4: One company's "special offer" may be another person's spam. Just click No to eliminate at least one kind of solicitation.

To minimize outright spam (that is, *un*authorized commercial e-mail), type **Mail Controls** into the keyword/address box and press Enter, choose Junk Mail in the dialog box that appears, and read up on how to report spam to AOL, how to control the mail you (and your children) receive, and how to use AOL-specific tricks to identify and minimize spam. Unfortunately, there's really nothing concrete here to *eliminate* spam, besides your Delete key.

Are You Experienced?

Now you can...

- ☑ **minimize your exposure to spam**
- ☑ **delete spam from your Inbox**
- ☑ **report spam to** `http://spam.abuse.net/`
- ☑ **obtain spam filtering software**
- ☑ **minimize ads on AOL**

APPENDIX A

GETTING STARTED

- Understanding direct and modem connections
- Finding the equipment you'll need
- Choosing a service provider
- Logging in and out
- Accessing Help

This appendix is here to help you if you're looking for an Internet service provider, if you need to get the equipment together for a dial-up account, or if you've already got an Internet account or access to Internet e-mail but you'd like to shop around for better services.

Different Types of Connections

To start with, we need to go over the different types of Internet connections. First, there are *direct connections* and *modem connections*. A direct connection is a computer attached to a network that is itself connected to the Internet. Many university accounts work this way, as do some work-related Internet connections. Direct connections to Internet gateways allow you to send and receive Internet e-mail but not much more. However, if your network administrator installs Web browser software for you, you can access the Web through your gateway, too.

There are several types of modem connections:

- PPP or SLIP accounts
- Client-access accounts
- Host-machine accounts (including freenets)
- Online services
- BBSs (Bulletin Boards)

A PPP or SLIP account is a dial-up account that puts your desktop computer, when you're connected, directly on the Internet. This modem connection makes your computer part of a network attached to the Net. This type of access is by far the most popular and, once you get it set up, the easiest to use (aside from online services).

A client-access account makes a temporary connection to a server and downloads your e-mail, Usenet news articles, and what-have-you and then logs off, allowing you to read and respond to your messages offline.

A host-machine account allows you to log on, using your desktop computer as a *dumb terminal* (a keyboard-and-monitor device that sends information to a larger computer, for example, a mainframe). In this case, the information would be sent to a host computer on the Internet. This account usually entails working in a Unix environment on the host machine, although there are many offline mailers and newsreaders available to help minimize your connect time and insulate you from the cryptic Unix commands. The host-machine account was once the most common type of access, but it has been superseded by PPP and SLIP accounts.

An account with an online service may offer anything from partial to complete Internet access through the proprietary interface of the service. America Online, CompuServe, and the Microsoft Network, for example, offer complete Internet access.

Bulletin boards allow you to log on and then select options from menus. They can provide Unix command-line access to the Internet, but they do not necessarily do so.

You can see that, depending on your type of access, you may be running programs in your desktop computer's native environment (SLIP, PPP, client-access, a host-machine account with offline readers), you may be working in a Unix environment (host-machine account), or you may be working in the interface provided by your online service or BBS.

This book covers the general procedures for using Internet services no matter what type of access you have, but it focuses on the most popular types of access: PPP/SLIP and online services.

Equipment You'll Need

If your computer is directly connected to the Net, then you don't need any special equipment. You run the client software installed on your computer for reading e-mail. If you don't have all the client programs needed to use other Internet services, such as the World Wide Web, Usenet, FTP, and so on, use a computer that has the right software to search for them on the Net.

NOTE

See Chapter 10, *Finding Stuff on the Web and the Net*, for tips on searching the Net.

Hardware

If you're not directly connected to the Net, you'll need a modem. More and more often, PCs and Macs are sold with a modem preinstalled. If you were not so lucky, then you'll have to make a few decisions about what type of modem to buy.

You have to decide first of all if you want an *internal* modem or an *external* modem. An internal modem is a circuit board with a modem chip on it that you have to install into a vacant slot inside your computer (or pay or cajole someone else to install). An external modem is a flat box that plugs into a port on the outside of your computer.

TIP

If at all possible, get a *Hayes-compatible* modem, since that's the most well-established standard. This should not be difficult, as most modems on the market are at least somewhat Hayes-compatible.

Internal modems cost a little less than external modems and take up less space, but they're a real pain to mess with if a problem develops. Internal modems draw their power from the computer's power supply, while external modems require a separate power supply. This means that for an external modem you'll need at least one more outlet on your powerstrip. Then again, it makes it easier to turn the modem off and on when it misbehaves. Expect to pay from eighty to a couple hundred dollars for your modem.

The next thing you need to consider is the speed of your modem. This factor limits the speed of operations when you're connected. Like all things computer-ish, this year's standard model is next year's dud; this year's supercomputer is next year's idler. But from where I stand right now, it looks like the best options are the 56.6 Kbps (kilobits per second) modems. Actually, the speed of communication is a function of two modems involved in the connection—the one attached to your computer and the one it dials up. Your connection will only proceed as fast as the slower of the two modems (if they differ in speed). Your 33.6 Kbps modem won't do you much good if you dial up a BBS with a 1200 bps Model T.

It goes without saying that once you install your modem, you must plug your phone into one of its jacks and plug the modem's phone cord (what we technical people like to call a RS-232 connector) into the wall jack. External modems have a cable that connects them to one of the COM *ports* (place where the cable plugs in) on the computer. Or, if you have one of those splitters that plugs into your single wall jack, you can plug your phone directly into the phone jack in the wall.

TIP

You may want to consider getting a fax/modem. A fax/modem is a type of modem that can send electronic information to fax machines and receive faxes as graphic images (though some can only receive and not send). They can be finicky, though, and you have to decide how much to burden your phone line with. In fact, if you are going to be using your modem a lot, you might want to get two phone lines, because when people call you and you are using your modem, they will get a busy signal and will not be able to leave a message, unless you have a premium phone service. If you have Call Waiting, you should turn that off, too, because an incoming call will disconnect your modem.

Software

If you'll be dialing up a connection with your modem, then you'll need to run some kind of communications software to communicate with the modem and to produce the terminal emulation so you can interact with the host computer. If you'll be dialing up a PPP or SLIP connection, then you'll need the software for the Internet programs you want to run. For PPP and SLIP, you will also need dial-up software (sometimes referred to as a *dialer* or as a *dial-up stack*), but you won't need a modem program. Your provider should give you the software you need.

If you have Windows 95 or 98, make sure your provider realizes this and gives you the correct software and instructions. Ask if there are any conflicts with existing software you might be using. You'll generally want to use the 32-bit version of most Internet software if you have a Windows 95/98 (or a Windows NT) connection.

NOTE NOTE NOTE NOTE NOTE NOTE NOTE NOTE NOTE NOTE NOTE NOTE NOTE NOTE NOTE

Online services, such as America Online and CompuServe, will provide you with software designed for their services.

You might also want to get an offline mail reader or newsreader so that you can make your connection, collect your messages, and then read and reply to them while offline. You should be able to find such programs (such as Eudora Light, a free e-mail program) on the Internet once you're connected. Client accounts offer this kind of service with their proprietary software.

No matter what kind of software you're running, you'll need to set it up the first time you run it. The software needs to know some crucial things about your modem and the type of connection it should make. The things you only have to tell it once include:

- Which COM (or serial) port the modem is connected to.
- What type of *parity*, *data bits*, and *stop bits* to use. Your provider will tell you the information you need, so you don't need to worry about understanding all the nitty-gritty details.
- What kind of terminal emulation to use for communication programs—most likely VT100.
- Some other Internet gibberish, which your provider should spell out for you in detail, since you'll never need to hear about it again once you've entered the information into the appropriate dialog boxes. Often enough these days, you only need to know which port your modem is attached to, and the software can figure out the rest.

Going Online with a Macintosh

A typical Macintosh bundle these days comes with the Internet Setup Assistant. The Assistant automates all the setup for a basic PPP connection to the Internet and provides you with a small list of available providers to choose from. Your Mac should come with Open Transport/PPP, or you can download FreePPP 2.6.2 from `http://www.rockstar.com/`. You specify a server to connect to, your account number, and your password.

Some Internet service providers will give you a version of Open Transport/PPP—or a similar program—already configured with your account information and password. Then all you need to do is start the program and open whichever Internet application you wish to use.

Finding a Service Provider

Once you have all the equipment you need, you've got to find a service provider. The greatest consideration for most people is cost. You should be able to find a provider who will charge a flat rate of around $20/month, depending on the competition in your local calling area. (AOL has a flat rate of just under $10/month for low-volume users.) One of the biggest cost factors can be the telephone charges for connect time.

If you can find a service with a dial-up number local to you, then you can reduce this charge to virtually nothing. If not, investigate several other options to see which will be cheapest for you. Look into services that provide 800 numbers or access via public data networks (such as CompuServe or AT&T). You'll have to compare total costs, including both phone charges and charges from the service. If you can't avoid phone charges, try to do as many of your activities offline as possible to minimize the charges.

WARNING WARNING WARNING WARNING WARNING WARNING WARNING WARNING

Although 800 numbers are free to call, your service will charge you extra to cover their cost, so choose carefully.

The next money issue is whether the service provider charges you based on how long you're connected or on a flat monthly rate. The other cost issues are the base monthly charge and a first-time setup charge, if any.

Located throughout North America, *freenets* are networks that charge nothing for an account or for connect time (although their public accounts may not always be available during hours of peak use). You'll still need to pay phone charges, unless the number you call is local.

TIP

If you're affiliated with a university, you can probably get a free (or at least cheap) university account.

Ironically, the best place to find up-to-date provider information is online. You could borrow someone else's access or connect to the Net through work and visit the sites I'll recommend in this appendix. You could also take one of the online services up on their offer of a free trial month and then spend some of that time hunting for a more permanent provider.

NOTE

AT&T WorldNet Service is offered to AT&T customers in some areas for free for a whole year (including e-mail and five free online hours per month). After the year, you have to pay a monthly charge. So far, there have been no reports of problems getting online with AT&T WorldNet, such as those that plagued another well-known online service provider after they offered lots of free access. Microsoft Network also has a cheap basic online rate of $4.95 per month with five free hours, but it's harder to establish a connection on MSN.

The Chicken or the Egg

Here are two Web sites you can visit to get updated service-provider information once you're already online.

One commercial service on the Web is making an effort to assemble the various lists of providers on a single Web page, allowing users to look for providers by region. To see the current state of this effort, point your Web browser at `http://www.tagonline.com/Providers/` (see Figure A.1).

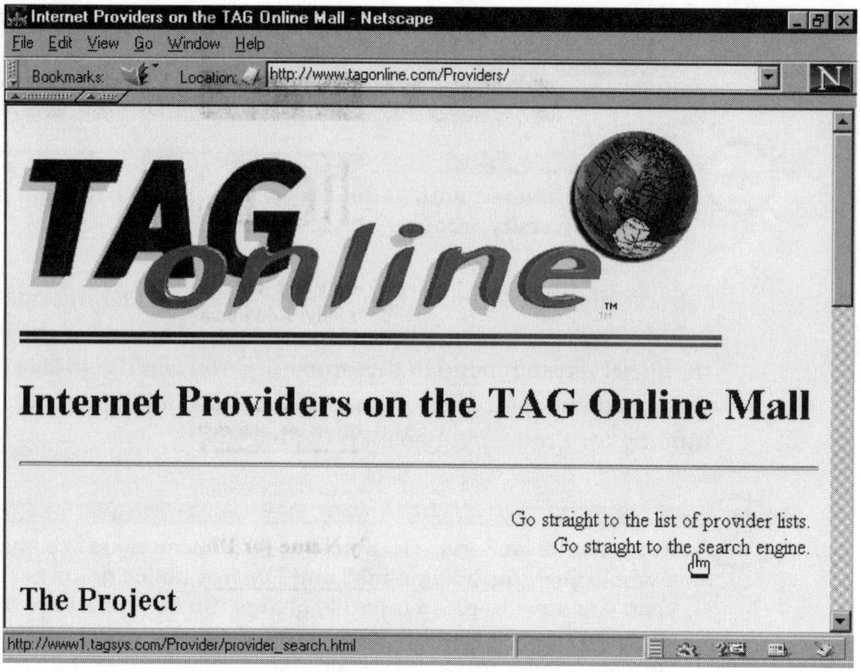

FIGURE A.1: TAG Systems' online listing of service provider

This is a searchable site you can browse based on services offered and area code (so you can get a provider that's only a local call away).

Another site you can try is called The List at `http://www.thelist.com/` (see Figure A.2). You can search by area code, as well as in various other ways.

When you do choose a provider, hold off on distributing your e-mail address to everyone you know until you're sure you're happy with the service. See if the connection works most of the time. (Nothing on the Net works all the time!) Notice how often you get a busy signal when you're trying to connect. Decide how helpful the support people are when you have questions or something isn't working. Be a good consumer and shop around until you find a provider you're satisfied with. *Then* spread your e-mail address around.

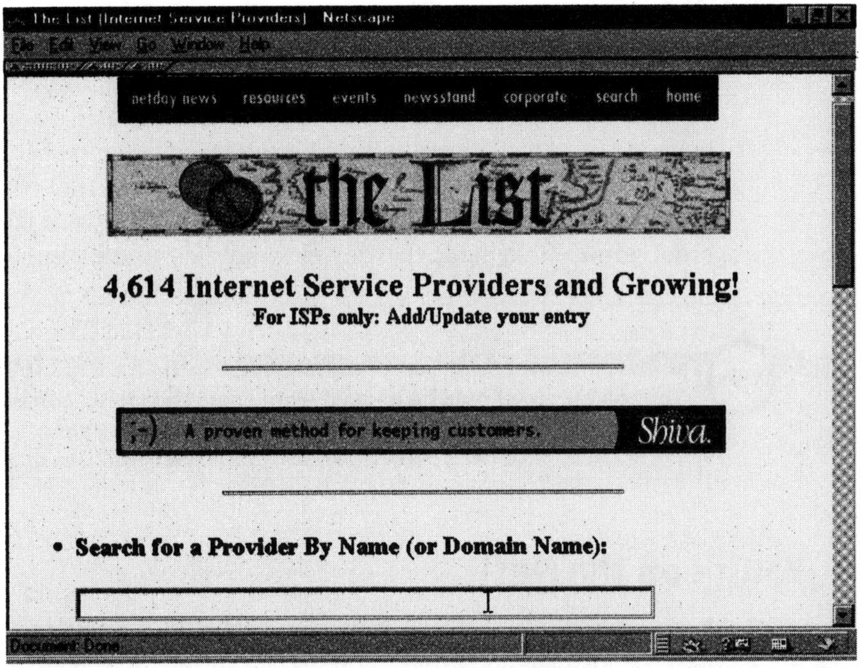

FIGURE A.2: MecklerWeb's The List site is another fairly comprehensive list of providers. (The List of Internet Service Providers [`www.thelist.com`] is owned and maintained by Mecklermedia Corporation. Copyright ©1996. Mecklermedia. All rights reserved. Image reprinted with permission.)

Getting Started

Whenever you want to connect to your provider, you'll run your dial-up or communications software, which will use your modem to phone your provider and make a connection.

Logging In

When you are connected, you will need to log in to your Internet account. First, type your login name (or username, your Internet handle), and then type your password. (Your password will not appear on the screen—a security feature so nobody can copy it.) Some software programs will remember your login information after you connect the first time and will, therefore, not require you to type it all in each time. (Having this capability means, though, that your Internet account is not secure, in the sense that anyone who runs your dial-up software will automatically be connected to your account, whether they know your password or not.)

TIP TIP TIP TIP TIP TIP TIP TIP TIP TIP TIP TIP TIP TIP TIP TIP TIP TIP TIP TIP TIP TIP TIP TIP TIP

Your password should be at least eight characters long, contain both letters and numbers, and be meaningless to other people (not your birth date, your partner's name, your pet's name, your driver's license number, or anything like that).

You're on the Net!

Now you're ready to do whatever you got on the Internet to do. Read the rest of the book for ideas and explanations. When you are finished with an Internet session, you should log off to tell your provider's computer that you're done. (Eventually your modem would hang up for you if you walked away, but that's sloppy and wasteful of resources and could conceivably cost you more money, too.)

You'll also want to hang up your modem (unless your software does this for you). Logging out is not hanging up. Even after you log out, your modem is still connected and charging time if that's how your phone system works. So after logging out, hang up. Then quit your software.

APPENDIX B

GLOSSARY OF INTERNET TERMS

If you've run into some jargon in this book that you don't understand, you should find an explanation here.

NOTE

If you want a more thorough compendium of Internet jargon, terminology, and culture at your fingertips, try another of my books, *The Internet Dictionary*, also from Sybex.

$0.02
Appended to the end of a **Usenet post**, this means "my two cents."

:-)
The basic **smiley** symbol; this is often used to mean "just kidding," "don't flame me," or "I'm being sarcastic," but it can also mean "I'm happy."

^]
This garbage symbol may appear on your screen, or in text-transferred files, from time to time. It's an uninterpreted Esc character. Ignore it.

acceptable use
Internet service providers require that all their users agree to some guidelines of acceptable use of Internet and **Usenet** resources. Acceptable use guidelines vary from provider to provider.

access
(n) 1. A connection to the Internet; 2. A type of Internet connection (network access, dial-up access, etc.); 3. The ability to perform certain activities or read privileged information, see also **access privileges**.
(v) 1. To connect to the Internet; 2. To connect to a site; 3. To open a file.

access privileges
The level of user capability assigned to each user authorized to gain **online** entry to another computer or **network**. Some users have greater access privileges than others and can enter almost any area of a network and make changes. Other users can only view materials, create files, or edit files, but cannot copy or delete files. These rights are assigned by the network administrator, the person managing the network for an organization.

account
A form of access to a computer or **network** for a specific **username** and password, usually with a home directory, an **e-mail Inbox**, and a set of **access privileges**.

ActiveX
Microsoft's answer to **Java**. A scripting language for including ActiveX controls in **Web pages**. These controls can perform animations or interactive functions.

address
1. The name of a computer (also called a **host** or **site** on the **Internet**, in the form `host.subdomain.domain`; 2. An **e-mail address** in the form `username@host.subdomain.domain`; 3. A **Web address** (**URL**) in the form `http://host.subdomain.domain/optionalpath/optional-filename.html`.

address book
In some **e-mail** programs, a list of abbreviations for e-mail **addresses**.

administrivia
Information regarding the administering of a **mailing list** or **moderated newsgroup** that is posted to the list or group.

AIFF
The Macintosh audio format on the **Internet**.

alias
1. An abbreviation for an **e-mail address**, sometimes called a *nickname*; 2. The term for a Macintosh shortcut to a file, folder, or program.

alt.
A quasi-**Usenet hierarchy** devoted to "alternative" topics. It is easier to create `alt.` groups than to create standard **Usenet** groups, and it's practically impossible to remove them.

alt.fan groups
Newsgroups devoted to a real-world or **Net** celebrity or villain.

America Online
The most widely used commercial online service.

Amiga
A line of desktop PCs, famous for their handling of graphics and the evangelical zeal of their users. Many Amiga users include an **ASCII**-graphic double-checkmark in their **.sigs**.

anchor
The highlighted area of a **Web page** (text or graphics) that, when clicked on, transports the viewer to another part of the same Web page, another Web **address**, or elsewhere on the **Internet** (often referred to as a **link**, or **hypertext link**). Anchors use HTML tags that begin with <A and can contain much information before the end bracket, >.

angle brackets
These arrow shaped brackets (< >) have a number of uses in the online world, but the one you will see most often is when they are used to enclose **HTML tags** used in coding text for use on the **World Wide Web**.

anon.penet.fi
The most well-known **anonymous remailer** service.

anonymous FTP
The most common use of **FTP**, the Internet **file transfer protocol**. **FTP sites** that allow anonymous FTP don't require a password for access—you only have to log in as anonymous and enter your **e-mail address** as a password (for their records).

anonymous remailer
A service that provides anonymity to users on the **Net** by allowing them to send **mail** and **Usenet posts** through the remailer.

***.answers**
Moderated newsgroups dedicated to the posting of **FAQs**. The "*" in `*.answers` stands for anything. `*.answers` newsgroups include `news.answers`, `alt.answers`, `rec.answers`, `misc.answers`, and so on.

AOL
America Online, a **commercial online service**.

application
A program (or piece of software) that isn't a **shell**, environment, or operating system.

Archie
A **client-server application** that gives users access to databases that keep track of the contents of anonymous **FTP** archives (hence the name).

ARPAnet
The legendary predecessor to the **Internet**.

article
A **Usenet** post.

.arts
A new Internet **domain** that can be used by *arts* organizations or artists.

ASCII
American Standard Code for Information Interchange; ASCII is a standard character set that's been adopted by most computer systems around the world (usually extended for foreign alphabets and diacriticals).

ASCII file
A file containing only straight text. ASCII files are easier and quicker to transfer than files with lots of formatting.

asynchronous
Not happening at the same time. **E-mail** is an asynchronous form of communication because the sender and receiver don't have to be involved at the same time, as compared with **chat**s, which are **synchronous**.

attachment
Any data file, in any form, that your **e-mail** program sends along with your e-mail **message**.

.au
A **Unix** audio format

Automatic AOL Sessions
See **FlashSession**.

AutoSurf
A **Mosaic** feature that will pull down and cache all the pages at a site, letting you browse them at your leisure.

.avi
A movie format native to the Windows platform.

back
1. In a **Web browser**, a command, often a shortcut button, for retracing your steps back to the previous **page** or **link**; 2. The command in a **Unix** paging program to go back one screen.

bandwidth
1. The amount of information that can pass through the wires in a certain amount of time; 2. Also, a more general term for what everyone is encouraged not to waste on the **Net**.

baud
Usually confused with **bps** (bits per second), baud is technically the number of times per second that your **modem** changes the signal it sends through the phone lines.

BBS
A **bulletin board system**. Many BBSs are connected to the **Internet**.

Bcc line
The portion of an **e-mail message** header where you list the recipients who will be sent blind copies of an e-mail. This means that the primary (and Cc) recipients will not see the names of people receiving blind copies.

binaries
Newsgroups that generally contain huge posts, each comprising part of a large **binary file**, usually a program, image, or other special-format file, as opposed to a **text file**.

binary file
As opposed to a **text file**, a file that contains more than simple text. It must be copied literally, bit for bit, or it will be corrupted. Also called an **image file**.

binary transfer
A **file transfer** in which every bit of the file is copied (as opposed to a **text transfer**, in which the text is transferred to whatever format the receiving machine prefers).

BinHex
A form of file **compression** native to the Macintosh. You can decompress BinHex files with StuffIt Expander (on either the MacOS, or Windows).

bitnet
A huge **network**, distinct from the **Internet**, but fully connected to it, used largely for **e-mail** and **Listserv mailing lists**.

bitnet.
A **newsgroup hierarchy** in the **Usenet** mold, comprising **newsgroups** that correspond to **bitnet** mailing lists.

biz.
A **newsgroup hierarchy** in the **Usenet** mold that expressly permits advertising (*biz* stands for business).

bookmark
1. In a **Web** or **Gopher browser**, a record of a destination that allows you to immediately get back there at any time. (Also called Favorites or Favorite Places in some browsers, and Items on a **Hotlist** in others.); 2. In a **Web page** or help file, a bookmark is a **hypertext link** that marks your place in the document and lets you jump there from other places in the document.

'bot
A robotic entity on the **Net** that automatically performs some function that people usually do.

bounce
When **e-mail** fails to reach its destination and returns to you, it is said to have bounced.

bozo filter
A **killfile** that allows you to filter out the bozos whose **Usenet posts** you don't wish to see.

bps
Bits per second; a measurement of **modem** speed. Kbps are kilobits per second and measure faster modem speeds.

browse
To skim an information resource on the **Net**, such as **Usenet**, **Gopherspace**, or the **Web**.

browser
The program you use to view **Web page**s.

BTW
By the way; shorthand for use in e-mail or **post**s to **newsgroup**s or **mailing list**s.

bulletin board
1. What some commercial online services call their discussion groups; 2. A bulletin board system, or BBS.

bulletin board system
A set of computers and **modem**s running **bulletin board** software that allows users to dial in, send **mail**, participate in forums, and (sometimes) access the **Internet** (often abbreviated as **BBS**).

cache
A form of memory storage on your computer where **Web browser**s save image files and other items from **Web page**s. The browser can access the page more quickly by retrieving material from the cache, but the cache may start consuming too much memory, so you may have to clean it out from time to time.

calendaring
Using scheduling software on a corporate intranet or on the big Internet to make appointments, plan meetings, and check the calendars of potential participants in these activities.

cancel an article
On **Usenet**, to delete an article after you've **post**ed it. It takes a while for the article to vanish everywhere, as the cancel message has to catch up with the propagating article.

cascade
A nonsensical series of one-line **follow-up post**s, each a play on the previous one and designed to create a huge triangle of >'s on the screen.

cc:Mail
A network-oriented **e-mail client** program.

Central Search Page
Most of the **Web browser**s have a shortcut to one or more **directory** or search pages built in to the program.

certificate

A piece of **encrypt**ed code appended to a **Web page**, **e-mail**, or **download**able file. Some certificate holders, such as Microsoft, also format their certificate graphically so that it resembles a paper "Certificate of Authenticity." This certificate is developed by the owner of the site or file and serves to verify that this file or site is authentic and originates with the owner of the certificate. Certificates can also be verified by independent security services. They are being implemented to increase **security** on the **Internet**, and to prevent unauthorized intrusion or release of **virus**es onto hard drives or **network server**s. Also known as a digital certificate.

CFV

Call for Votes, a step in the creation of a **Usenet newsgroup** that comes after the **RFD** (Request for Discussion) step.

channel

1. In **chat** parlance, this refers to an active **discussion group**, or topic area, where users can enter and leave the conversation; 2. A newer meaning relates to **Webcast**ing, where a **Web site** becomes a channel that can be selected by users to be **download**ed and updated on a regular basis as new content becomes available on the site.

character-based browsers/readers

Internet programs, generally used in **Unix** systems, that can display only characters (and no graphics).

chat

Synchronous, line-by-line communication over a **network**.

client

An **application** that communicates with a **server** to get you information.

client-server application

An **application** whose process is distributed between a central **server** and any number of autonomous **client**s.

clueless newbie

A derogatory term for a beginner who SHOUTS IN ALL CAPS or betrays some ignorance of the **Net**. We were all clueless newbies once.

collaborating

The practice of online sharing of applications over the Internet or an organizational intranet.

.com

An **Internet domain** that stands for *commercial*.

COM port
A communication port in your PC. Your **modem** plugs into one.

command-line
The place in a character-based **shell**, such as a **Unix** or DOS shell, where you can enter commands directly (usually at the bottom of the screen).

commercial online service
A private, proprietary **network**, offering its own content and access to other network members, such as **CompuServe**, **America Online**, Prodigy, and Microsoft Network.

comp.
A **Usenet hierarchy** devoted to computers.

compress
1. The act of squishing a file; 2. A **Unix** program that squishes files.

compression
The method of squishing a file or the amount of squishing.

CompuServe
A popular commercial online service.

conferencing
A groupwide **online** communication process, conducted either via the **Internet** or an organizational intranet. The individual hosting the conference will call all of the other participants. Each conference participant can view online presentations made with **whiteboard** software, and can communicate with other conference participants via **chat** software. One-on-one communication can also occur during the online conference when two individuals have audio software and microphones for their computers.

connect time
The amount of time you spend logged in to a **commercial online service** or **ISP**. Connect time used to be very important because you were charged for every minute of access above a certain limit. However, some service providers are moving to a flat-fee monthly service charge with unlimited connect time, or access.

cookie
Information about your system that is collected by **Web browser** software and sent to the **Web server** that contains the **Web page** you are examining. The cookie is often stored in a cookie folder on your hard drive so that the information is available to the Web server the next time you access that page. The server can then adjust the way the page is displayed to match your system's capabilities. Some people consider cookies an invasion of privacy.

copyright
Legal protection for intellectual property (original content, technology, or art). People debate how existing copyright law applies to articles posted to **Usenet** or to texts in general made available on the **Internet**. Some people attach copyright notices to their **post**s. See also **fair use**.

cracker
A **hacker** who breaks into computers.

crosspost
To **post** a **Usenet article** to several **newsgroup**s at once. Crossposting takes up less disk space than posting it separately and repeatedly.

CU-SeeMe
A **protocol** that enables anyone with a video camera and enough memory to play video images in their computer to see and talk to other people via the **Internet**.

cyberspace
A term, popularized by author William Gibson, for the shared imaginary reality of computer **networks**. Some people use cyberspace as a synonym for the **Internet**. Others hold out for the more complete physical-seeming, virtual reality of Gibson's novels.

daemon
In **Unix**, a program that runs all the time, in the background, waiting for things to do (possibly from Maxwell's Demon). When you post an article to a `*.test` newsgroup, daemons all over the world send you **e-mail** confirming they received your post.

data bits
One of the things you have to define before you first use your **modem**. Usually set to 7 or 8; it depends on the modem you're calling.

decoding
Retranslating a file from some encoded format to its original format.

decrypt
To remove the **encryption** from a file or **e-mail message** and make it readable.

DejaNews
A service for searching **Usenet** (at `http://www.dejanews.com/forms/dnq.html`).

delurk
1. Coming out of **lurk**ing to **post** to a **list** or **newsgroup** for the first time; 2. A first post to a newsgroup or list after the writer has lurked for a while.

dial-up account
An **Internet account** on a **host** machine that you must dial up with your **modem** to use.

B

digest
A collection of **mailing list posts**, sent out as one message.

direct-access ISP
An **Internet service provider** (usually just called an **ISP**) that offers direct **Internet** access, as opposed to a **commercial online service**.

directory
A **Web site** where other Web sites are listed by topic and subtopic, something like a yellow pages phonebook.

discussion groups
Any "place" on the **Net** where discussions are held, including **mailing lists** and **Usenet newsgroups**.

domain
The short code in an **Internet** or **Web address** indicating whether the **address** is a business (`.com`), a non-profit organization (`.org`), a university (`.edu`), a branch of the US government (`.gov`), a part of the US military (`.mil`), an international organization (`.int`), and so on. New domain names, such as `.firm`, `.store`, `.arts`, `.rec`, `.web`, and `.nom` (people, names, and nomenclature) are in the works.

download
To transfer a file over a **modem** from a remote computer to your desktop computer.

.edu
An **Internet domain**; it stands for *educational*.

EFF's Guide to the Internet
Formerly Big Dummy's Guide to the Internet, **EFF**'s excellent and free **Internet** guide is available via the **Web** (`http://www.eff.org/papers/eegtti/eegttitop.html`).

EFNet
The traditional **IRC network**.

Electronic Frontier Foundation (EFF)
Founded by Mitch Kapor and John Barlow, the **EFF** lobbies for the preservation of freedom on the **cyberspace** frontier.

elm
A popular **Unix mail** program.

emacs
A **Unix** operating environment that doubles as a **text editor**.

e-mail
Electronic mail, but you knew that already, didn't you?

e-mail address
An **Internet address** that consists of a **username** (also called a **login**, a logon name, a userID, an **account** name, and so on), followed by an "at" sign (@) and then an address in the form `host.subdomain.domain`.

emoticons
Those little **smiley** faces people use to indicate emotions in **e-mail messages** or **posts**.

encoding
Any method of converting a file into a format for attaching to **e-mail messages**.

encrypt
To scramble the contents of a file or **e-mail message** so that only those with the **key** can unscramble and read them.

encryption
A process of rendering a file or **e-mail message** unreadable to anyone lacking the right encryption **key**.

Eudora
An **e-mail** program.

fair use
The legal doctrine in U.S. **copyright** law that allows limited quotation of other people's work if the use of their work does not undercut its market value.

FAQ
1. Frequently asked questions; 2. A file containing frequently asked questions and their answers, also sometimes called a FAQL (Frequently Asked Question List). To find FAQs, look in the ***.answers** newsgroups or the **FTP** archive at `rtfm.mit.edu`. Many newsgroups post their own newsgroup-specific FAQs.

Fetch
An **FTP** program for the Mac.

FidoNet
A network of **BBS**s with **Internet e-mail** access.

file transfer
To copy a file from one computer to another. See also **FTP**.

film at 11
A common tag in **Usenet follow-up post**s mocking the timeliness of the news. Often follows **Imminent death of the Net predicted!**

filter
A feature found in recently released **e-mail** programs that allows you to sort your messages according to criteria such as the sender, the date received, the subject, or other facts useful for organizational purposes.

B

finger
A **Unix** command that reports back on the status of a user or a **network**.

.firm
A new **Internet domain** for companies.

flame
1. An ill-considered, insulting **e-mail** or **Usenet** retort; 2. An insulting **post**.

flamebait
A **mailing list** or **newsgroup post** designed to elicit **flames**. Flamebait can be recognized by the fact that it goes beyond the premises of the list or newsgroup. Nobody objects to provocative or even argumentative posts, but posts to the `alt.fan.frank-zappa` newsgroup saying that "Zappa was a no-talent, potty-mouthed dweeb" betray a lack of legitimate interest in the subject at hand.

flamer
One who **flames** or likes to flame others.

flame war
An out-of-control series of **flames** and counterflames that fills up a list or **newsgroup** with **noise**. Traditionally, flame wars end when Nazis are mentioned.

FlashSession
An **AOL** process (in earlier versions) that enables its users to work **offline** and then send and receive **mail** and **newsgroup articles** and **download** files all at once, minimizing connect time. These sessions are called Automatic AOL Sessions in the most current version of AOL's software.

FOAF
Friend of a friend; shorthand for **e-mail** and **posts**. Often pointed to as the source of a **UL**.

follow a link
In graphical **browsers**, following a **link** entails positioning the mouse pointer over the link (the pointer will change to show you that you're over an active link) and then clicking once.

follow-up
A **post** that replies to and possibly quotes an earlier post.

follow-up line
In **Usenet articles**, if there is a follow-up line, follow-up articles will be posted to the **newsgroups** listed there, and not necessarily to the original newsgroups. Always check the follow-up line before posting. Pranksters sometimes direct follow-ups to `*.test` groups, resulting in thousands of automated replies stuffing the **Inbox** of anyone hapless enough to follow up without editing the follow-up line.

FQA
Frequently questioned acronyms.

freenet
A free public **network** (also written with a hyphen, *free-net*).

freeware
Free software available for downloading on the **Net**.

FTP
File Transfer Protocol, the standard **Internet** way to transfer files from one computer to another.

FTP site
A computer on the **Net** containing archives and accessible by **FTP**.

FTPmail
A way to use **FTP** by **e-mail** if you don't have an FTP **application**.

FTPmaster
The human being responsible for managing an **FTP server** or **site** and to whom information requests for access should be addressed (`ftpmaster@`*`address`*).

full name
Your full name as it appears in **e-mail** messages and **Usenet post**s.

full-screen editor
A **text editor** that enables you to move the insertion point or cursor all over the editing window, as opposed to a **line-at-a-time** editor that always keeps the insertion point at the bottom of the screen.

FUQ
Frequently unanswered questions.

FWIW
For what it's worth; shorthand for **e-mail** and **post**s.

<g>
Indicates the author is grinning, similar to **:-)**.

garbage characters
Nonsense characters that **modem**s sometimes spit out.

gate
Short for **gateway**, a computer that transfers files or **e-mail** from one **network** to another, or from a **newsgroup** to a **list**, and vice versa.

gated
Said of a **newsgroup** or **mailing list** that is connected to a mailing list or newsgroup, respectively.

B

gateway
1. A computer that connects one **network** to another, for the purpose of transferring files or **e-mail** when the two networks use different **protocols**; 2. A computer that transfers **post**s from a **newsgroup** to a **list**, and vice versa.

GIF
1. A **compress**ed graphics (image) file format (*GIF* stands for graphics interchange format) invented by **CompuServe**; 2. A file in the `.gif` format.

gnu.
A **hierarchy** in the **Usenet** mold devoted to the Free Software Foundation and to **emacs**.

gopher
A **client-server application** that performs **FTP** transfers, remote **log ins**, **Archie** searches, and so on, presenting everything to you in the form of menus. This saves you from having to know (or type in) the **address**es of the **Internet** resources being tapped. You run a gopher **client** program to get information from a gopher **server** running at a gopher **site**.

Gopherspace
A collective name for all the **gopher server**s on the **Net**, so called because all the servers can connect to each other, creating a unified "space" of gopher menus.

.gov
An **Internet domain** that stands for *government*.

green-card lawyer
A derogatory term for people who **spam** the **Net** with unwanted advertisements and then go on TV to defend their actions.

<grin>
Equivalent to **<g>** and the **:-)** emoticon.

group
A **newsgroup**.

gunzip
The Unix **uncompression** program for **Gzip**ped files.

Gzip
A file **compression** program.

hack
To dig into some computer activity, going beneath the surface and reinventing things when necessary.

hacker
A computer adept. Among hackers, anyone who can bend a computer to his or her will is a hacker, whereas people who break into computer systems are called **crackers**. In the rest of the world, people generally refer to those who break into computers as hackers.

Hayes-compatible
Modems that understand the Hayes AT instruction set are said to be Hayes compatible. (*Hayes* is a name-brand modem maker.) If you're buying a modem, make sure it's Hayes compatible. Most are these days, so that shouldn't be difficult.

hierarchy
1. In file storage, the arrangement of directories or folders into a tree of parents and children; 2. In **Usenet**, the organization of **newsgroups** into general areas, topics, and subtopics.

^H
In the standard **VT100** terminal emulation, Delete is used to erase characters, and Backspace either backs up over the previous character (without deleting it) or produces this character on the screen. It's a sign that a **clueless newbie** has tried to erase something and failed.

history
A record of your last so-many actions. In a **Web browser**, a list of all the **pages** you've been to since you started your Web browsing program. The history list will actually show you only the pages you've visited in a straight line from your starting point. Any time you back up and then follow a different **link**, you will lose the original history path from that point forward.

$HOME
In **Unix**, a variable that means your **home directory**.

home directory
The **directory** you start off in when you **log in** to your **Unix account**.

home page
1. The **page** you begin with when you start your **Web browser**; 2. The main **page** of a **Web site**; 3. A personal **Web page**.

host
A computer on the **Internet**.

HotJava
A **Web browser** made by Sun Microsystems.

hotlist
A **bookmark** list (especially in **Mosaic**).

HTML
Hypertext Markup Language; the **hypertext** language used in **Web page**s. It consists of regular text and **HTML tag**s that tell the **browser** how to display the page and what to do when a **link** is activated.

HTML source
The underlying source file, revealing all of the **HTML tags**, that makes a **Web** document look the way it does in a **Web browser**.

HTML tag
Codes enclosed in < > **angle brackets** that are used to mark text in an **HTML source** file. These codes control formatting and tell the **browser** what files to jump to when **hyperlink**s are clicked.

HTTP
Hypertext Transfer Protocol; the **Web protocol** for **link**ing one **Web page** with another.

hyperlink
A **link** (highlighted text, images, or parts of images) that, when clicked on, sends the user to another portion of the current document or file (a **bookmark**), another **URL**, or elsewhere on the **Internet**.

hypermedia
Linked documents that consist of other media in addition to plain text, such as pictures, sounds, movies, and so on.

hypertext
Text that contains **link**s to other text documents.

hypertext link
A **link** from one text document to another.

image file
A **binary file**.

image map
A graphic on a **Web page** that contains links to other Web pages or addresses. Users click on various portions of the image to reach the links.

IMHO
In my humble opinion; shorthand for **e-mail** or **post**s.

Imminent Death of the Net Predicted!
A parody of the perennial warnings that traffic on the Net has gotten to be too much. Often followed by **film at 11**.

IMNSHO
In my not-so-humble opinion; shorthand for **e-mail** or **post**s.

IMO
In my opinion; shorthand for **e-mail** or **post**s.

Inbox
A file containing your incoming **e-mail**.

info
Many **Internet** providers have an info **address** (`info@`*`host.subdomain.domain`*).

.info
A new **Internet domain** for information providers.

Internet
The worldwide **network** of networks. The Internet is a way for computers to communicate. It's not a place; it's a way to get through to other computers.

Internet address
See address.

Internet Explorer
Microsoft's **Web browser**.

Internet Phone
A **protocol** that enables anyone with a microphone, speaker, and sound card in their computer to talk to other people via the **Internet**.

Internet Resources Meta-Index
A useful starting point on the **Web**.

Internet service provider (ISP)
A company that offers "just" access to the **Internet** and no local content (or only very limited local information and **discussion groups**).

InterNIC
The Internet's Network Information Center, a repository of **Internet** information. A resource worth knowing about.

intranet
A network of linked computers maintained by a corporation or other organization. Employees or members of the organization can **access** information specific to the company or organization on the intranet.

IP
Internet Protocol; the **protocol** that allows computers and **network**s on the **Internet** to communicate with each other.

IRC
Internet relay chat; a **protocol** and a **client-server application** that allows you to **chat** with people all over the **Internet**, in channels devoted to different topics.

Ircle
A Macintosh **IRC** program.

ISP
See Internet service provider.

Java
A programming language from Sun Microsystems that's a variant of C++. With a special Java-savvy **browser** such as **HotJava**, **Netscape Navigator** 2 and higher (or earlier versions of Navigator with a Java **plug-in**), or Microsoft Internet Explorer 3 and higher, users can interact with fully operational programs (called applets) inside the browser window.

JavaScript
A scripting language that can be embedded into **Web page**s to provide simple controls.

JPEG
A **compress**ed file format for images that uses the extension `.jpg`.

Jughead
An index of high-level **gopher** menus.

k12.
A **hierarchy** in the **Usenet** mold, devoted to kindergarten through 12th grade education.

Kermit
A protocol for download and upload file transfers.

key
In **encryption**, a code that allows you to **decrypt encrypt**ed text.

keyword
A word used to search for a file, document, or **Web page**. The search program will look for files, documents, etc., that contain the keyword.**killfile**
A file containing search instructions for automatically killing or **autoselect**ing **Usenet post**s. See also **bozo filter**.

Knowbot
An information service on the **Net** that, among other things, helps find **e-mail address**es.

Kbps
Kilobits per second, a measurement of **modem** speed.

LAN
A **local-area network**. A computer **network** usually confined to a single office or building.

lharc
A file **compression** program for DOS.

library catalogs
Most university and public library catalogs are available via **Telnet** (and some via **Gopher**). **Hytelnet** has an excellent index of library catalogs.

line-at-a-time
Said of programs (such as **text editors**) that, as the name suggests, only allow users to see one line of type at a time.

link
On **Web pages**, a button or highlighted bit of text that, when selected, jumps the reader to another place in the document or another page on the Web.

list
A **mailing list**.

Listserv
A type of **mailing list** software that runs on **bitnet** computers.

local-area network
A small, local network of computers, such as in an office (**LAN**).

log in
To start a session on your **Internet account** (also referred to as log on, or sign in/on).

login
A **username**, the name you **log in** with.

log out
To end a session on your **Internet** account (also log off, sign out/off).

LOL
Laughing out loud; shorthand for **e-mail** or **posts**.

lurk
To read a **mailing list** or **newsgroup** without **posting** to it. You should lurk for a while before posting.

Lynx
An excellent, text-based, **Unix browser** for the **Web**, developed at the University of Kansas.

^M
In **text file**s transferred from DOS to **Unix** as **binary file**s, this character will sometimes appear at the end of each line. Get rid of it with the dos2unix program (or delete them one-by-one).

mail
On the **Internet**, synonymous with **e-mail**.

mail box
A folder or area in a **mail** program where **message**s are stored.

mailing list
A list of people with a common interest, all of whom have signed up to receive all the **mail** sent, or **post**ed, to the **list**.

.mailrc
A resource file for **Unix mail** programs, other than **elm**.

mail reader
A program that allows you to read and reply to **e-mail**, and to send out new **mail** of your own.

mail reflector
A computer that sends copies of **mail** to a list of **address**es.

majordomo
A type of **mailing list** software.

message
1. An **e-mail** letter; 2. A comment sent to a specific person on **IRC** and not to the entire channel.

MIDI
Musical Instrument Digital Interface. This is a sound file format. You can listen to these sound files if you have MIDI software or a MIDI **plug-in** for your **browser**.

MIME
Multipurpose Internet Mail Extensions, a **protocol** that allows **e-mail** to contain more than simple text. Used to send other kinds of data, including color pictures, sound files, and video clips.

.mil
An **Internet domain** that stands for *military*.

mIRC
A Windows **IRC** program.

mirror site
A secondary **FTP site** that maintains the exact same files (updated regularly) as another site, in order to reduce the communications load (traffic) on the primary site.

misc.
A **Usenet hierarchy** devoted to whatever doesn't fit in the other hierarchies.

modem
A device that connects your computer to a phone jack and, through the phone lines, to another modem and computer. (It stands for modulator/demodulator.)

moderated
Said of **lists** and **newsgroups** whose **posts** must pass muster with a **moderator** before being sent to the **subscribers**.

moderator
The volunteer who decides which submissions to a **moderated list** or **newsgroup** will be posted.

Mosaic
A **Web browser**, developed by NCSA, for graphical user interfaces.

MOTAS
Member of the appropriate sex; shorthand for **e-mail** and **posts**.

MOTOS
Member of the opposite sex; shorthand for **e-mail** and **posts**.

MOTSS
Member of the same sex; shorthand for **e-mail** and **posts**.

motto!
A **follow-up post** on **Usenet** proposing the previous post as a motto for the group.

MPEG
A **compress**ed file format for movies with the extension `.mpg`.

MS Exchange
A Microsoft **e-mail** program.

MUD
A multi-user domain/dimension/dungeon. A role-playing game environment that allows people all over the **Net** to play together in something like interactive text adventures.

MUSE
A multi-user simulation environment (for role-playing games).

My
Appended to the beginning of a brand name, this indicates a customizable, personalized version of the generic product.

my two cents
A tag appended to **Usenet** or **list posts**, indicating "this is just my opinion," or "I just wanted to get my two cents in" (also written as **$0.02**).

Ncftp
A more sophisticated **Unix FTP** program than Ftp, the basic Unix FTP program.

NCSA Mosaic
The original graphical **Web browser**, developed at the National Center for Supercomputer Applications and distributed for free.

NCSA What's New Page
The unofficial newspaper of the **Web** (found at `http://www.ncsa.uiuc.edu/SDG/Software/Mosaic/Docs/whats-new.html`).

Net, the
Often used as an abbreviation for the **Internet** or for **Usenet**, the Net is really a more general term for the lump sum of interconnected computers on the planet.

.net
An Internet domain that stands for *network*.

Netcasting
A new technology that uses Webcasting software to **subscribe** to **sites** on the Internet and Web and **download** content from these sites on a regular basis.

net.celebrity
A celebrity on the **Net**.

net.cop
Someone accused of trying to control others' **posts** in **mailing lists** or in **Usenet newsgroups**.

NetCruiser
Netcom's all-in-one **Internet** access software.

Netfind
An **Internet** resource for finding **e-mail addresses**.

netiquette
The traditional rules of civilized behavior **online**.

netizen
A citizen of the **Net**.

net.personality
A somewhat well-known person on the **Net**.

.netrc
A file of **FTP** archive **site** names, **usernames**, and passwords, used by Ftp and **Ncftp** to automate the FTP **log in** process.

Netscape Communicator 4
An integrated suite of **Internet applications**, including **Netscape Navigator** 4, Netscape Collabra, Netscape Conference, Netscape Composer, Netscape Messenger, and Netscape Netcaster.

Netscape Navigator
Hands-down the most popular **World Wide Web browser** program. It works very much the way **Mosaic** does, but with a number of additional features and improvements.

net.spewer
A new contributor to a group who **spews** hundreds of **posts**, following up every **thread** that's around and attempting to start new ones.

network
A set of computers and computer equipment that are connected together.

newbie
A beginner, not as derogatory as **clueless newbie**.

newsfeed
The packet of news articles passed along from one computer to the next on **Usenet**.

newsgroup
A **Usenet** discussion group.

.newsrc
The list of subscribed and unsubscribed newsgroups for a Unix newsreader.

newsreader
A program used to read **Usenet articles**.

NewsWatcher
A **newsreader** for the Macintosh.

News Xpress
A **newsreader** for Windows.

B

NFS
Not to be confused with **NSF**, NFS is the Network File System **protocol**, developed by Sun Microsystems, for transferring files over a **network**.

NIC
A **network** information center.

Nn
A Unix **newsreader**.

node
Any computer on the **Internet**, a **host**.

noise
Useless or unwanted information (as in **signal-to-noise ratio**).

.nom
A new **Internet domain** reserved for people, names, and nomenclature.

NSF
The National Science Foundation; maintainers of the **NSFnet**.

NSFnet
A high-speed backbone of the **Internet** (crucial but not essential) maintained by the **NSF**.

Ob
A prefix added to an obligatory addendum to a **Usenet** or **list post**.

offline
Not currently connected to the **Net**.

offline mail reader
A **mail** program that connects to the **Net**, **download**s your **e-mail**, and then disconnects, allowing you to read, reply to, and send mail without being charged for very much connect time.

offline news reader
A **newsreader** that connects to the **Net**, **download**s all unread **article**s in all **subscribed newsgroup**s, and then disconnects, allowing you to read, reply to, and **post** articles without being charged for much connect time.

online
Currently connected to the **Net**.

Online service
See **commercial online service**.

.org
An **Internet domain** that stands for (non-profit) *organization*.

page
A **hypertext** document available on the **World Wide Web**.

pager
A **Unix** program that presents text one screenful at a time.

parent directory
The **directory** for which the current directory is a **subdirectory**.

parity
One of the things you have to set to use your **modem**. It's usually set to None or Even, but it depends on the modem you're calling.

Pegasus Mail
A free **e-mail client** program.

pgp
A **shareware encryption** program (it stands for Pretty Good Privacy).

Pico
A **Unix text editor** based on the text editor built into the **Pine mail reader**.

Pine
A popular **Unix mail** program.

ping
A somewhat obsolete **Unix** command that checks on the status of another **network**.

pkunzip
The **uncompression** program for **pkzip**ped files.

pkzip
A DOS file **compression** program.

platform
A type of computer or system.

players
Programs, also called **viewers**, used to display multimedia file formats.

plebiscite
Literally, *popular vote*. In a **newsgroup**, it means polling the readership.

plonk
A **follow-up post** that means, "I just put you in my killfile." (It's supposed to be the sound of the bozo falling into the **killfile**.)

plug-ins
Programs that can be plugged into a **Web browser** to add multimedia capabilities to it.

point at
To start a **client** program, such as a **Web browser**, by supplying it with an address, as in "Point your Web browser at `http://ezone.org/ez` to see the latest episode of Enterzone."

POP
1. Point of Presence; a local access number for a **service provider**; 2. Post-Office Protocol, a standard way to **download** and **upload e-mail**.

POP server
A type of **mail server** that "speaks" the Post-Office Protocol.

portal
A Web site whose traffic depends on its success as a jumping-off point, as an essential starting place for at least some types of users on the Web.

post
To send a **message** to a **mailing list** or an **article** to a **newsgroup**. Also, the message that is posted. The word *post* comes from the **bulletin-board** metaphor, in which scraps of paper are posted to the board, to be read by anyone who comes by.

Postmaster
The human being responsible for information requests for a **mail server** (`postmaster@`*`address`*).

PPP
Point-to-Point Protocol; a **protocol** for an **Internet** connection over a **modem**.

private key
In **key encryption**, the **key** that allows you to **encrypt** your outgoing **messages**.

.project
A **text file** that might be displayed when someone **finger**s your **e-mail address**. Not all fingers check for a `.project` file. You can use the file to describe your current project.

propagation
The process of dissemination for **Usenet post**s, as they are passed from computer to computer. Propagation delays are responsible for the sometimes confusing situation that occurs when you read a **follow-up** to an original post that hasn't yet appeared at your **site**.

protocol
Any agreed-upon method for two computers to communicate.

/pub
A **Unix directory** often found on **FTP hosts**.

public data network
A public data network allows you to make a local call to connect to a national **network**.

public discussion area
See **discussion groups**.

public key
In **key encryption**, the **key** that allows you to verify the **encrypted signature** of the person who has sent you **mail** or to **decrypt** a **message** from that person, given out to anyone who asks.

push
Also called Webcasting, the already out-of-fashion method of sending updated Web content to a portion of a user's screen.

query
A search request submitted to a database.

queue
A list of **messages** waiting to be sent.

QuickMail
An **e-mail client** program designed for **networks**.

QuickTime
A movie format originally on Macintoshes only.

RealAudio
Progressive Networks' **streaming** audio format.

real name
Your full name as it appears on **e-mail messages** and **Usenet posts**.

real time
The time it takes real people to communicate, as on a telephone.

rec.
A **Usenet hierarchy** devoted to recreation.

.rec
A new **Internet domain**, short for *recreation*.

remote login
Logging in to another computer over a **network**. See also **Telnet**.

reply
An **e-mail message** or **Usenet post** responding to, and possibly quoting, the original.

repost
To **post** again. A subsequent post of the same information.

-request
Human-administered **mailing lists** have an **address** for sending administrative requests (such as subscriptions), with `-request` appended to the **username** for the list. The administrative address for the imaginary list `epictetus@netcom.com` would be `epictetus-request@netcom.com`.

RFC
Request for Comments; one of a set of documents that contain **Internet protocols**, standards, and information, and that together, more or less define the Internet in an open way. The standards contained in them are followed carefully by software developers (commercial, **shareware**, and **freeware**). The name Request for Comments can be confusing, since the contents are settled (i.e., the comments are already there), but they arrived from free and open discussion on the **Net**.

RFD
Request for Discussion; a stage in the creation of a new **Usenet newsgroup**, preceding the **CFV**.

Rlogin
A **Unix** program that allows you to **log in** to another Unix machine without having to give your password.

Rn
A nonthreaded newsreader for Unix.

root
1. The **directory** with no parent, at the top level. 2. An **Internet address** at a **network** usually monitored by a **system administrator**.

ROTFL
Rolling on the floor laughing; shorthand for use in **e-mail** and **posts**.

RTFM
Read the f***ing manual! (shorthand for use in **e-mail** and **posts**).

sci.
A **Usenet** hierarchy devoted to science.

search engine
A program, usually reachable through a **Web page**, used to search a Web **site**, the entire **Internet**, or some **domain** in between.

security
The means by which users and networks are shielded from unauthorized intrusion. Security can take many forms, from anti-**virus** software employed by individual users **downloading** files from the **Web** to **encryption** and **certificates** used to ensure the safe transmission of files and **applications**.

select articles
In **newsreaders**, to choose ahead of time (by their titles or authors) which articles you want to read.

semi-anonymity
Because you'll never see the vast majority of people whose **post**s you read on the **Net**, this creates a veil of semi-anonymity.

server
A **network application** providing information to **client** programs that connect to it. They are centralized repositories of information or specialized handlers of certain kinds of traffic.

service provider
A company that provides access to the **Internet** (an **Internet service provider** or ISP).

shareware
Software that is available (often by **download** from the **Net**) for a free trial period. You're expected to register and pay for it, if you decide to keep using it.

shell
A computer operating environment.

shell account
An **Internet account** that gives you access to a **Unix shell**.

SHOUTing
Typing portions of your **e-mail message** or **post** in all capital letters for emphasis. Excessive SHOUTing is considered very rude and a violation of **netiquette**.

.sig
A signature file.

signal-to-noise ratio
An engineering term adapted as a metaphor for the proportion of useful information to junk on a **list** or in a **newsgroup**.

signature
A few lines of text, usually including your name, sometimes your postal (snail mail) address, and perhaps your **e-mail address**. Many people also include quotations, jokes, gags, and so on. Signatures (also called sig blocks, **signature files**, **.signatures**, or **.sigs**) are a little like bumper stickers in this respect. Some **e-mail** programs do not support signature files.

.signature
A **signature file** (so spelled because of the convention used for **Unix** signature files).

signature file
A **text file** that is automatically attached to the end of your **e-mail messages** or **Usenet posts**, usually containing your name and other pertinent information about you.

site
An **Internet host** that allows some kind of remote access, such as a **Web site**, **FTP site**, **gopher** site, and so on.

SLIP
Serial Line Internet Protocol; a **protocol** for an **Internet** connection over a **modem**.

SlipKnot
A program made by MicroMind that provides graphical access to the **Web** for people with character-based **Unix accounts**.

smiley
Sideways smiley faces, such as **:-)** and **;^)** and **=%7o** that are used to indicate emotions or facial expressions.

SMTP
Simple Mail Transport Protocol; this **protocol** is what enables **Internet e-mail** to flow so freely.

snail mail
Internet slang for surface mail.

SO
Significant other; shorthand for use in **e-mail**, **posts**, or personal ads.

soc.
A **Usenet hierarchy** devoted to society (and usually sectarian groups in it).

spam
To **post** (or **robopost**) huge amounts of material to **Usenet**, or to post one **article** or **message** to huge numbers of inappropriate groups, thus creating a nuisance.

spew
To **post** excessively.

stand-alone program
For **online services**, a program that runs separately from the main access program, but one that can use the connection established by the main program.

stop bits
One of the things you have to set to use your **modem**. Usually set to 1 or 2, but it depends on the modem you're calling.

.store
A new **Internet domain**, to be used for online buying and selling.

streaming
When files are sent a little at a time and start playing almost immediately.

subdirectory
A **directory** that is the child of another directory.

subdomain
A named portion of an **Internet domain**, usually a **network**, university, or company. In one of my **e-mail address**es, `xian@netcom.com`, *netcom* is the subdomain.

subscribe
To join a **mailing list**, to start reading a **newsgroup**, or to set up your **Netcasting** software to **download** content from a **site**.

surf
To **browse**, following tangents. You can surf **Usenet** and **Gopherspace**, but the best place to surf is the **Web**.

synchronous
Happening at the same time. **Chat** is a synchronous form of communication.

sysadmin
A **system administrator**. Someone who runs or maintains a **network**.

sysop
A system operator.

system administrator
Someone who runs or maintains a **network**.

B

system operator
A type of **sysadmin** who runs a **BBS**.

talk
One-to-one **synchronous chat**ting over the **Net**.

talk.
A **Usenet hierarchy** devoted to discussion, argument, and debate.

tar
1. The act of lumping a bunch of files together in an archive; 2. The **Unix** program that does the said lumping.

TCP
Transmission Control Protocol; a **protocol** that transmits information over the **Internet**, one small piece at a time.

TCP/IP
The Internet protocol using TCP.

Telnet
A **protocol** for **remote login**, and the name of most programs that use that protocol.

***.test**
Usenet newsgroups, such as `misc.test`, `alt.test`, and so on, used for posting test **message**s to see if they propagate properly. If you **post** something to a `*.test` newsgroup, be prepared for a mailbox full of confirming replies to your post, sent back by **daemon**s as your post propagates around the world.

text editor
A program for editing **text files**; less fully featured than a word processor.

text file
A file containing text only.

text transfer
A transfer of straight text over a **modem**, from a remote computer to a **text file**.

thread
A series of related **post**s and **follow-up**s in a **newsgroup** or a **mailing list**.

threaded newsreader
A **newsreader** that organizes **post**s according to a **thread** and allows you to read your way up or down from response to response.

time out
To fail, as a **network** process, because the **remote server** or computer has not responded in time.

Tin
A threaded newsreader for Unix.

Trn
A threaded newsreader for Unix, similar to Rn.

troll
To deliberately **post** egregiously false information to a **newsgroup**, in hopes of tricking dense know-it-alls into correcting you. Also, such a post itself. If you follow up a bizarre post to point out that Grover Cleveland Alexander was never president of the U.S., you may see an even more confusing reply to your post saying just "YHBT. YHL. HAND." This stands for "You have been trolled. You have lost. Have a nice day."

TrueSound
Microsoft's own **streaming** sound format.

TurboGopher
A **Gopher** program for the Mac.

UL
An **urban legend**; the **Internet** is a perfect communication medium for tracking down and verifying or debunking urban legends.

uncompress
To unsquish a **compress**ed file. Also, a **Unix uncompression** program.

uncompression
The process of unsquishing a file.

Undernet
A smaller, more community-oriented alternative **IRC network** than **EFNet**.

Uniform Resource Locator (URL)
An **Internet address**. It consists of a **protocol**, a **host**name, a port (optional), a **directory**, and a file name.

Unix
An operating system common to workstations and on which most **Internet protocol**s were developed.

Unix shell account
An **Internet account** that provides access to a character-only **Unix command line**.

unmoderated
Said of a **newsgroup** or **list** whose **articles** are not vetted by a **moderator**.

unselect articles
To remove the selection tag from **Usenet article**s selected for reading.

B

unsubscribe
To remove yourself from a **mailing list** or to stop reading a **Usenet newsgroup**.

untar
To separate a **tar**red file into its component parts.

upload
To transfer a file over a **modem** from your desktop computer to a remote computer.

urban legends
Stories passed around and always attributed to a friend of a friend (a **FOAF**), frequently (but not always) based on a kernel of falsehood. The **Usenet newsgroups** `alt.folklore.urban` and its less noisy cousin `alt.folklore.suburban` are the homes of **UL** debunkers.

URL
See **Uniform Resource Locator**.

Usenet
1. The collection of computers and **networks** that share news **articles** (from User's *Net*work). **Usenet** is not the **Internet** (though they overlap to a great extent); 2. The **hierarchy** of **newsgroups**.

username
Also called a **login** or userID. The name a user logs in with. Also the first part of your **e-mail address** (up to the @).

UUCP
Unix to Unix Copy. A **protocol** and a program for intermittent **network** connections and file and mail transfers.

UUdecode
1. The act of turning a **UUencode**d file back into its **binary** form; 2. The **Unix** program that does this.

UUencode
1. To convert a **binary file** into a text form that can be sent as part of an **e-mail message**; 2. The **Unix** program that does this.

Veronica
An index of **Gopher** menus that you search. The results are presented to you as a **Gopher** menu.

Vi
A common Unix text editor.

viewers
See **players**.

virus
A program that deliberately does damage to the computer it's on.

.VOC
The audio format for the SoundBlaster sound card.

VRML
Virtual Reality Modeling Language; VRML files usually have a `.wrl` extension.

VT100
A terminal type, originated by DEC, that has become the standard terminal. If you dial up a **Unix shell**, then your communications program probably emulates a VT100.

w3
An abbreviation for the **World Wide Web**.

WAN
A wide-area **network**. A computer network spanning a wide geographical area.

.WAV
Wave format, from Microsoft; perhaps the most widespread sound format on the **Internet**.

Web
The **World Wide Web**.

.web
A new Internet **domain**.

Web address
A **URL**.

Web browser
A **Web client** program that allows you to view **hypertext pages** and follow **links**.

Web page
A **hypertext** document on the **Web**.

Web server
A **Web application** that allows you to store **home pages** and make them available via the Hypertext Transfer Protocol (**HTTP**). If you lack access to a Web server but have access to an **FTP site**, then you can store your home page there and make sure that **URLs** pointing to it use the `ftp://` protocol instead of `http://`.

whisper
A private **message** to someone in an **IRC** session.

whiteboard
A feature of **conferencing** software that enables **online**-meeting participants to all see the same presentation and to share a drawing tool to scribble diagrams or make changes to images collectively.

WhoWhere?
A **Web site** from which you can look for people.

WinZip
A **compression** program for Windows.

wizard
1. An expert, usually one willing to help **newbies**; 2. Interactive help screens that assist users in installing new software or performing a complicated operation, such as publishing a **Web page**.

working directory
The current **directory**. The directory you're "in" right now.

World Wide Web
A collection of **hypertext** documents and associated files, **link**ed together, that spans the **Internet** (and hence, the globe).

WRT
With respect to; shorthand for **e-mail** or **post**s.

WSGopher
A **gopher** program for Windows.

WS_FTP
1. An **FTP** program for Windows; 2. A **Unix**-based **Web browser** developed at CERN, the European particle physics laboratory where the **Web** was invented. It is the original text-based Unix **browser** for the Web.

X window
A graphical user interface for **Unix**.

Yahoo!
The most popular **Web directory**.

YMMV
Your mileage may vary; shorthand for **e-mail** or **post**s. Can be taken as a precautionary statement about how long it will take to do something on the Internet, or more generally, that your experience may differ from that of the person posting.

zip file
A **compress**ed file with a `.zip` extension.

Index

Note to the Reader: First level entries are in **bold**. Page numbers in **bold** indicate the principal discussion of a topic or the definition of a term. Page numbers in *italic* indicate illustrations.

Numbers and Symbols

A

B

C

F

G

H

I

J

K

L

M

N

Q

R

S

V

W

Y

Z